MW00606344

Bruce brings a lifetime of sharing Jesus wit
to the reading of the Bible. The grand story
nations is evident on every page as he wall
God's interactions with humanity. This boo. ....up un readers develop a biblical missiology that propels them to share the Gospel with all nations.

Jonathan Bornman
Eastern Mennonite Missions Christian/Muslim Relations Team
Peacemakers Confessing Christ

If you would read the Bible fifty times, carefully taking notes to find the meaning of the whole, and if you would sell your possessions and live for twenty
years in the Middle East to bring the gospel of Jesus Christ where the need for
God's love is so great, and if you would go to graduate school to study the Bible
and culture with one of the greatest missions faculties ever assembled, and if
you disciplined your mind to write every day for ten years on every book of the
Bible, and if you would devote your heart to the art of moving your readers to
examine themselves to see whether they are obeying the upward call of God,
then you might have what it takes to put together a masterpiece, like Bruce
Heckman has in this book. Here, for our generation, is a biblical theology of
missions and kingdom that will inform the young and remind the elders of the
glorious unity of the Bible.

Robert A. Blincoe, PhD
US Director, Frontiers

A true "Biblical Theology" of Mission, Bruce unpacks Scripture from Genesis to
Revelation to reveal God's amazing plan throughout history. A very insightful
read that centers mission in the context of the Kingdom of God. The stories of
the Bible become understandable when seen through the lens of God's mission.
If you want to know why you are on the earth, or why you seem to feel there
is something great you should be able to discover about your future, you need
to read this book. It will help you make sense of what God is up to and why the
most exciting thing you could do with your life is to get involved.

Barry Wissler
President
HarvestNET International

God's Heart and Mandate for Mission is written by a man who has dedicated his
entire life to the process of seeing the nations come to Jesus. Bruce is not just
another author. Bruce is an ongoing practitioner who continues to increase his
knowledge and experience working single-mindedly to both engage Muslims
in his community as well as to mentor younger leaders into the mission of the

Kingdom. As I read God's Heart and Mandate for Mission, I was drawn to this book's discussion of suffering. The reality of suffering as a way of life for most followers of Jesus in the Muslim, Buddhist and Hindu worlds is barely recognized or acknowledged in western Christendom. If the Word and history are indicators, suffering is something we should learn to expect, and learn it quickly. This book is a must read for Kingdom conscious followers of Jesus.

Francis Patt
Northeast Regional Director
US Center for World Mission

God's Heart and Mandate for Mission

The call to live beyond ourselves

Bruce Heckman

Foreword by J. Dudley Woodberry

God's Heart and Mandate for Mission
by Bruce Heckman

© 2014 by Bruce Heckman
Second Edition 2016

Published by
Partnership Publications
A Division of House Publications
11 Toll Gate Road, Lititz, PA, USA
Tele: 717.627.1996
www.h2hp.com

ISBN-10: 0983156077
ISBN-13: 978-0-9831560-7-9

Unless otherwise noted, all Scripture quotations in this publication are taken from the Holy Bible, New International Version (NIV). © 1973, 1978, 1984 by International Bible Society. Used by permission of Zondervan Publishing House. All rights reserved.

All Qur'anic quotations in this publication are taken from the Qur'an, published by Muhammad Ali Beydoun, Beirut, Lebanon: Dar Al-Kutub Al-Aalamiya. Translation or interpretation from the Arabic is the author's.

Acknowledgments

In the early 1970s, God laid a burden on my heart to bring the news of Jesus the Messiah to Muslim people. My life was radically transformed by simply saying "yes" to the call of God. At that time, I had almost no concept of mission; all I knew about Muslim people was that they were without Jesus, without hope, and had very few people who cared about them.

Don Richardson spoke at a mission seminar I attended in Europe in 1984. He spoke about the twofold call of God on Abraham: "blessed to be a blessing." I confess my amazement that God spoke of mission to the nations in the Old Testament, and also made it incumbent upon each believer to have both blessings of Abraham.

This fascination with a mission concept in the Old Testament eventually led me to a Master of Arts Degree at Fuller Seminary's School of World Mission, now called the School of Intercultural Studies. Studying Biblical Theology of Mission under Dr. Arthur Glasser convinced me that background in mission theology is necessary to both sustain workers in the field and teach them how to flow with the call of God when the landscape of need changes around them. I studied Islam under Dr. J. Dudley Woodberry which deepened my missionary zeal and helped me understand the parameters of my calling. Both of these men, and others, have offered their shoulders for us us to "stand upon" and move forward in our mission task. They have helped me find my role to prepare the next generation of mission workers to Muslim background peoples.

My interest in compiling *God's Heart and Mandate for Mission* came out of new discoveries for me in the Word of God. Major themes in the Bible grabbed me with God's mission heart. In a new way, I understood that the Bible had a clear mission story line and was not simply a compilation of fragmented stories with God at work in them. It is my desire in writing this book to place that mission story line (mission theology) into a form that is teachable. Therefore, this work is not highly referenced to theological works, allowing the reader to easily reference the material with his or her Bible, hopefully making it more readable.

"Part 1: Creation Through The Captivity" was written while on the field in the Middle East. Living among the people of the Middle East helped me read my Bible in the light of its cultural setting. "Part two: The Captivity to John the Baptist" was completed while working with DOVE Christian Fellowship as mission director. I am indebted to Jane Fasnacht for her proofreading, typing, and attentiveness to details. "Part 3: The Ministry of Jesus in the Four Gospels," and "Part 4: The Formation and Expansion of the Church" were written in conjunction with my work for IMMERGE, as I teach this material annually to field bound missionaries. Jessica Kurtz read, typed, and corrected the New Testament sections of the material. My thanks also to Larry Filbert and Joan McManness for proofreading with their missiological backgrounds and for their tips to make the material more practical. Jacqueline Hagy poured over the entire book with numerous hours of proofreading and tying themes together. A special thanks to Joyce, my wife and best friend, for her years of encouragement in ministry, and her help in organizing my thoughts which have been hammered on the anvil of Scripture.

It is my prayer that this book will be of great help to each one who reads it. I pray that you will press on to do great works for Jesus in the Kingdom of God and that you will continue to be transformed by Scripture. All Scripture references are taken from the NIV translation, unless otherwise noted.

Bruce Heckman

Abbreviations for the Books of the Bible

Genesis .... Ge	Isaiah .... Isa	Romans .... Ro
Exodus .... Ex	Jeremiah .... Jer	1 Corinthians .... 1 Co
Leviticus .... Lev	Lamentations .... La	2 Corinthians .... 2 Co
Numbers .... Nu	Exekiel .... Eze	Galatians .... Gal
Deuteronomy .... Dt	Daniel .... Da	Ephesians .... Eph
Joshua .... Jos	Hosea .... Hos	Philippinas .... Php
Judges .... Jdg	Joel .... Joel	Colossians .... Col
Ruth .... Ru	Amos .... Am	1 Thessalonians .... 1 Th
1 Samuel .... 1 Sa	Obadiah .... Ob	2 Thessalonians .... 2 Th
2 Samuel .... 2 Sa	Jonah .... Jnh	1 Timothy .... 1 Ti
1 Kings .... 1 Ki	Micah .... Mic	2 Timothy .... 2 Ti
2 Kings .... 2 Ki	Nahum .... Na	Titus .... Tit
1 Chronicles .... 1 Ch	Habakkuk .... Hab	Philemon .... Phm
2 Chronicles .... 2 Ch	Zephaniah .... Zep	Hebrews .... Heb
Ezra .... Ezr	Haggai .... Hag	James .... Jas
Nehemiah .... Ne	Zechariah .... Zec	1 Peter .... 1 Pe
Esther .... Est	Malachi .... Mal	2 Peter .... 2 Pe
Job .... Job	Matthew .... Mt	1 John .... 1 Jn
Psalms .... Ps	Mark .... Mk	2 John .... 2 Jn
Proverbs .... Pr	Luke .... Lk	3 John .... 3 Jn
Ecclesiastes .... Ecc	John .... Jn	Jude .... Jude
Song of Songs .... SS	Acts .... Ac	Revelation .... Rev

Introduction

The word "theology" can sound cumbersome or like something studied from a former era. Some young people even have an aversion to this word because it brings to mind a lifeless bondage that is void of the joy of the Spirit of God. Theology is simply defined as 'the knowledge of God,' and this knowledge can come either from studying and meditating on the Word of God, or it can come from other sources. The truth is, however, that everyone has a theology, right or wrong, and that theology directs the way each of us lives our life.

Many themes are present in the Bible and each one will form our theology along a particular line. Looking carefully at a theme, such as Biblical Theology of Mission, necessitates maintaining a single-minded focus. If one considers all themes simultaneously, the clarity of each will be blurred. However, it must also be recognized that extracting and isolating one theme from the Bible is not really possible either. Missiology requires an understanding of soteriology, Christology and biblical ethics.

My goal in writing *God's Heart and Mandate for Mission* is twofold. My first goal is to help the Body of Christ understand God's love for all people and His teachings on how each believer must express that love to others. Missionaries who have lived many years in a given location, as well as those embarking on their first journey, benefit from a fresh understanding of biblical missiology. My second goal is to produce a text that can be easily understood, translated into other languages, and taught by others.

Many of my thoughts come from working among unreached peoples. It is my sincere prayer that the knowledge of God (theology) within each of us compels us to take the gospel, the Good News, to new regions and to people groups who have never yet known the joy of God's forgiveness nor heard God's invitation to become a member of His family.

Roy Whitman, a missionary in Jordan for sixty-six years, once told me that everyone needs to read the Bible before someone else molds their theology. Believers need a clear understanding of the entire Bible in order to make decisions that reflect the heart of God. They also need to understand what God is speaking to them before someone else influences the way they look at the Bible. I invite you, the reader, to meet daily with God in the pages of Scripture.

The Bible is a large library of many books, written by many people over a long period of time. Understanding the mission of God and His invitation to work with Him takes us into a task of multiple readings of every part of the Bible in order to comprehend and categorize the volumes of material. Because the Bible was written over many years, one of our categories will relate to time periods. "Part 1: Creation Through The Captivity" and "Part 2: The Captivity to John the Baptist" will help the reader enter into the progressive revelation of Scripture which has taken place over hundreds of years. God worked with His people in ancient times before Moses wrote the first five books of the Bible. God also formed a people through whom He sought to bless the world. These categories lead us to an examination of "Section One - Ancient History" and "Section Two - The History of a People". These two sections are imbedded in Parts 1 and 2 and span the Old Testament.

The four gospel writers are very unique in that they introduce us to the person of Jesus, the Incarnate One. His life and declaration of the Kingdom of God is thrilling. "Part 3: The Ministry of Jesus in the Four Gospels" examines His incarnational life in a world living as "sheep without a shepherd." The call of the Father on our lives beckons us to bring the Shepherd to a desperate world.

The coming of the Holy Spirit recorded in the Book of Acts brought each believer into contact with the Creator. The spark of God and His mandate to all people will be examined in "Part 4: The Formation and Expansion of the Church."

Our task in not humanly possible. We need the zeal of the Lord to accomplish great things for Him. God's zeal, however, will require serious knowledge and understanding of the path He has called us to follow (Proverbs 19:2).

Table of Contents

Part 1: Creation Through The Captivity 19

1. Introduction and Purpose of Mission Theology 21

Section One - Ancient History

2. Creation, the Fall, and Depravity 31
   Cain and Abel
   The Flood and Covenant

3. Job: A Case of Stolen Identity 39

Section Two - The History of a People

4. The Patriarchs 53
   Abram, Covenant and Mission
   God Will Bless and Protect
   Circumcision, Obedience Through Shed Blood
   Isaac, Bearer of the Promise
   Jacob, Strife and Blessing
   Joseph, Provision and Healing
   Major themes of Genesis

5. The Exodus 67
   Moses Called and Sent
   Sinai and the Law
   Missiological Implications
   Israel Set Apart
   Three Annual Feasts

6. Israel and the Nations 81
    Joshua
    Rahab
    Ruth
    King David
    Absalom
    The Gibeonites
    David's Mighty Men
    King Solomon

7. Prophets and Kings 95
    Elijah and Elisha
    The Hebrew Servant Girl
    Jonah
    Amos: Shepherd and Prophet
    King Hezekiah
    Hosea

8. Isaiah: Message for the Nations 111
    The Lord is Righteous
    Light to the Gentiles
    Messiah and Kingdom of Messiah
    Peace
    Gentiles are Included

9. Jeremiah: Prophet to the Nations 125
    Called to the Nations
    The Heart of God for Judah
    The Vision of Captivity
    God's Letter to the Captives

Charts and Tables

Hebrew Festivals and Calendar --79
Captivities of Israel and Judah-- 103
Kings of Israel and Judah (Appendix) ---------------------------------- 136
Early Prophets During a Troubled Kingdom ---------------------------------137

Prophets of a Troubled Kingdom, Decline and Future Hope ------------ 138
Prophets During Decline, Captivity and Future Hope --------------------- 139
The People of the Nations -- 140

Part 2: The Captivity to John the Baptist 141

10. The First Captivity of Judah 143
    Daniel - Life and Mission in Babylon and Persia
    God Prepares His Servants for Ministry
    The Cross in Obedience (The Furnace)
    God's Five Visions Given to Daniel
11. The Second Captivity of Judah 157
    Ezekiel
    The Theology of Ezekiel
    An Allegory of His People
    The Sin of Sodom
    Sin will be Judged
    Who Owns the Land?
    Many Sheep, But not all Fed
    One Flock from Two Sticks
    Rebuilding of the Temple
12. Exiles First Return 175
    Zerubbabel - Rebuilding the Second Temple
    Temple Construction Revived
    Prophetic Message of Haggai
    Prophetic Message of Zechariah
13. Esther: Life and Mission in Persia 187
    Introduction
    Seven Principles for Cross-Cultural Ministry
14. Ezra: The Exiles Return 193
    Ezra Sent to Jerusalem
    Fasting
    Intermarriage

15. Nehemiah and the Unprotected City 199

    Introduction

    Strategy

    The Ways of the Enemy

    God's Qualifications

    This Isn't My Responsibility!

    Translation Projects

    Reinstatement of the Feasts and Life

    Conclusion

16. Malachi 209

    Introduction

    Is That an Offering?

    Four Messengers Sent

17. Intertestamental Period 215

    Introduction

    The Synagogue

    Persian Rule

    Greek Rule

    The Seleucids

    The Maccabean Response

    The Sadducees

    The Pharisees

    The Zealots

    The Essenes

    The Herodians

    The Rule of Rome

    Conclusion

18. John the Baptist.. 223

    Introduction

    Elijah has Come!

    Set God's Plan in Motion!

    Conclusion

Charts and Tables

Prophets During Captivity and Future Hope..................................172
Prophets of Post Exile and Future Prophetic Insight 173

Part 3: The Ministry of Jesus in the Four Gospels.. 227

Introduction to the New Testament 229

19. Introduction to the Gospel Narratives and Acts 233
        The Genealogy of Jesus
         The Visitation of Angels
        Adoption
        The Infancy Narratives
        The Birth of Jesus
        Dedication in the Temple
        The Boy Jesus

20. Jesus Inaugurates the Kingdom 249
        John's Baptism and The Kingdom
        A New Society
        Look, The Lamb of God!
        Miracle in Cana
        Proclamation of the Kingdom in Nazareth
        Growing Popularity of Messiah
        The Rejection of Messiah
        The Arrest and Crucifixion of Jesus
        The Resurrection--Real Proof
        Jesus as Resurrected Lord

21. The Kingdom and Restoration 275
        Kingdom Battles with the Enemy
        Kingdom Clashes with Religious and Political Institutions
        Reactions to the Announced Son of God

22. Discipleship in the Kingdom of God 289
     The Calling of the First Disciples
     The Cost of Discipleship
     Disciples Called Apostles
     This is Not Discipleship!
     Discipleship and the Nations
     Discipleship Requires a Fresh Start
     Discipleship and All Professions
     The Vision of Disciples

23. The Kingdom and Forgiveness.............................303
     1. Forgiveness and the Blood of Jesus
     2. Repentance
     3. Reconciliation with Other People
     4. Generosity Rather than Being Exacting
     5. Forgiveness Received and Given
     6. Do not Judge
     7. Forgiveness and the Welcome Mat
     8. Forgiveness of Sins and Healing
     9. Forgiveness and Compassion
     10. Continuous Forgiveness
     11. Forgiveness and the Nations
     12. Unforgiven and the Hard-Hearted

24. Jesus Teaches on the Kingdom.............................321
     How did Jesus Teach?
     Kingdom Teaching - The Sermon on the Mount
     The Parables
     Kingdom Values and Worldly Values – Luke

25. The Ministry of Jesus 343

Old Testament Ministry Types
     Jesus as Prophet, yet Greater
     Jesus as Priest
     Jesus the King
     Jesus as Servant King
     Jesus as Suffering Servant

New Kingdom Ministries
    Messiah, Our Healer
    Jesus the Evangelist Shepherd
    Jesus the Teacher
    Jesus and His Ministry of Prayer

26. Jesus, the Kingdom, and the Nations 359
    The Kingdom and the Nations - Matthew
    The Kingdom and the Nations - Luke
    The Kingdom and the Nations - John

27. The Coming Kingdom 389

Part 4: The Formation and Expansion of the Church 395

The Acts of the Apostles - Introduction 398

28. The Spirit and The Nations 401
    Pentecost and Mission
    The Spirit and All People
    Samaritans Receive the Spirit
    The Spirit and God's People

29. Theology in Context 413
    Peter and Theology in Context
    James and Theology in Context
    Paul and Theology in Context

30. Leadership, Obedience, and the Kingdom of God 421
    Leadership and Transitions
    Peter at Pentecost
    Leadership at the Beautiful Gate
    Discipline and Church Expansion
    Leadership, Obedience, and the Seven

31. Acts and Missionaries to the Nations...........................429
    Peter and Change

Paul, the New Missionary
Ananias and Light to the Nations
Barnabas and Light to the Nations
Antioch, A New Gentile Church
Missionary Principals
32. Decisions through Conflict 455
Jerusalem Council I
Questions Resurface - Jerusalem Council II
33. Fruit and Suffering in the Kingdom 463
Peter, the Apostles, and Suffering
Paul, His Mission Team, and Suffering
Suffering from Jealousy and Slander
Suffering as a Result of Obedience
34. Revelation, Epic Battles and Ultimate Victory 471
To the Churches: Repent, Be Strengthened
Worthy is the Lamb of God
The Bridegroom and the Bride

Selected Bibliography 481

Scripture Index...485

Illustrations

Abraham Greets Three Visitors (Ayad Karaboush)...............................20

Nebuchadnazzar's Amazement (Ayad Karaboush)......................... 142

The Road to Emmaus (Joyce Heckman) 228

Saul's Encounter with Jesus (Joyce Heckman)................................ 396

Foreword

The goal of this book, according to Bruce Heckman is, first, to help the Body of Christ understand God's love for all people and how each believer must express that love to others. Second, it is to produce a text that is easily understood, translated, and taught by others. For the first goal, he notes those at Fuller Theological Seminary's School of World Mission who "offered their shoulders" for students "to stand upon" as they moved forward in their mission work.

From their shoulders it is obvious that he saw still more as a missionary in the Middle East where he came to understand better the cultures that the biblical authors reflect. Then he added the additional perspectives of being a mission director and a teacher of new missionary recruits. His second goal he has accomplished both in content and format by reaching down to make it easily accessible. Throughout the biblical survey he shows God working out his purpose through the ages in a text interspersed with highlighted missiological principles and questions for group interaction or personal reflection.

The theme of the book is the theme of all history—the outworking of God's plan to redeem the world through his people and establish his Kingdom of justice, peace, and righteousness. As he traces God's purpose and work through the Bible, he highlights the divine concern not only for Israel but also that it in turn be a light to the nations. The author draws helpful lessons for the church in its mission from the biblical accounts of God's people under Persian, Greek, and Roman rule, and the clash of God's Kingdom with religious and political institutions. He identifies the issues that arise when churches shift from being predominantly among one ethnic/cultural group like the Jews to another ethnic/cultural group like the Greeks or become a mixture of two or more groups.

Then he moves on to the epic battles and victory of the future described in Revelation—issues that can give understanding and encouragement in these days when Christians are being killed and their churches burned by radical Muslims in places like Africa and the Middle East, yet where we are seeing a greater number of Muslims turning to Christ than in all of history.

Throughout the text the author identifies missionary principles that are derived from the biblical accounts on such diverse issues as the leading of God, facing demonic opposition, learning cultural lessons, developing leaders, facilitating transitions between leaders, expressing theology in different cultural contexts, translating Scripture, and developing strategy.

A few years ago my wife Roberta and I walked on the Roman road out of Tarsus that Paul would have taken on his second and third missionary journeys. There were milestones along the way that would have marked the missionaries' progress. We are now at one such milestone in the Church universal's missionary progress. Recently we celebrated 200 years since the founding of the first foreign missionary sending institution in the United States, the American Board of Commissioners for Foreign Missions, and the sending of their first missionaries, Adoniram and Ann Judson. At that time 20% of the world was Christian, and 90% of Christians were Europeans. Now 33% of the world are Christians, and only 25% of those Christians are Europeans.[1] Global Christianity has shifted from the West to the Global South with many cross-cultural missionaries from Asia, Africa, and Latin America as well as the West. This volume helps to meet these present changing needs. In keeping with its two-fold purpose, it shows God's unchanging heart and mandate for mission throughout the Bible, with its implications for us. And it is presented in a way that can be easily understood, translated, and taught by others.

J. Dudley Woodberry
Dean Emeritus and Senior Professor of Islamic Studies
School of Intercultural Studies, Fuller Seminary
Pasadena, California

---

[1] Todd M. Johnson, "North American Mission: From Judson to Global Christianity," Mission Frontiers, 34(2012), no. 3, 10-12.

Part 1:

Creation Through The Captivity

Abraham looked up and saw three men standing nearby. When he saw them, he hurried from the entrance of his tent to meet them . . .

Part 1: Creation Through The Captivity

Chapter 1 - Introduction and Purpose of Mission Theology

Two platforms seem common among Bible believers. The first implies that rarely do we find someone so foolish as to claim he or she has mastered the Bible. This is healthy as long as no one plateaus or becomes complacent. The second platform, which is less verbalized, suggests that most believers feel comfortable with their general knowledge of the Bible and with their perception of how it does or does not seem to fit together as a whole work. We need both the humility to hunger for a freshness in God's Word and a desire to understand how this Book of all books fits together. Our purpose is to delve into the Bible and experience the call of God on our lives. A poor knowledge of the Word of God, or a misunderstanding of God's character, will produce poor missionaries.

A challenge we all encounter is to make the leap from the biblical text, which means our reading and receiving instructions in the Scriptures, to its application in our personal lives. For years, I read the account of the Children of Israel wandering and complaining in the desert, often wondering how they could be so foolish, so filled with unbelief. Yet my own needs, while living in the Middle East, brought me to cry out to God with a sense of urgency rather than ask with peace and confidence for His provision. I needed to learn to make the connection between "Why did you bring us up out of Egypt to make us and our children and livestock die of thirst?" (Ex. 17:3) and fearfully asking God for provision while in "the land of my calling." When I saw myself as complaining in unbelief--so similar to the Children of Israel--I learned to look to the Lord and ask, "Would you split a rock for me?"

This is an example of making a connection between the text and life experience. When you compare your life to those in the stories of the Bible, situations are not identical, but they are similar. A missionary must make connections between biblical truth and his or her own personal life in order to fulfill God's purposes. In what areas of your life do you need to bring the truth of God's Word home in order to demonstrate your faith?

Areas Requiring Theology in Context

We must be able to make decisions based on truths found in the Bible rather than looking at circumstances through the lens of our personal backgrounds. Many people read the Word and say, "I believe!" Their believing, and whether or not it includes life application, is evidenced in the way they live their lives. The question for both you and the people you will disciple will be, "Do your life decisions reflect Jesus, or do they reflect the society in which you find yourself?" God wants your knowledge of Him to "trump" the influence society has upon you. Because Peter read, ". . . may another take his place of leadership" (Ps. 109:8), he came to the conclusion that someone needed to take the missing seat of Judas Iscariot. This is an example of theology in context.

Leadership must be influenced by God's Word in our context today. Modern day "Daniels" find themselves in influential positions and are challenged to give God glory regardless of society. On the other hand, Qur'anic leadership influences leaders to look back to the Golden Days of the Prophet, requiring adherence to a seventh century image of society.

Prophetic influence on your team and on your audience requires theology in context. The Bible draws us to seek a fullness of the Holy Spirit and reject a fullness of self in order to make decisions. A fullness of self blinds us to pride and develops a pushy, hard-headed individual. The fullness of the Spirit, however, helps us to remember that without Him we can do nothing, and with Him we are filled to be His witnesses.

Bible stories draw the listener into the text! I recently told the story of Jesus healing the paralytic who was lowered through the roof. When I came to the part, "The Pharisees and the teachers of the law began thinking to themselves, 'Who is this fellow who speaks blasphemy? Who can forgive sins but God alone?'" (Lk. 5:21), a woman jumped (into the story) and exclaimed, "That's right!" She knew no one except God could forgive sin. But when I completed the story, "But that you may know that the Son of Man has authority on earth to forgive sins...(v. 24)," she was now very quiet. Her theology was challenged in the context of Scripture.

The following are questions we carry with us into our reading of the Word of God.

Where in the Bible are we told about mission? We are familiar with the Great Commission in Matthew 28 and in Mark 16. Many look to Paul as an example of an early missionary. We need to answer two questions to begin this study in God's Word: (1) What does the whole Word of God have to say about mission and, (2) How do I begin my life in mission with the strength and power of God?

What is the mission of God? Mission in the Bible is not limited to witnessing, preaching, and disciple gathering. Find the ways God expressed His love and compassion to all peoples... to the needy, the unfortunate, and those without voice. Find yourself working as your Father works. Along with recognizing God's mission in the Bible, we need to ask ourselves, "What participation is expected from us?" Does a "mission mandate" exist in the Bible? Remember, Jesus did not just talk about faith in God, but He did the works of Him who sent Him. You and I also need to jump into the action with Him and do the works.

Do we recognize the Kingdom of God? What are the signs of the Kingdom, and who are the people who belong to the Kingdom? A post-reformation struggle which exists in the minds of believers today is the conflict between "faith" and "action." Biblical faith requires action and cannot be left as a mental acceptance of propositional truth. The difference is seen in the disciples who believed, but found the price too high to follow Jesus, and those who left everything behind and followed Him. Signs of the Kingdom of God will be faith, transformation, community, reconciliation, joy, forgiveness, and authority over dark powers. It will be radically different from the world in which we presently live.

Purpose of Mission Theology

We will discover that mission themes are present throughout all of Scripture. These themes will require our response, not simply an acknowledgment of their existence. Our purpose is not to force our desire for mission into Scripture that does not address this topic. This means that parts of the Bible, and possibly some entire books, will not directly lend themselves to mission thought. We accept this, knowing that God addresses a variety of specific themes throughout the pages of Scripture. Our purpose is to understand the mission of God and then to ask if we are invited to enter into His works and vision. Our purpose is not limited to searching for examples of people doing "mission activities." The following are three settings in which the study of mission theology will be applied.

1. One purpose of understanding mission is to foster God's purpose within a local church setting or within a community of believers. Mission activity is reaching out with one hand to the people to whom God has called you to minister, and reaching with your other hand to bring the Body of Christ with you into that call of God. We need the Church with its faith, its prayers, and its financial involvement in our ministry. The Church needs mission understanding in order to expand its focus and remain vibrant.

2. Short-term teams benefit from understanding God's Word which brings meaning and direction to their role. Loving the widows and orphans and feeding the hungry become more purposeful, and take on greater significance, when mission themes are understood by the volunteers.

3. The biblical foundation of mission is necessary in the career missionary's life. Each person called by God to impact the world for Jesus needs the necessary fuel to accomplish his or her task. The Bible puts into our lives the fiber required to complete the tasks given by the Lord. Without such fuel or nourishment, the temptation to look elsewhere for new guidance, to move on to other locations, or to return "home" can be overwhelming.

Not the Purpose of our Study

I will not validate the canon of Scripture. Such a study is outside the scope of this book. I assume that those desiring an overview of the Bible in relation to mission believe the Bible to be the Word of God. I take for granted that you accept the Bible as inerrant and giving direction to your life, and that you are willing to change your life to conform to fresh revelation. I will not cover all of mission theology. This brief introduction will simply move us, within our current belief setting, to see Kingdom values in a broader scope.

Some themes in the Bible

Revelation and History

The Bible speaks of much more than timeless rules and sweeping statements of human error in light of God's holiness. Throughout the Bible, we clearly see an involved Creator, Sustainer, Father, Lover, and Redeemer. We know He is the Refiner of His people and the Judge of sin. He is the One who empowers the humble to do great things and the One who removes power from the proud. God is involved throughout history; He is involved in our lives today.

Biblical history spans particular lives and does so within a time frame. The time span from Moses to John the Baptist is a mere one thousand five hundred years. In contrast, Hindu history covers millions of years which cannot be charted. It cannot trace the lineage of a person because the time frame of reference shrouds the past in an unknown time.

Salvation history is a particular theme of our God in history. God's work of searching for the lost and redeeming them back to Himself is clearly found throughout the biblical record. "Return faithless Israel, declares the Lord, I will frown on you no longer" (Jer. 3:12) touches our hearts today with a Creator who calls the wayward to Himself. "O Jerusalem, Jerusalem, you who kill the prophets and stone those sent to you, how often I have longed to gather your children together, as a hen gathers her chicks under her wings, but you were not willing" (Mt. 23:17) describes God's heart that longs for the salvation of a people who did not want Him. God's patience and His carrying a people who refuse His ways are not a Qur'anic view of God.

> And (Allah) punishes the hypocritical men and hypocritical women, men and women that believe Allah has a partner, and those that think an evil thought about Allah, upon them is the turn of evil events and Allah was angered at them and cursed them, and has prepared for them hell, an evil end to their journey. (Surah 48:6)

Revelation and Culture

No human culture is completely bad or completely good. The Scriptures were written in Hebrew, Aramaic, and Greek over the course of approximately two thousand years by men conditioned by their cultural surroundings. Their culture is reflected in their writings.

Because God's revelation comes into any language, spoken or written, we understand the following:

1. God is not asking us to conform to one particular aspect of culture presented in the Bible. A person does not need to pray in Hebrew or wear a particular robe to be pleasing to the Lord. Biblical expressions of culture range from Job in Iraq to Paul in Rome. Selecting one expression by which to live is random, unclear, and does not represent a God who is comfortable with meeting us in the context of different languages and cultures.

2. The message presented through us must flow into the language and understanding of the people we are to reach. God asks us to bring His Kingdom and His Word to people who speak all languages.

3. His revelation requires cultures to conform to a higher standard, leaving none untouched. One must take note that the inverse of tolerance is not intolerance as today's society would want us to think. God is long-suffering yet not tolerant of sin. Baal worship must go! He is also not requiring our vote of approval. His Kingdom is not a democracy. "For my thoughts are not your thoughts, neither are your ways my ways, declares the LORD" (Isa. 55:8).

Revelation and Biblical Criticism

Many theological works begin by asking questions concerning the authenticity of the biblical records and seeking verification of authorship. Questioning authorship and examining biblical records in light of other historical documents is not the intent of our present task. We believe that the God of the Bible spoke to humans in human languages, recorded for the benefit of all who would believe. The platform with which we begin is that God's Word is true and must be obeyed.

Revelation and Hermeneutics

Hermeneutics examines the cultural understanding and communal application of revelation. This presents a twofold task: to understand what the authors of the original writings meant in their ancient setting, and to translate their understanding into the thought and language of a particular culture, preserving the meaning and bringing application. The result is that a believing community understands the Word of God and responds in obedience.

Revelation and the Kingdom of God

God has not given us one theme with which to run. The diversity of God's leading brings us to the theme of Kingdom. The Kingdom of God is the rule and reign of God. God is not looking for just one response to the needy world from our lives. He wants His Kingdom to come, His will to be done. Therefore, many aspects of "Kingdom" are reflected in the Bible. Practically, this means that we preach the Word, stop the abuse of the societal weak (children, women, slaves), help the needy with food, disciple believers, find methods to provide clean water, foster a new respect for all, and live with overflowing joy before the world. Our tasks cover many aspects of life.

Kingdom and Mission

It is important we view Scripture in light of God's work in our lives and allow overflow to others. In one way or another, all Scripture will strengthen our understanding of mission. Mission is not just one aspect of the Kingdom we seek to identify through Scripture. We are led by Scripture; we do not lead Scripture. This allows mission to become a multifaceted calling that has clear levels of importance. One must never search Scripture to validate one's life as did the teachers of the law (Jn. 5:39). We acknowledge our need to grow in the Kingdom of God and to humbly receive from others instruction that lines up with the Word.

Failure to understand God's total concern for the nations will lock us into one type of expression and overlook the valid calling of God on groups or individuals in our own midst. On the other hand, not recognizing God's priorities will wrongly make all tasks of equal value, thus missing His heart for those who still do not know Him. We need to change our priorities and embrace the main concerns that are on God's heart.

Our understanding of Kingdom and Mission has changed greatly throughout the centuries. The Church of the Reformation was initially intent on understanding its theology rather than its mission. Hence the Catholic Orders carried the Gospel to regions beyond for nearly three centuries before the early Protestant workers found their way eastward and to the south. Our challenge today is to grasp scriptural understanding and allow it to be applied in an expanding expression of Kingdom involvement in the world.

1. With whose Kingdom are we involved?

Occasionally, this question needs to be asked to keep each of us from sliding into serving a system (e.g., a church or a mission) instead of the Kingdom of God. Our God-given task is to keep up with obedience to the Holy Spirit, refusing to establish our own Kingdom. Some church denominations and mission organizations will hold their belief systems to be the ones closest to the truth and look down upon other denominations as less accurate. The Kingdom of God is broad enough to welcome all who hold Jesus as the center of their existence. Remember that the Kingdom of God has deposited expressions of faith throughout the centuries and via a multitude of cultural expressions. It is natural for communities of faith that began in India centuries ago to look very different from communities of faith that began in Algeria in just the last ten years.

2. Who is, therefore, in charge of the direction?

We must remind ourselves that we serve under the King of Kings in His Kingdom. The Spirit of God is free to use different groups in the way He sees best. This frees us to obey God in our calling without the need to bring all Kingdom expressions into the likeness of *our particular* calling. It is good to describe one's calling without pushing others to serve in exactly the same manner. God will reinforce His ability to judge His people and the world. Judgment is in the hands of God and we acknowledge that all His judgments are righteous.

3. Who is sending messengers?

Throughout Scripture, we find messengers sent by God to speak to particular kings or nations. At times, God sent needy people to find the prophet or messenger of God, looking for an answer or for healing. Today, God is still the one who sends messengers to inform and teach peoples or nations. He still draws people to seek out the messenger of God to find answers for life's challenges. God is free to move His messengers into a nation for the time and purpose He so desires.

Look throughout the pages of Scripture for expressions of God's mission.

- Note God's compassion for the needy. What does He say about the poor, the widows, the naked, or those without justice? What are we as His people to *do* about the needy; not simply *believe* about the needy?

- God will use a person or a messenger. Look for the Adam, Noah, or Abraham whom God is using to accomplish His task. God still searches for individuals to do His will among the nations.

- What is God's method in mission? How did the Lord move Joseph into Egypt and then into a position to fulfill His purposes? What is the method He used to bring David into leadership? Is your life ready for movement into position for ministry?

- God opens doors to usher people into their ministries. What doors do you recognize God opening in Scripture, and how will you recognize and use these opportunities in your service?

- God desires to develop a people or a nation. God exerted great effort with Israel across many centuries. His desire is still to develop many peoples and many nations that honor Him.

- What is the message conveyed? The Lord conveyed many messages throughout the years of prophetic recording. He told Noah to build an ark in order to save a family of eight and two of every animal in existence. He spoke to Joseph in Egypt to store grain in preparation for mass famine. His message of purity is always with us. He is not limited to a monochromatic picture of what He speaks to the human race.

• What does "light to the nations" mean? The theme of light is developed in Scripture. How are we to understand the meaning of light, and how are we to become that light for God?

Challenges in Old Testament Theology

The Old Testament describes salvation history and God's dealings almost exclusively with Israel. It is divided into two major time blocks:

1. Primeval history (Ge. 1 - 11)

This time period covers the life of Adam and the moment sin entered the world. It covers Noah and the ancient kingdoms resulting from Noah's descendants.

2. Particular history (Ge. 12 - Mal.)

Particular history begins with Abraham who lived approximately 2000 B. C. Particular history is measurable, describing the lives of the Patriarchs and introducing us to Moses who recorded both ancient history and the beginning of particular history. A text that spans thousands of years brings us to an understanding of God and His interactions with people. This is quite different from interpreting all actions from one time frame, or worse, from one prophetic voice in time.

Speaking about "Bible times" in the Old Testament is as vague as speaking about the time from Abraham to the present day, which covers over four thousand years. Wearing particular clothing such as a yamaka or a prayer shawl, for example, references a very particular time frame and cannot be taken as "biblical dress."

The placement of the Old Testament books in the canon of Scripture challenges the student of the Bible with the task of sorting out chronology. Job, most likely the oldest book in the Bible, is placed next to the poetry books of Psalms and Proverbs. Daniel and Ezekiel are larger books and are placed with the "Major Prophets," or the larger books of the Old Testament. Chronologically, Daniel and Ezekiel are more suited for placement at the end of Chronicles. The book of Obadiah is placed near the end of the Old Testament with other books of its size (Minor Prophets), even though Obadiah, himself, was a contemporary of Elisha. Nehemiah deals with issues that fit the time frame of Malachi, but is found with the "History Books" after Chronicles. Reading Scripture without any time reference will confuse the purpose of God for His people. This study will attempt a chronological approach to Scripture.

At times, names in the Old Testament vary from one book to another. Some are a translation from the Hebrew, while others refer to a Persian or an Aramaic name. The historical names and dates of kings are important in order to understand the Word of God. With the dates, we are able to catch a glimpse of God's great patience and piece together the characters who fit into the chronology of the story.

Section One - Ancient History

Chapter 2 - Creation, the Fall, and Depravity

God is the God of Creation (Ge. 1-2)

We have a tremendous message for people! Because we know the God of creation, it is a message of hope and of freedom from fear and guilt. Unfortunately, the message of creation is less often heard today than it was before evolution and random selection became acceptable in school curriculums. The message of evolution is deeply opposed to a creative God who designed the entire universe. Evolution does not answer the longing of hearts for morality, and it denies the existence of guilt. On the other hand, the God of creation builds order into both a physical and moral world. Modern secularists, who are also created in the image of God, will long to know the Creator and will desire to understand His purposes for them, though at times these longing are suppressed and denied.

Creation highlights humans as the pinnacle of God's creation in a physical realm. Sometimes animal rights activists wrongly believe that animals have the same "rights" as do humans. The difference lies in whether we believe the story of creation as recorded in Genesis or reject this story and the God behind it. Abortionists deny the significance of human life for their personal convenience. The creation story demonstrates a respect for all life but places higher significance on the lives of humans because they are created in God's image (Ge. 1:27). Humanism has little to say about human supremacy without the solid backing of God's creation. Only in light of creation are humans superior to animals, especially while under the rule of the Creator.

The story of creation, recorded in the first two chapters of Genesis, is a challenge to the worldview of other religions. The Genesis account challenges the Hindu worldview on several levels. One level is the supremacy of humans, both male and female, over any animal life. This point will drive those who believe in Creation to use animals to search for cures to diseases rather than afford microorganisms or rodents the same freedom to live. Creation by one God in six days is opposed to the Hindu understanding of endless cycles over millions of years to bring the world into existence. The creation story of Genesis tells us that everything in the sea reproduces "according to their kinds" (1:21). Land creatures reproduce after their kind (v. 24), and to humans God gave this command:

> God blessed them and said to them, 'Be fruitful and increase in
> number; fill the earth and subdue it. Rule over the fish of the
> sea and the birds of the air and over every living creature that
> moves on the ground' (Ge. 1:28).

Hindus need to hear the message concerning the order of creation and the beauty of God's authority given to humans. Creating order and giving both man and woman the authority to rule over creation challenges the impersonal animistic world.

Creation in Genesis refutes the Islamic concept of God: His person, His image, and His character. It also refutes the Islamic position regarding the status of women. The twist is subtle but evident. The Qur'an does state that the world was created in six days.

> Your Lord, Allah, created the heavens and the earth in six days,
> then was firmly seated on the throne, veils the day with night
> in rapid succession; and the sun, moon, and stars are subju-
> gated by his commands. (Surah 7:54)

The Bible tells us

> God created man in his own image, in the image of God he cre-
> ated him; male and female he created them (Ge. 1:27).

Man in this case is a collective term, showing that God created both male and female in His image. This declaration is very important. God's image is evident and to be respected in both man and woman. Lowering this respect in any way will devalue the beauty of God's creation. The Qur'an twists the creation order, describing man created in God's image and woman created to bring pleasure to the man. This injects an expectation for both men and women that harms both the value of creation and the relationship between men and women which will follow.

> Your wives are as a tilth unto you; so approach your tilth when or
> how ye will; but do some good act for your souls beforehand; and
> fear God. And know that ye are to meet Him (in the Hereafter),
> and give (these) good tidings to those who believe. (Surah 2:223)

The contrast between the Genesis declaration of both created in the image of God and the Qur'anic declaration of the husband's complete possession of property is noteworthy. The former draws out a fullness of purpose; the latter formulates subjugated souls under carnal demands.

God creating a world with order also counters Buddhist beliefs. The world is far from simply an illusion with plant and animal life lacking boundries. Creation is the reality that an eternal and unchanging God set in motion. The Lord created vegetation and trees that reproduce ". . . according to their kinds" (Ge. 1:12), all birds and fish that reproduce after their kinds (v. 21), land creatures that produce according to their kind (v. 25), and humans with the directive from God to rule "... over all the earth" (v.26). When God told the man and woman to "Be fruitful and increase in number; fill the earth, and subdue it" (v. 28), He placed His desires in the hearts of people. The Buddhist belief to reject all desire dissolves in light of God's command.

Our Cultural Mandate

In light of God's creation of all people in His image, no human clique or cultural grouping can claim either superiority or inferiority to others. Our security is in the one God who gave life to all. Because all are created in the image of God, it is our duty to train and uncover talents in people which will, in turn, help others. Helping those whom God has created is a mandate. We who follow the living God must grasp that people of every culture and language are created to love God and fulfill His purposes. On the other hand, living for oneself or for personal and selfish pleasures are not options. God creating all people in His image is the beginning of His Cultural Mandate for family, community, order, communication, and civilization. This commission by God requires us to bless those who are deprived of basic dignity. Biblically based believers must be involved in meeting the needs of people stuck in squalor.

The Cultural Mandate is God's requirement of believers. It is not, however, a movement toward a welfare state in which the underprivileged are locked into financial dependency. His Cultural Mandate is not an excuse to exercise colonial control over subjugated people.

Sin Entered the World

Sin entered the world when humankind sought personal goals instead of God's commands. Adam and Eve were commissioned to rule over God's creation (Gen. 1:28-31), but sinned by rejecting God's authority over their lives. "Therefore, just as sin entered the world through one man, and death through sin, and in this way death came to all men, because all sinned" (Ro. 5:12). This sin in the heart of humankind disrupted communication between the Creator and His people, and it opened the door for darkness to corrupt creation. Sin now challenged the Cultural Mandate with personal desires esteemed above the desires of the Creator. World order was twisted and intimacy with God was stifled.

Adam and Eve were judged by God for their act of disobedience. God did not turn to Adam and Eve and ask them to do one act of goodness to balance out their one act of rebellion. The Islamic concept of a balance scale is not part of the biblical account. They could not atone for their act of rebellion; atonement needed to come from the outside.

> And I will put enmity
> between you and the woman,
> and between your offspring and hers;
> he will crush your head,
> and you will strike his heel (Ge. 3:15).

God immediately intervened with a hope for the future that one born of the woman would crush the works of Satan. God's desire to completely eradicate the works of Satan is a major theme in Scripture. "The reason the Son of God appeared was to destroy the devil's work" (1 Jn. 3:8).

Unregenerate people seek to use this world and its people to further their personal goals. This is contrasted to a life in harmony with the Creator; a life lived in responsible and sacrificial relationship to others and to the world.

Seeking after the lost is the heart of the Father

Mission began with God seeking after Adam in the Garden: "But the LORD God called to the man, 'Where are you?'" (Ge. 3:9). God alone sought after this couple in the Garden. His mission to bring back the lost was in place and very important to Him. The Mission Mandate for His people will be developed in the coming pages of Scripture. All of God's people are to have His heart for those outside His covenant and are to bring the lost back into relationship with Him.

God judged Adam and Eve and punished them with expulsion from the Garden of Eden. Adam and Eve's sin, and subsequent expulsion from the Garden, meant that future generations would reap the effect of their sin. Sin has a communal component; it is not just an individual matter.

Implications for Mission

Four implications for mission come through the story of the Fall and God's quick response.

1. This one God who created all things should be honored as our Source with thanksgiving and worship. Thankfulness is a quality we can bring to an unthankful and self-centered world.

2. Our mission cannot simply be a human-centered attempt to improve society, but rather it is a clear call for all people to repent from their sins (Ac. 17:30).

3. The rebellion of humankind is complicated by the presence of spiritual evil in the world. Any overview of our world's condition must conclude that the degree of suffering and degradation far exceeds simple human error or mischief. Our efforts to combat rebellion must go beyond recognizing human error or imposing external laws.

> For what the law was powerless to do in that it was weakened by the sinful nature, God did by sending His own Son in the likeness of sinful man to be a sin offering. And so He condemned sin in sinful man, in order that the righteous requirements of the law might be fully met in us, who do not live according to the sinful nature but according to the Spirit (Ro. 8:3-4).

4. The biblical mandate is a call to moral response in the Kingdom of God. It is essential that humans recognize their disconnect from a relationship with God and the necessity for God to initiate the ability to reconnect.

Cain and Abel - Presenting Hope While Facing Tragedy

This is the tragic story of the first murder. Cain and Abel were the sons of Adam and Eve. One brother became jealous of the other's accepted life and offering. God had clearly entered into both men's lives before this tragedy. God entered into Abel's life by receiving his offering with favor. God's confrontation with Cain was a picture of a father's heart pleading with a son not to commit to a foolish path, the murder of his brother. This is the heart of God in mission that we embrace. We plead with the couple before they divorce. We urge the pregnant woman not to abort her baby. We also present the hope found in Christ before it is too late. Entering God's mission means we point out the potential evil in a situation and warn individuals to consider the outcome.

Like Cain, not everyone will hear and understand the message presented. As God's messengers we understand the pain people will encounter when they choose foolish paths, especially when they ignore the invitation to overcome evil and to know God's pleasure.

Case Study - He walked away

A young man, with whom I had worked over a period of nine years, had made a commitment to follow Jesus and was seemingly being changed by the Lord. Then he abandoned all reason to follow his own path. I cried out to the Lord: "Lord, I spent so much time with this young man. I thought he was doing well." Immediately a man's face flashed through my mind. This man had been an elder in a church where we were members. He had left his wife and children for his secretary, who also had left her husband and children. The Lord said, "I spent a lot of time with him as well." God feels the pain of people in their willful rebellion. When individuals do not listen to our counsel and go after their own lust or anger, it is not always because we failed in our communication. God knew how to communicate with Cain, but Cain clearly refused God's admonition.

Then the Lord said to Cain, "Where is your brother Abel" (Ge. 4:9)?

It is important to notice that God's question, "Where is your brother Abel?" was not asked because God was unaware of Abel's whereabouts. God asks questions that solicit a response. Cain's response, "I don't know," added a lie to hatred and murder.

God protected Cain from certain judgment by other people. Cain lived out his life and built a city which he named after his son Enoch (Ge. 4:17). We have no word of any reconciliation or sense of peace in Cain's life.

The Flood and Covenant

God's Wrath

The Biblical record of the flood shows us God's wrath and ability to deal with sin on a cataclysmic level. We see His patience in preparation for the flood. The ark could have taken more than one hundred years to build and prepare. (Read Genesis 5:32 and 7:6.) We also understand God's willingness to use a man and his family to keep His creation from being completely annihilated.

What was God's mission in the story of the flood? His mission was to eradicate the human race and to start over with Noah's family. We have many questions in light of the Ark being constructed over such a long period of time. Could others have been included if they had turned to the Lord? How did Noah remain faithful to God in such a depraved society? How much interaction did Noah and his family have with the people living around them? In this story, we clearly see that God's judgment was just and did not take place in a fit of rage.

God's Display of Grief

Believers need an understanding that God's sorrow and grief are also part of His anger. We know He was sorry that He had created the human race (Ge. 6:6-8). God's feelings are deeply touched by events on this earth. Every believer in the one true God must commit to never bring grief to the heart of the Creator who has obviously suffered so much. Our sins bring pain to the heart of God, in part because He sees the end results of those sins.

Some glibly say, "God hates the sin but loves the sinner." This is not evident in the story of the flood. It follows the understanding of the Psalmist:

> The arrogant cannot stand in your presence; you hate all who do wrong. You destroy those who tell lies; bloodthirsty and deceitful men the LORD abhors (Ps. 5:5-6).

A Commitment to Holiness

God brought obliteration to a society that was destroying itself (Ge. 6:13). Noah was found blameless and walked with God (Ge. 6:9). Any desire to understand the heart of God must be backed by an honest commitment to holiness. God took Noah, a righteous man, into His confidence and told him about His plans. God also made a covenant with Noah, pledging to deliver him and his family from the waters of the flood. Noah obeyed the Lord in "holy fear" (Heb. 11:7) and built the ark. He entered into obedience by actively carrying out the will of God in the face of persecution. Here, God's mission was to destroy the world but save one family and two of every species of animal. God's mission was to start over.

God's Redemptive Heart

The visible sign of the rainbow was given to remind Noah and all of his descendants that God would never again destroy the world by flood. His rainbow continues to be a symbol of beauty and covenant that cannot be misconstrued by human agendas. God does, however, promise to destroy the world with intense heat (2 Pe. 3:12). Never question God's resolve to judge the wickedness of the human race.

Questions for Review

What is the Cultural Mandate?

Why is there a Cultural Mandate?

What are examples of God's commitment to holiness?

Is purity an option in our commitment to the Lord?

Chapter 3 - Job: A Case of Stolen Identity

Background

Many believe the book of Job to be the oldest book in the Bible. Moses recorded the Books of Genesis, Exodus, Leviticus, Numbers, and Deuteronomy nearly five hundred years after the time of Abraham. Given Job's age of approximately 200 years old (Job 42:16), we conclude that he did not live in ancient history nor in the pre-flood era. Nor is he of the time frame of David and the Psalms, "The length of our days is seventy years—or eighty, if we have the strength" (Ps. 90:10). The book of Job makes no mention of the patriarchs. So, this man of the East seems to fit neatly into our chronology at the end of Genesis Chapter 11, before the mention of Abraham.

Chapter 1 gives us insight into Job and his life, which must be interpreted within the context of his time frame. The text says, "He was the greatest man among all the people of the East" (1:3). Job was a very rich man, but not as one would think of "rich" in our current century. Riches today are often measured in personal, gluttonous extravagance. Some Hollywood figures come to mind with their rows of garages for exotic cars, their massive homes that would rival some hotels in size, and ocean-worthy yachts, complete with crews awaiting the perfect day to sail.

Job had three thousand camels, which meant employment for the crew who would take care of and work with the camels. As beasts of burden, camels carry large loads over long distances. Job was the local long distance shipper who could move goods in and out of the entire region. Think of his camels as three thousand trucks. Additionally, his seven thousand sheep were not held in pens for Job to look at and say, "Look at all my sheep!" Sheep meant work for milkers, cheese makers, shearers, those who dyed the wool, clothing makers, butchers, and of course, many shepherds. Job employed hundreds of people and fed an entire region. His five hundred yoke of oxen were really five hundred small tractors. Job employed people to feed and care for the oxen as well as those who plowed hundreds of fields. Agriculture was a large part of Job's life, and his influence on the entire region was a blessing. Five hundred donkeys would be used as beasts of burden for smaller loads and shorter distances than those covered by the camels. Job had the equivalent of five hundred pick-up trucks for local hauling. When the text states that he "had a large number of servants" (1:3c), it appears to be an understatement when compared to today. Job was indeed a man of great influence who employed and fed much of the region. He was also honest, upright, and walked with a fear of the Lord. The ruin of Job is the ruin of the entire region in terms of employment, food, clothing, and any future hope for life.

The Character Of God

The Book of Job forces us to ask the hard questions in order to understand the knowledge and character of God. Why do the innocent suffer? Is God to be blamed for the diseases and deformities in our world? These age-old questions continue to trouble some believers and keep others out of relationship with a God they blame. Is God to be blamed, or are other forces at work to carefully bring blame to a righteous God? The problem we face is that we attempt to place too many questions of life into too few categories.

Some have mistakenly viewed this story as a struggle between God and Satan with the unfortunate victim, Job, placed in the middle as a test case. This wrong view is like God and Satan playing a tennis match with Job as the tennis ball. The Bible clearly does not describe dualism between good and evil forces. God, who is all-powerful, never struggles in overcoming evil. Therefore, that interpretation of this story cannot be correct. Another errant opinion was expressed by Job's friends. These counselors placed the blame squarely on Job for his own misfortunes, and wrongly believed God to be justifiably responsible for the following:

1. The Sabeans attacked, stole his oxen and donkeys, and killed his servants (1:14-15).

2. Fire from the sky burned up the sheep and the servants (1:16).

3. The Chaldeans raided, stole Job's camels, and killed the servants (1:17).

4. A mighty wind swept in from the desert, collapsing the home of one son where all of Job's children died (1:18-19).

5. So Satan went out . . . and afflicted Job with painful sores from the soles of his feet to the top of his head (2:7).

Each of the first four incidents is joined to the others with the phrase, "While he was still speaking." Bad news came to Job as multiple crushing blows of destruction which could not be received as coincidental. Job responded after these four tragic events:

At this, Job got up and tore his robe and shaved his head. Then he fell to the ground in worship and said: "Naked I came from my mother's womb, and naked I will depart. The LORD gave and the LORD has taken away; may the name of the LORD be praised." In all this, Job did not sin by charging God with wrong-doing (Job 1:20-22).

Who caused the destruction of Job?

Some Christians believe that God brings both blessings and calamities to their lives. Struggles that the righteous encounter in this life and the judgment of God on sin are not to be placed in the same category. Many also believe that God removes blessings to test or to get a point across. Some have referred to car accidents, broken legs, or sickness as acts of God to teach them lessons or to punish them. The book of Job is quoted as the reference to show God's destructive intentions in an effort to refine Job. But God said of this man, "There is no one on earth like him; he is blameless and upright, a man who fears God and shuns evil" (1:8). Interestingly enough, some have gone so far as to be afraid of being "too good or too righteous" because it might catch God's attention and precipitate disaster. The battle is actually for the true knowledge of God's character, which has been maligned repeatedly. Misunderstanding the character of God will drive believers into mediocre service, foolish decisions that lead them to further mistrust God, and to misrepresent Him to a desperate world. The book of Job must be examined in light of God's character as demonstrated in the Bible.

When "God called to the man, 'Where are you?'" (Ge. 3:9), it was not because God was unable to locate Adam. It was a question He asked knowing that Adam and Eve were hiding as a result of their sinful actions. Similarly, when "The LORD said to Satan, 'Where have you come from?'" (Job 1:7), it was not because God was unaware of Satan's activity. Satan desired to ruin the works of God. He entered into the perfect world of the Garden of Eden and the perfect harmony of the Creator with His creation, Adam and Eve, seeking to destroy that in which God delighted. (Satan still enters into the harmony between God and His people, seeking to corrupt any sense of peace and trust.) Satan gave a terse response:

Does Job fear God for nothing? Satan replied, Have you not put a hedge around him and his household and everything he has? You have blessed the work of his hands, so that his flocks and herds are spread throughout the land. But stretch out your hand and strike everything he has, and he will surely curse you to your face (Job 1:9-11).

Satan was already seeking a way to destroy the man Job: his positive economic influence in the region, his vast agricultural provision, his family, and ultimately the confidence Job had in God. Make no mistake in the intent of this deceptive attack. Satan's desire was that Job would curse God to His face. This could only be achieved if Satan could bring Job to believe lies about God's character and intent.

Question

How do we respond to crushing blows to our lives or to our ministries?

A frequent misunderstanding of this exchange between God and Job is believing that Job is on trial. It is actually God who is on trial. God is accused by the Accuser (Satan) of unfairly protecting His own. This accusation against God goes further to state that God will be cursed by His creation if problems occur in the lives of His people. Satan tried unsuccessfully to initiate God's action against Job (1:11-12). Notice that God gave permission to Satan to harm, "everything he has," but not to harm Job himself (op. cit.). The point we must retain is that God is accused of only garnering love and respect when life is good for His people. God's identity was wrongly connected to Job's crushing problems. The point is not whether Job was righteous. God fully expected Job to remain His humble servant. He expects the same of us even when we do not understand the difficulties surrounding us.

My Grump Walk

I ran a business in the Middle East for a number of years. Our regional office for an American based manufacturing company was in a very difficult position. My "prayer walk" one November morning was actually a "grump walk." My heart was very heavy with the financial pressures and lack of interest in our machines from the local businessmen. As I walked I said, "This is impossible! They think the equipment is too expensive. They accuse our company of having ties with Jews. They do not approve of the way the machine operates. The economy is so bad that I cannot even take a job to demonstrate the operation of the machine, let alone sell it. This whole section of their industry is under the scrutiny of the Muslim Brotherhood. This is impossible!"

As I walked, Heaven was very quiet. I turned to enter the stairwell of our apartment building to go up to our second floor apartment and heard the question,

"Do you have food on your breakfast table?"

    "Yes, we do. Thank you Lord," I replied.

"Your rent is paid for the coming year."

    "You are right, thank you."

"You have central heating in your apartment, not everyone does."

    "Yes, thank you for that too."

"And your fuel tank for the central heating is full of fuel."

    "Yes Lord, I appreciate that too."

"And your children are all in private schools."

    "Yes, they are."

"And their tuition is paid."

    "Thank you Lord for that."

"This is not impossible, you are just uncomfortable."

The reality was that I blamed God for leading me into a situation that was not prosperous in my economy or in my time measurement. God was working for me and for the people I was reaching. My struggles, though real, had everything to do with an opposition to my presence and to the presence of God living through my life. That prayer walk was humbling.

Source of Destruction

Consider the destruction that Job faced. We read that the Sabeans attacked and carried off the oxen and the donkeys (Job 1:15). That was five hundred pairs of oxen and five hundred beasts of burden. All the servants associated with these animals were murdered except for one who reported the events. Does God use theft and murder, overt acts of evil, to get His way? Is God both good and evil at the same time? Do we not read the account of how God, who is pure and cannot associate with evil, is slandered with another set of character qualities? James wrote, "When tempted, no one should say, 'God is tempting me.' For God cannot be tempted by evil, nor does he tempt anyone" (Jas. 1:13). It is not possible for God to use evil to carry out His plan, nor to use evil to bring temptation to the lives of believers or unbelievers. The Qur'an places God in a different light, stating that He uses deception to tempt people to sin (Surat Al-Araf 7:163). The Qur'an also tells us that God embraces truth and deception at the same time (7:89). The question is clearly greater than whether we believe in God. The important question is what do we believe God to be like? Muslims believe in God, but they believe in a God who is distant, unconcerned about their daily lives, and one who gives but also comes to take away in order to test their hearts. Blessings are held in fear that He will destroy. Muslims, and many other people, use clever animistic countermeasures to keep blessings and ward off potential destruction.

The statement in Job 1:16 given by a servant who survived a disaster must be understood in light of God's character. He said, "The fire of God fell from the sky and burned up the sheep and the servants, and I am the only one who has escaped to tell you!" The verse says "the fire of God." If the fire was from God, then God and Satan were working together to ruin Job, which must be completely rejected in light of Scripture. God's moral boundaries prevent us from confusing God's work with Satan's work. The Bible gives other examples of people who interpreted events with only partial understanding. Solid believers, filled with the Holy Spirit, told the servant girl, Rhoda, that it could not be Peter, but rather his angel at the door (Ac. 12:15). This interpretation is recorded in Scripture, but we know they were wrong in their understanding of events. It does not fit our theology to believe that people's angels sound like them or knock on doors. Our struggle with the passage in Job is that it describes miraculous power that is normally only attributed to God.

Jesus tells us that "false christs and false prophets will appear and perform great signs and miracles to deceive even the elect--if that were possible" (Mt. 24:24). The warning Jesus gives alerts us to the fact that not all miracles are from God. Miracles can be deceptive, when we no longer ask their purpose or apply our knowledge of the character of the God we know to them. Many today attribute all miraculous power to "heaven," which removes any sense of discernment. It is extremely important to know the source of miraculous power and the purpose for which it is used. If not, we will also fall into the delusion of misunderstanding God and, therefore, will misrepresent Him. Paul tells us to beware of the one who will come without any moral boundaries; who draws power from Satan to perform miracles.

> The coming of the lawless one will be in accordance with the work of Satan displayed in all kinds of counterfeit miracles, signs and wonders, and in every sort of evil that deceives those who are perishing. They perish because they refused to love the truth and so be saved. For this reason God sends them a powerful delusion so that they will believe the lie and so that all will be condemned who have not believed the truth but have delighted in wickedness (2 Th. 2:9-11).

God has moral boundaries. We too must have a sense of morality that keeps us from deception. A miracle seemingly from Heaven, but with immoral implications or performed by someone associated with evil, is not to be attributed to God. Truth must remain our guiding commitment. Therefore, our testimony of Jesus must remain at the forefront of our lives. The description of the power given to the Beast in the book of Revelation grabs our attention, particularly the description of fire coming from the sky. Note the similarity of this description with the Book of Job and the resulting conclusions wrongly drawn from this sign.

> And he performed great and miraculous signs, even causing fire to come down from heaven to earth in full view of men. Because of the signs he was given power to do on behalf of the first beast, he deceived the inhabitants of the earth (Rev. 13:13-14).

What does it mean to deceive the inhabitants of the earth? Is it not the interpretation that any being who can call fire from the sky is supreme and must be honored and followed? God is calling us to remain vigilant to our surroundings and committed to our knowledge of Him and His pure, moral character. God's character is maligned by quoting Scripture out of context and applying that misunderstanding to our present state of mind. Solomon in cynical disorientation wrote, "Man's fate is like that of the animals . . . All go to the same place; all come from dust, and to dust all return" (Ecc. 3:19-20). Quoting Scripture out of context will certainly bring error to understanding the character of God.

The other calamities in Chapter 1 of Job refer to the theft and murder committed by the Chaldeans (1:17) and the mighty wind that caused death and destruction (vv. 18-19). The source should be clear to us. The Chaldeans were incited to do evil, as were the Sabeans, to fulfill their own selfish gain. The mighty wind cannot be confused with the wind of God in Chapter 2 of Acts that brought an anointing to spread the true knowledge of God. This destructive wind in Job can be attributed to the ruler of the kingdom of the air (Eph. 2:2). It is followed by those who live in disobedience and deny the truth of God.

Job remained fixed in his integrity and in his honor of God. The next level of destruction brought "sores from the soles of his feet to the top of his head" (Job 2:7). Satan's use of physical sickness brings us to the enormous topic of the satanic re-engineering of God's creation for destructive purposes. Many diseases are very intricate and require the study of the human body, created in God's image, in order to discover cures. Rather than blaming God, we are to find cures for all diseases (Lk. 9:1-2). This brings us to the conclusion that God wants people cured rather than painfully struggling with poor health until death finally conquers. Entering into the works of God to destroy the works of Satan takes on a broad and fulfilling challenge.

The battle is for the pure character of God to be proclaimed. Preaching Jesus--His life, His death, and His resurrection--must come with the backing of the eternal God who suffers because of this fallen world. God loves the world He created; He longs to redeem the inhabitants of the earth, but He cannot stoop to use destruction and immorality to bring redemption. His clean and pure judgment cannot be confused with the immoral calamities of the evil one. We are to proclaim the true character of God and not, as Job's counselors, be misrepresenting God (Job 42:7-9).

What About Us?

God's people face overwhelming struggles at times. Some have gone through the fire of multiple blows which have destroyed their families and possessions. Job's utterance, "The LORD gave and the LORD has taken away," misses the delicate point that God is not always behind this destruction. Selfishness, fire from the sky, destructive wind, and bacterial infestation are only part of Satan's arsenal. Dr. Ralph Winter, a noted missiologist, author, and founder of the US Center for World Mission, believes that Satan is not only behind diabolical distortions of God's creation, but he also uses diabolical delusions to cover his tracks (Winter 2007:6-7). The knowledge of God requires we no longer blame Him for the corruptions of bodies or the decay of creation.

Satan desires to corrupt the works of God as was evident in the Garden of Eden. Humans are not in the place of the Creator, but God *has* granted us intelligence to study bacteria and carefully design antibiotics that save lives. Likewise, our intelligence can be used to form biological weapons that kill masses of people. The chemical properties we devise can both clean an operating room to save a life or burn the flesh and lungs of enemies. How many forms of bacteria, viruses, plant and animal life (including types of worms) has Satan re-engineered for destructive purposes?

The sin of humankind has placed all of us under the curse and corrupting influences of a decaying world. Neither Satan's hatred for God nor a corrupted world can be blamed on a just and loving God.

Insights from the Book of Job

The Book of Job, neither offering a look at dualism nor a strange co-laboring of God and Satan, must then offer insights into the Kingdom of God and His ways. It also offers an ancient understanding into how Satan works and masquerades with false identity.

God could have evicted Satan from the throne room with overwhelming force the day the angels came to present themselves (Job 1:6), but He did not. The Lord knew Satan's heart was bent on accusing Him of wrong, wanting to prove that even God's servants are only faithful when everything goes well. This deep bitterness of Satan unfolds in the text. The Lord can, and will, utterly defeat Satan, and He has chosen to use simple godly humans to participate in this defeat.

> I have given you authority to trample on snakes and scorpions and to overcome all the power of the enemy; nothing will harm you (Lk. 10:19).

We are also told in the Book of Revelation that Satan will be hurled down (12:9) and that His people overcame the works of Satan. It states, "They overcame him by the blood of the Lamb and by the word of their testimony; they did not love their lives so much as to shrink from death" (12:11).

First Conclusion: The Kingdom of God does not advance by raw power.

Job's case was brought to the supreme court of the universe. It is so important to understand the reasoning behind the Lord asking Satan if he had considered His blameless servant Job. Job was God's recommendation for the witness box and was not a toy given by God to be crushed by Satan. God could not prime Job for his task as a witness. Telling Job what would happen would have been seen as witness tampering. God could not tell Job, "Only seventeen months of destruction by Satan, and I will personally make sure you are restored. Just speak well of me." Again, to do so would have been tampering with the witness.

The Qur'an moves freely beyond the story of Job in blaming God's character for all misfortune. It places in the minds of Muslims the idea that all misfortune is predetermined, and therefore from God.

> No misfortune can happen on earth or in your souls but is recorded in a decree before We bring it into existence: That is truly easy for God. (Iron 57:22)

The Qur'an agrees with Job's counselors that his destruction was an act of God. Job did not know the final outcome; neither do we. Job did not know the length of time he would suffer; neither do we. The Kingdom seems to advance by holiness and righteousness against the Prince of Darkness.

Second Conclusion: God and His identity were on trial.

This book gives us amazing insight into the work of Satan (Job 1-2). Satan continues to work behind the scenes, outside of the throne room of God. In Job 4 we read of Eliphaz trying to convince Job of his sinfulness and just punishment by God. The Enemy will try to push his agenda into the lives of people closest to you. Eliphaz told Job, "Consider now: Who, being innocent, has ever perished? Where were the upright ever destroyed" (Job 4:7)? Our fallen world is filled with examples of people who love God and face tremendous difficulties. Noah suffered ridicule, and those who stand for righteousness face persecution. The Qur'an is actually in agreement with Eliphaz and his revelation.

> As to those who believe and work righteousness, verily We shall not suffer to perish the reward of any who do a (single) righteous deed. (The Cave 18:30)

Islam teaches that the righteous cannot suffer because God protects them. This means inversely that anyone who suffers is reaping justice for their evil deeds.

Eliphaz went on to describe his revelation in the night and how it came to him.

> A word was secretly brought to me, my ears caught a whisper of it. Amid disquieting dreams in the night, when deep sleep falls on men, fear and trembling seized me and made all my bones shake. A spirit glided past my face, and the hair on my body stood on end (Job 4:12-15).

Several items of his revelation grab our attention. A "secret" word given "Amid disquieting dreams in the night" should disturb us. Dreams or visions that rob our peace, unless it comes as a personal rebuke to our moral failure, must be questioned. A revelation that comes "with fear and trembling," to the point that his bones shook, is an indication of our human world intersecting with the world of dark, evil spirits rather than with the Spirit of God. Fear that comes in the form of "A spirit glided past my face and the hair on my body stood on end" needs to be stood against and commanded to flee, rather than received. The confusion in the Book of Job was that people did not yet have categories for the work of dark, lying spirits.

The fear with which the revelation was brought does not reflect the Good Shepherd who leads us beside quiet water (Ps. 23). This revelation given to Eliphaz did not come with the "do not be afraid" spoken to Zechariah, as Gabriel announced the coming birth of John (Lk. 1:13); to Mary, hearing and seeing Gabriel (Lk. 1:30); to Joseph, hearing God's plan (Mt. 1:20); to the shepherds, who saw angels (Lk. 2:10); to the women at the tomb Easter morning (Mt. 28:5); to Paul, as he faced shipwreck (Ac. 27:24); nor to John, as he received the revelation of Jesus on Patmos (Rev. 1:17). Once we know this Shepherd, we will not follow another.

> He calls His own sheep by name and leads them out. When He has brought out all His own, He goes on ahead of them, and His sheep follow Him because they know His voice. But they will never follow a stranger; in fact, they will run away from Him because they do not recognize a stranger's voice (Jn. 10:3-5).

Content of the revelation given to Eliphaz:

Eliphaz went on to relate the revelations given in the night.

> It stopped, but I could not tell what it was. A form stood before my eyes, and I heard a hushed voice: Can a mortal be more righteous than God? Can a man be more pure than his Maker? If God places no trust in his servants, if he charges his angels with error, how much more those who live in houses of clay, whose foundations are in the dust, who are crushed more readily than a moth! Between dawn and dusk they are broken to pieces; unnoticed, they perish forever (Job 4:16-20).

The revelation came with a hushed voice asking, "Can a mortal be more righteous than God? Can a man be more pure than his Maker" (Job 4:17)? The questions are good. One must agree that we as humans are not more righteous nor more pure than God. Once we agree with these two assertions, the next statement comes that God places no trust in His servants (v. 18a). Is this true? Does God place no trust in His servants? Lies are crafted with partial truth to bring deception to the listener. This false statement is prefaced with two true comments to gain the listener's confidence.

The voice went on to say that if God charges "His angels with error, how much more those who live in houses of clay" (vv. 18b, 19a). God, who made us out of the dust of the ground, would never despise our origin because He is the one who chose to form us as He willed. The one who would look down upon our humble origin must be another part of creation, like an angel. The content of this revelation reflects a proud, disgruntled angelic being who was charged with error. Eliphaz was listening to either the one who was "... roaming the earth and going back and forth on it ..." (Job 1:7), or to one of his messengers. The content of the revelation also claims that humans have a meaningless, unnoticed death. Jesus said that a sparrow cannot fall to the ground without the notice of our Heavenly Father (Mt. 10:29), and we are worth so much more. Understanding the dark source of Eliphaz's revelation helps us understand Job's wife telling her husband to "Curse God and die" (Job 2:9), the very words Satan boasted that Job would speak. A spouse needs to hear direction from God and not respond through hurt or anger toward God. Job's wife was also suffering the loss of her children and all of her possessions. A spouse needs to hear from the Lord in both good times and in times of trouble. The close relationship of a spouse brings opportunity for either encouragement from the Lord or for the crushing blows of the enemy.

Neither the way the revelation was conveyed to Eliphaz nor the content of the message reflect the character of God we know and trust. This information is very important as we bring the knowledge of the true God to a world that has not yet met the Good Shepherd.

Third Conclusion: Not every revelation is from God! Know God's character and do not be conned.

God was angry with the three counselors because they misrepresented Him! God extended grace (forgiveness) to Job's counselors based on the prayers of Job for them (Job 42:8-10). This is an example of intercession and the Lord's mercy based on a righteous man's prayer. This is a very important point for us to receive. We are to represent Him correctly to the world. Faulty or immature revelation is not an excuse.

Another level upon which grace was extended through Job and his witness through suffering, was that the knowledge of God spread. The goodness of the true God was made clear. This is a God whom you can trust and not blame for misfortune. The knowledge of God also opens the eyes of believers to the work of Satan, to his influences in the world, and to his attempts to distort the image of God.

Job spoke an anointed prophetic utterance in the middle of his pain through loss, physical agony, and the torment of accusers. He prophesied that his living redeemer, God Himself, will stand on the earth in the resurrection. This oldest book of the Bible tells us that the Redeemer is involved with the resurrection of the dead.

> I know that my redeemer lives,
>   and that in the end he will stand on the earth.
> And after my skin has been destroyed,
>   yet in my flesh I will see God;
> I myself will see him
>   with my own eyes—I, and not another.
>   How my heart yearns within me (Job 19:25-27)!

Fourth Conclusion: When the righteous suffer, grace is extended to the undeserving.

Grace was extended to the entire region with the fresh knowledge of the God whom all could trust. This grace was spread to the Chaldeans from whom Abram traced his background. Grace would eventually be extended to the entire world through the Righteous One who would suffer in our place.

Questions

What was God's mission in the Book of Job?

What should Job's response have been?

What is your response when life brings difficult circumstances?

Are you a witness for God or against God?

List several ways we can reveal and defeat the works of Satan.

Section Two - The History of a People

Chapter 4 - The Patriarchs

The lives of the Patriarchs set the Old Testament scene for God to develop a people. This section addresses the lives of Abram, who became Abraham; Isaac; Jacob, who later became Israel; and Esau, his brother. It will also give us a picture of the lives of Jacob's twelve sons and one daughter. God's general promise given in the Garden will take shape as He develops a people.

> And I will put enmity between you and the woman, and between your offspring and hers; he will crush his head, and you will strike his heel (Ge. 3:15).

Abram: Covenant and Mission

Abram was born 292 years after the flood, nine generations removed from a major mark in history. After nine generations, stories can begin to fade or even be doubted. We know Abram's father Terah worshipped other gods (Jos. 24:2), so how Abram came to such unquestioning faith in the one true God is unclear. It seems reasonable to speculate, however, that Job left a powerful impression on the peoples of the East, influencing a young Abram to trust in the nature and character of God.

The Promise to Abram

Abram left his home region with his father, traveling from southern Iraq to northwestern Iraq (Ge. 11:32). This man from the East was challenged by God with a promise.

> The LORD had said to Abram, 'Leave your country, your people and your father's household and go to the land I will show you. I will make you into a great nation and I will bless you; I will make your name great, and you will be a blessing. I will bless those who bless you, and whoever curses you I will curse; and all peoples on earth will be blessed through you' (Ge. 12:1-3).

Before we look at the promise of God, we must see His call in light of mission. Abram was challenged to leave his people and his family and travel with a blank itinerary. We, like Abram, follow a clear calling of God to new places, not knowing how life's events will unfold. Entering uncharted regions is an act of faith in the God we trust.

A Two-Part Promise

The call of God, "Leave your country, your people and your father's household and go to the land I will show you," precedes the blessing of God. Jesus told His disciples to "go" and then promised to be with them (Mt. 28:19-20). The call of God precedes His promise. Desiring the blessing of God without the obedience to the call of God is a fundamental misunderstanding.

The promise of God to Abram began by God saying that He would make Abram into a great nation. Just imagine, this was spoken to a man without children. The Lord also promised in a general way to bless Abram. When God speaks, we listen. For God to give a general blessing is very precious, and we can receive it because God does not lie, whimsically change His mind, or twist His words. In contrast, general words from people can feel superficial because we know they have the ability to fall short of fulfilling a promise. God also promised to make Abram's name great. The citizens of Babel built a tower to make a great name for themselves (Ge. 11:4). We must learn early in life that striving to make a name for ourselves is a useless task whose foundation is pride. God's blessing to make a great name is something Abram just received.

The second part of the blessing was a purpose clause. When God blesses us, the purpose is that many will also be blessed through us. God's promise continued with ". . . and you will be a blessing" (Ge. 12:2). Abram was not just to receive, but he was to be a channel of blessing. God promised ". . . all peoples on earth will be blessed through you" (Ge. 12: 3). The fact that this would happen was certain because God had promised. How Abram and the nation to come from him would be a blessing to the whole earth had not yet been revealed.

This promise was so powerful because it was clearly for Abram, his descendants, and all peoples on earth. This blessing with a purpose, given to Abram, promised God's blessing to the world. Yet the sentence, "I will bless those who bless you and whoever curses you I will curse," raises questions in our minds. What does it mean to "bless Abram?" Today, some use this phrase to garner political support for the nation of Israel without scrutinizing any of Israel's current actions. Others use this phrase to raise finances to build houses in the West Bank for returning

Jews, which displace Palestinians. In this context, does blessing Abram simply mean showing kindness and hospitality to him, his herds, and his servants? Could blessing Abram imply joining with the faith of Abram?

People within Abram's household did not become a "blessing to all peoples on earth" by simply belonging to the family. God's blessing did not describe a club with bloodline membership, but a promise/covenant between two parties. This meant that those within Abram's household were to actively seek to represent the God of covenant and thus become a source of blessing to the nations. They could not treat the nations as inferior to themselves. In a similar thought, how did one outside of Abram's household bless Abram? Do we not err in our thinking when we invite those outside Abram's household to help Abram to prosper, yet allow them to die without entering God's covenant promise? Is it not also folly to help the children of Abram simply find a new home and not share with them the gospel, the true covenant?

Questions

- Does the covenant between God and Abram bring blessing? How?
- Is it possible to bless Abram and his descendants by joining with them and the covenant made with them?
- Does cursing Abram and his descendants mean ridiculing them or refusing to enter into covenant with them?

God will Bless and Protect

This two-part blessing must be absorbed into our subconscious and received as a word spoken over all who walk with the God of Abram.

1. **Abram receives the blessing. Abram's descendants (through the promise of family) receive the blessing.**

2. **All people receive the blessing of God through this man and his family.**

Almost every nation's currency includes coins. Coins have a front side we call "heads" in English, and a back side we call "tails." Some countries call the front side "crowns" or "the king" and the back side "the eagle." A coin with only one side is either counterfeit or defective. Likewise, the blessing of God comes with two sides: we receive the blessing and we give the blessing. Wrongly desiring the blessings of God, without offering those same blessings to others, is one sided and counterfeit or defective theology. Our faith cannot receive the blessings of God without finding a way to also become a blessing to the nations.

"I Am Your Reward"

A key element of the first half of this blessing we receive is that God Himself is our shield and our very great reward (Ge. 15:1). In looking only for material comforts, we will miss the deeper meaning and purpose of this great blessing to Abram and his entire family who follow in the faith of Abram. God is our protection, our "shield of faith" (Eph. 6: 16). He Himself is the greatest possible reward. Our mission is not simply going in His Name but bringing with us the presence and knowledge of our reward, God Himself. The blessing we offer to the nations is a God who comes to surround them with His protection. The image of a shield reminds us of "the shield of faith." The beauty of this promise to Abram is that the Shield is not dependant upon just Abram's faith or on ours, but upon God's promise.

God promised Abram, ". . . a son coming from your own body will be your heir" (Ge. 15:4b). It is evident that Abram was already thinking of servants who could receive the promise and blessing, such as Eliezer of Damascus (v. 2). God's promise went on to say,

> Look up at the sky and count the stars—if indeed you can count
> them. Then he said to him, So shall your offspring be (Ge. 15:5).

No doubt Abram related this promise to his wife Sarai. Imagine the struggle of faith she had to have had within her soul to acknowledge her aging body and lack of children as she repeatedly heard the words, "as numerous as the stars in the sky." In a similar way, we will face times when God speaks, and we see no evidence of His promise. Stories like Abram's and Sarai's are meant for us to read and put into the context of our own individual lives.

The Birth of Ishmael

The story of Ishmael must be placed in its Middle Eastern context. It was common for a man to have children with his wife's maidservant in Abram's time. This cannot be viewed as something lewd. Sarai told Abram:

> The LORD has kept me from having children. Go, sleep with
> my slave; perhaps I can build a family through her (Ge. 16:2b).

There was a desperation in Sarai that could have been motivated either by her knowing the promise, "as numerous as the stars in the sky," or possibly by believing that Abram could not have children with Hagar. Her anger with Abram and her mistreatment of Hagar certainly speak to her inner struggles (vv. 5-6). How do we respond to a word of faith before us that we, like Sarai, are incapable of fulfilling? Indeed, if we have the ability to fulfill a particular promise, does it even require our faith?

Abram was not from a bloodline of people through whom God had worked in the past, at least for numerous generations. Neither Sarai nor Hagar were chosen because of bloodline or rejected because of bloodline. Abram was chosen because of his faith and obedience to God. Sarai, as we later learn, was chosen as the mother to bear the child of promise (17:15).

Hagar fled into the desert because of mistreatment (16:6-15). It was the angel of the Lord (or the Lord Himself) who named Ishmael, "God hears." After the birth of Isaac, Sarah bristled at the mocking of an adolescent boy toward her son. It seems her laughter and joy were not extended to Hagar and Ishmael.

> Get rid of that slave woman and her son, for that woman's son
> will never share in the inheritance with my son Isaac (21:10).

The result was a mother and her thirteen-year-old son banished to the desert with little food and a skin of water (21:14). The scene is one that should draw great pity from our hearts, and it requires a response, even today, to the many banished and lost sons of Ishmael. The response from God was so tender. He heard the crying of the boy in the desert, thus fulfilling the prophetic name given to Ishmael, "God hears." Is it possible that today we have so wrongly labeled Ishmael and his children as unworthy of either land or kindness that we are unable to hear the cry that God hears? Some have wrongly blamed this child for the rise of Islam. There were nearly two thousand six hundred years between the birth of Ishmael and the birth of Muhammed, making that link impossible. Many sons and daughters of Ishmael walk with Jesus today and have never come under Islam. Others have responded to the voice of God and live today in harmony with Him through the Messiah. The religion of Islam encompasses many people and nations far beyond the confines of this story of Ishmael. Be very careful to acknowledge that God "so loved the world," (Jn. 3:16) which includes all sides of politically charged areas about which many truly know very little.

Self Protection and Fear

It is important we trust the Lord--without twisting the truth--in order to find acceptance. Abraham's embarrassing description of Sarah (given the name Sarah by God in Ge. 17:15) as his sister was not acceptable to God and was awkward with Pharaoh (Ge. 12:13-20) and later with Abimelech (20:11). Never make plans based on fear. Honesty is not a shell game that you hope the local officials will not discover. The world runs on half-truths and seeks personal protection. God wants to protect us and to be honored for that protection.

Circumcision: Obedience Through Shed Blood

Including Eliezer of Damascus and Ishmael (Ge. 17:23-27)
God told Abraham to circumcise every male in his house, born to him or acquired by him, in order to be part of the covenant promise. This covenant already included Gentiles from the nations. The covenant included slave and free, Abraham's house, and the many nations under his influence, including his natural descendant Ishmael. This son entered into covenant when he was thirteen-years-old. Many Arabs continue today with the tradition of circumcision when sons reach the age of thirteen. This tradition has spread widely into many Islamic circles desiring to be obedient to God.

All Uncircumcised Will Be Cut Off From Israel
Any belonging to the house of Abram were cut off from belonging to Israel if they were not circumcised. This was true of native born and those added to the household through purchase. There were no favorites; there were no exceptions.

Isaac: Bearer of the Promise

Isaac was circumcised when he was eight days old (21:4); the son of promise became a son of covenant. Abram obeyed God's call to take his son to ". . . the region of Moriah . . . on one of the mountains I will tell you about" (22:2) and offer him as a sacrifice. Mount Moriah was considered to be Temple Mount on which Solomon's Temple (2 Ch. 3:1) and later, Ezra's restoration project were built. It is absolutely amazing to think that "one of the mountains I will tell you about" is most likely what is today called the place of the Skull, or Golgotha, which is not far from Temple Mount. Abraham, a man like us, came to the realization that God could raise the dead, something no one had yet seen at that time.

> Abraham reasoned that God could even raise the dead, and so in a manner of speaking he did receive Isaac back from death (Heb. 11:19).

Abraham's prophetic word, "On the mountain of the LORD it will be provided," (Ge. 22:14) is a foreshadowing of the provision of God's Lamb to come nearly two thousand years later. Abram would be used by God to bless all people, every tribe, and each nation (22:17-18). Nations receive the blessing as a result of Abram's and our obedience. The unfolding revelation of God for all nations was beginning to be seen through the promise to Abraham and would be repeated in the Prophets and in the New Testament. Every tribe, language, people, and nation will be blessed with redemption as a result of Christ's obedience through shed blood.

Isaac received the blessing of Abraham from God (Ge. 26: 3-6). It is significant that Isaac heard from the Lord and did not simply hear his father pass the blessing on to him. Each generation needs to hear the voice of God to confirm the covenant of blessing. Isaac heard the Lord bless him and promise that his descendants would be as numerous as the stars in the sky. God promised to bless him with land, and He promised that all nations on earth would be blessed through his offspring. Jacob received the blessing from Isaac while deceiving him (Ge. 27:27-29) and again as he was departing the region (28:1-5). He heard the promise from God in Bethel (28:14-15) that confirmed his father's word. All nations would be blessed through the descendants of Abraham, Isaac, and Jacob.

Jacob: Strife and Blessing

The call of God given to Abraham was not only for him but for his descendants. This means that it is important to pass on the specifics of the call to the children of each generation. Hope must be instilled that the descendants will become a great nation. This necessitates unity. They will be blessed and protected, and all nations will be blessed through them. Each generation will need to look for ways to bless the nations around them. This hope seems to be elusive in some of the lives of the Patriarchs and their families.

The Patriarchs are often looked to as the fathers of faith. Some were more so than others. Isaac's wife came from his mother's relatives and needed to enter the call of God which was already in motion. The Lord spoke a prophetic word to Rebekah describing strife between the twins she was carrying. Isaac must have remembered the friction in his family between Sarah and Hagar and the subsequent banishment of his brother Ishmael.

> Two nations are in your womb,
>   and two peoples from within you will be separated;
> one people will be stronger than the other,
>   and the older will serve the younger (Ge. 25:23).

The passage later speaks of Isaac's enjoyment of eating wild game from the son who had brought it to him (v. 28) and Rebekah's attention to the other son. The family appears to be polarized in affections. Husband and wife need to work together at family unity and not overcompensate for a spouse's failure. Unity in raising children is a necessary platform in family harmony. It is very important that parents take time to appreciate the talents of each of their children and not fall into the blunder of preferential love. Patterns established in the home often go into the next generation's home if left unchecked. Esau married two Hittite women that "were a source of grief to Isaac and Rebekah" (26:35). The vision Abraham passed to Isaac, son of the promise, was not demonstrated through Esau's life choices. No doubt the family had discussions regarding who would make an acceptable wife, and no doubt the family was frustrated with Esau's decision. Pick a mate who shares God's vision and His hope for His Kingdom to touch the nations. Pass this valuable teaching on to your children.

Strife came to a head when Jacob connived with his mother, Rebekah, for Esau's birthright (27:31) and for the "first born" blessing (27:13-29). Jacob did receive the blessing of Isaac: heaven's dew (or favor), the prosperity of life, fullness of crops, prominence and authority among the nations, and authority over "the sons of your mother" (27:28-29). He remained unmarried for several years after his twin brother married into the Hittite clan. The blessing given to Esau was certainly one that intensified the anger he felt toward Jacob. His blessing was almost the opposite of that given to Jacob.

> Your dwelling will be away from the earth's richness,
>   away from the dew of heaven above.
> You will live by the sword and you will serve your brother.
> But when you grow restless, you will throw his yoke
>   from off your neck (vv. 39-40).

Life is not always fair. We know people who are blessed with doors of opportunity that seem to open without difficulty. Others seem to strive with life itself, feeling cheated or abandoned. No one has the right to give up on the goodness of God and His willingness to free us from the pressures around us. Bitterness destroys the fabric of families and darkens the soul. Life is not based on luck, good or bad. The opportunities to serve God and to make life choices that further the Kingdom of God in our families and in the world bring fullness and blessing that surpass family background.

Jacob was no doubt physically slighter than Esau and, with his mother's counsel, chose wisely to keep his life and leave the area. She wanted Jacob to marry from her family of origin and not from the Hittite women of the area where they were living (27:46). Isaac blessed Jacob with the blessing of Abraham as he departed for Paddan Aram. The text tells us that Esau finally realized how displeasing his Canaanite wives were to his parents. For some, learning lessons is a difficult process which sometimes requires some emotional blows in order to gain understanding. Difficult children need the reassurance that God deeply loves them and has hope for their futures. Individuals must take responsible steps to obey what they know is right, realizing that a stubborn past may have rendered many poor decisions.

God spoke to Jacob through a dream at Bethel during his journey north to Paddan Aram. God identified Himself as the God of Abraham and the God of Isaac. He promised Jacob that his descendants would be as numerous as dust, and that all peoples on earth would be blessed through him and his offspring" (28:15). The significance of this dream is that God personally passed onto Jacob the promise given to Abraham. It was Jacob's family who was chosen to carry the blessing to the nations and to be blessed with the protection and watchful eye of God Himself. Jacob vowed to make God his God if he had provision granted during his journey and if he returned to his father's house safely. We see Jacob making a conditional agreement with the Lord for God to be called the God of Abraham, Isaac, and Jacob. This proposition certainly looked after his personal interests and did not enter into a commitment to God's promise. His outlook on life and attention to God's direction does not appear to have the depth of Abraham's commitment. Do we approach God with conditional commitment like Jacob or with abandoned love like Abraham?

Jacob's story of marriage to Leah, and then to Rachel through Laban's trickery, seems to put Jacob in a place where he cannot get his own way. God has ways of bringing all of us to a point of surrender; our hearts molded by His hand. Leah was unloved by her husband (Ge. 29:31), yet she bore him Reuben, his first-born; Simeon, the hostage in Egypt; Levi, father of the priesthood and temple workers; and Judah, from whose line the blessing of the Messiah will come. God's blessing was certainly upon the marriage of Jacob and Leah. We, too, must take note when part of our life seems mundane or even forced; when we are unaware of the blessings God is working out for us and for His Kingdom. Our prayer, "Your Kingdom come," needs to be invited into all of life, including areas we believe are out of our comfort zone. This includes people with whom we prefer not to deal in business, family members, and government officials who grant visas. Jacob could have done a better job encouraging his family.

Animism or Faith?

Jacob was granted ". . . every speckled or spotted sheep, every dark-colored lamb and every spotted or speckled goat" as his wages from Laban (30:32). Jacob's actions are curious, placing fresh-cut poplar, almond, and plane branches with spotted, speckled and striped marks before mating sheep and goats (vv. 37-43). God did bless Jacob with the increase of herds with spotted, speckled, and striped markings according to the agreement with Laban. Did God bless Jacob in spite of his actions or as a result of his actions? Did Jacob place the branches in front of the sheep and goats in obedience to the Lord or as a herdsmen's practice? The text does not say. Repeating this action will take people into animistic beliefs or magical hope in order to change the genetics of animals or people through what the male or female, mother or father, look at when conceiving or when pregnant. A common practice in the Middle East is for pregnant women to stare at something they desire (*tawaahim*) in the hope that their unborn child will have that particular quality or feature. For example, they believe that staring with desire at strawberries places rosy color on the child (or possibly a birth mark). Staring at a person with a particular hair color brings that coloring to the unborn child. This is very similar to Jacob's action. Magical systems are counter to prayer to a God who is free to bless and protect us as His children.

Laban cannot be understood to be a follower of the "God of Abraham." He was still an idolater with "household gods" (Gen. 31:19) whom his daughter Rachel considered worth possessing. His promise before the heap of stones shows his lack of clarity toward God and His singular nature.

> May the God of Abraham and the God of Nahor, the God of their
> father, judge between us (31:53).

We know God spoke to Abraham and called him: "Go from your country, your people and your father's household to the land I will show you" (12:1). Terah, Abraham's father, "worshiped other gods" (Jdg. 2:19), which most likely meant idols. The faith of Nahor is not understood from Scripture. We know he was

Rebekah's grandfather (Ge. 24:24) and Abraham's brother. Faith in our God means we are part of a new family. Old family ties are not sufficient to claim membership in the family of God. Family members need to sort out for themselves their allegiance to the God who calls them to follow Him exclusively.

Jacob wisely changed the name of his son from Ben-Oni (son of my sorrows) to Benjamin (son of my right hand). Children need to know they are included in the family and blessed by their parents; not that they are cursed with a bad memory. Rachel's choice of a name for the boy in a painful, personal moment would have created a life of pain for the child. Take careful steps in life to bless people. Some parents have called their children "stupid," or they have thoughtlessly remarked, "you will never amount to anything." God wants the curse reversed and hurting people welcomed in as sons and daughters of His right hand.

Joseph: Provision and Healing

Jacob allowed the preferential treatment he knew from family history to become part of his family. He loved Joseph, first born of Rachel and eleventh son to be born, more than any of his other sons (37:4). Joseph's dream of eleven sheaves bowing to his sheaf infuriated his brothers (vv. 7-8). His next dream of his parents and brothers bowing to him brought even greater anger to his brothers. Many of us have experienced family strife, but few on the scale Joseph experienced. Being sold to the Ishmaelite traders and living as a servant in Egypt was a tremendous blow to his life. His integrity, honor of God, and honor of Potiphar kept him from adultery (39:8-10) but not from false accusations. Many of us will be tempted with evil financial deals, sexual temptations, and opportunities for power. We must keep God and His ways before us at all times in order to keep us from walking into sin and having God's blessing taken away.

Lord – You prospered Joseph!

During my time in business in the Middle East I faced many struggles. It seemed everything I attempted had tremendous opposition. Financially we were stretched. It was a time when there was little response from people with whom we shared our faith. There were fried computers, burnt boards on the printer, equipment that we had marketed was breaking down in the desert, and we were exhausted from both work and ministry. In my mind it seemed everything was crumbling and lacked blessing. In my heart I did not feel blessed and certainly did not see that everything I did was receiving a blessing. I could only see the break downs, the expenses, and the opposition. Then I remembered the story of Joseph and that "the LORD was with him and the LORD gave him success in everything he did." In frustration I looked toward heaven and said, "You blessed Joseph and everything he did!" I told God, "Look, it is right here," turning to the story of Joseph, as if God needed to be reminded of the Genesis account of a young man's life in the Middle East. I turned to the text and read the following:

> But while Joseph was there in the prison, the LORD was with him; he showed him kindness and granted him favor in the eyes of the prison warden. So the warden put Joseph in charge of all those held in the prison, and he was made responsible for all that was done there. The warden paid no attention to anything under Joseph's care, because the LORD was with Joseph and gave him success in whatever he did (Ge. 39:20-23).

I remembered Joseph's success, but somehow forgot that a part of his success was the result of his confinement in prison. My understanding of God's idea of success suddenly changed. I knew I was living for Him as His representative in a foreign land among a people who desperately needed Him. Much of the opposition I felt was not because of God's lack of interest, but because of buffeting opposition to God Himself. Then the thought came to my mind, "Do you want to be successful like Joseph?"

Joseph was sent by the Lord to Egypt. God's mission included saving the lives of people in the whole area affected by famine. Joseph entered Egypt with the experience of two prophetic dreams. God's anointing on Joseph to interpret dreams grew during his time in prison. God was preparing his anointed person for something greater.

> After they had been in custody for some time, each of the two men—the cupbearer and the baker of the king of Egypt, who were being held in prison—had a dream the same night, and each dream had a meaning of its own. When Joseph came to them the next morning, he saw that they were dejected. So he asked Pharaoh's officials who were in custody with him in his master's house, "Why do you look so sad today?" "We both had dreams," they answered, "but there is no one to interpret them." Then Joseph said to them, "Do not interpretations belong to God? Tell me your dreams" (40:4-8).

Joseph matured as a man as a result of his prison experience. His language skills improved as well. The provision of a cupbearer and a baker helped him to speak properly in the court of Pharaoh. Joseph was also a person who brought forgiveness. His frustrations were overcome by his grasp on the goodness and call of God.

> God sent me ahead of you to preserve for you a remnant on
> earth and to save your lives by a great deliverance (Ge. 45:4-7).

God saved nations from starvation as a result of Joseph and his anointing. God also saved Jacob's family from strife and hatred through the humbling and repentance that touched their lives.

Major principles of Genesis 11:26 through chapter 50

The Kingdom of God reflects the nature of God. The following principles are part of the lives and experiences of the Patriarchs. Each is worth noting, with an understanding that God's ways and character do not change.

- We understand the necessity of covenant promise with the living God, and His destruction of wicked people.

- Homosexual and extramarital behavior are always sin.

- Scripture teaches us that a life of faith does not come without testing; and then testing yet more for God to know our hearts.

- God's purposes prevail regardless of our manipulation.

- Righteousness is a prerequisite for intercession.

- God can bring you to recognize your limitations.

- God provides even in famine and uses His people to bless others.

- Success in God's eye is not the same as success in human terms.

- God speaks through dreams. He reveals understanding to His people.

- Blessing our children brings God's blessing.

Exercise

Which stories illustrate the above-mentioned principles learned during the days of the Patriarchs?

Do some principles change with time?

If so, which ones, and upon what basis do they change?

Chapter 5 - The Exodus

Moses: Called and Sent

Moses was raised in a desperately evil setting. The state of the Israelites in Moses' day required social justice. We know they were initially "segregated" from proper society because of their background (Ge. 46:31-34). In nearly four hundred years they had multiplied greatly in population (Ex. 1:7). This great expanse in population led many Israelites to develop their own cities. Fearing a takeover, the Egyptians enslaved them with harsh labor (Ex. 1:10-11). The Hebrew midwives were required to kill the male babies (1:15). When that was unsuccessful, the subsequent law was for the Egyptians to personally throw the live male babies into the Nile (1:22). In the depth of depravity, a nation legislated death on the male children of an ethnic minority. This written record of Egyptian decadence differs from abortion today in that the Egyptians targeted unwanted minority babies. Today, abortion legally allows people to dispose of their own unwanted children. The Egyptian society of that time period is shocking, yet our own society has sunk to even lower levels of moral failure.

Moses grew up in a land that oppressed his ethnic background. Never think that God called Moses to be a freedom fighter, which is similar to a modern "Jewish Anti-Defamation League" position. God placed His people in Egypt (Ge. 50:18-19) with a purpose for the nations.

Before God called Moses, Moses had killed an Egyptian (Ex. 2:12). This was the result of human indignation rather than heavenly directive. We do not hear the text condemn Moses for his murder of this Egyptian (2:13). It is clear that neither deliverance nor social reform was achieved through Moses' violent act. Several lessons are brought to light through this text.

- Neither mission nor salvation will be achieved through humanly initiated efforts.

Moses actually made himself a fugitive. The evil he committed would have required his death if Pharaoh had captured him (2:15). His self-made revolutionary style did not attract his fellow Hebrews (2:14).

- Deliverance requires God as the central figure rather than a human hero.

The call, purpose, and mission were spoken by God to Moses at the burning bush:

> So now, go. I am sending you to Pharaoh to bring my people the
> Israelites out of Egypt (Ex. 3:10).

This is the beginning of the call of God on Moses rather than self calling through his own zeal. Mission, too, must be a God-centered, God-initiated plan. The sending of Moses began with God's vision of how deliverance would be accomplished. Moses was overcome with thoughts of his role in leading Israel out of slavery and returning to a land where he was wanted for murder. How does a fugitive shepherd face the Pharaoh? God's response is necessary for us to comprehend.

> And God said, "I will be with you. And this will be the sign to you
> that it is I who have sent you: When you have brought the people
> out of Egypt, you will worship God on this mountain" (Ex. 3:12).

This clear word from God stated that when it happened and was successful, when the people found deliverance, they would know it was the Lord! This is also our need in guidance: We believe the God who calls us when we are personally unable to accomplish the task. We are also to move forward in obedience against overwhelming odds in a human sense. God and any believer make a majority. The Creator is capable of means we never knew existed.

Equipping for the Task

Moses was given the following signs:

1. The burning bush (Ex. 3:2)

2. God's name revealed, "I am who I am" (3:14)

3. The promise that Pharaoh would be hard-hearted, and that God would strike Pharaoh and his people (3:19-20)

4. God would change the heart of the Egyptians to become favorable to the Israelites (3:21)

5. The Israelites would plunder the Egyptians (3:22)

6. The sign of the staff turned into a snake (4:2-4)

7. The miracle of the leprous and clean hand (4:6-7)

8. The sign of the Nile waters turned into blood (4:8-9)

Moses' response?

> Moses said to the LORD, "O Lord, I have never been eloquent,
> neither in the past nor since you have spoken to your servant.
> I am slow of speech and tongue."
> The LORD said to him, "Who gave man his mouth? Who makes
> him deaf or mute? Who gives him sight or makes him blind? Is
> it not I, the LORD? Now go; I will help you speak and will teach
> you what to say." But Moses said, "O Lord, please send someone
> else to do it." Then the LORD's anger burned against Moses and
> He said, "What about your brother, Aaron the Levite? I know he
> can speak well (Ex. 4:10-14).

Moses received the call of God with eight compelling proofs, but he was still not
convinced. Unfortunately, our response to the call of God can be similar to that
of Moses. Even with the signs promised from the Lord, Moses still reverted to his
insecurities as his excuse not to obey the Lord. Insecurities can have a powerful
effect on our ability to make good decisions.

Questions

- How do you respond to the clear call of God?

- What would help His voice to become more clear in your life?

- Do insecurities hold you back from obeying His call on your life?

- Do you live with insecurities, or do you deal with them?

The Purpose of God

God's purpose through the Exodus of Israel from Egypt was to reintroduce Himself to humankind. The Lord simply wanted the nations to know He was in control, not the creation nor any created being. His purpose was never to erase

Egypt from the earth in favoritism to Israel. This message must be understood and proclaimed in mission.

> Then the LORD said to Moses, Get up early in the morning, confront Pharaoh and say to him, This is what the LORD, the God of the Hebrews, says: Let my people go, so that they may worship me, or this time I will send the full force of my plagues against you and against your officials and your people, so you may know that there is no one like me in all the earth. For by now I could have stretched out my hand and struck you and your people with a plague that would have wiped you off the earth. But I have raised you up for this very purpose, that I might show you my power and that my name might be proclaimed in all the earth (Ex. 9:13-16).

God was clear on several points:

1. He was in charge. This was not a negotiation nor a democratic vote. God is always the best leader and is very sure of His plan.

2. God wanted Pharaoh, all of Egypt, and the world to fear Him and know Him. The confrontation with the great nation of Egypt and its Pharaoh was on such a large scale that all surrounding nations were forced to take note.

3. God's plagues destroyed the gods of Egypt and did not annihilate the Egyptians. The gods of the Egyptians and their sorcerers were powerless before the plagues of God. God does not play favorites with any people.

4. He did not want to eliminate Egypt or remain an enemy to Egypt. There is a distinction between the fear of the Lord and the hatred of God. His desire is to place the former in the hearts of all people. Hating God keeps us at a distance from Him and renders us unaffected by His character.

5. His purposes went beyond freeing Israel. The reintroduction of God into the lives and everyday speech of people would certainly take place through this confrontation. We will read later of the fear of God coming upon the people of the Middle East because of His power.

Interaction Assignment
There is a clear distinction between the "chosen people" and the "favorite people" or "best people." Write a one and one half to two page paper supporting

your understanding of these terms. Give references to support your argument. Include how proper understanding of the terms will help or hinder church planting today. (Compare and contrast with Surat Al-Imran 3:110.)

The Judgment of God

The judgment of God in the final plague was to fall upon every firstborn of both humans and animals and ". . . on all the gods of Egypt" (Ex. 12:12). Blood of the sacrificial lamb--seen on both door posts and on the top of the door frame-- would be the only means of salvation to escape the Angel of Death. Salvation was through the sign of the blood of the lamb and not limited to the Hebrew section of the city. We have reinforced in our minds that obedience for us today is required in order to be counted as the Lord's people.

Passover Night

We read that ". . . many other people went up with them" which was a sign of the inclusive nature of the Exodus (Ex. 12:38). There were several reasons that people joined this emerging nation, previously just a group of oppressed slaves under rule of genocide. The "gods" of Egypt were not only powerless; they were ruined. So was Egypt. Leaving Egypt and joining Israel was the immediate correlation on the surface. Walking away from the "gods of Egypt" and following the Lord is the mission concept we must present. The former is a misguided political move, forgetting that Israel was a huge band of runaway slaves. Joining them was a deeper longing to follow God. We believe that the Kingdom of God will meet people from all nations and call them to covenant. Those included in "many other people" could have included Egyptians, who brought their slaves and livestock inside for shelter before the promised hail (Ex. 9:20). It could have included other nationalities who claimed their freedom that same night. The significant aspect of this inclusion is that others were welcomed. Provision needed to be made to receive people of other backgrounds.

The Passover was to be a solemn ceremony for all generations. Any foreigner could partake of the Passover with the following prerequisites (Ex. 12:43-51):

1. All males in the homes of foreigners had to be circumcised prior to eating the Passover. This meant that the foreigners "cut covenant" with God.

2. The Passover had to be eaten within the house.

3.   No bones of the lamb could be broken, neither by native-born Hebrew nor by a foreigner.

4.   The foreigner, when completing these regulations, was the same as native-born.

What does native-born mean in this passage? All nationalities were leaving Egypt together, and most were likely born in Egypt. Native-born is a special connotation that signifies "belonging." In the passage through the Red Sea and in the wanderings in the desert, these people belonged both to Israel and to the Lord. In a sense, the nations that joined during the night of the Passover entered into the Promise.

Passover and Communion

The symbolism between the Passover and communion is powerful.

1.   All are accepted in the One Covenant. The Old Covenant was a basis for commitment between God and His people. Even though the covenant has changed, it is still the only basis on which we are accepted.

2.   All enter into covenant through the blood of the Lamb, who offered Himself on our behalf.

3.   No bone of the Passover lamb--nor of Christ's body--was broken. The Passover lambs prophetically pointed to the future Lamb without broken bones (Ps. 22:17).

4.   The Angel of Death has no power over us. We remain alive in God. This is an assurance we carry daily and is not simply a reference to a past event.

We eat of the "Passover" within the one house of faith, never outside of community in isolation. A believer in isolation was not an option in the Exodus and is not an option in the era of the Church. Faith in God and commitment to other believers are both necessary. This is reiterated in the New Testament, which pushes this concept further to include our commitment to seek those who do not yet know the joy of fellowship with the Lord and His community.

> But if we walk in the light, as He is in the light, we have fellowship with one another, and the blood of Jesus, His Son, purifies us from all sin (1 Jn. 1:7).

This verse clearly points us to walking in the light and in fellowship with other believers, necessary for Christ's blood to purify us from all sin. This message from the Old Testament is expanded and clarified through the New Testament.

Sinai and the Law

The Lord worked powerfully for His people en route to Mount Sinai. God Himself led them by day with a pillar of cloud and by night with a pillar of fire (Ex. 13:21). This one pillar of two types never left them (Ex. 13:22; cf. Heb. 13:5, Dt. 31:6, Ps. 118:6-7). The Lord showed Himself as a crafty warrior at the Red Sea, setting up Pharaoh and his army (which was the strongest in the world at that time) for utter defeat. The powerful Egyptian army chased seemingly defenseless runaway slaves. God planned that He would be the only defense for Israel. Many times in life, we find ourselves in a similar position where only God can protect us from disaster.

Each aspect of the text is readily applicable to mission. When you count the cost to follow God, be sure to remember His omnipotence. Overwhelming odds are both routine and His delight. Fear forgets the previous examples of His greatness (i.e. plagues, Passover and present freedom). When we view the Children of Israel, we often see ourselves, quickly forgetting the work of God in the past. Fear and doubt at the Red Sea now paralyzed the Israelites. God's response was threefold:

1. "Why are you crying out to me" (Ex. 14:15)?

2. "Move ahead and raise your staff, I will part the Red Sea for you" (Ex. 14:16).

3. Both the angel of the Lord and the pillar of cloud withdrew from in front of Israel and went behind them, separating them from the Egyptian army (Ex. 14:19-20).

These three responses speak volumes to those of us who follow God. God is never caught off guard, and He expects us to trust Him in overwhelming circumstances. God has a plan even before we cry out to Him; our need is to ask Him calmly for His plan. Devising a human plan will overlook the miraculous and always keep God from showing Himself among the nations. The protection offered by the Lord to Israel was a fulfillment of His promise to Abram to be his shield (Ge. 15:1). This is a promise to all who follow the faith of Abram.

Missiological Implications

The journey to Sinai shows God as our compass. He personally leads us in paths we have not considered. He is our Provider, Sustainer, and Shield. He will be made known among the nations. The "many other people" who joined Israel experienced God distinguishing between them and the Egyptian army. God has no favorites. Your past performance helps you make decisions today, but it is not a substitute for obedience.

Israel Set Apart

The Inclusion of All Peoples

God's plan for His people and the nations became even clearer at Mount Sinai. His people are a "called out" people. God's treasured possession is a reflection of His promise to be Abraham's great reward. He has a love relationship that requires mutual commitment and offers intimate joy. The called out nature of this people included the "many other people." It was never exclusive and blood line specific.

> Now if you obey me fully and keep my covenant, then out of all nations you will be my treasured possession. Although the whole earth is mine, you will be for me a kingdom of priests and a holy nation. These are the words you are to speak to the Israelites (Ex. 19:5-6).

The "kingdom of priests" referred to in the above passage included more than the descendants of Levi. All Israel and all foreigners joining Israel were a nation of priests to the world. Women and children were also included in the kingdom of priests. We have a glimpse into God's plan for the whole earth which belongs to Him. This plan is to send His priests to represent His true nature and character. His priests are equipped to tell His story and invite others to also be welcomed as "native born." They will know that God is their provider, their shield, their great reward. They will also know that they are the treasure of God's heart.

The Old Testament has a few people who come on the scene with a knowledge of God and who are used by God. One example of God's work among other people is Jethro, a priest from outside of Israel and Moses' father-in-law (Ex. 18: 10-11). His inclusive nature is also shown through Joseph's wife, Asenath, and their two sons, Ephraim and Manasseh, and through Moses' wife Zipporah and their two sons.

Guidelines were given by God to set apart this kingdom of priests from the rest of the world. These Ten Commandments are to this day a powerful tool in sharing the knowledge of God with people of all backgrounds. No culture is exempt from the commands of God. Each commandment, given 3,500 years ago, provides guidelines and boundaries to societies. The idolatry of the East, the profanity and adultery of the West, the command for Sabbath rest, the honoring of parents... each brings needed correction and shows the weakness of human attempts to improve society without God's involvement.

The Three Annual Feasts

The Lord commanded that three annual feasts were to be kept by the whole community of Israel. These instructions were given to Moses while on Mount Sinai, along with the Ten Commandments and the communal laws. The three annual feasts lead us to understand God's heart for the nations.

Scriptures from Exodus 23, Leviticus 23, Deuteronomy 16

Three times a year you are to celebrate a festival to me. Celebrate the Feast of Unleavened Bread; for seven days eat bread made without yeast, as I commanded you. Do this at the appointed time in the month of Abib, for in that month you came out of Egypt. No one is to appear before me empty-handed. Celebrate the Feast of Harvest with the firstfruits of the crops you sow in your field. Celebrate the Feast of Ingathering at the end of the year when you gather in your crops from the field. Three times a year all the men are to appear before the Sovereign LORD (Ex. 23:14-17).

From the day after the Sabbath, the day you brought the sheaf of the wave offering, count off seven full weeks. Count off fifty days up to the day after the seventh Sabbath, and then present an offering of new grain to the LORD (Lev. 23:15-16).

Three times a year all your men must appear before the LORD

your God at the place He will choose: at the Feast of Unleavened Bread, the Feast of Weeks and the Feast of Tabernacles. No man should appear before the LORD empty-handed: Each of you must bring a gift in proportion to the way the LORD your God has blessed you (Dt. 16:16-17).

The Feast of Unleavened Bread

The feast of Unleavened Bread begins at Passover and lasts for seven days. This feast focuses on the unleavened bread, pure and without contamination, broken for us. Annually, it points to the message of removing impurity and, ultimately, to the message of Christ's body to be broken for the redemption of the world. It begins with the Passover; the protection of all who trust in the blood of the lamb to save their house from death. The implications are that the first feast of the Hebrew calendar year directs every household to clean out the yeast (Ex. 13:7) and to remember the salvation God brought by the blood of the lamb. This theme is reinforced throughout the Word of God.

The Feast of Weeks

The Feast of Weeks or the Feast of First Fruits begins seven weeks after the barley harvest and at the beginning of the wheat harvest. This celebration rejoices in the beginning of the wheat harvest or the first fruit of the wheat harvest. These first fruits are not to be kept but are to be given to the Lord as an offering. This feast is celebrated fifty days after the beginning of the Feast of Unleavened Bread or fifty days from Passover. The Leviticus passage tells the people:

> . . . do not reap to the very edges of your field or gather the gleanings of your harvest. Leave them for the poor and for the foreigner residing among you. I am the LORD your God (Lev. 23:22).

This "fiftieth" day is referred to in the Hellenic world as Pentecost. This feast of the first fruits rejoices in the abundant harvest to come. It requires waiting for that day to come and only having a down payment in hand to offer to the Lord.

The outpouring of the Holy Spirit on the fiftieth day is for the nations and not to be kept for the believers. The reference to the coming of the Holy Spirit in Acts tells the disciples why this anointing is given to them: "But you will receive power when the Holy Spirit comes on you; and you will be my witnesses . . ." (Ac. 1:8).

The Feast of Tabernacles

The Feast of Tabernacles is one week of celebration for the harvest. It is also called the Feast of Booths or the Feast of Ingathering. The Hebrews were to take the fruit of the harvest, wave it before the Lord, and rejoice before Him for seven days (Lev. 23:39-40).

The Hebrew people moved out of their established homes and into simple shelters, remembering that they were strangers and aliens. The Lord told the people that this was to remind them that their ancestors lived in tents when they came out of Egypt (Lev. 23:42-43).

Missiological Implications

The people were to remember three feasts annually:

1. The Feast of Unleavened Bread which began with the Passover

2. The Feast of Firstfruits or Weeks

3. The Feast of Tabernacles or Ingathering

These three feasts remind us that:

1. The crucifixion of Jesus the Messiah leads us to clean out our old ways (leaven) and begin anew. Discipleship requires addressing specific areas of "old leaven" and breaking these influences on our lives. It also reminds us of our salvation from death, of the blood of the Lamb, and of His body given for our health.

2. The instruction for the Feast of Weeks was to leave the gleanings and edges of the field for the poor and the foreigner living in the area (Lev. 23:22). This concept is minimized if relegated only to farmers. All professions need to care for the needy and the foreigners. This feast takes on new meaning in the Holy Spirit because all are called to bless the needy and the nations. The Holy Spirit is not for us to hoard but to share willingly and with great joy. This fullness today is only a taste of what is to come.

3. The reality of the harvest is linked to a life called to pilgrimage. We are to hold our homes and possessions lightly, remembering we are strangers and aliens.

Holding our possessions lightly is directly linked to the great ingathering.

Requirements of Mission

Mission to the world requires a message of Christ redeeming the world through His blood. It requires a fullness of the Holy Spirit to pour abundant grace upon those coming to faith. Mission requires that we hold lightly our homes and the locations in which we live for the sake of the lost. Obedience to the Lord often requires a change of location.

Questions

- When are self-examination and the blood of the Lamb linked together?

- How has the fullness of the Holy Spirit changed your ministry?

- Is pilgrimage in this life an option for you?

> Then Moses commanded them: At the end of every seven years, in the year for canceling debts, during the Feast of Tabernacles, when all Israel comes to appear before the LORD your God at the place He will choose, you shall read this law before them in their hearing (Dt. 31:10-11).

Every seven years God commanded a cancelling of debts between His people. The interesting link for debt cancellation is the Feast of Tabernacles and the seventh year. Holding our own possessions lightly helps us to release others' debts and allows them to go free. Mission to the world will bring many opportunities to forgive those who have debts against us. Business without any debt collection is not reasonable. But times do come when old debts are cancelled. It is important that the one forgiven not take advantage of a kind creditor. God also commanded His people not to steal.

Hebrew Festivals and Calendar[1]

Sacred Sequence Begins	Hebrew Month (Post-exelic Name)*	Modern Solar Month Equivalent	Biblical References	Growing Seasons	Feasts
1	Adib; (Nisan)*	March-April	Ex 12:2; 13:4; 23:15; 34:18; Du 16:1; Ne 2:1; Est 3:7	Spring rains; barley and flax harvest begins	Passover; Unleavened Bread; Firstfruits
2	Ziv (Iyyar)*	April-May	1 Ki 6:1,37	Barley harvest continues, dry season	
3	Sivan	May-June	Est 8:9	Wheat harvest	Pentecost (Weeks)
4	Tammuz*	June-July		Tending grape vines	
5	Ab*	July-August		Ripening of grapes, figs and olives	
6	Elul*	August-September	Neh 6:15	Processing grapes figs and olives	
7	Ethanim (Tishri)*	September-October	1 Ki 8:2	Autumn rains; plowing	Trumpets; Atonement;
8	Bul (Marcheshvan)*	October-November	1 Ki 6:38	Sowing of wheat and barley	Tabernacles (Booths, or Ingathering)
9	Kislev*	November-December	Ne 1:1; Zec 7:1		Hanukkah (Dedication)
10	Tebeth*	December-January	Est 2:16	Winter rains begin	
11	Shebat*	January-February	Zec 1:7		
12	Adar*	February-March	Ezr 6:15; Est 3:7, 13; 8:12; 9:1; 15, 17, 19, 21	Almond trees bloom; citrus harvest	Purim

[1]Adapted from New Bible Dictionary, 1986, pg. 158

Chapter 6 - Israel and the Nations

Joshua

The book of Joshua makes an important transition from Moses to the new leadership. This transition is crucial in understanding God's ongoing work with the nation of Israel and His acceptance of people from other backgrounds. The transition from Moses to Joshua is also important to our understanding of mission. How would new leadership respond to the mandate to take the land? What role did the nations have in Joshua's military thrust?

Joshua's Challenge

The Lord commanded Joshua:

> Be strong and courageous. Do not be terrified; do not be discouraged, for the Lord your God will be with you wherever you go (Jos. 1:9).

This command is a great encouragement for all "sent ones" who enter new areas, face cultural change, and begin to see an expression of the kingdom of God. God's word to Joshua, "Be strong and courageous," is not only a word for leaders but also for those venturing into new areas. The actual military conquest of Joshua is difficult to understand in our times, especially with a broad western understanding of tolerance. If God simply desired to destroy the nations, He could have done so at any time. He could not allow Israel to enter the land they were not worthy to inherit. To do so would be showing favoritism without a righteous reason.

> In the fourth generation your descendants will come back here, for the sin of the Amorites has not yet reached its full measure (Ge. 15:16).

Joshua and Caleb were present with Moses when Israel failed to enter the land. Just before Israel was sent into the wilderness for forty years, these men spoke from an understanding of God's character.

> If the LORD is pleased with us, He will lead us into that land, a land flowing with milk and honey, and will give it to us. Only do not rebel against the LORD. And do not be afraid of the people

of the land, because we will swallow them up. Their protection is gone, but the LORD is with us. Do not be afraid of them (Nu. 14:8-9).

Joshua understood the necessity of God's people to walk in holiness and in faith. There is no room to claim any people as favorite, or that God's laws are less binding on a certain nation.

Rahab

A Prostitute's Act of Faith
Rahab was known to be a prostitute (Jos. 2:1). The actions of this courageous woman spoke of her faith that God was with the people of Israel. The two spies promised her, or made covenant with her, that her life and the lives of her entire family would be spared (2:12-14). Rahab believed God and worked with the "spies" sent from Israel to Jericho. This Gentile woman of faith was a prostitute, yet her act of faith saved her entire family from destruction (6:22).

Mission Preparation
As Israel prepared for God to destroy the city, two major events took place. The first was a personal recommitment to the Lord and renewal of the covenant vows through circumcision (Jos. 5:2-5). God is a God of covenant promise who allows none to walk in a favored status. The second event, Joshua meeting the commander of the angelic hosts, challenges our mission concepts.

For Us or For our Enemies?
As Joshua approached Jericho, he saw a man with a drawn sword in his hand (Jos. 5:13-15). The man was obviously a warrior and ready for battle. The question Joshua asked was significant, "Are you for us or for our enemies?" The answer brought the entire thinking process into line for Joshua and all Israel.

> "Neither," he replied, "but as commander of the army of the LORD I have now come." Then Joshua fell facedown to the ground in reverence, and asked him, "What message does my Lord have for his servant?" The commander of the LORD's army replied, "Take off your sandals, for the place where you are standing is holy." And Joshua did so (Jos. 5:14-15).

Missiological Implications

This significant answer of "neither" sets the order straight: God is not with Israel nor with any one specific nation. He is God. The real question to be asked is, "Are you with the Lord?" This message is true today worldwide. Nations that reflect God's heart will follow His directives. God shows no favoritism. He will use the nations to fulfill His purposes.

When the city was taken, Rahab and her entire household were spared. The people of Israel kept their promise. Reaching out to people of a different background was a challenge for Israel, and it still is for us today. The way in which Israel handled this new family raises many questions.

> So the young men who had done the spying went in and brought out Rahab, her father and mother, her brothers and sisters and all who belonged to her. They brought out her entire family and put them in a place outside the camp of Israel (Jos. 6:23).

This household was clearly brought into the family of God, but their current status within the community of Israel still lacked integration. Living outside the camp of Israel meant that social interaction and community events would not start immediately. Intermarriage would not be possible at this time. This same question of integration will be a topic in the New Testament when Gentiles are brought into the community of faith.

In other words, the family was saved from destruction, but not yet integrated into Israel. The text continues with a note of later including Rahab and her family into Israel (Jos. 6:25). Rahab's act to shield God's plan is remembered as a mighty act of faith (Heb. 11:31, Jas. 2:25). The Lord clearly approved of her faith by listing her in the genealogy of Christ (Mt. 1:5, Heb. 11:31, Jas. 2:5).

Questions

- How did Israel accept a Gentile woman and her family?
- How did they deal with a former prostitute?
- What would be your response as a elder in Israel to accept a family received on a covenant basis?

Ruth

Ruth was a Gentile from a Moabite background (Ru. 1:4). Her love for her mother-in-law was beyond measure, even after losing her husband, brother-in-law, and father-in-law. Her commitment to Naomi, her people, and her God was exemplary.

> Don't urge me to leave you or to turn back from you. Where you go I will go, and where you stay I will stay. Your people will be my people and your God my God. Where you die I will die, and there I will be buried. May the LORD deal with me, be it ever so severely, if anything but death separates you and me (Ru. 1:16-17).

Ruth was making a verbal commitment to her mother-in-law's people. This is an example of someone willing to make cultural adaptations in order to be adopted into a family. She was also entering into a commitment to the God of Naomi. In this case, commitment was to God and to the adopted people group. In the New Testament, a similar question will challenge our thinking: Can God move among a people without them adapting to the village norms of Bethlehem?

A Gentile Included

Boaz was a curious person in the story of Ruth. He was a wealthy landowner and likely the most eligible bachelor in the region. The question of why this man was not yet married is illuminated in the New Testament: "Salmon the father of Boaz, whose mother was Rahab, Boaz the father of Obed, whose mother was Ruth, Obed the father of Jesse" (Mt. 1:5). Common questions regarding marriage in a Middle Eastern setting are "Who are the parents? Is the family respectable? Are the siblings healthy?" Rahab's former life complicated the marriage of her son Boaz to local ladies. Boaz was half Canaanite and half Hebrew. Ruth was a Moabitess. Their son, Obed, was half Moabite, one fourth Canaanite and one fourth Hebrew. The ancestry to which Jesus was named was inclusive of the nations (Ru. 4:17, Mt. 1:5). Matthew was careful to focus on the historic and prophetic nature of the Christ. He clearly included two women from outside Israel as though they were "native born."

Reflection

Why did God allow a famine which would force Naomi and her husband Elimelech to leave their native Bethlehem and move to Moab?

Ruth is a foreigner who arrives in ". . . Bethlehem as the barley harvest was beginning" (Ru. 1:22). It also states in the following verse,

> So Ruth stayed close to the servant girls of Boaz to glean until the barley and wheat harvests were finished. And she lived with her mother-in-law (2:23).

The calendar of events helps us to understand the story of Ruth.

1. Ruth entered Israel at the time of Passover. The timing tells us of redemption, freedom from the fear of death, and God's protection offered to His people.

2. Ruth entered Israel at the beginning of the barley harvest and was present during the feast of weeks.

3. She received grain as a gift from "Israel," which is symbolic as a gift to the nations during the feast of weeks. She received six measures of barley (3:16) as first fruits, symbolizing a tithe to the nations.

4. Pentecost is the receiving of the Spirit as a down payment, either to be used as a gift to the nations or to be His witnesses.

5. Ruth married Boaz and into his family, Israel. The ingathering of the nations and incorporation into the Body of Christ have many similarities.

King David

Messianic Symbolism

David was a shepherd boy anointed by God to shepherd Israel. This rich symbolism reflects the heart of God for all His people. He cares for us as a shepherd cares for His sheep. David was also placed in positions that resembled those of the coming Messiah.

1. David was anointed king (1 Sa. 16), yet waited patiently to receive his kingdom (2 Sa. 2).

2. His kingdom was not established through impatience or selfishness (1 Sa. 24:1-5, 2 Sa. 3:28-34).

3. His kingdom would last forever (2 Sa. 7:5-17). This is only true in Christ, David's descendent.

Line of Sight

At this point, one can mistake the present Israel and the prophetic insight into the eternal Kingdom of God. This is likened to mountain ranges seen by an observer who does not realize the distance between the ridges.

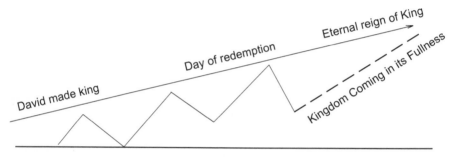

Prophetic insight into David's kingdom, the future influence of Messiah, the age of the Church, and the ultimate eternal rule of God are often seen simultaneously in Scripture. When are prophetic events to take place, and what is the time between events? These questions have been discussed for centuries.

- Aliens will shepherd your flocks (Isa. 61:5)

- The Spirit of the Sovereign Lord is upon me (61:1)

- The wolf will live with the lamb (11:6)

- You will be my people and I will be your God (Jer. 7:23)

Some of the Jews missed the advent of the Messiah because they understood He would remain forever (Jn. 12:34). How is it possible that Messiah would die or "be lifted up?" Our challenge today is to live in obedience to the King, and acknowledge God as the one who will usher in the events of the Kingdom.

Mission in the Psalms

The Psalms have rich insight into God's heart for the nations. "I will make the nations your inheritance . . ." (Ps. 2:8) reveals God's heart through the coming Messiah. No inheritance is ever considered dross. Jesus' inheritance from God the Father is rich, valuable beyond all imagination. We must be set free from the concept that "inheriting the nations" has any relation to enslaving the nations.

By definition, Psalm 67 is tied to Genesis 12:3. Psalm 67 was sung at the Feast of the First Fruits (or at the beginning of the wheat harvest). It was also called the Feast of Weeks, being seven weeks after the barley harvest and 50 days after Passover. This was, in fact, the Pentecost of the Jews.

> "May God be gracious to us and bless us and make His face shine upon us," always has this purpose -- "that your ways may be known on earth, your salvation among all nations" (Ps. 67:1-2).

This is the first of the harvest, given to the Lord for the nations. We enter the Jewish festival of God's initial blessing (first fruit) knowing it is for the people around us. Fast forward into the Pentecost of Acts where we also see that the down payment of the Holy Spirit is ". . . that you may be my witnesses . . . ." Our blessing, our anointing, our harvest, and our finances are for the ingathering of the nations.

The Psalms are rich with hundreds of references to "the nations," and "the peoples." The prophetic nature of the Psalms encourages us with God's love for all people. Psalm 126 refers to the restoration of the fortunes of Israel. What are the fortunes of Israel; by what type of wealth are they to be measured?

> When the LORD restored the fortunes of Zion,
>   we were like those who dreamed.
> Our mouths were filled with laughter,
>   our tongues with songs of joy.
> Then it was said among the nations,
>   The LORD has done great things for them (Ps. 126:1-3).

Absalom

David's children in conflict, and lack of parental leadership, resulted in Absalom harboring hatred, murdering, and fleeing for his life. The separation and inability to come into his father's presence reflects the dilemma of a sinful world unable to enjoy fellowship with the Father. This separation also reflects David's inability to truly forgive Absalom. Joab, commander of the army, encouraged a wise woman to help David see the necessity of reconciliation. Her words show God's heart for the lost and His hope of uniting with His creation.

> Like water spilled on the ground, which cannot be recovered, so we must die. But God does not take away life; instead, He devises ways so that a banished person may not remain estranged from Him (2 Sa. 14:14).

God's heart for a banished world is reconciliation. God clearly will devise ways for reconciliation where none have previously existed. This also tells us He will work out the means for individuals to be brought into fellowship. Our world is one of refugee and immigrant populations, many of whom are unreached people. Are these people "spilled water" that cannot be recovered, or are they people God has desired to bring to Himself? Are we part of the process of reconciliation?

Absalom stole the hearts of the men of Israel from his father the king (2 Sa. 15:6). The death of Absalom was not a day of rejoicing for David (2 Sa. 18:33). This conflict allows us to see the heart of David in seeking a lost son rather than the destruction of an enemy. In a similar way, God's heart will never rejoice over the destruction of the wicked. Rejoicing in the Kingdom of God will take place as a result of reconciliation (Lk. 15:7,10).

The Gibeonites

During the reign of King David, a famine occurred for three consecutive years (2 Sa. 21). After seeking the face of God, the understanding came to David that Israel had broken covenant with the Gibeonites. These non-Jewish people feared destruction and tricked Israel into making a promise to keep them alive (Jos. 9). God is faithful to His promises and does not change His mind from one people to the next. He expects His people to also remain faithful to their word. King Saul tried to annihilate the Gibeonites, ". . . in his zeal for Israel and Judah . . . " (2 Sa. 21:2). His desire to annihilate the Gibeonites is a form of ethnic cleansing. The resulting judgement on Israel is significant to our understanding Israel in our present day. Some radical opinions call for the cleansing of Israel from all non-Israeli elements.

David's Mighty Men

The role of David's mighty men was very significant during his reign and the expansion of his kingdom, both in terms of loyalty (2 Sa. 23:13-17) and of shear courage (23:20-23).

David had a very different approach from that of Saul in building a kingdom. He endeared people to himself and gave them a purpose in life. One of his mighty men, Ishmaiah, was one whom Saul would have preferred dead. ". . . and Ishmaiah the Gibeonite, a mighty warrior among the Thirty, who was a leader of the Thirty" (1 Ch. 12:4), tells us that David developed both loyalty and leadership qualities in many people's lives.

King Solomon

The life of Solomon exemplifies both the greatness of God's blessing and the folly of being led astray. The abundance within Solomon's household (1 Ki. 4:20-28) is quickly contrasted with the burden laid upon the nation (1 Ki. 12:10-11). For our purposes we will look at the significance of the Temple.

The Temple

King David desired to build a temple as a permanent resting place for the ark of God.

> Here I am, living in a palace of cedar, while the ark of God remains in a tent (2 Sa. 7:1).

David wanted to show his zeal for the Lord in building a grand temple. God's initial reply shows the nomadic heart of the Almighty among His people. This response also gives us insight into the value of the Feast of Tabernacles and God's call upon our lives to remain flexible in where we live for Him.

> This is what the LORD says: Are you the one to build me a house to dwell in? I have not dwelt in a house from the day I brought the Israelites up out of Egypt to this day. I have been moving from place to place with a tent as my dwelling. Wherever I have moved with all the Israelites, did I ever say to any of their rulers whom I commanded to shepherd my people Israel, "Why have you not built me a house of cedar" (2 Sa. 7:5-7)?

> Nathan replied to the King, "Whatever you have in mind, go ahead and do it, for the Lord is with you" (2 Sa. 7:3).

Questions & Implications

- Was Nathan speaking for himself or for the Lord?
- Explain your understanding of 1 Ch. 22:8-10.
- What do we understand from Uzziah's life (2 Ch. 26:16-23; Nu. 16:39-40; 18:1-7)?

Missiological Implications

God moves with His people. This is clear. He also lives among His people. Wherever the people of God go, God travels with them. We in mission need to grasp this truth. A fixed temple structure speaks of permanence and that His people are always in one location. People asked me at times while living in the Middle East, "How can you stand to be away from church and worship?" This question assumes that a fixed place of meeting and a particular style of worship are essential to a walk with God. God calls us as His people to a life of pilgrimage, "Blessed are those whose strength is in you, who have set their hearts on pilgrimage" (Ps. 84:5). Worship without following God's call is very empty. Following His leading is a form of worship. His promise is to come and make His dwelling with us (Rev. 21:3-5). The word dwelling (σκηνή) refers to the dwelling place--the tent or tabernacle--among His people.

Pilgrimage is very important to mission. Are we willing to recognize that our lives are not in our "fullness" yet. Sacrifice and simplicity are what God requires. We can break loose from our comfort. Going to bring "light to the nations" will require such an understanding of this present life.

Prayer of Dedication

Solomon prayed a prayer of dedication after the Temple was built and the ark was brought into it, requesting six areas of blessing from the Lord (1 Ki. 8:31-53). Solomon prayed in many ways that the people would be restored as they confessed their sins and turned to the God represented by the Temple. One part of his prayer was for the nations, to welcome and to never exclude the foreigner.

1. May people be found innocent or guilty as they come to the Temple with disputes.

2. Hear and forgive your people when they are defeated because of sin.

3. Relieve the drought that is caused by our rebellion as we confess our sin in this Temple.

4. Heal us from famine or any disaster as we confess our sins here.

5. Hear the prayer of the foreigner who comes to this Temple that all may know you as Israel does.

> As for the foreigner who does not belong to your people Israel but has come from a distant land because of your name—for men will hear of your great name and your mighty hand and your outstretched arm—when he comes and prays toward this temple, then hear from heaven, your dwelling place, and do whatever the foreigner asks of you, so that all the peoples of the earth may know your name and fear you, as do your own people Israel, and may know that this house I have built bears your Name (1 Ki. 8:41-43).

6.   When we sin and turn toward this Temple in prayer, hear us and restore us.

Solomon clearly prayed that all people would know the Lord on an equal level. The inclusion of "the foreigners" in Solomon's prayer is quite different from the exclusion of the foreigners from the Temple in the Gospels and in Acts. Our understanding of the inclusive nature of God should come from the inception of the Temple rather than from the attitude of the Pharisees. Drawing the nations to the Temple of God is a gathering or centripetal attraction. Gathering people to the work of God is one expression of mission. Another expression, centrifugal or scattering of the believers to the people, will be understood in later parts of the Old Testament.

Three Annual Feasts Reiterated
Solomon singled out the three annual feasts and sacrificed burnt offerings to the Lord.

> On the altar of the LORD that he had built in front of the portico, Solomon sacrificed burnt offerings to the LORD, according to the daily requirement for offerings commanded by Moses for Sabbaths, New Moons and the three annual feasts—the Feast of Unleavened Bread, the Feast of Weeks and the Feast of Tabernacles (1 Ch. 8:12-13).

Solomon reminds us:

1.   The feast of Unleavened Bread starts at Passover and lasts for seven days. It is the unleavened bread, sinless and pure, which is broken for us. The Passover Lamb guards us from death and is eaten within the house.

2.   The Feast of Weeks, or the Feast of the First Fruits, is a time of rejoicing before the Lord and giving Him our first fruit. This is our Pentecost. It is the outpouring of the Holy Spirit on the fiftieth day for the nations.

3.   The Feast of Tabernacles rejoices for one week at the harvest God has granted. It is linked with the years of living in pilgrimage in a tent.

Temple Questions

- What does it mean to you when the nations are drawn to the Temple?

- How will the nations hear about the work of God at the Temple?

Chapter 7 - Prophets and Kings

Elijah and Elisha

Elijah and Elisha were prophets who traveled frequently. Their ministries were never linked to a location, but rather to obedience to the Word of the Lord. They heard God speak and relayed His message to the people or kings to whom they were sent. In some ways, these two prophets symbolize the apostles to come in the Book of Acts.

Elijah

Elijah came from the eastern side of the Jordan river, the region of Gilead (1 Ki. 17:1). The nature of Elijah's ministry is descriptive of mission from many aspects. A word of rebuke from Elijah to King Ahab of Israel shows the obedience of this prophet. He feared the Lord and not people, especially at the beginning of his ministry.

> As the LORD, the God of Israel, lives, whom I serve, there will be neither dew nor rain in the next few years except at my word (1 Ki. 17:1).

Elijah knew the direction God gave for the nation of Israel and could pray to stop the rain and dew from coming. His prayer life was one from which we all must learn. The rebuke given to Ahab brought Elijah into hiding near a stream. A man or woman of God may have times of challenge, hiding, financial stress, or imprisonment. It could even be great faith in God that brings a person into a realm of new pressures.

The Lord "ordered the ravens" (17:4) to feed Elijah. Ravens, like crows, are scavengers. The food in their claws is not appetizing to anyone, and certainly unclean to a Hebrew like Elijah. God's provision for Elijah could not be refused as unclean. God then prepared a Gentile woman to provide for Elijah saying, "I have commanded a widow in that place to supply you with food" (v. 9). It is possible that God used the experience of the ravens to prepare Elijah to receive food from a Gentile woman. In a similar way, many missionaries find themselves adapting to food and cultural habits that are new.

God provides for His workers in a variety of ways. The provision of God for Elijah was often miraculous. His provision through ravens and a woman in Zarephath

(South Lebanon) were certainly not linked to offerings from the Temple. In the midst of miraculous provision, we must never assume independence or superiority over others. But neither should our provision force political subservience.

Jesus mentioned the widow of Zarephath and her provision of food during the three and one half year famine. God's provision of food was for Elijah, the widow, and her son. Her obedience to God, by giving all she had, opened the door for God's abundant blessing of food. In Luke, we see the enraged members of the synagogue trying to kill Jesus for speaking of God's provision to a Gentile (Lk. 4:28-29).

The miracles during Elijah's ministry included raising a Gentile woman's son from the dead (1 Ki. 17:17-24). This speaks of the coming resurrection and the inclusion of all people who follow the Lord. The woman's cry of anguish, "What do you have against me, man of God? Did you come to remind me of my sin and kill my son?" is typical of people who believe God is vindictive. Reminding of sin and forgiving sin are complete opposites. Satan reminds us of past failures, but the forgiveness of God moves us into restoration. The reinstatement of her son's life brought her to confess, "Now I know that you are a man of God and that the word of the LORD from your mouth is the truth" (v. 24).

Elijah traveled about, rebuking the wickedness of the northern kingdom of Israel (1 Ki. 18). Standing against evil is a mandate from the Word of God. Preaching peace and forgiveness is part of our message. The other part is to point out the depravity in the societies to which we are called.

This prophet also faced people who worshiped other gods (1 Ki. 18). Unlike unreached people who have never been enlightened, Israel left its walk with the Lord and followed Ahab and Jezebel's deception.

Elisha

Elisha was discipled by the prophet Elijah. He received the double anointing for which he had asked when his mentor was taken to heaven in a whirlwind (2 Ki. 2:9-10). Both of these prophets were required to walk in holiness and obedience before the God they personally knew. Both were able to pray, knowing that God would hear and answer. They also experienced miraculous signs and wonders which are still granted today to all who walk with Christ. Both of the prophets were a foretaste of the ministry of Jesus and His followers. Elijah discipled Elisha and the result appears to have gone very well. Elisha was hungry for God and for anointing, and he became the servant of the Lord. Elisha discipled Gehazi, but Gehazi's selfishness was his ruin (2 Ki. 5:27). Gehazi lived one way with Elisha present and another way when he thought no one was watching. Gehazi remained simply the servant of Elisha.

Discipleship is a joint commitment. However, it is important not to take personal credit when someone does well in God. It is also important that we do not take personal blame for someone who lives selfishly. We will meet different types of people in ministry and must give our all to discipleship.

Elisha's miracles laid a foundation for recognizing the miracles of Christ. Raising the son of the Shunammite in 2 Kings 4 is a glimpse of God's power available in Elisha's day. When Jesus raised the widow's son in Nain (Lk. 7:11-17), it quickened the residents of that city to realize a prophet was among them. Nain and Shunam were only two kilometers apart.

Elisha also had provision in Shunem through a couple who fed him and built a room for his use (2 Ki. 4:8-10). In this case, provision came through people who loved God and saw Him at work through Elisha. We, too, find individuals and communities involved with the ministries to which God calls us.

Naaman, the captain of the Syrian army, was healed of leprosy (2 Ki. 5). Jesus healed many lepers in His day (Mt. 8:2, Mt. 10:8, Mk. 1:40, Lk. 5:12, Lk. 17:12). Naaman's significance is that this Gentile was also commander of an army that oppressed Israel. God chose to show His greatness to this man from another nation and also from another religious background (2 Ki. 5:18-19). Naaman is a symbolic type of believer in the God of Israel who faced conflict between his new faith and the former religious system. He is also symbolic of the foreigner who returned to give thanks (Lk. 17:18).

Naaman made two requests:

He asked for two mule loads of earth from Israel to take back to Syria. This is an odd request, but appears to be linked with his vow to ". . . never again make burnt offerings and sacrifices to any other god but the LORD" (2 Ki. 5:17). Apparently, the earth will be used as a basis on which he will build an altar of sacrifice.

He asked to be pardoned when he entered the temple of Rimmon. How does this request parallel similar requests of young Muslim Background Believers? Elisha's response "Go in peace" (v. 19) cannot be taken as a complete word for all people of other religious backgrounds. We do understand from the context that Naaman would be required to accompany the king of Aram into their temple, and already felt a sense of uneasiness.

The Hebrew Servant Girl

Contained within the story of the healing of Naaman is the powerful example of cross-cultural witness. Her family was not mentioned, nor do we know if her village was destroyed. The captive girl was made a servant to the wife of Naaman (2 Ki. 5:2-3). She knew the power of God available to Elisha. This girl overcame her potential bitterness, loss of family, and loss of community to express hope and health for her captors. **This "captive witness" became a channel of God's grace and exemplifies mission.**

Reflection
How many people are in the story of Naaman and his cleansing? Which of the people mentioned helped Naaman find healing? Who was clueless about God's work?

Israel's Short-Sighted Vision

The kingdoms of Israel and Judah continued their decline. The self-centered ways of these people had little regard for the nations around them. Several prophets with amazing messages of God's mission to the world came from this time period.

Jonah

Jonah was a prophet from the Northern Kingdom of Israel. His ministry began in approximately 785 B.C. Only 52 years later, Israel would be taken captive to Assyria. God devised a way for the people of Nineveh to be brought back from destruction.

Jonah was a prophet at whom we can easily look and upbraid for his hard heart. That is, until we realize "we are Jonah." This phrase was remembered yearly by the Jews during the feast of Weeks or Harvest. Are we like Jonah? We are when we, as committed Christians who live in ease, look at the situation in the world, or at the waves of immigrants coming to our country, and sigh in disgust, wishing these people would go away, or even worse, be wiped off the earth. God's heart for the unreached, "who cannot tell their right hand from their left" (Jnh. 4:11), needs to become our heart.

God called Jonah to the city of Nineveh ". . . because its wickedness has come up before me" (Jnh. 1:2). The two major themes of this book are: God's heart for the unreached and the struggles of working with His people who do not love the nations. Jonah was no doubt acquainted with the force and cruelty of the Assyrian Empire whose capital was Nineveh. Fifty-six years before his ministry began, the Assyrian King Shalmaneser attacked Damascus, crushing armies back as far as Tyre in Lebanon (New Bible Dictionary 1986:99). Assyria received tribute from several of the surrounding nations and later required tribute from Samaria.

Jonah was called to the largest empire of his time to speak against its evil ways. Tarshish, Jonah's choice of destination, has two possible locations. One is the city of Tartessus on the Spanish coast, which was renamed Tarshish in the 9th century B.C. (op. cit. p 1165). Another possible location could be on the Red Sea coast in Africa. Solomon built ships that returned with goods common in Africa.

> The king had a fleet of trading ships at sea along with the ships
> of Hiram. Once every three years it returned, carrying gold, sil-
> ver and ivory, and apes and baboons (1 Ki. 10:22).

The Hebrew word for "trading ships" is tarshish. Because Jonah fled toward Tarshish, the former location is more acceptable. This means that Jonah fled westward when God called him eastward. Unlike the Hebrew servant girl in Elisha's day, Jonah could not overcome his fears of the Ninevites and considered them unworthy of God's message.

Jonah did not reflect an understanding of the Psalmist's prophetic call to "Declare his glory among the nations, his marvelous deeds among all people" (Ps. 96:3-4). He did reflect the common cultural attitude of Israel toward the nations that is accentuated in a post-captivity, Pharisaic disgust toward unclean Gentiles. Jonah also seemed to understand God as the God of Israel, possibly territorially linked to the land of Israel. The text says, "But Jonah ran away from the Lord and headed for Tarshish (Jnh. 1:3). If God is territorially linked to the land of Israel, fleeing westward toward Gentile Spain would, in Jonah's mind, remove the conviction of God's words upon his life! His prayer from the belly of the fish indicates that God hears prayer from His Temple. "I remembered you, Lord, and my prayer rose to you, to your holy temple" (2:7).

Jonah was found in a deep sleep during a furious storm at sea. Deep sleep during a crisis is often a sign of depression. Fleeing from God is a sure cause of depression, as is anger toward God or wrongly sensing God's rejection. His confession to the crew that he had disobeyed the God of heaven brought teaching to their lives (1:9-10). The crew actually learned to fear the Lord more quickly than Jonah when the sea became calm (v. 16). The text both amazes and shames us to see people from a background of false gods learn to fear the Lord. It is possible that this can happen to a reluctant missionary. We are humbled to realize that peoples of the world are, at times, ready to receive truth with which the people of God seem to struggle in their hearts.

God's patience with stubborn people should never be read as indifference. His ability to bring any person to his or her senses must be taken seriously. We know that "the fear of the LORD is pure, enduring forever" (Ps. 19:9). The fear of the Lord means that life is not befuddled or mixed up; it is pure and has clear direction. Jonah was a missionary who lacked the fear of the Lord, but a missionary with a strong dose of the fear of man. God raised up a great fish that became his prison for three days. The prophet cried out to God and vowed to obey Him. The Lord released Jonah when He was convinced he would obey.

The message of Jonah, "Forty more days and Nineveh will be overthrown" (Jnh. 3:4), could be the message that God gave to him to proclaim (v. 2). It does seem to convey sure judgment, without any understanding of the sins God wanted to address. The king's address to the people gives us some insight into the need.

> By the decree of the king and his nobles:
>
> Do not let people or animals, herds or flocks, taste anything; do not let them eat or drink. But let people and animals be covered with sackcloth. Let everyone call urgently on God. Let them give up their evil ways and their violence. Who knows? God may yet relent and with compassion turn from his fierce anger so that we will not perish (3:7-9).

On one level, the king seems to exhibit more understanding than Jonah. He somehow knows violence is wrong and that God may relent with compassion. Some unreached people possess an understanding of the ways of God, which causes us to marvel. Do not underestimate your audience's ability to grasp the truth of your message. On another level, the king's decree showed ignorance of God and His ways. His order for fasting and sackcloth was for both humans and animals. Imagine denying food to cows and chickens, or placing sackcloth on goats and sheep? Jonah could have explained the message more fully, or blessed the people with more understanding through discipleship. Always be ready to teach and train the people to whom God has called you. This is one of the clear messages of the book.

Jonah was unmoved by the repentance of one hundred twenty thousand people. He seemed more concerned that the words he spoke did not come to pass. His anger toward both God and his ministry came to light. Jonah knew the character of God to be "gracious and compassionate" and one "who relents from sending calamity" (4:1-3). He was in conflict with God's character on the one hand, and the message presented of impending destruction on the other. Conflict between understanding either God or His message is a sign that we need to grow. It is God's character that should fuel our ministry rather than buffet our ministry.

God's question, "Is it right for you to be angry?" (4:4), comes to many of us at different times in life. It could be lack of fruitfulness or sickness that leads to anger toward God. Jesus told His disciples that He, unlike a fox, has no place to lay His head (Mt. 8:20). He did not promise to make us rich or pay for our retirement packages. He is faithful, and He is our great reward. We have no reason for anger toward God. Asking questions of the One who loves us is healthy. Anger toward God is unhealthy because it blocks our ability to understand His heart.

God took time to tenderly explain His heart for the people and animals of the city, all of which He created, and all of which would have died in judgment. The provision of a vine Jonah did not plant, and its withering the following day, brought him again to intense anger. God was willing to work with Jonah, and He is willing to work with each one of us, forming us into the image of His Son.

Reflection or Group Discussion

You are team leader to Nineveh. The people hear of God's pending judgment and repent. What four steps will you and your team take in ministry?

Jonah's struggle tells us that God is far more concerned about the inhabitants of Nineveh hearing His word than He is with the personal comfort of His prophet. We also must grasp that the preaching in Nineveh took place after the "resurrection" of Jonah's ordeal of three days and three nights in the fish. Both of these truths will become pronounced as we continue our journey through biblical mission history.

Amos: Shepherd and Prophet

God was set to judge the nations and revealed His words of sentencing through Amos. Biblical prophets revealed God's words, and God carried out the action. Judgment was delivered, at times through natural disasters and at other times through invading armies. Amos knew that God spoke, and he was very clear about the message given to him. Senseless shepherds do not know when God speaks and, therefore, lead people astray (Jer. 10:21). The voice of the Lord that Amos heard was compared to a roaring lion (Am. 1:2), compelling the prophet to speak. We, as servants, need to know His voice and not fill in with what we assume He might say. The former takes humility to keep listening; the latter is done in pride, presuming God's thoughts are like our thoughts.

Amos delivered a sentence of destruction or captivity to nine nations of the region (Damascus, Gaza, Ashdod, Ekron, Tyre, Edom, Ammon, Moab, and Judah). He rebuked Judah and then turned the force of his message upon Israel. Judgment was inevitable. Amos received the word of the Lord approximately 760 B.C., or twenty-five years before the first captivity of Israel to Assyria.

> Does a lion roar in the thicket when it has no prey?
> Does it growl in its den when it has caught nothing (Am. 3:4)?

Amos used several illustrations of cause and effect: traps do not spring on their own (v. 5), and trumpets sound for a reason (v. 6). His point is that disaster comes to a city because of God's judgment on its evil ways. The proclamation to Israel was that she would fall, never to rise again (5:2). This would be accomplished as God sent Israel ". . . beyond Damascus" (5:27), which we know meant deportation to Assyria.

Think of the pain God suffered at Israel's depravity (5:10-12). The Flood brought destruction in the days of Noah to a corrupt world, but Israel was groomed by God. Israel saw the miracles and was present when the Law was given at Sinai. Their depravity after the Lord's input over centuries was overwhelming. What can be said of the Church which lives in the age when the Messiah has been revealed and the Scriptures made available in thousands of languages? If Israel is judged for its wickedness, are we not responsible to live in the purity of Christ and in the fear of the Lord?

The Lord showed Amos swarms of locusts coming to completely devour the land (7:1). Amos interceded and the Lord changed His mind. He then showed Amos a consuming fire that would wipe out the entire Mediterranean (7:4). This judgment, too, was held back as Amos interceded. The power of God must be kept in front of our eyes, both His power to bless and create, as well as His power to judge.

Amos faced opposition from Amaziah, priest of Bethel (7:10). Amaziah officiated in Israel's cult practice of worshipping golden calves (2 Ki. 10:29). Expect that the words God gives us will also find opposition from those in cultic religious practices. Amos feared the Lord rather than people. We must have the resolve of Amos to carry out our ministry.

The strongest judgment proclaimed against Israel went beyond destruction of property or the deportation to Assyria. God refused to talk to these people.

Captivities of Israel and Judah

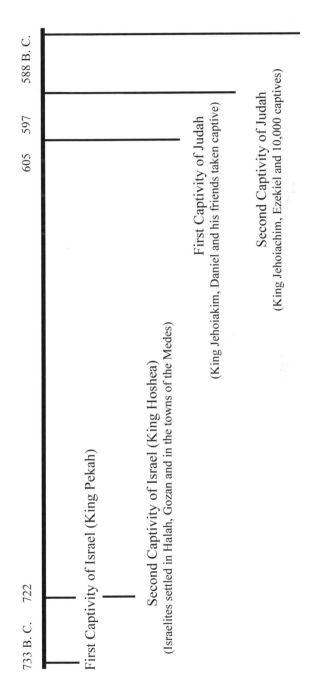

733 B. C.   722

First Captivity of Israel (King Pekah)

Second Captivity of Israel (King Hoshea)
(Israelites settled in Halah, Gozan and in the towns of the Medes)

605   597   588 B. C.

First Captivity of Judah
(King Jehoiakim, Daniel and his friends taken captive)

Second Captivity of Judah
(King Jehoiachim, Ezekiel and 10,000 captives)

Destruction of the Temple in Jerusalem
(King Zedekiah and the rest of Jerusalem taken)

> The days are coming, declares the Sovereign LORD, when I will
> send a famine through the land— not a famine of food or a
> thirst for water, but a famine of hearing the words of the LORD
> (Am. 8:11).

People we encounter in mission will not be familiar with the Lord or with His Word. Many have been given another direction through another voice. It is our calling to bring the truth that can set them free and transform their lives.

The future hope spoken about by the Lord was that He would restore "David's fallen tent" (9:11), which was symbolic of the restoration of not just one people but all people. Note that His Word linked this promise with "all the nations that bear my name" (9:12). The hope about which Amos spoke was the hope of all nations--to belong to the Lord. This future hope is our hope today, and an encouragement that our calling to the nations will not be fruitless.

King Hezekiah

His Life in Context
Hezekiah was raised by one of the most vile kings recorded in scripture. The story of his father, King Ahaz, is recorded in 2 Chronicles 28. Listed among the sins of Ahaz are:

- Casting idols
- Worshiping Baals
- Sacrificing his sons in fire to pagan deities
- Establishing pagan worship throughout the land
- Sacrificing to the gods of Damascus, whom he thought to be more powerful

Hezekiah grew up in a household knowing that some of his brothers were sacrificed to foreign gods. He was aware of the destruction that came to his native Judah from Rezin, King of Aram (Damascus), and later from Pekah, King of Israel. When Hezekiah was thirteen-years-old, the Northern Kingdom of Israel was taken into their first captivity. This young man saw the terror of war and knew firsthand of God's judgment on their lives when they worshipped other gods.

King Hezekiah - Life of Obedience
Hezekiah ascended the throne at age twenty-five (2 Ch. 28:1), and he invited God into his life and reign at the first opportunity. He turned the Kingdom of Judah around as no other king had done before him. His heart to serve the Lord, regardless of family background, is portrayed in Scripture.

In the first month of the first year of his reign, he opened the doors of the temple of the LORD and repaired them. He brought in the priests and the Levites, assembled them in the square on the east side and said: "Listen to me, Levites! Consecrate yourselves now and consecrate the temple of the LORD, the God of your fathers. Remove all defilement from the sanctuary . . .

They began the consecration on the first day of the first month, and by the eighth day of the month they reached the portico of the LORD. For eight more days they consecrated the temple of the LORD itself, finishing on the sixteenth day of the first month. Then they went in to King Hezekiah and reported: "We have purified the entire temple of the LORD, the altar of burnt offering with all its utensils, and the table for setting out the consecrated bread, with all its articles. We have prepared and consecrated all the articles that King Ahaz removed in his unfaithfulness while he was king. They are now in front of the LORD's altar" (2 Ch. 29:3-5, 17-19).

The Temple consecration was finished in only sixteen days. Years of neglect took a toll on the people, but the Temple was now functional. Do you mean business with God on this level of intensity? Regardless of how your "temple" was used, regardless of family history, God today gives you the strength to turn your life into something useful to His Kingdom. Each generation must walk with God. Many, like Hezekiah, had very bad examples to follow. God gives strength to move forward for His purposes.

Purification of the Temple

Purification began with the Temple. The same is true in our lives. The speed at which the Lord's house, lying in defiled degradation, is put in order is breathtaking. God asks us to clean up our house. His plans go far beyond restoring ritual. Once our house is in order, He is then able to make our lives and ministries useful.

Reflection

- Does your "temple" need rededication to the Lord?
- What areas of your "temple" need to be cleaned?

We are all called to a life of obedience, knowing neither the future nor the span of our lives. Our ministries today cannot be taken for granted. The open doors for effective service can close for a number of reasons. Evangelism and outreach cannot be tabled for another season as though these ministries are optional.

Cleansing and Rededication

Two sections of this story unfold in an intriguing manner. The first breakthrough was God's heart expressed through Hezekiah to celebrate the Feast of Unleavened Bread and Passover in Jerusalem. At this point we need to remember that the Feast of Unleavened Bread begins with the mandate to clean the yeast completely from each house (Ex 13:7). The old ways will affect our lives today unless they are completely removed. Salvation by the blood of the Lamb, without the cleansing of former patterns of life, will not bring the result the Lord requires of us. The message for us is to clean up our old ways and actively serve Him. The people gathered

> . . . in Jerusalem to celebrate the Feast of Unleavened Bread in the second month. They removed the altars in Jerusalem and cleared away the incense altars and threw them into the Kidron Valley (2 Ch. 30:13-14).

The purity that results from true discipleship cannot be separated from salvation. Passover and Unleavened Bread are within the same feast. Our message is only complete when salvation and repentance from former works are spoken in the same context. In Hezekiah's day, cleansing and rededicating the Temple included cleaning up society from perversion and idolatry. Purity for our personal lives will also mean cleaning and dedicating the temple of the Holy Spirit and removing symbols of degradation from our societies. This is God's mission in our present age, just as it was in the days of Hezekiah.

Reflection

Name three areas in which our society needs to be cleansed.

Invitation to Return to the Lord

The second breakthrough came with God's invitation for the Northern Kingdom of Israel to rejoin Judah (2 Ch. 30:5-9). Hezekiah overcame his awareness of Israel rampaging Judah (2 Ch. 28:5b-8) and the years of animosity between the two peoples. Hezekiah invited Israel to return to the Lord and celebrate the Passover. He had vision for changing lives beyond the borders of Judah. Reminding them that the captivity of their countrymen to Assyria was because of rebellion, he urged them to turn to the Lord so that God would have mercy and restore the captives to the land of Israel.

Four years later, judgment fell on the house of Israel. It is important to note that we, too, do not know the time allotted for us to serve in a particular nation.

> In King Hezekiah's fourth year, which was the seventh year of Hoshea son of Elah king of Israel, Shalmaneser king of Assyria marched against Samaria and laid siege to it. At the end of three years the Assyrians took it. So Samaria was captured in Hezekiah's sixth year, which was the ninth year of Hoshea king of Israel. The king of Assyria deported Israel to Assyria and settled them in Halah, in Gozan on the Habor River and in towns of the Medes. This happened because they had not obeyed the LORD their God, but had violated his covenant—all that Moses the servant of the LORD commanded (2 Ki. 18:9-12).

Israel was removed and scattered in cities throughout the Assyrian Kingdom. Some who ate of the Passover and rejoiced greatly in the God of Israel were now forced to live in exile. Did they take their hope in God with them into captivity?

The custom of the conquering power in this time period was to deport the conquered people into other areas, thus breaking their nationalistic allegiance. The intermarriage between the Israelites in Assyrian towns and the intermarriage of the nations listed above with the remnant in Israel produced the people we know in the New Testament as the Samaritans.

> The king of Assyria brought people from Babylon, Cuthah, Avva, Hamath and Sepharvaim and settled them in the towns of Samaria to replace the Israelites (2 Ki.17:24).

The people of the five listed nations met wild beasts in the cities of Israel. The report came to the king of Assyria telling him that the reason for the lions killing the new inhabitants was because "The people you deported and resettled in the towns of Samaria do not know what the god of that country requires" (2 Ki. 17:26). This led the king of Assyria to send an exiled priest back to " . . . teach the people what the god of the land requires" (2 Ki. 17:27). At first, this looked like a wonderful opportunity to tell people of five nations the ways of the true and living God. The opportunity was missed, however, and became an example of syncretism in the Old Testament.

> They worshiped the LORD, but they also appointed all sorts

of their own people to officiate for them as priests in the shrines at the high places. They worshiped the LORD, but they also served their own gods in accordance with the customs of the nations from which they had been brought. To this day they persist in their former practices. They neither worship the LORD nor adhere to the decrees and ordinances, the laws and commands that the LORD gave the descendants of Jacob, whom He named Israel (2 Ki. 17:29-34).

Notice that the old shrines used by Israel became a stumbling block to the new inhabitants (v. 29). Each of the five nations are listed with the gods they served in syncretism along with the Lord. The priest who came to the five peoples needed to speak against their former cultic ways and not simply describe Hebrew rituals. We, too, need to understand the people to whom we are sent and be able to point out evil aspects of their practices.

Missiological Implications

- Hezekiah turned wholeheartedly to the Lord, even with a very wicked father. We, too, can believe for complete transformation of a person's life, regardless of background.

- He reinstated the commands of the Lord and removed the foreign idols and altars of sacrifice.

- Turning to the Lord requires giving up old ways and paths upon which we formerly relied. Old altars of our lives will be picked up by people with whom we come into contact. Your old 'trash' will cause others to stumble.

- Preaching the good news must be accompanied by preaching the bad news, highlighting specific sins of the community.

Questions

- Hezekiah invited Israel to return to the Lord. How far do we take this thought? Can we also believe for the Assyrians and Babylonians? Are the Persians also able to be changed when they follow the Lord? What will the other nations need to give up as they come into the knowledge of the Lord?

- How do you share the gospel with people of a different religious background?

- Do you teach ritual observance to the Lord? (i.e. baptism, marriage, Easter, Christmas, burial?)

- How do you approach their former "rituals and faith?"

Hosea

Hosea prophesied to Assyria during a span of seven to twelve years after the second captivity of Israel. His prophetic voice spoke to a nation that had undergone total deportation and subsequent replacement with peoples of the nations. He exemplified a person who had participated in God's sufferings (Php. 3:10) by marrying Gomer, an adulterous wife (Hos. 1:2). God intensely loves us and also deeply grieves over our wayward lives. So intense is God's jealousy for us that He likens spiritual waywardness to adultery. No other picture placed in our minds can convey His deep hurt. He feels like a faithful husband with an unfaithful wife who has left him for another lover. The names of Hosea's children, "Punishment" and "Not Loved," reflected God's utter contempt for the House of Israel. Future hope, which always characterizes God's judgment, tells us:

> Yet the Israelites will be like the sand on the seashore, which cannot be measured or counted. In the place where it was said to them, 'You are not my people,' they will be called 'children of the living God.' The people of Judah and the people of Israel will come together; they will appoint one leader and will come up out of the land, for great will be the day of Jezreel (Hos. 1:10-11).

God welcomed those who were once told, "You are not my people." His vision was to "show my love to the one I called 'Not my loved one.' I will say to those called 'Not my people,' 'You are my people,' and they will say, 'You are my God.'" The divorce and remarrying of Israel is one application of this promise. Gathering the nations to Him, or those not previously called by His name, is another application. Both interpretations are acceptable.

Future hope is always conditionally offered to God's people. At times, future hope is offered on a worldwide scale, tucked into the present questions people face. Knowing the character of God keeps us from the world's utter despair. Future hope also speaks of the miracle of transformation to come. Hosea spoke intensely of the rift between God and the destroyed Israel. Then the mind of God turned to a future date of complete restoration, "After two days he will revive us; on the third day he will restore us, that we may live in his presence" (6:2). The change is beyond measure! Taking us from "not my people," to "live in his presence" is a miracle of God.

The condition to "live in his presence" can only be understood at this time in an Old Covenant context. We link restoration on the third day with life in His presence, knowing the work of the Messiah to come. The word after the promise of life in His presence, "Let us acknowledge the LORD; let us press on to acknowledge him" (6:6), is far more rewarding than fulfilling ritual obligations. The offer of His presence brings with it the protection, the provision, and the joy only the Creator can supply.

He longs for people to display a sincere heart of mercy toward their fellowman far more than observance of religious rituals. His word, "I desire mercy, not sacrifice, and acknowledgment of God rather than burnt offerings" (6:6) is put into story form by Jesus, describing a compassionate Samaritan. This prophetic verse is one God looks for in our lives. Mercy and love speak to a world far more effectively than a religious debate.

The many sins of Israel were beyond human repentance or restitution and needed God's intervention. This message is also true for the world. Israel was condemned, yet the hope offered was to live in His presence. A glimpse was offered of God's plan to make this possible by defeating death, bringing life to those without hope.

> I will deliver this people from the power of the grave;
> I will redeem them from death.
> Where, O death, are your plagues?
> Where, O grave, is your destruction (13:14)?

Life in His presence and triumphing over death is an offer of eternal life. This is future hope that overcomes present stress in this world.

Hosea ends his prophetic word with an abundance of God's love and promises. In this outpouring of encouragement, God leaves the door open for Israel to return. He so longs for them to be healed that He teaches what to pray. Look at this prayer in light of their captivity and in light of the prayer Jesus taught us to pray.

> Say to him: . . . "Forgive all our sins and receive us graciously,
> that we may offer the fruit of our lips. Assyria cannot save us;
> we will not mount warhorses. We will never again say 'Our
> gods' to what our own hands have made,
> . . . for in you the fatherless find compassion" (14:2-3).

Chapter 8 - Isaiah: Message for the Nations

The prophet Isaiah spoke of Israel's failure and impending judgment. Several themes of mission make this book a deep source from which we can draw knowledge of how we must live. This prophetic book reveals God's love for all nations. Isaiah clearly described the coming Messiah, the Messianic Kingdom, and God's yearning for Israel to be a "light for the nations." Throughout Isaiah's prophetic writing was a call to righteousness. The outcome of righteousness would affect the nations. Isaiah's prophetic ministry spanned the reign of four kings of Judah (Isa. 1:1). The words he spoke and recorded helped the people of his day to understand Messiah and the future rule of the Kingdom of God. We also benefit by recognizing our role in the Kingdom of Messiah.

Themes in Isaiah

This book describes God's activities and future vision. Themes are often intermingled. Messiah and the Kingdom will bring about many changes simultaneously. Five themes in Isaiah describe our God and His hope for the nations. (1) Isaiah tells us that **God is completely righteous**, and His judgment on Israel and the nations is completely fair. If we respond to the Lord, there is future hope. Despair is not of God because it discounts His outstretched, loving arm. (2) Israel is to be a **light for the nations** or a beacon of hope through obedience to God. How Israel will affect the nations is a theme that will be expanded upon in this book. (3) Isaiah speaks frequently of the **Messiah, the Kingdom of Messiah**, and the changes to look for "In that day." (4) **Peace** is described as life without war or peace after all wars. Swords become plows and spears become pruning hooks. Culture will be transformed "in that day" from a defensive life to life in His presence. This future hope is an encouragement to all of us and part of the message we proclaim in Christ, whom Isaiah called the Prince of Peace. (5) God clearly announces that **the Gentiles are included** in faith and in the people of God as both recipients and vessels carrying the light. They are considered holy and welcomed and are to engage in righteous acts of service in the Kingdom of Messiah.

The Lord is Righteous

Isaiah opens with the theme of many nations learning the ways of the Lord from Israel and carrying their new faith and hope to other Gentile areas (Chapter 2). Five conditions for Israel to be a blessing to other peoples are found in Isaiah 1. God requires His people not only to repent but to take steps to do what is right.

1. Wash, remove your sin and evil deeds (v. 16).

2. Learn to do what is right (v. 17).

3. Seek justice.

4. Encourage the oppressed.

5. Defend the cause of the fatherless and the widow (v. 17).

The judgment upon Israel was almost a complete removal of their population through death and captivity. God allowed a few survivors, unlike His total judgment on Sodom and Gomorrah (1:9). The reasons they faced captivity and death should drive us to action with a fear of the Lord to do what they failed to do. They made unjust laws "to deprive the poor . . . and withheld justice from the oppressed" (10:2). Our gospel must include encouragement to the poor and laws that protect them from cruelty. Israel ignored the plight of the widows and orphans (v. 2); we must take special note of people with no voice or defender.

Judgment of Judah and Jerusalem began by removing internal harmony creating discord (3:5-7) with the intent to bring them to recognize their need for the Lord (v. 7). Judah was also guilty of plundering the poor (3:14-15). The Lord promised that, "In that day" He would remove their luxury and bring them into poverty (vv. 18-22). Future hope "In that day" is declared in the same breath with the Messiah wiping the bloodstains from Jerusalem, which meant that the memory of judgment would be forgotten. The phrase "In that day" was used by Isaiah as a day to come. He saw the days of judgment and the days of hope in the coming Messiah separated by a span of time. The length of time between the "days coming" was unclear. What *was* clear was that judgment was pronounced with future hope.

God's judgment upon Jerusalem was depicted as judgment upon His vineyard. He promised to remove its "hedge" and allow its destruction (5:5). Judgment was coming because of injustice, violence, distress (v. 7), and turning a blind eye to justice through bribes (v. 23). Within this prophecy was a depiction of captivity; "great houses will become desolate" (v. 9), and "my people will go into exile" (v. 13). He prophesied of the coming capture of Jerusalem's leaders (22:3) and promised the defeat of her enemies (29:3-8). This mention of captivity to Judah was a reminder of the devastation to the Northern Kingdom, and seemingly a warning of what could happen to Jerusalem if they continued in their darkness.

God was angry with Assyria, the nation He used to judge Israel. His purpose was for Assyria to "seize loot and snatch plunder, and trample them down" (10:6). Assyria went beyond this and came "to destroy, and to put an end to many nations" (v. 7). The mission of God is not to put an end to many nations but to bring the hope of the Messiah to many nations and people. This concept instructs us to encourage the growth of the Kingdom of God in a way that honors people and cultures different from our own. Discernment is needed to keep away from syncretism while maintaining the flavor of the many redeemed nations in whom God delights.

Righteousness and Future Hope

Despair and hopelessness reign among people who do not know the Lord and His covenant promises (Eph. 2:12). They also grip those who have a distorted view of Him (Job 7:6). Our righteous God does not want despair among His people. His discipline is not meant to shun but to bring growth. None who come to Him remain in ashes or in mourning. His praise displaces despair. His transformation turns a lost people inside-out in renewal to:

> provide for those who grieve in Zion— to bestow on them a crown of beauty instead of ashes, the oil of joy instead of mourning, and a garment of praise instead of a spirit of despair. They will be called oaks of righteousness, a planting of the LORD for the display of his splendor (Isa. 61:3).

Judgment and Future Hope

God promised judgment to the house of Israel (Isa. 5), comparing it to His personal vineyard. He judged the Israelites for calling evil good and good evil (vv. 20-23). The next writing of Isaiah related his vision of a holy God (Isa. 6) and His call to a stubborn people. They will face captivity "until the cities lie ruined and without inhabitant" (vv. 11) but with the promise of a remnant (v. 13). "Comfort, comfort my people, says your God. Speak tenderly to Jerusalem, and proclaim to her that her hard service has been completed" (40:1-2) presents both judgment and future hope. Future hope is often linked with ultimate hope in the coming Messiah. Valleys filled and mountains were flattened to prepare for Messiah (vv. 3-5). We are promised that the Sovereign Lord will rule with power (v. 10), which is the establishment of the Kingdom of God.

Reflection

God asked for someone to speak truth to a needy people. The Lord said, "Whom will I send" (Isa. 6:8)? The clear call to Isaiah is a mission theme; God calls us. Do we respond with the "Here am I. Send me." as Isaiah responded?

For what did Isaiah ask before responding?

What do you require before you respond to God's call?

Light to the Gentiles

God's heart for the non-Jewish areas is clearly laid out by Isaiah. His love for the nations must be understood by His people and become one of the major factors that form our calling. His hope for the nations is often mixed with a prophetic description of the coming Messiah.

> Nevertheless, there will be no more gloom, for those who were in distress. In the past He humbled the land of Zebulun and the land of Naphtali, but in the future He will honor Galilee of the Gentiles, by the way of the sea, along the Jordan (Isa 9:1).

God does not desire gloom in Israel nor in the world. He cares when people, any people, sit in depression. Humanism wrongly believes that isolated people are happy in their present conditions. Freedom from animistic bondages requires the light of the world entering their lives. He promises to honor the area of the Gentiles. Future hope is for the world and not simply for Israel.

Light is symbolic of the true understanding of the God of Israel going forth to the whole earth: "The people walking in darkness have seen a great light" (v. 2). He plans to engulf the dark area of despair into His Kingdom of light. Mission is unavoidable. Great light on earth cannot be seen from long distances, which leads us to conclude that His people need to carry the light into regions beyond their borders.

"You have enlarged the nation" (v. 3) cannot be understood as a pro-Israeli drive to engulf Assyria, Babylon, Egypt, and Cush in a military conquest. This is the Kingdom of Light going forth with power to the areas of darkness. The result, "and increased their joy," is never the case with a military conquest. Enlarging the nation brings us to realize that citizens of the Kingdom are welcomed in whatever land they currently live—the Kingdom grows, regardless of political borders.

The true Israel, or the light and knowledge of the Lord, increases or expands as salvation in Messiah comes to the ends of the earth. The expansion of the nation is endless, because:

1. Light continues to spread to areas of darkness.

2. The harvest is exposed to the "Light" and gathered or brought into safety.

3. The harvest becomes part of the next generation, carrying Light to new regions beyond.

This cycle depicts Gentiles turning to God and reaching new areas with the light they now radiate: "You have shattered the yoke that burdens them, the bar across their shoulders, the rod of their oppressor" (Isa. 9:4). Nation after nation will experience increasing freedom from former taskmasters as yokes are shattered. This is also futuristic. Many taste freedom in the Lord in spite of temporary persecution and imprisonment.

Hope of the coming Messiah is the hope for the nations. "For to us a child is born" (9:6a) is intertwined with light to the Gentiles. Unfortunately, many have heard Isaiah read, yet missed the beauty of God's gift in the Messiah for all nations (Lk. 4:24-30; Ac. 2:21-22). Peace and the expansion of His Kingdom are dynamically related. "Of the increase of His government and peace there will be no end" (Is 9:7a). The increase of His government means that we carry the light into regions filled with darkness. Darkness does not welcome the expanding light of the Kingdom of God. This brings us to the conclusion that "peace without end" is to be realized in the middle of battle with the darkness that opposes the light. How often do we seek peace, a personal private peace that avoids a battle? His increasing Kingdom is tied to peace, but to a different definition of peace than is normally understood.

Carrying the light into dark regions, church planting, is the will of God. This is the call of God upon His people. The battles faced when pushing out the darkness are also a part of His calling. We are designed for battle, not on a human level but against opposing powers (Mk. 3:15; Lk. 10:19).

At times, God's people have taken one aspect of the Kingdom (peace) at the expense of the direction of the Kingdom (carrying light). What is required is laying down our false understanding of "peace" (personal comfort, isolation) for the increase of His Kingdom! The gospel of peace is much broader than focusing on one aspect of peace, such as personal comfort or a tolerant lack of conflict.

Personal comfort and tolerance to sin hardens hearts to the truth; they work against the Kingdom.

We are lambs sent among wolves (Lk. 10:3). Responding as Jesus would to those of an opposite spirit is required to exemplify the Kingdom of God. But make no mistake! It will be a battle with both demons and selfish people when national issues of slavery, abortion, child prostitution, and homosexuality are addressed.

The ends of the earth will know the Lord. Isaiah prophetically described God both mandating light to the Gentiles and making provision in order for this light to be carried to them.

> And now the Lord says – He who formed me in the womb to be His servant to bring Jacob back to Him and gather Israel to Himself, for I am honored in the eyes of the Lord and my God has been my strength. It is too small a thing for you to be my servant to restore the tribes of Jacob and bring back those of Israel I have kept. I will also make you a light for the Gentiles, that you may bring my salvation to the ends of the earth (Isa. 49:5-6).

This prophetic word to the preincarnate Christ tells us that gathering Israel is good, but it's too small a job. It is not the end product for the Messiah. The other part of the job is to carry this Light to the ends of the earth. The message to every tribe, nation, people, and language is an anointing on Messiah. The Father is anointing the Christ for mission to the world. Jesus said, "As the Father has sent me, so I send you" (Jn. 20:21). We, His people, must embrace this two-fold calling of gathering the people of God and salvation to the ends of the earth. The amount of emphasis on the former overwhelms the needed emphasis on the latter. His calling is our calling. We carry a twofold calling to both God's people (here Israel, or for us, the Church) and to the regions yet unreached (Gentiles to the ends of the earth).

Questions

- Did Jesus accomplish this work during His lifetime?
- Does He not live out the fulfillment of these prophetic words through all who believe?
- Are you willing to be part of the fulfillment of that vision?

Carry the Light

Many parts of the book of Isaiah speak of carrying the good news that brings joy. Carrying the light to the Gentiles is honored by God.

> How beautiful on the mountains are the feet of those who bring good news, who proclaim peace, who bring good tidings, who proclaim salvation, who say to Zion, your God reigns (Isa. 52:7)!

This passage brings encouragement to the weary feet and bodies who will carry the good news of salvation. Our message must always contain the news of salvation available only through Christ, the son of David. News of salvation cannot be replaced by humanitarian aid to a people. New homes and flourishing fields that sit in darkness are not God's vision for the world.

God wants the nation enlarged. He wants other people to enter the Kingdom. If we look only at a political Israel, we cheer it on to take Syria and Iraq. Such thinking is pointless!

> Enlarge the place of your tent, stretch your tent curtains wide, do not hold back, lengthen your cords, strengthen your stakes, for you will spread out to the right and to the left; your descendants will dispossess nations and settle in their desolate cities (54:2-3).

The only time we need to enlarge the tent is when the family grows. God wants us to take many nations into our family. This is a powerful picture of the body of Christ, expanding without prejudice against any nation or color or language!

Today, how do we read Scripture that describes dispossessing other nations? Do you look for Israel to expand into the nations; or is it the Church that spreads to the right and to the left? God has called us to move into desolate areas that need the Lord Jesus.

> Surely you will summon nations you know not, and nations that do not know you will hasten to you, because of the Lord your God, the holy one of Israel, for He has endowed you with splendor (Isa. 55:5).

Missiological Implications

Nations will come to Jesus. How many nations are presently in the world? What draws nations to want to know your message of salvation?

Messiah and the Kingdom of Messiah

Isaiah conveys a rich understanding of the coming Messiah, which is useful in explaining our faith and trust in Him. Our faith in the one and only Messiah is not simply based upon His life, but upon the prophetic promises that describe His character and authority. Unlike a human prophet or king, the Messiah is to be born of a virgin and be called Immanuel (7:14), meaning "God with us." God's promise to live among His people is fulfilled in the Messiah, which is expanded revelation to the words of the prophets. Immanuel needs to be understood as "God living among us" and must not be misinterpreted as "God is on our side."[1] The list of names given to this child to be born--"Wonderful Counselor, Mighty God, Everlasting Father, Prince of Peace" (9:6)--describes God in human form. This, too, is a new word from the prophets.

We learn that He is the ruler (9:6) and judge to come (11:3-5). His place of judgment is described as "with righteousness he will judge the needy" (v. 4). This brings us to understand the One who will make things right on this earth. He will also, "strike the earth with the rod of his mouth; with the breath of his lips he will slay the wicked" (op. cit.). This makes Him the ultimate ruler on judgment day.

Messiah will gather the nations, Israel, and Judah (11:12). He is the one who will be the head to whom all nations will look for leadership. Jesus later said, "I have other sheep that are not of this sheep pen. I must bring them also. They too will

---

[1] "God with us" must be taken in the context of the Bible. Joshua asked the commander of the army of the LORD, "Are you for us or for our enemies" (Jos. 5:13)? The answer, "neither," is revelation that God does not validate a person or nation. We must follow Him and be on His side. Immanuel literally must mean "God living among us" and cannot be misinterpreted as "God is on our side." Israel's fatal mistake was believing that they possessed the Kingdom.

> But when the tenants saw the son, they said to each other, 'This is the heir. Come, let's kill him and take his inheritance.' So they took him and threw him out of the vineyard and killed him (Mt. 21:38-39).

This parable spoken by Jesus describes the "tenants" as unyielding to authority and having possession of the vineyard. Wrongly believing "God is on our side" brings a people to believe that they are validated, and they will close their minds to true authority. God chose Abraham and formed a people. Mistakenly saying God is Jewish would bring that nation to believe that they are "the Kingdom." The Qur'an takes the mind of a Muslim down a closed path by saying, "The religion of Allah is Islam" (Surah 3:19). This brings a Muslim to believe his or her path is validated without question, no longer needing discernment for God's will today because the lines between God's will and the person's will are blurred.

listen to my voice, and there shall be one flock and one shepherd" (Jn. 10:6). All are united in the Messiah.

The description of Jerusalem clothed with "garments of splendor" (Isa. 52:1) appears to be a precursor to the picture of the prepared bride "dressed for her husband" (Rev. 22:1). The woman later referred to as the widow is told:

> You will forget the shame of your youth
> and remember no more the reproach of your widowhood.
> For your Maker is your husband—
> the LORD Almighty is his name—
> the Holy One of Israel is your Redeemer (Isa. 54:4-5).

Widowhood is not the same as divorce or rejection. The husband is the Maker or Creator, the LORD Almighty, the Holy One of Israel, the Redeemer. The death of the husband lies between the words of the bride in Isaiah 52 and the widowhood of Chapter 54. The description of the death of the beloved in Chapter 53 gives insight into the reality of Messiah. God incarnate is our husband who suffered and had "laid on Him the iniquity of us all" (53:6). We rejoice that He rose (v. 11) and that He intercedes for us (v. 12c).

In that Day

Isaiah uses the phrase "In that day" to describe many aspects of the Messiah's Kingdom to come. We read, "In that day the Branch of the LORD will be beautiful and glorious, and the fruit of the land will be the pride and glory of the survivors in Israel" (4:2). The survivors will have their sins cleansed, and they will have "a cloud of smoke by day and a glow of flaming fire by night" (v. 5). This reference to the cloud by day and fire by night is a restoration of the pillar that followed the Children of Israel out of Egypt. Messiah's protection is from heat, storm, and rain, which could be a reference to protection of the remnant during war. This protection is present in God now and is also to be received in the age to come.

Isaiah refers to a time when Gentiles will gather around the Messiah. "In that day the Root of Jesse will stand as a banner for the peoples; the nations will rally to him" (11:10). This reference has had its fulfillment from the time of the Book of Acts to the present, and it will continue. Gentiles gathering around the Messiah was an odd concept in Isaiah's day and unthinkable by the Jews in the Gospels and even into the Book of Acts (Ac. 11; 15; 21). Isaiah continues with this theme, proclaiming that in that day, the message of Messiah's accomplishments will be proclaimed among the nations (Isa. 12:4).

References to "in that day" include the destruction of "Leviathan the gliding serpent" (27:1), the destruction of all God's enemies (vv. 7-11), and the ingathering of His people at the sound of the trumpet (v. 13). God grants peace to followers of the Messiah, understanding the culmination of His warfare against His enemies and future victory. Sorting out the mountain tops about which Isaiah spoke, and the sequences of events, necessitates the New Testament.

Peace

He will be the end of all disputes. The effect of the Word of the Lord is that fighting ends between nations. Agricultural equipment will replace weapons of war. This is a picture of the future Kingdom. Such a description of peace must draw the world to long for the Kingdom.

> He will judge between the nations and will settle disputes for many peoples. They will beat their swords into plowshares and their spears into pruning hooks. Nation will not take up sword against nation, nor will they train for war anymore. Come, O house of Jacob, let us walk in the light of the LORD" (Isa. 2:4-5).

Peace is described as a new world without fear. The concept of "The wolf will live with the lamb" (11:6) is describing a new world in which the nutritional habits are restored to the Garden of Eden. The stomach and digestive order of a lion will need to change because "the lion will eat straw like the ox" (v. 7). The complete harmony of all creation, including humans, symbolizes peace beyond our current imaginations.

Gentiles are Included

When God's people reflect His Kingdom, others will become hungry for that which satisfies the longing of every person. His hope for the nations is to learn His ways.

> Many peoples will come and say, "Come, let us go up to the mountain of the LORD, to the house of the God of Jacob. He will teach us His ways, so that we may walk in His paths." The law will go out from Zion, the word of the LORD from Jerusalem (Isa. 2:3).

There is a drawing of outsiders to the knowledge of God through "Come, let us go up . . . to the house of the God of Jacob." There is also revelation of God's desire to scatter His people to fulfill His blessing of the nations. "The law will go out from Zion." This word clearly tells us that many peoples want to be taught the way of the Lord, and many peoples will also carry the knowledge of God to new areas. Learning the ways of God changes the behavior of people.

Centrifugal and Centripetal Mission

Mission is presented in Scripture as centripetal (drawing) and centrifugal (scattering). Isaiah portrayed a picture of the nations streaming to the city of Jerusalem in the last days. "Come, let us go up to the mountain of the LORD, to the house of the God of Jacob" (Isa. 2:3) seems to indicate the nations coming to the house of God in Jerusalem. The magnetic draw to a location could be understood from "Who may live on your holy hill" (Ps. 15:1b)? Rather than a pilgrimage to Jerusalem, it is a hunger for God that will draw people to His righteousness. It is God and His people who draw the nations to know Him and His ways. It is not a geographic location. We should not misunderstand God's intent in Isaiah to encourage pilgrimage to Jerusalem to find truth. Nor should we wrongly proclaim Jerusalem as the only geographic center involved in the work of the Lord.

The knowledge of God sent out to the nations is described by "The law will go out from Zion, the word of the LORD from Jerusalem" (Isa. 2:3b). The scattering of God's people who are filled with the Holy Spirit is, in a sense, the scattering of the temple of the Holy Spirit (1 Co. 6:19). This transforms our concept of mission: The Body of Christ, filled with many temples of the Holy Spirit, is a gift to the nations through training and sending.

Does God draw the nations to a particular location to know Him and His ways, or are we to take His message to the nations? Has God asked the nations to come to us, as the animals came to the ark in Noah's time? Waiting for people to come to us will only count those we discover in our location. Going to the nations will bring us to search for those living in darkness, those without the knowledge and morality of the Sovereign Lord. In one sense, the people of God must attract others to the light of God in any location where they find themselves. Both gathering and scattering are part of God's plan to reach the nations. How we position ourselves will either pacify us or invigorate us to enter into God's call to mission.

The product of only centripetal mission will be the formation of communities that are oblivious to people living beyond their proximity, like the Essenes. Centripetal mission will form a "saved" community that may or may not allow others the opportunity to join. Becoming Amish, for example, is no small task and is rarely attempted. Other cultural expressions will almost always be judged and therefore required to be left at the gate upon entry. This will also be true with language. Others will need to understand the language of the "saved" community in order to enter and be accepted.

Centrifugal mission will have a heart that breaks for ". . . those living in the land of the shadow of death . . ." (Isa. 9:2). God's grief over the moral condition of our planet will compel us to go into the world. Living a life for Jesus in "the land of the shadow of death" will present opportunities to live for Jesus in other cultural settings. Isaiah continued to say that those nations taught of His ways would go forth from that city with the Word of the Lord in them. Second generation mission must be sown in the hearts of all coming to the light of God.

Reflection

- Are both centrifugal and centripetal mission necessary?
- What is the result of only centripetal mission?
- How would you characterize Israel at this point in Isaiah?
- What is the result of only centrifugal mission?

All Are Welcome!

Isaiah 56 speaks of God's invitation to all people to enter covenant with Him. Mission concepts are gleaned from the following verses of this chapter.

- God accepts foreigners who are bound to Him (v. 3).

- Eunuchs who follow God's laws will be given a memorial name within the Temple (v. 5). Foreigners who worship God, keep the Sabbath, and hold true to the covenant will be brought to the mountain of God and given joy in His house of prayer (vv. 6-7).

- God will accept the offerings of Gentiles (v. 7). He accepts their sacrifices on His altar.

- God's house is a house of prayer for all nations (v. 7; Mk. 11:7).

- The "robbers den" can be the market that blinds us to the needs of others, the social advancement that distracts us from our calling, or the entertainment that we allow to steal our time.

- God will gather others to belong to "Israel" (Isa. 56:8).

God's vision is a global vision and one which requires all people to hold to the covenant. Israel missed the vision and used the house of prayer for a market place in Jesus' day. Isaiah also tells us that foreigners will shepherd the flocks and work the fields (Isa. 61:5). Room will be made for responsibility and leadership for those from the nations. They will be included in both faith and leadership.

God is the God of all the Earth

Isaiah repeatedly writes of the prophetic knowledge that God is not simply the God of Israel; He is the God of the whole earth. We know from the Genesis account that God created the whole earth. Isaiah repeats this theme, letting it be known that God made everything (Isa. 40:28, 41:5). Look for this description of God to later come out of the mouths of Gentiles.

Now with the imminent threat of captivity, Isaiah prophesies that God's praise will go to the ends of the earth (Isa. 42:10). This prophetic look into the spread of the knowledge of the Lord goes against the idea of one Temple, one place of gathering.

The idea of God's praise going to the ends of the earth includes more than the children of Israel traveling to many places. This includes the salvation of the "Gentiles to the end of the earth" (Isa. 45:22-25, 52:10). Light is not only carried or scattered; it must also be received and allowed to transform lives.

Chapter 9 - Jeremiah: Prophet to the Nations

Jeremiah's voice was heard as Jerusalem was taken into captivity. His written prophecies later brought hope to the captives (Da. 9:2). This prophet witnessed God's judgment come upon Judah and prophetically spoke of the return of the captives. Jeremiah's anointing was "over nations and kingdoms to uproot and tear down, to destroy and overthrow, to build and to plant" (Jer. 1:10). Too often the words of the prophets are heard as rebukes calling for judgment. It is important we also hear the words to build and to plant. Look for the prophetic voice to declare God's power for nations to change and a Kingdom to be planted.

Called to the Nations

Jeremiah began his writings by acknowledging his call from God. He believed what the Lord said.

> The word of the LORD came to me, saying, "Before I formed you in the womb I knew you, before you were born I set you apart; I appointed you as a prophet to the nations" (Jer. 1:4-5).

Prophets like Elijah had a specific calling to Israel. The ministry of Jeremiah went beyond speaking to Judah. He was called to be a prophet to the nations! This is the clearest articulation of a ministry to the Gentiles in the Old Testament. Isaiah's theme of "light to the nations" took on new meaning with Jeremiah and his anointing. Further provision was made for the Gentiles to know God as Israel knew Him (1 Ki. 8:43).

Concept of Calling

The Lord touched Jeremiah's mouth (Jer. 1:9) which brought the anointing of prophetic words. Isaiah had a seraphim touch a live coal to his lips (Isa. 6:6), pronouncing his freedom from guilt and atonement. Both prophets deepened their ministries after their commissioning. The point is significant for all who enter ministry. Each of us needs a touch of God, an anointing, and a commissioning. None can move into a holy work because it is a good idea. It must be God's touch. Earnestly pray for an anointing of the Spirit of God, without compulsion to repeat another person's experience.

Verbalizing the call of God upon your life is a statement of faith that acknowledges God has spoken. Jeremiah knew he was set aside for ministry before his birth. From the time of formation in his mother's womb, he knew he was called to the nations. Notice the similarity of Jeremiah to Paul, who was called to be an apostle to the nations from the womb (Gal. 1:15). The difference in language is (1) called to be a prophet before formation in the womb and (2) called to be an apostle from the womb. God's burden to be made known among the nations is very clear through His raising up people specifically for this task. The commission of God upon our lives to reach the nations is rooted deeply in His Word. Many of us, like Paul, look back on foolish or sinful paths that diverted our lives from God's calling. Yet like Paul, we also acknowledge that the ministry we have to the nations is that for which we were set aside from birth.

The words given to Jeremiah at his commissioning can be applied to our ministries. We are called to do the will of God, not to fulfill our own plans. Neither is the call of God something one picks up at will or sets down at will. Jeremiah was told, "Get yourself ready! Stand up and say to them whatever I command you" (Jer. 1:17). Our walk with God needs this level of obedience.

The Heart of God for Judah

Jeremiah is a book revealing the intense love and heartbreak of God for His people. Israel and Judah brought heartache to a holy God as a result of numerous types of sins. God abbreviates the list against Judah into two categories:

They have forsaken me, the spring of living water, and

(They) have dug their own cisterns, broken cisterns that cannot hold water (2:13).

God comes to His people as a spring of living water. Jesus said,

> . . . whoever drinks the water I give them will never thirst. Indeed, the water I give them will become in them a spring of water welling up to eternal life (Jn. 4:14).

He promised that the spring would be available when we drink of Him or believe in Him (Jn. 7:38). The struggle of Judah was that its people wearied of daily depending upon the spring of living water. Like their forefathers in the desert (Ex. 17), they carved out their own system to contain religious life. A religious system appears to work; it has ritual, a calendar of events, a list of officials, and even contains sacred writings. Without "living water," however, the human-made system is a broken cistern that cannot satisfy. Fear that the "spring" is not consistent seeks a religious system rather than the humility and repentance needed to place God first.

Jeremiah captured the intensity of God's pain. God described Himself as a bereaved husband with an adulterous wife (Jer. 3:26). The captivity of Israel was spoken of as a certificate of divorce (3:8), sending her away. And now God's justice would not allow Judah, who was less righteous than Israel (3:11), to go unpunished. The emotions of God are greater than we can understand and are on full display in this book.

God was in deep anguish because of the destruction coming upon Judah. It was not His pleasure to bring disaster, and He described it as "the agony of my heart" (4:19)! The message we grasp is that God does not coldly call for punishment. He has tried to pursue His bride for centuries.

The level of rebellion in Judah shocked God.

> I had planted you like a choice vine of sound and reliable stock.
> How then did you turn against me into a corrupt, wild vine
> (2:21)?

The "choice and reliable stock" is a reference to the family of Abraham that God had cultivated for over fourteen hundred years. Cultivating a people means that they have a history of seeing His miracles, of knowing His protection from their enemies, and of receiving the blessing of His provision. God's question shows frustration that people who knew His ways would live without reflection of their past.

The people learned to live with their broken cistern and seemed happy without any need for the "spring of living water." God knows the destructive consequences of living with false hope based upon lies. He also knows the pride of people acting upon their own authority. The question He asked showed the pain of His heart.

> A horrible and shocking thing has happened in the land: The
> prophets prophesy lies, the priests rule by their own authority,
> and my people love it this way. But what will you do in the end
> (5:30-31)?

Living without God's direction leads to death (Pr. 14:12). Judah, like Israel, preferred to live with a broken cistern rather than live under God's authority. God felt alone in His anguish, not comforted by the judgment to come.

> Oh, that my head were a spring of water and my eyes a foun-
> tain of tears! I would weep day and night for the slain of my
> people (Jer 9:1).

Spring and fountain in this case were not health and life for the nation, but the tears of a broken heart. The pain experienced in Jeremiah is expressed using figurative words so that we who follow God understand His emotions.

> My tent is destroyed; all its ropes are snapped. My children are
> gone from me and are no more; no one is left now to pitch my
> tent or to set up my shelter (10:20).

Vision for the expanding tent to bless the nations (Isa. 54:2-3) was now a great disappointment. This could also be a reference to the tent of meeting prior to the days of the Temple in Jerusalem. No one cared about the will of God or even listened to His rebukes. The human desire to form a good system did not end with Israel. People in churches today can also forget the necessity of drinking from the spring of living water and carrying God's vision for the nations to know Him. The message from Jeremiah is applicable today.

Is Hope Available?

Was captivity inevitable for the people of Judah? Jeremiah prophesied of their impending captivity, knowing God's mercy was more than sufficient to relent of His anger. Any change depended upon their response to God. "Return, faithless people; I will cure you of backsliding" (Jer. 3:22). Hope seemed to be obtainable at this point.

> This is what the LORD says to the people of Judah and to Jeru-
> salem: Break up your unplowed ground and do not sow among
> thorns. Circumcise yourselves to the LORD, circumcise your
> hearts, you people of Judah and inhabitants of Jerusalem, or
> my wrath will flare up and burn like fire because of the evil you
> have done— burn with no one to quench it (4:3-4).

God wanted Judah to return to Him and be the blessing of "light to the nations" for which it was intended (4:2). The blessing of God through this nation would require its immediate response. Unplowed ground referred to the empty areas of life which should be used. Sowing among the thorns was placing importance on things that were not profitable. Respond to whatever God asks from you to fulfill your calling in Him. Place priority upon that which is on His heart rather than your personal desires. Never take His conviction of sin casually, assuming that grace without consequences is available.

The Vision of Captivity

God came to a decision point that Judah would go into captivity. Jeremiah was told to stop praying for the people (14:11). Jeremiah knew God's heart of mercy. Was there any possibility for him to move God through intercession? Jeremiah believed this and pleaded with God on the basis of His throne and His covenant (v. 21). He interceded with God on the basis of His true nature (v. 22). The decision was final!

> Then the LORD said to me: "Even if Moses and Samuel were to stand before me, my heart would not go out to this people. Send them away from my presence! Let them go (Jer. 15:1)!

Jeremiah was told that two great prophetic intercessors could not even move His heart. This word was not to belittle Jeremiah, nor us in our intercession. Knowing the time to stop praying requires hearing from the Lord. Captivity was the only option left for this rebellious people. What would become of God's plan for the nations?

God's vision went beyond the pain of captivity. He placed a vision before Jeremiah that revealed His heart for the nations.

> The LORD showed me two baskets of figs placed in front of the temple of the LORD. One basket had very good figs, like those that ripen early; the other basket had very bad figs, so bad they could not be eaten. Then the LORD asked me, "What do you see, Jeremiah?"
>
> "Figs," I answered. "The good ones are very good, but the bad ones are so bad they cannot be eaten."
>
> Then the word of the LORD came to me: "This is what the LORD, the God of Israel, says: 'Like these good figs, I regard as good the exiles from Judah, whom I sent away from this place to the land of the Babylonians (24:1-5).

This vision revealed God's plan for the captivity. In his vision he saw:

1.   Good figs in a basket

2.   Rotten figs in a basket

3.   Both baskets placed in front of the Temple

Jeremiah saw something that challenges our conclusions of the captivity of Judah. It was not the rotten figs, the unworkable people of Jerusalem and Judah, that were to be sent to Babylon. God was sending what He considered to be good figs to the land of the Babylonians. His purpose went beyond the punishment of His people. The bad figs "which are so bad they cannot be eaten" (v. 8), included King Zedekiah, his officials, and those not taken into captivity. These would perish regardless of what action they attempted. For the bad figs, judgment was final.

The vision included the Temple which we know would be destroyed in the third captivity of Jerusalem. The basket of figs en route to Babylon would need to do without the Temple, the only place on earth that, at that time, expressed their religious ideas. God would do away with the broken cistern and bring His people into a new fullness through new promises.

Reflections

- God's plan for the captives became clear (24:4-7). What was His plan?

- What was His plan for those not going into captivity?

- What was His plan for the Temple? (The Temple was removed. Central worship as an exclusive form of worship in Israel was removed.)

Promises to The Captive Figs

God's heart for the nations is seen in the following promises and in the inferred results of captivity from Jeremiah 24.

1.   They experienced a forced removal from their homeland. The people whom God considered to be good figs would suffer as they left their homes for a foreign land.

2.   The good ones were picked by God; the rotten ones were unusable.

3.   God regarded the exiles He sent to Babylon as good (v. 5). We must conclude

that God had a specific purpose for the people to fulfill in Babylon.

> I will watch over them for their good, and I will bring them back to this land. I will build them up and not tear them down; I will plant them and not uproot them. . . for they will return to me with all their heart (Jer. 24:6-7).

4. Exiles had opportunity to find their roots in serving God in whatever nation or circumstance they lived. Obedience to His calling has more rooting effect than location.

5. They could not be planted outside of God's calling. Left to their own will, the people reflected a wild vine rather than the vineyard of God. Life in the vineyard requires commitment to God and to His purposes.

6. Good figs (like Daniel, Shadrach, Meshach, Abednego) would fulfill the purpose of God. Nations would be affected by the power of God. People would learn to acknowledge Him as the God of all the earth (Da. 5:21).

7. God broke the tradition of temple worship. The creation of the synagogue was a result of their captivity. Neighborhood meetings were now a necessity to keep faith alive, rather than a broken cistern of activity.

8. They longed for home (Ps. 137). They longed for freedom from their oppressors. God used their captivity to leave a deposit of the knowledge of God and His Kingdom. The pre-captivity excitement to "Declare his glory among the nations, his marvelous deeds among all peoples" (Ps. 96:3) will be put into practice.

9. Learning the language and customs of the people would be required to communicate. The record of God's people in Babylon and Persia tells us of language learning, understanding literature, and adapting to customs.

Reflection

- How do the previous nine points relate to your life in mission?

- God desires us to live with His kingdom in mind, not the nation of our origin.

People who say such things show that they are looking for a country of their own. If they had been thinking of the country they had left, they would have had opportunity to return. Instead, they were longing for a better country—a heavenly one. Therefore God is not ashamed to be called their God, for He has prepared a city for them (Heb. 11:14-16).

The charge to us is not to compare nation with nation, but rather to long for the heavenly Kingdom. Foreign workers who ridicule the nation of their calling miss the joy of representing the Kingdom of God. National pride of comparing nation with nation makes God ashamed to be called our God.

Application for Today's "Figs"

Missionaries are carried into the service of the Lord. We see similarities between the first wave of captives from Judah to Babylon and missionaries in their land of calling. You are called to carry the light of God to people living in darkness. Sacrifice is required in a variety of ways, depending upon the nation in which you live. Leaving home is not the result of your nation being uprooted, but a result of your obedience to His call. Communities of faith in your nation of origin pray for your calling to impact a people. The joy of people coming to faith in Christ more closely resembles those in the Book of Acts than the captives in Babylon (Ac. 11:18).

Each person is hand picked. It is healthy to picture yourself in God's basket as He sends you to the nations. God needs to be calling us and anointing us for His work. Paul wrote, "we are co-workers in God's service; you are God's field, God's building" (1 Co. 3:9). Our contribution in partnership with God is small in comparison to His, which makes acknowledgment of His leading all the more important.

Guard yourself from comparing one nation to another. The standard is the Kingdom of God and His righteousness, not the nation of your origin. Jesus went through many changes to come from the throne of God to live in first century Palestine. Your life in a desolate city is considered good because the Lord wants to bring transformation (Jer. 10:20). Some of the transformation will be within *your* life. Learning the language and culture of the new nation will open doors for effective communication. Part of the transformation will be the creation of new communities of faith. These communities will impact the way people around them are treated. The oppression in their community and beyond will be lifted.

God calls us to a life of pilgrimage (Ps. 84:5). Our service to Him brings a level of fulfillment in life that the world cannot offer. He builds us and plants us in our calling. Those who form the direction of their lives without God receive their payment in full in this life. Serving Jesus requires we set our sights on a higher standard and on our eternity with Him.

God's Letter to the Captives (Jer. 29:4-7)

Jeremiah dictated a letter from God to the captives in Babylon. He desired to bring structure to their lives and overcome the words regarding a quick return, about which the false prophets had spoken. The letter from God to His captive figs is one that ministers to missionaries today. He told them to build houses, settle down, plant gardens, marry, and have children. The captives were to have meaning in their lives rather than just quickly getting through their time of service. The people were to realize that they would be in their new nation for a long time. Their lives, and the lives of their children, needed meaning. This also holds true for missionaries today. It was wrong in Jeremiah's day for the people to despise the new nation or the new people among whom they lived. Children in mission today also need to be blessed with a healthy understanding of their nation and people. Life that is "temporary" will take its toll on children.

Let your children learn the language of the land to which God sends you. They will thrive with friendships and also gain insight useful in conveying the truth of Jesus. Moral boundaries must be in place for all people but should not become a fence that excludes friendships with nationals.

God's directive to marry and have children must be taken within the context of Scripture (Ge. 24:1-4). Marriage is not to be with someone outside of faith. Abraham selected a wife for his son and brought her into his land of calling. Life should become normal in your new context, complete with children, the holidays you choose to celebrate, and vacations.

The next instruction is healthy for any one serving God in another land: "Seek God's peace and prosperity for the nation to which I have carried you into exile. Pray to the Lord for it . . ." (Jer. 29:7). This would be difficult for Hebrews who had a siege mentality or a fear of being defiled. The same is true for workers today. You will prosper as your new land and people prosper. Do not give up on its Gentileness, or seeming lack of understanding of God's love for them. This is the reason God sent the captives to Babylon and now sends you to the nations. Believe for change--that cruelty and sin will be transformed into the likeness of Jesus.

The peace and prosperity of the nation will most likely require not only practical expressions of love but also a message. A spiritual message needs to be accompanied by practical love. God will give us practical ideas including clean water, marketing their products, helping with education, and hundreds of others. Peace and prosperity will also mean victory over the ways of Satan, which include fear of spirits and protection sought through animistic practices.

Missiological Implications:

The desire of the Creator is to bring a moral standard to all nations. He longs for praise from the inhabitants of the world. In His great power, God can bring the nations to His people or His people to the nations. He still looks for willing hearts to respond to His bidding.

Self-centeredness and nationalism are tools that work against the purposes of God. Patriotism and national identity are only healthy when the priorities of the Kingdom of God are held supremely high.

No people or nation should ever view itself as God's favorite, therefore breaking the commands of God. His will is more righteous than ours. We must seek His will and affirm His will continually.

Ministry Lessons in Jeremiah

Jeremiah saw himself as too young to receive God's call on his life (1:6). God's words of anointing and confidence encouraged this prophet who had begun with timidity. Jeremiah spoke the words of God, but the plot on his life, even though the Lord protected him (11:18-24), left him shaken and frustrated. Chapter 12 is the record of a man of God in turmoil. He saw injustice and did not understand why God allowed it (v. 1). God speaks to us in our struggles, just as He did to Jeremiah. The words were for Jeremiah and may not appear comforting if applied in the wrong context. God told Jeremiah that he needed to be tougher than other men and able to navigate over a terrain of thickets (v. 5). A coach saying, "You should be much tougher," will normally crush the spirit of one struggling. God's word often takes us back to what He has already said. His promises to Jeremiah were to strengthen him, to be with him, and to rescue him (1:8). We must walk with the revelation that God has given us and not forget part of His promise when life is difficult.

Jeremiah faced another crisis when God decided that intercession would not move Him. Jeremiah, like any of us during a time of tremendous pressure, told God that he was trying, and that he had remained obedient to the Lord. Now, however, he saw that all was going to be destroyed (15:15-18). His struggle was that he saw himself as a failure because the people did not listen and turn back. He would be without a country and without a people. His question to God was one of fear: "Will you be to me like a deceptive brook, like a spring that fails" (15:18b)? This question challenged God's nature and His promise to be a spring of living water. The response to Jeremiah was one for all in mission who accuse God of possible abandonment.

> If you repent, I will restore you that you may serve me; if you utter worthy, not worthless, words, you will be my spokesman. Let this people turn to you, but you must not turn to them (15:19).

We are not to accuse God; those are unworthy words. The Lord is not like a human who is moved by a flair of emotions. He requires that we make decisions based on truth. This is also a ministry point that cannot be stated lightly: the people can turn and become like us, but we are never to become like them. This is not a cultural point, but a clear mandate to take our faith and moral standing very seriously, never giving it up because times are difficult. God Himself will make us strong enough that people will not be able to stand against us. The purpose is that His Word is known and lives change to honor God.

Conclusion from Jeremiah

God longs for the nations to know Him. He used a difficult people, even in their captivity, to become part of the fulfillment of "light to the nation." Jeremiah was picked as a young man to be a prophet to the nations. He suffered with God in the destruction of Jerusalem and Judah. God used this man to bring hope to His people in a massive thrust into Babylon. We conclude that we, too, are called to fulfill the purposes of God among the nations. It will require our taking the time to learn language and to make life for our families an expression of God's goodness.

Appendix
Kings of Israel and Judah

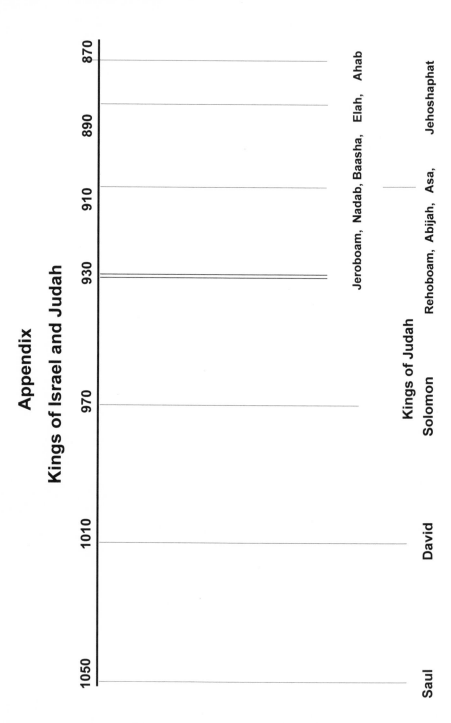

Early Prophets During a Troubled Kingdom

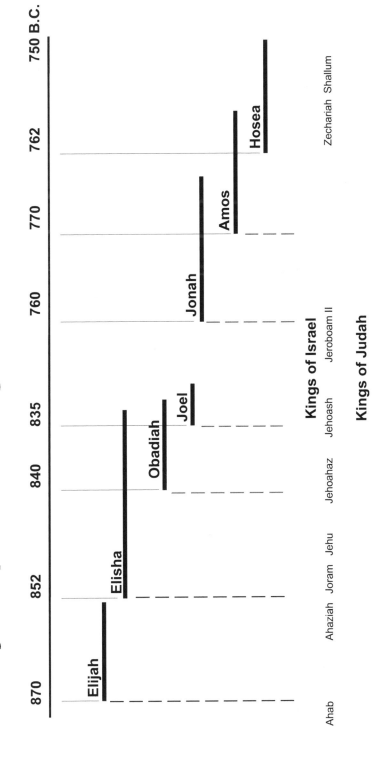

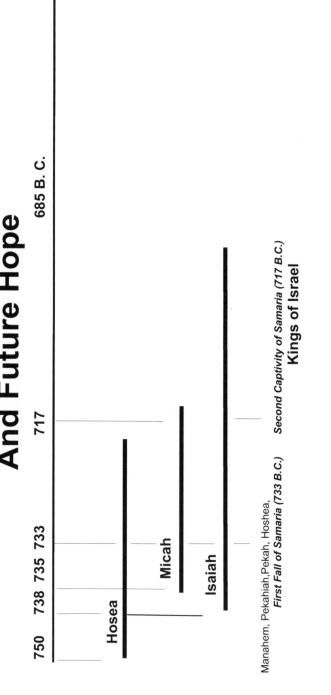

Prophets of a Troubled Kingdom, Decline And Future Hope

750   738 735 733   717   685 B. C.

Hosea

Micah

Isaiah

Manahem, Pekahiah, Pekah, Hoshea,
First Fall of Samaria (733 B.C.)   Second Captivity of Samaria (717 B.C.)

Kings of Israel

Jotham,   Ahaz,   Hezehiah,   Manasseh

Kings of Judah

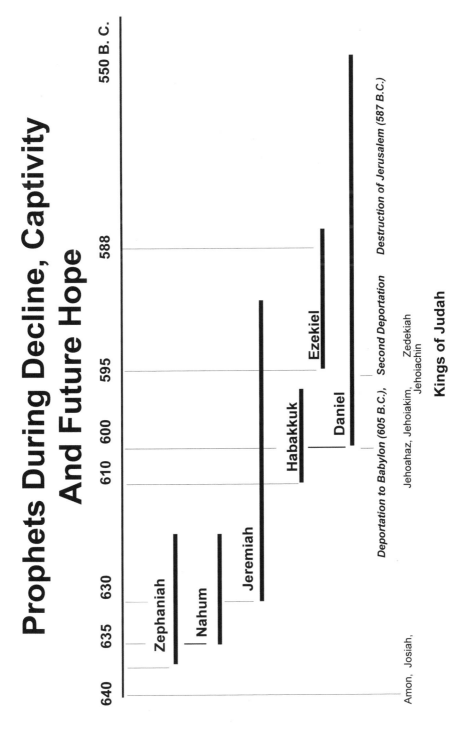

Prophets During Decline, Captivity And Future Hope

Review - The People of the Nations

What do you know of the nations mentioned in the pages of Scripture? Who are these people today?

The Assyrians

The Chaldeans

The Babylonians

The Medes

The Persians

Part 2:

The Captivity to John the Baptist

He said, "Look! I see four men walking around in the fire, unbound and unharmed, and the fourth looks like a son of the gods."

Part 2: The Captivity to John the Baptist

Chapter 10 - The First Captivity of Judah

Daniel - Life and Mission in Babylon and Persia

Introduction

Daniel is an exciting book with a lions' den and a blazing furnace. The protection of God is as captivating now as it was when we first heard the story in Sunday school. How does one understand the book of Daniel and apply it to mission? Is this book a random collection of miraculous stories and prophecies? Do miracles and prophetic insight while in a "foreign land" have significance for us today? What effect did the obedience of Hebrew captives have on the Babylonian people? The book is broken into major events that require our attention.

The Book of Daniel is a precursor to the Book of Acts where,

> On that day a great persecution broke out against the church at Jerusalem, and all except the apostles were scattered throughout Judea and Samaria . . . .Those who had been scattered preached the word wherever they went (Acts 8:1, 4).

One difference from the church in Acts is that the Prophet Jeremiah remained in Jerusalem, and the useful lives of Daniel and his friends were scattered into Babylon. This God-designed struggle in captivity is similar to the persecution in the Book of Acts in that God's people were thrust out to fulfill the "light to the nations" mandate. Both stories tell us that God is more concerned about salvation spreading to the nations than He is about the personal comfort of a people.

Daniel and the Hebrew boys mentioned in Daniel Chapter 1 were part of the first wave of captivity in 605 B. C. They were placed under Ashpenaz, chief of the king's court officials, in order to bring them into the king's service. Ashpenaz was to teach them " . . . the language and literature of the Babylonians" (Da. 1:4b).

Missiological Implication

The captivity is a clear demonstration of God's goodness to the Babylonians; not just His punishment of the Hebrews. His people, filled with the knowledge of God, aware of His laws, and understanding something of His Kingdom, were placed in Babylon. Their background and love for God were placed into the local Babylonian language. This was mission to the nations in its best form so far. The effectiveness of the Hebrews would depend on their ability to live for God rather than wallowing in self pity in their new environment. This is very true for missionaries as well.

The four Hebrew young men were given new names:

Original Name	Meaning	New Name	New Meaning
Daniel	God is my Judge	Belteshazzar	"Bel" - chief god of Babylon
Hananiah	The Lord shows grace	Shadrach	Servant of Aku, the moon god
Mishael	Who is equal to God?	Meshach	Who is this?
Azariah	The Lord helps	Abednego	Servant of Nego, the god of wisdom or the morning star

Daniel, Hananiah, Mishael, and Azariah had to become citizens of Babylon in order to serve the king. The new names were given to them as they became citizens of a new kingdom. Notice the similarity with mission: A relevant message requires that we learn to fit into our new nation.

Reflection

Many missionaries change their names to fit into a new society. If you pick a name, what should it express? Example: Yousef, or Joseph in the Bible, is a name used by people of many backgrounds. Mehmet is the Turkish equivalent for Muhammad. Its connotations are quite different from a name like Joseph. The name I adopted meant the father of my oldest son's name, which is the name of an Old Testament prophet. It was so different from local names that it opened opportunities to share repeatedly about the Kingdom of God.

"But Daniel resolved not to defile himself . . ." (Da. 1:8).

Each one of us will need to decide what is permissible and what is not permissible in taking on the likeness of another people. Daniel and his friends were well fed, but not with food that defiled their consciences. Form and meaning are two concepts that challenge us in cultural adaptation. In this case, how closely did the meaning (well fed) reflect the form (eating the king's food)? The Hebrew men had good results with other means. They learned the ways of the Babylonians and became loyal citizens of the new land. They took on new names. But the line they drew was with the food offered to them. Mission will require us, and new believers, to ask the following three questions about customs:

1. Is the custom acceptable? Can I participate in the custom?

2. Must the custom be modified?

3. Is the custom unacceptable, unredeemable, and therefore to be eradicated?

These three questions are not easily answered, especially in pre-service training. Questions answered from one social background may be strange or unacceptable in a new social setting. Examples help us understand the significance of these questions.

- Eating with utensils or eating with your hands is a custom that does not need to be addressed. A North American will eat a casserole with utensils but a hamburger with his hands. A Middle Easterner will eat some meals with the hands and some with utensils. At times, a spoon is chosen over a fork, but changing the custom has no value.

- Finding protection from evil spirits is a real need. This "custom" needs modification rather than eradication. People want protection, but the way in which they seek protection must be brought under the protection of Christ.

- Immorality and violence in a society must be rejected by all believers and not overlooked as being normal.

God anointed these men to move into needed positions in society. Entry strategy was not a question for them. They were God's handpicked tools for service. Their equipping can teach us a lot about missionary preparation.

God Prepares His Servants for Ministry

God gave wisdom and the ability to interpret dreams to His servants.

> To these four young men God gave knowledge and understanding of all kinds of literature and learning. And Daniel could understand visions and dreams of all kinds (Da. 1:17).

Remember, all four men were equipped with:

1. The language of the Babylonians

2. Knowing the literature (customs and folklore)

3. Systematic thinking about the people

4. God's anointing to use in the nation

Each of the above areas of preparation is necessary for ministry. Knowing the new language without an anointing for service, or vice versa, is insufficient to reach a people. Daniel was granted a particular ministry gift. He was given God's anointing to interpret dreams and visions.

Questions
Daniel, Hananiah, Mishael, and Azariah were prepared for ministry. What does ministry preparation mean to you? Is it language study? Is it living in community with people outside of your immediate family?

Nebuchadnezzar's Dream

God gave Nebuchadnezzar a dream at a particular moment in time. Why did God not give the dream five years earlier? Do you believe that God waits for His people to be in place and prepared with language in order to interpret dreams and to preach before He moves upon an unreached people with miraculous signs? Your answers to these questions could possibly build your faith, expecting God to go before you in preparation. The dream came as a dividing line between the former "magicians" and the knowledge of the Most High God.

Daniel's Faith in God

Daniel exercised his faith in the Lord by stepping out and speaking to officials. He did not exercise his faith by remaining submissively silent. Some wrongly believe that silence and trust in God's will is always the answer, missing the point that we are called to change societies for the better. Daniel first stepped out by asking permission from the chief official not to be defiled with the king's food (Da. 1:8).

Daniel heard about the king's edict to execute all of the wise men of Babylon (2:12).He promptly went to the king to ask for time in order to receive the dream and bring the interpretation (2:16). After he was committed to receiving revelation regarding the dream, he told his three friends of the plan! This is knowing God and walking in His direction. In this example, it was either faith or certain death. Clearly one cannot be a spectator and aspire to ministry.

Daniel quickly pointed out that no person had the ability the king required (2:27), but that there is a God in Heaven who knows all mysteries (2:28). The response was similar to Joseph's response to Pharaoh (Ge. 41:16). God must receive the credit when you find yourself in a similar circumstance.

Result of Daniel's Faith

Nebuchadnezzar was deeply moved by the knowledge of God and His anointing upon Daniel, falling ". . . prostrate before Daniel . . ." (Da. 2:46). The situation was ideal and could not be fabricated. Our faith is built, knowing that the highest person of the land in a different nation requested a dream to be interpreted. It can happen again. The bold faith of Daniel also brought King Nebuchadnezzar to confess, "Surely your God is the God of gods and the Lord of kings and a revealer of mysteries, for you were able to reveal this mystery" (2:47). Pharaoh recognized the Spirit of God in Joseph's life and made decisions based upon his words (Ge. 41:26). Nebuchadnezzar appeared to be moved to the point of a personal faith in the God of Daniel. Daniel's faith also opened the door for his three friends to serve in administration in Babylon. Helping others find their way in a new country has biblical roots. Faith is vocal, willing to approach the highest ruler of the land. Never judge your faith or your effectiveness by the response of an official! Moses had the opposite experience when Pharaoh rejected his demands.

Questions

God delights in people of many backgrounds coming to an understanding of His greatness.

1. Who will be honored by people knowing the one true God through your life?

2. How do you ascribe honor to the Lord, moving it away from yourself?

The Cross in Obedience (The Furnace)

Suffering in the life of the believer

Serving the Lord can bring us to imprisonment, torture, or death. The three Hebrew men, Shadrach, Meshach, and Abednego refused to worship an idol. These three messengers of God understood the consequences of actions appearing to snub the king. They submissively accepted the potential of dying for their God rather than altering His laws.

> If we are thrown into the blazing furnace, the God we serve is able to save us from it, and He will rescue us from your hand, O king. But even if He does not, we want you to know, O king, that we will not serve your gods or worship the image of gold you have set up (Da. 3:17-18).

People die for their faith in the one true God. If a disciple of Jesus bows to an idol with "crossed fingers," it is not a "contextual witness!" We cannot justify things that grieve the Lord because it allows us to live longer. We cannot tell a lie, for example, or deny Christ in order to spare our life because we think that doing so justifies the fact that we can have many more years to do good and to give testimony. Sometimes God requires our integrity--to the death. Ultimately, God does deliver us from an eternal judgment. Jesus did not circumvent the cross. Those who suffer and die for the testimony of Jesus are given special honor for eternity.

> I saw thrones on which were seated those who had been given authority to judge. And I saw the souls of those who had been beheaded because of their testimony for Jesus and because of the word of God. They had not worshiped the beast or his image and had not received his mark on their foreheads or their hands. They came to life and reigned with Christ a thousand years. (The rest of the dead did not come to life until the thousand years were ended.) This is the first resurrection. Blessed and holy are those who have part in the first resurrection. The second death has no power over them, but they will be priests of God and of Christ and will reign with Him for a thousand years (Rev. 20:4-6).

There is always excitement over God's miracles in delivering His people from prison and martyrdom. But we must remember that deliverance is not the ultimate sign of God's covenant with His people. Identifying with Christ in His shame and in His death is an honor. God is God. He must choose whether He is glorified through your death or through your deliverance. It is God's choice, not ours, if a "Nebuchadnezzar" will have Christians die before him or realize there is a higher King in charge.

Result of Shadrach, Meshach, and Abednego's Obedience

The three Hebrew men were willing to refuse idolatry and sacrifice their lives to maintain their integrity. Many have died as martyrs for their faith, refusing to weaken their resolve to walk with God. Honesty and integrity are necessary; the outcome is in God's hands.

> Then Nebuchadnezzar said, "Praise be to the God of Shadrach, Meshach and Abednego, who has sent His angel and rescued His servants! They trusted in Him and defied the king's command and were willing to give up their lives rather than serve or worship any god except their own God (Da. 3:28).

This was Nebuchadnezzar's second major revelation and accompanying confession. God is patient, but He also expects us to live according to the light we receive. Revelation comes with consequences.

The King was Humbled

Nebuchadnezzar dreamed of a tree cut down and a word from heaven making this once noble person like an animal (Da. 4:1-18). Daniel interpreted the dream to be speaking about the king himself. The word did not come with a consequential warning to walk in humility. One full year later, the king boasted pridefully of his greatness and the word from heaven was spoken; Nebuchadnezzar lost his mind. God wanted Nebuchadnezzar to know Him. His will was not to destroy the king but to humble him. This king had been exposed to the power of God on three occasions, each with a lesson to be learned.

1. God can reveal a dream and interpret the meaning. God holds the future in His hands and will ultimately rule.

2. God is able to save His people from fire and from a king's foolish decision.

3. The Lord can remove our minds or grant us wisdom. Pride is foolishness.

After Nebuchadnezzar was humbled, he said,

> At the end of that time, I, Nebuchadnezzar, raised my eyes toward heaven, and my sanity was restored. Then I praised the

Most High; I honored and glorified Him who lives forever. His dominion is an eternal dominion; His kingdom endures from generation to generation. All the peoples of the earth are regarded as nothing. He does as He pleases with the powers of heaven and the peoples of the earth. No one can hold back His hand or say to Him: "What have you done?"

At the same time that my sanity was restored, my honor and splendor were returned to me for the glory of my kingdom. My advisers and nobles sought me out, and I was restored to my throne and became even greater than before. Now I, Nebuchadnezzar, praise and exalt and glorify the King of heaven, because everything He does is right and all His ways are just. And those who walk in pride He is able to humble (Da. 4:34-37).

God has the ability to give someone intelligence and wisdom. Conversely, God has the ability to remove someone's mind in an act of judgment. It is important to discern an act of judgment from either human frailty or a demonic entrance to the mind. Daniel did not seek personal greatness in interpretation and neither should any of God's workers. The Lord seeks people who can hear His voice in humility. There is no limit to what the Lord can do with a life fully given over in obedience to Him.

Daniel Read the Handwriting on the Wall

Belshazzar, son of Nebuchadnezzar, drank from the goblets of the Lord's Temple in Jerusalem and ". . . praised the gods of gold and silver, of bronze, iron, wood and stone" (Da. 5:4). Daniel read the handwriting that judged Belshazzar's refusal to acknowledge the Lord (5:22). God is in charge. Pride is always judged. Swift judgment came that night with the king's death. Waiting for guidance as plain as "handwriting on the wall" is not a good sign. Even the Lord's handwriting had to be interpreted by Daniel because God would not speak directly to this king. God uses people of covenant to reveal His will to the world. Know that He has you in place, among a particular people, to reveal Himself as Master and Savior. God will honor your ministry and speak interpretations through you.

Daniel Continued to Pray

Darius the Mede was the third king, or possibly governor of Babylon, under whom Daniel served. Jealousy led men in government to find a way to eliminate Daniel. His relationship with his God was the only fault they could find in him. The question here, as it is with mission today, was loyalty toward God over anyone or anything else. This confrontation, and resulting night with the lions, is similar to the previous encounter between Nebuchadnezzar and the three Hebrew boys: worship me or die. Jesus was confronted with the same question (c.f. Mt. 4:8-9; Lk. 4:6-8). Believers are not immune to the temptations to tone down their witness, hide their prayer meetings, or worship in silence to avoid detection. The quietness or openness of an Algerian or Saudi Arabian fellowship is not easily judged by an outsider. Judgment on how nationals respond to any of these cases needs to be made only after one gains an understanding of the stresses they face. Judgment of your personal response is much easier to make.

King Darius issued the following decree as a result of Daniel's deliverance from the lions:

> I issue a decree that in every part of my kingdom people must fear and reverence the God of Daniel. For He is the living God and He endures forever; His kingdom will not be destroyed, His dominion will never end. He rescues and He saves; He performs signs and wonders in the heavens and on the earth. He has rescued Daniel from the power of the lions (Da. 6:26-27).

Lions' dens and furnaces are not our first choice as believers. Our hearts must be willing for God to be made known, whatever the cost. How will God touch nations like Saudi Arabia or Afghanistan today? Do we recognize His work in Iraq and in Iran in our days?

God's Five Visions Given to Daniel

The Ancient of Days

The vision given to Daniel clearly places the "Ancient of Days" as Lord Almighty over all creation (7:9) and Judge of all (7:10). Daniel went on to describe "the son of man, coming with the clouds of heaven" (7:13). This is nearly identical to the description of the returning Christ (Rev. 1:7; Mt. 24:30-31; 26:64). Jesus, using this phrase, sealed His fate before the Sanhedrin. He identified Himself as the "son of man" referred to in Daniel. Daniel's vision in Persia saw both the enthroned Ancient of Days and what we now understand to be the Christ in His second coming. The "son of man" was led into the presence of the "Ancient of Days," clearly signifying the relationship and level of communication between the two (7:13). Daniel then laid out the goal of mission concerning the one known as the "son of man:"

> He was given authority, glory and sovereign power; all peoples, nations and men of every language worshiped Him. His domin-

ion is an everlasting dominion that will not pass away, and His
kingdom is one that will never be destroyed (Da. 7:14).

Daniel's revelation coincided with the level of the knowledge of the Lord being
made known among the nations of Babylon, Persia, and Media. "Light to the nations" was now, more than ever before, a reality through those taken as captives.
We know the following from this vision:

1.   All nations and languages worship the "son of man."

This is the will of God: that all peoples, men of every language, know Him. We
must conclude that God searches for people of every language and desires that
they understand Him and live according to His ways. It seems fitting that a vision
for all nations be given to God's people while in a foreign land. Our mission to the
world is made clear through the Book of Daniel.

2.   His Kingdom is eternal.

Daniel prophetically understood that the Kingdom of this "son of man" is eternal.
He who appeared to be a man had divine attributes. Daniel was seeing events we
understand to be expressions of the Trinity. In his description, an eternal being,
who appeared to be a man, walked into the presence of the Ancient of Days--God
Almighty. One of the questions posed to Jesus was:

> We have heard from the Law that the Messiah will remain for-
> ever, so how can you say, 'The Son of Man must be lifted up'?
> Who is this 'Son of Man' (Jn. 12:3)?

No single Scripture can be interpreted alone. The "everlasting dominion" and "the
LORD has laid on him the iniquity of us all" (Isa. 53:6) must both be true.

Vision of Struggle

Daniel's vision of the ram and goat described the power of a goat coming through
the air, not touching its feet to the ground, and overcoming the ram. In its strength
it:

1.   threw some starry host down to the earth (Dan. 8:10),

2.   set itself up to be "as great as the Prince" (8:11),

3.   took away daily sacrifice to the "Prince" (8:11),

4. lowered the importance of the sanctuary (8:11), and

5. threw truth to the ground (8:12).

The insight given to Daniel was very specific and of the distant future. Some have tried to pinpoint this revelation to mean that the Babylonian empire would be overthrown by Media and Persia. These kingdoms were subsequently taken over by Alexander the Great of Greece, whose kingdom split into four sections, each led by one of his four major generals. This definition is very narrow, leaving little room for insight into the culmination of events on earth.

Our present age has lowered the authority of Jesus the "Prince." Our daily sacrifice of meeting with Him should not be lessened through busyness or intellectual pride. Truth today is believed to be relative, which leads to the false conclusion that truth is nonexistent. This can become a difficult struggle for many in school. Truth is truth and must always be so for everyone and for every situation. Truth is established by God and has nothing to do with evolution, which is random. Our present days fit the prophecy of Daniel very well.

Daniel's Prayer and Vision

Daniel was known as a man of prayer. We previously read that it was his prayer to God that had him thrown into the lions' den. He requested God's revelation and guidance for every area of his life. The following aspects of prayer mark this Hebrew missionary's life:

1. Daniel understood from Jeremiah's prophecy that Jerusalem would be desolate for seventy years (9:2). He honored Jeremiah and knew the Word of the Lord was in his mouth and pen, acknowledging Jeremiah's writings as Scripture.

2. Daniel prayed in humility with fasting, sackcloth, and ashes (9:3). His example is for us today.

3. Confession of sin is never third party; it is always personal (9:4-5). God will never listen to our confession of sin that blames someone else. Intercession is identification in prayer with your people.

4. Daniel proclaimed that God is just in His judgments (9:11-14). This is acknowledging God's righteous judgment over Israel. His prayer was turning toward the restoration of Jerusalem and the Hebrew people.

5. He asked God to turn from His anger (9:16). Prayer to turn God's righteous judgment away is just the opposite of Jonah's desire for swift destruction. How do you apply this in your prayer life?

6. Daniel pleaded with God based on His mercy rather than human righteousness (9:18).

The prophetic word brought by Gabriel is applicable to our lives. Today we understand the end of sin and its atonement, coinciding with the sacrifice of the Anointed One (the Christ). "Seventy sevens" or four hundred ninety years are required until the atonement arrives. Jerusalem would be destroyed once again, with war continuing until the end of all things.

Vision of a Man

Daniel received a vision during the reign of Cyrus, King of Persia, the fourth king under whom Daniel served. The vision tells us that answers are given when we first cry out to God with a humble heart (10:12). Territorial opposition, here referred to as the Prince of Persia, opposed the Word of the Lord sent to Daniel (v. 13). Territorial opposition is evident in many places where God's people serve as light in unreached areas. The world in which we live has never been a simple, physical world. This is a world in which spiritual forces wage war and oppose the will of God. We are encouraged to persevere in prayer and fasting, believing God is good and wants to bring the answers we need. We also know God is all powerful, and the struggle is not on an equal level.

Questions

- What are territorial spirits?
- Where is their domain evident?

Vision of the End Times

Daniel's vision continued with knowledge of the end times.

1. We are told that we will witness distress greater than any other time in the history of the world (Da. 12:1). Deliverance will be given to all those whose names are written in the book. This does not say specifically how deliverance will be accomplished, but simply that it will occur.

2. We are told of the resurrection of the multitudes; some to everlasting life, others to everlasting shame (v. 2). (Compare with John 5:28-29.)

3. "Light to the nations" has deeper meaning in that the ". . . wise will shine like the brightness of the heavens, and those who lead many to righteousness, like the stars for ever and ever" (Da. 12:3). Leading people into the knowledge and righteousness of God will be blessed. God rewards those who follow His command to carry the knowledge of the Son of Man to the nations. This vision for mission requires God's people to aspire to His calling in active participation.

4. Those who are ". . . purified, made spotless and refined," will understand the ways of God (12:10). The wicked will not understand. A growing dichotomy between those who understand and those who are clueless will define the days before the end.

5. The final word of this prophesy given to Daniel told him that he would rest (die physically) and be raised to life at the end. Daniel would receive his inheritance in the resurrection. This clear word confirms in the heart of all missionaries that our reward is with the Lord, not in this life. Daniel's hope for the resurrection is also our hope. The Bible is a book of resurrection. The Book of Daniel pierces this hope deeply into our hearts.

Conclusion

Daniel and his believing friends overcame the shame and disgrace of God's judgment which came upon their generation, upon the city of Jerusalem, and upon the Temple of God. Throughout their lifetime, they faced many challenges living in a foreign land, but they continued to faithfully serve, worship, and pray to their God. They spoke the languages required to convey the truth of the one and only true God in Babylon and later in Persia. In this mission story, Daniel was given revelation into the future, highlighting that the nations would worship the Lord. He also wrote of the final judgment to come. The resurrection will be for all; some to everlasting life, others to everlasting humiliation.

The Challenge of Integrity

Daniel knew how to work. He was not a meditating holy man who was detached from typical daily life. God used Daniel in civil leadership in a foreign nation. His integrity was above reproach. Joseph, in a similar way, rose from prison to national leadership. Only God knew Joseph's integrity through testing him. Joseph's pure integrity was more important to him than living it up in Egypt. Integrity is required to shun evil and to live as a stranger in the foreign land where God has placed you. Your purity and motives will be tested. God will know the extent to which He can trust your responses. The Book of Daniel does not allude to sin in Daniel's life or to his being tested in order for God to know his heart. Daniel's purity before God challenges us today. Daniel encourages us to believe for people of God to be placed in positions of government among the unreached.

Chapter 11 - The Second Captivity of Judah

Ezekiel

Introduction

Nebuchadnezzar returned to Jerusalem in 597 B. C. and took 10,000 captives to Babylon. Ezekiel was part of this second wave of captives taken from Judah to Babylon. Eleven years later, Nebuchadnezzar returned to destroy the city of Jerusalem and the Temple and to bring more inhabitants back to Babylon.

Content of the Book - Message and Mission

Ezekiel's visions frequently referred to the appearance of a "man" on the throne (i.e. Eze.1:26). Ezekiel prophetically saw God in human form, ruling over all of heaven and earth. His vision of "a man" and Daniel's description of one appearing as "a son of man" were one and the same.

Ezekiel was clearly called by God to Israel (2:3). His ministry prophetically spoke of God's desire to form a holy people, completely free from the gods of this world and completely committed to the one true God.

> He then said to me: Son of man, go now to the house of Israel and speak my words to them. You are not being sent to a people of obscure speech and difficult language, but to the house of Israel— not to many peoples of obscure speech and difficult language, whose words you cannot understand. Surely if I had sent you to them, they would have listened to you (Eze. 3:4-6).

We infer from this passage that God's direction for some of His people was different from that to which He was calling Ezekiel. Some would be called to people of obscure and difficult speech, and to people of many different cultures, religious backgrounds and worldviews. All of these people are in the mind of the living God. Yet the main thrust of the mission of God in the book of Ezekiel was the house of Judah, which still had not repented. The seriousness of God's call was made plain in this book. Ezekiel was to be held accountable to deliver a message to the unrepentant (3:18-21).

Missiological Implications

When we couple the understanding that Ezekiel would be held responsible to speak God's words to a wayward nation with Christ's command to preach the gospel worldwide, we must conclude that God will hold us responsible for our apathy! Faith leads to obedience; unbelief to disobedience. It is our responsibility to bring the messasge of God's Kingdom to this world. Those living in sin are still God's concern. He wants them restored.

God's judgment comes in waves. Ezekiel heard God describe the sin of Jerusalem and the coming judgment on its inhabitants (Eze. 9). Judgment is always meant to turn us around toward the Lord. Judgment does not mean we have paid our debt and can now live as we desire with additional freedoms. Jerusalem had experienced two traumatic waves of captivity by the invading Babylonian army. The remnant felt forsaken by God. (Forsaking His people goes against the very character of God.) They believed He was no longer watching their actions (9:9), like looters when the lights go out. The Lord was grieved by the sin of this remnant of Jerusalem. The glory of the Lord moved to the outer threshold of the Temple (10:4). God's glory moved away from the Temple (v. 18), traveled to the eastern gate (v. 19), and departed. The destruction of Jerusalem and the Temple were now imminent.

Questions

1.   Are we obeying the Lord today?

2.   How do we know He is present with us and pleased with our lives?

3.   Is the life you live a road map for future generations to follow?

The Theology of Ezekiel

God's Priorities

The book of Ezekiel is very important to us in our study of mission because we are able to examine God's priorities for His people living in a foreign land. Ezekiel is a book filled with biblical theology. God's broken heart is laid bare before the reader to know both His sorrow and His punishment. This is not a book that easily lends itself to our study of mission, but it does direct us as God's people in paths of obedience. It also quantifies our previous conclusions regarding God's use of the captivity to reach the nations. Many taken captive to Babylon were not usable in God's hands! Changing locations to engage in cross-cultural mission is only reasonable when the disciple has shown dedication to obeying the Lord. The following themes construct our understanding of God's dealing with the people of Judah in Ezekiel's day. These themes also shake us loose from complacency in our day. The Lord is against the following forms of evil, both then and now.

False Prophets

God hates false prophets who prophesy out of their own imagination (13:2). Prophecy is on the increase in our present day. With the blessing of prophecy also comes the necessity to judge every word that is spoken, and it requires every word be placed under the light of the Word of God. If we are slow to judge prophecy in our own nation, it will be difficult in a mission context. Words are not to be received because they are uttered by a well-known personality. Neither can a word be received because it fits with the present political climate of a nation. Do the words spoken correct our lives and direct us in personal involvement in the Kingdom of God? Do the prophetic words honor the Creator and His Kingdom, or do they affirm a particular group or individual?

A Whitewashed System

God will send His wrath against a flimsy religious system constructed by religious leaders. His anger is against a whitewashed system that does not clearly honor the Lord (13:15). Jesus called the Pharisees whitewashed tombs (Mt. 23:27). These weak religious systems were the ones about which Jeremiah spoke, calling them "broken cisterns that cannot hold water" (Jer. 2:13). A faltering religious system tries to contain the fountain of living water in a man-made container. The end result is stagnant water that smells and old spiritual food that, like yesterday's manna, becomes worm infested. No system can be centered around the personality of the day or around a "priest" who holds an office without having a burning heart after God. At the core of true religious systems must be leadership which is a) deeply committed to the Word of God, b) deeply committed to preaching righteousness, and c) deeply committed to obedience.

Magic Charms

The Lord is against magic charms (Eze. 13:18). This includes any symbol that is used to insure success or ward off evil. Magic charms are evil because they replace the trust and confidence that must only be placed in the one true God. All societies are susceptible to using symbols that insure protection. These symbols are present from the most animistic of South American villages to the most modern of North American and European homes and businesses. Placing trust in anything other than God breaks both the first and second commandments: "You shall have no other gods before me . . ." and "You shall not make for yourself an idol . . ." (Ex. 20:1-6).

Modesty

God is against women dressing to lure men (Eze. 13:18). Modesty is not old-fashioned. Present day societies are not unique in forming their fashion markets around sexual statements. "What is hot and what is not" is not a biblical value. Sexual appeal is not universal and is often defined by a society. A provocative type of dress in one society may be modest in another. Any society has the ability and means to express itself with dignity and modesty. Although the Bible does not present a dress code for all societies, modesty is expected among God's people. Youth need role models in all societies.

A Perverse Justice System

God hates reversing the justice system; calling good evil and evil good (13:19). Tolerance of sexual perversion is a sign of fallenness rather than openness. Is someone considered evil in a society when opposing homosexual behavior or abortion on demand? Can obscenities and pornography be acceptable because they meet the standard of freedom of speech and freedom of the press? These questions are the result of formed opinions in our limited and warped minds, rather than those based on the timeless Word of God. The inability to speak up and judge your own society will make you ineffective in speaking to another.

Disheartening the Righteous with Lies

God abhors disheartening the righteous with lies (13:22). A righteous life is not lived in a vacuum or in a monasatic retreat. Rather, we know that God's people are a blessing to society, the light and the salt to which Jesus referred. Each one of us needs to bring encouragement to others in the household of faith and not discourage the righteous. Ask yourself if you are an encourager of God's people. God knows the work required to speak the truth in opposition. He knows the effort required for fathers and mothers to train their children in the sea of society's evil. He also knows the effect of lies hammering on the lives of His people daily. This lying is common within societies that are based upon false religious concepts. It is also common within atheistic and secular humanistic nations. "Open societies" that present evolution, atheism, and relativism are often critical of Christians and Christian values.

Idols

God opposes idols set up in hearts (Eze. 14:3). Idolatry is often wrongly equated with statues of gold in other nations. What constitutes an idol? Is something that consumes our thoughts, love, affection, and money able to be contained in our hearts? Almost anything can become an idol when our hearts feed it and treat it with worship. Objects, people, media, projects, attention, and even our own stomachs can become idols that rob God of His place in our lives. The danger of an idol is that it is an object of worship, and it dulls our hearing the voice of the One who should have our undivided attention.

God demands purity of heart and of speech. He hears the prayers of the righteous. Noah, Job and Daniel are named as those whose prayers were heard and answered (14:14-20). Mediocre prayers by part-time saints do not impress the living God. Yet the Lord tells Ezekiel that even these three men could not move His heart from destroying Jerusalem. His mind was made up! The Lord was about to unleash His four dreadful judgments against the city of Jerusalem: the sword, famine, wild beasts and plagues (14:21).

This judgment to be released came after the first captivity of 604 B.C. and after the second captivity of 597 B.C. The few who were to be spared would also come into captivity. Ezekiel was comforted when he saw these few survivors. Ezekiel's comfort would not be the result of seeing more countrymen arrive! Ezekiel's comfort would not be because he returned to his homeland or because of a rebuilding project that restored Jerusalem. This brings us, as servants of the Creator, the King of kings, to ask ourselves the meaning of comfort.

Ezekiel's comfort acknowledged that God was righteous in His judgment of Jerusalem. He was comforted by observing the depth of depravity within the newly arrived captives to Babylon (14:22-23). His comfort was knowing that His people deserved the wrath of God poured out on their land; the destruction of both the city and the Temple! This message of God's righteous judgment will affect some world Christians as they hear of the destruction of their city or nation of natural birth. Our citizenship in heaven is intensified by this account in Babylon. Ultimate comfort is knowing that God is righteous. Our eternal assurance is knowing the universe must come under the righteous rule of the one and only holy God.

An Allegory of His People

Limitations of Language

Human languages have communication limits. Learning a second or third language quickly reveals the areas where one language is stronger than another. God communicates with the human race within the confines of the many different languages. The allegorical language used is God's way of putting His feelings into words that we can understand.

Israel, the Abandoned Baby

Ezekiel records the lament and anger of God toward a people in whom He took a personal interest--from their earliest beginnings to their development as a nation. Israel is described as a nation neglected by all but God on the day of her birth (Eze. 16:1-6). Through language, he paints the image of an abandoned baby who was thrown into a field to die and left without so much as even the cut umbilical cord. The Lord took pity on this child, and through the years He protected and nurtured her, bringing her into His own family. This is a picture of Israel entering the family of God through adoption; it is not a picture of a natural birth.

Israel, the Prostitute

God poured out His heart, describing Israel as a prostitute who used the gifts lavished upon her by her rightful husband to purchase cheap lovers. Spiritual lovers come to the people of God and are paid for by the very gifts He has lavished upon them. This deep lament by the living God was spoken to a prophet during the days of captivity in Babylon. He was Israel's husband, as He is the bridegroom of the body of Christ. This vivid language must grip our hearts as believers and followers of Christ. Flirting with things that not only take our attention, but also weaken our resolve in the Lord, are truly foreign lovers. All that we have in life is a gift from our Creator and not to be used to buy distractions that lessen our covenant with Him. Even in this, God promised future hope to His people. He promised to remember the covenant that they had abandoned (16:60). He promised atonement that would forever humble and silence His people who were wayward.

> ## Reflection
>
> Is our "post Christian" society any different than the description God gave to Ezekiel? Our guilt is multiplied beyond that of Israel because of the amount of light and truth once embraced by many of our ancestors. The knowledge of the crucifixion and resurrection, if thrown aside for personal passions and selfish ambitions, will also be a standard by which those breaking covenant will be judged. God's grace is still extended but is not to be trifled with. At times, sweeping judgment comes with the fury of God's jealously. Remember, He is never interested in sharing His people with other lovers.

The Sins Of Sodom

Introduction

At times, references to particular names of cities and regions in Scripture are illusive. Sometimes, Babylon, Egypt, Rahab, Edom, Sodom and Ephraim are used interchangeably, focusing on sinful people and their various types of rebellion. It is God speaking which makes His analogies very specific and discriminate. The reference to Samaria, the older sister in the North, makes this passage name and location specific (Eze.16:46). The following reference to Sodom would then appear to be the Sodom destroyed in the days of Abraham (Eze. 16:49-50; Ge. 18, 19). The sins listed for Sodom should strike the fear of God into our lives today. The people were arrogant, overfed, unconcerned, not helpful to the poor and to the needy, and they committed detestable acts.

Personal Indulgences

When remembering the cities of Sodom and Gomorrah, it is usually the sins associated with sexual perversion which come to mind first. There are, however, sins that lead to perversion. We are challenged to take the call of God seriously with each sin mentioned. Personal indulgences distract God's people from their goals and calling to the nations.

Selfish Pursuits

Arrogance and self-sufficiency require judgment rather than approval from God. Arrogance is evidenced by "faith" in evolution as the creator of all and in the superiority of a society equated with tolerance of sin. As a sin, "overfed" may never have more clearly described a people better than it does today. Lack of satisfaction in many areas produces overfeeding. Food, entertainment, sexual hunger and toys of many kinds come into our lives in gluttonous quantities. "Overfed" points to a hunger to please self rather than a hunger to please God who has called us to His gospel. "Overfed" also describes Christians who add to their own knowledge without either applying it to the society around them or without involving themselves with unreached people.

Are you concerned for the things that concern God? All people have concerns. Priorities are meaningless without receiving God's perspective on priorities. He is concerned that the gospel be carried to the ends of the earth; that every nation would know Him. Is that the concern you carry? He is also concerned for the rights of those unable to defend themselves: the poor, the orphans, the widows, and the unreached. We must not ignore these unfortunate people and leave them without a voice!

This list ends by highlighting detestable acts. Perversion is the end of the road; it is rarely the initial sin that brings destruction. Paul reiterates this by writing that those who neither glorified God nor thanked Him were given over to sexual perversion (Ro. 1:21, 24).

Sin Will Be Judged

Sin and Judgment

Righteousness in the past does not cover over sin committed today (Eze. 18:24). Holiness is not a commodity that is stored in order to pay for future sins. This categorically denies the "balance system" of Islam, which describes paying for past, present, and future sins with a "good work." Sin requires judgment. A righteous man who sins will be judged. Once again, God has no favorites. He is not bought off, allowing close friends to indulge a few freedoms. This is necessary for all ministers of the gospel to comprehend. Some have stumbled, believing God owes something to His servants. Faithful ministers of the gospel are not allowed a few dark areas of life overlooked by God's holy eye.

> When you offer your gifts—the sacrifice of your sons in the fire—you continue to defile yourselves with all your idols to this day. Am I to let you inquire of me, O house of Israel? As surely as I live, declares the Sovereign LORD, I will not let you inquire of me (Eze. 20:31).

> ## Reflection
>
> Sin blocks our access to the Lord. He will not let people inquire of Him while they remain in sin. We know God hears the prayers of sinners; we all are a testimony to His ability to hear a sinner's prayer. The difference comes in hanging onto sin while seeking God contrasted with the prayer from a repentant heart.

Sins of Jerusalem

Ezekiel heard God's judgment pronounced against Jerusalem. The destruction of the city was now coming (Eze. 21). Chapter 22 tells us that the destruction of the city occurred because the people

- treated their fathers and mothers with contempt (v. 7),

- oppressed the alien (v. 7),

- mistreated the fatherless and the widow (v. 7),

- desecrated His sabbaths (v. 8),

- slandered others (v. 9),

- ate at pagan shrines in disregard of God's ways (v. 9),

- committed lewd sexual acts (v. 9),

- slept with their father's wife (v. 10),

- violated women during their menstrual periods (v. 10),

- had sex with their neighbors (v. 11),

- had sex with in-laws (v. 11),

- committed incest (v. 11),

- took bribes to murder the innocent (v. 12),

- took excessive interest (v. 12),

- extorted (v. 12), and

- forgot the Lord (v. 12).

Isolated Believers

It is impossible to see such a list and not reflect upon our own society. Remember, neither you nor Ezekiel can say you are free from such sin. An intercessor is required to identify with the sins of the people and confess the needs of the nation. God looks for a people whose hearts are fully committed to Him, not a group of scattered individuals who are only interested in personal holiness. Holiness in isolation from society produces a cocooned believer. Imagine the difference between Ezekiel and Daniel confessing the sins of their nation and asking for God's mercy, and a Pharisee telling the Lord of his personal righteousness. God's heart for a nation must become our heart. Personal holiness is required in intercession while identifying with the sins of society.

Questions

- Is there a nation for which you pray?

- How do you pray for that nation?

God Seeks Intercessors

The Lord searched for an intercessor to pray and to stand in the gap for the city of Jerusalem. He could not find one (22:30-31). This is one of the saddest descriptions of God's people in the Bible. Filled with sin and without an intercessor, the city was destroyed on the tenth day of the tenth month (January 15, 588 B.C.). Today, God looks for intercessors with a burden for the gospel to have its full effect, who will pray for specific people or nations. Prayer, combined with preaching the Word and discipleship, are all required to transform a people. Isolation from society, with a concentration on personal or group purity, produces an inward focus. The intercessor is a watchman who not only prays, but also clearly and distinctly warns a people of impending judgment (33:1-6). This is an outward focus. Prayer requires interaction with people to avoid becoming an isolated or mystical movement.

Who Owns The Land?

God's Judgment on the Land

The discussion of who rightfully possesses the land of Israel is beyond the confines of this course. Blanket statements of possession rights, both in Ezekiel's day and today, must be challenged in light of the conditions God places upon those living in this land. The challenge is not finding a worthy people to claim the Lord's favor, but rather the humility to live together.

> Then the word of the LORD came to me: "Son of man, the people living in those ruins in the land of Israel are saying, 'Abraham was only one man, yet he possessed the land. But we are many; surely the land has been given to us as our possession.' Therefore say to them, 'This is what the Sovereign LORD says: Since you eat meat with the blood still in it and look to your idols and shed blood, should you then possess the land? You rely on your sword, you do detestable things, and each of you defiles his neighbor's wife. Should you then possess the land?' "Say this to them: 'This is what the Sovereign LORD says: As surely as I live, those who are left in the ruins will fall by the sword, those out in the country I will give to the wild animals to be devoured, and those in strongholds and caves will die of a plague. I will make the land a desolate waste, and her proud strength will come to an end, and the mountains of Israel will become desolate so that no one will cross them. Then they will know that I am the LORD, when I have made the land a desolate waste because of all the detestable things they have done" (Eze. 33:23-29).

An International Community

Possession of the land was not according to the quantity of Abraham's descendants. The sins of breaking the covenant in dietary laws, idolatry, violence, and adultery were all enough to bring God to tell His people that they were not worthy to possess the land. It is important we do not jump to the conclusion that Israel is the home of Jewish descendants only, and that ethnic cleansing is required to please God. Setting the land aside simply because of blood lineage rights is not Scriptural. The Israelites were commanded to distribute the land among themselves and among the aliens living among them (Eze. 47:21-23). The Israelites were to consider the aliens living among them as native-born Israelites.

The naturalized aliens were to have inheritance rights along with the Israelites. "'In whatever tribe the alien settles, there you are to give him his inheritance,' declares the Sovereign LORD" (Eze. 47:23). This is in sharp contrast to some opinions today that exclude all non-Jews from life in Israel, even if they were born there. Believers in Christ have also experienced rejection from Israel based on their lack of Jewish heritage.

Many Sheep, But Not All Fed

God's Judgment on Injustice

Ezekiel heard the Lord speak about some sheep which were overfed and others which were pushed aside from pasture. There appeared to be both enough pasture and water for all sheep, but some had priority, and there was unconcern for others. Who were the other sheep which were left without food and water? Are we guilty in mission of feeding some areas and allowing others to starve? For example, there is an island in the Caribbean that currently has five thousand missionaries, twice the number of missionaries in the entire Muslim world. It is not my place to suggest that fewer workers be sent to this area, but rather to ask why so few are sent to the unreached elsewhere.

> As for you, my flock, this is what the Sovereign LORD says: I will judge between one sheep and another, and between rams and goats. Is it not enough for you to feed on the good pasture? Must you also trample the rest of your pasture with your feet? Is it not enough for you to drink clear water? Must you also muddy the rest with your feet? Must my flock feed on what you have trampled and drink what you have muddied with your feet?
> Therefore this is what the Sovereign LORD says to them: See, I myself will judge between the fat sheep and the lean sheep. Because you shove with flank and shoulder, butting all the weak sheep with your horns until you have driven them away, I will save my flock, and they will no longer be plundered. I will judge between one sheep and another. I will place over them one shepherd, my servant David, and he will tend them; he will tend them and be their shepherd. I the LORD will be their God, and my servant David will be prince among them. I the LORD have spoken (Eze. 34:17-24).

Fat and lean sheep speak of the inequity of priorities. Some areas of the Kingdom have so many resources that the "overfed" condition speaks of waste. Other areas of the Kingdom are "hungry," lacking resources to accomplish their tasks. The picture of "you shove with flank and shoulder" speaks of the misuse of power, wealth, and priorities.

One Shepherd - One Flock

This passage goes beyond the point of leaders who are well fed and followers who are lean. The "one shepherd" to be placed over all the sheep speaks of different flocks coming under the one shepherd in Christ. Jesus told us, ". . . There shall be one flock and one shepherd" (Jn. 10:16). The Messiah will shepherd the flocks and raise up leaders with a shepherd's heart. This word applies to all of God's people, both in Ezekiel's day and in ours.

Missiological Implication

Some sheep are overfed and are unconcerned about the spiritual and physical hunger of other flocks. God's heart for all His sheep is that they are provided for and fed. How do we justify feeding overfed disciples, while others have not had the opportunity to hear the gospel even once? There is enough of God's grace to cover the earth. What are you doing with your knowledge of the Shepherd? It is imperative that we search for the spiritually starving and feed them!

One Flock From Two Sticks

Unity in the House

God is concerned that all people come into the fullness of His covenant promise. Ezekiel is told to join two sticks in his hand, making one stick.

> The word of the LORD came to me: "Son of man, take a stick of wood and write on it, 'Belonging to Judah and the Israelites associated with him.' Then take another stick of wood, and write on it, 'Ephraim's stick, belonging to Joseph and all the house of Israel associated with him.' Join them together into one stick so that they will become one in your hand" (Eze. 37:15-17).

Two Interpretations

1. There are two interpretations of this prophetic act. One interpretation is the joining of the house of Judah with the house of Israel. Israel was, at times, referred to as Ephraim. This was an invitation to both Northern and Southern Kingdoms to come under one head in the Lord so that they would never again be referred to as two kingdoms (v. 22).

2. The other interpretation goes beyond Judah and Israel in Ezekiel's day. Ephraim was also the son of Joseph and Asenath, daughter of the priest of On. Their son represented the bringing of other ethnic people into the family of God. This interpretation is the joining of Jewish and Gentile believers into one people of God. Paul tells us, "There is neither Jew nor Greek, slave nor free, male nor female, for you are all one in Christ Jesus. If you belong to Christ, then you are Abraham's seed, and heirs according to the promise" (Gal 3:28- 29). There is a joining of Jew and Gentile in Christ. This is not a joining in humanism nor good will to the nations. The joining is in Christ and in His hands that were pierced for all people. All share the guilt of piercing those hands, and in those hands all are welcomed. Paul goes on to tell us that Gentiles were formerly aliens and strangers, yet they were welcomed into the household of faith in Christ (Eph. 2:11-22). The dividing barrier was now taken away, joining the two into one. Most likely both interpretations must be considered valuable. Oneness reflects the strength of the Lord, not the good intentions of man.

The Rebuilding Of The Temple

Significance of the Temple

God desires a sanctuary among His people forever. His sanctuary or dwelling place in light of Scripture means that He dwells with His people.

> . . . and I will put my sanctuary among them forever. My dwelling place will be with them; I will be their God, and they will be my people. Then the nations will know that I the LORD make Israel holy, when my sanctuary is among them forever (Eze. 37:26-28).

Does this speak of rebuilding the Temple with one place of permanence among His people; or does He speak of a sanctuary among His people? Some have taken this verse to substantiate the necessity of the Temple being rebuilt. One must question the significance of a single Temple for the lives of believers scattered throughout the nations of the world. A permanent temple, complete with animal sacrifices, would displace Christ and His sacrifice for the sins of everyone, everywhere.

God's Universal Temple

God desires to "tabernacle" with His people or to "dwell" among His people. We also know our bodies are the temple of the Holy Spirit (1 Co. 3:16, 6:19). The reference in Ezekiel is far broader than one temple in one location of the earth. God declares that His desire is to place His sanctuary among His people. Every tribe, language, and nation will have God's sanctuary placed among them forever. All have the opportunity to enter into the sanctuary of God, regardless of location.

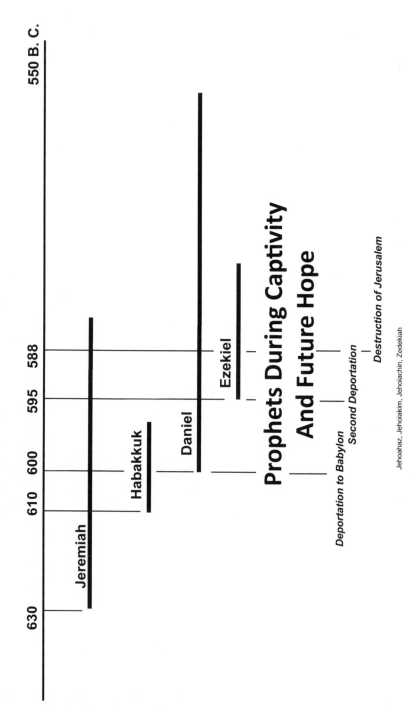

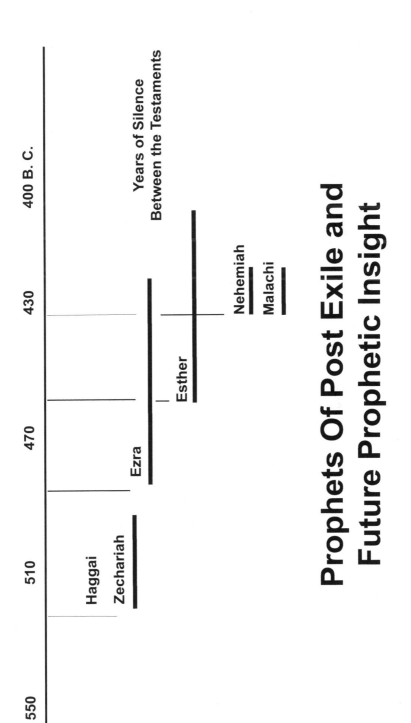

Prophets Of Post Exile and
Future Prophetic Insight

Chapter 12 - Exiles First Return

Zerubbabel - Rebuilding the Second Temple

Chronologically, the book of Ezra is divided into two sections with the time of Esther falling between the two. The first section of Ezra focuses on the return of the exiles to Jerusalem and the rebuilding of the Temple. The second part of Ezra records his journey with the returning captives and the effort to put life back into order.

Introduction

Daniel remained in Babylon until the first year of King Cyrus (Da. 1:21). He influenced both Babylonian and Persian kings. He also understood the prophetic words of Jeremiah which indicated that the captivity would end after seventy years (Jer. 25:11-12). After sixty-six years in Babylon, in the year 539 B. C., Daniel saw the first captives returning to Israel and specifically to Jerusalem.

The Decree of Return

Cyrus issued a decree allowing the Hebrews to return and rebuild the Temple in Jerusalem. In this marvelous confession, note how he refers God in various ways.

> The LORD, the God of heaven, has given me all the kingdoms of the earth and He has appointed me to build a temple for Him at Jerusalem in Judah. Anyone of His people among you—may his God be with him, and let him go up to Jerusalem in Judah and build the temple of the LORD, the God of Israel, the God who is in Jerusalem. And the people of any place where survivors may now be living are to provide him with silver and gold, with goods and livestock, and with freewill offerings for the temple of God in Jerusalem (Ezr. 1:2-4).

Cyrus wrote of the LORD, which is a Hebrew term for the Sovereign Lord over all the earth. The God of heaven in our minds depicts God as the King over all the universe. What Cyrus meant by heaven and the God of heaven, or God's rule over the nations, is not clear. God is a personal God through the king's description, "may his God be with him." Is God also able to be personal to non Hebrews? Cyrus also wrote of "the God of Israel and the God who is in Jerusalem." Once again, we read the king's words and easily agree from our own worldview. But is God also the God of Persia? Is God the personal God of Cyrus?

Cyrus opened the treasury and released the gold and silver articles taken by the former Babylonian king, Nebuchadnezzar. We must note that the Babylonian kingdom lasted for only seventy years, coinciding with the captivity of Judah. God is able to raise up any nation for His purpose and pull down any kingdom as He sees fit. The legal command to return, and the financial provision to accomplish this task, came from the Persian Empire. It is possible to conclude that Zerubbabel and his returning team had the Persian Empire as their sending base.

The Book of Ezra begins by describing the families returning to the nation of Israel. It specified the Levites (2:40), the singers (2:41), the gatekeepers (2:42), and the Temple servants (2:43-60).

> The following came up from the towns of Tel Melah, Tel Harsha, Kerub, Addon and Immer, but they could not show that their families were descended from Israel: The descendants of Delaiah, Tobiah and Nekoda 652.
> And from among the priests: The descendants of Hobaiah, Hakkoz and Barzillai (a man who had married a daughter of Barzillai the Gileadite and was called by that name).
> These searched for their family records, but they could not find them and so were excluded from the priesthood as unclean. The governor ordered them not to eat any of the most sacred food until there was a priest ministering with the Urim and Thummim (Ezr. 2:59-63).

Those who could not verify their family records could not minister as priests in the most holy things, but they were not excluded from Israel. The distinction is important to keep us from assuming that to belong to Israel meant a tight family lineage.

Co-laborers with the Lord

Those who returned for this enormous venture gave from their personal finances to accomplish the task before them (2:68). All of us entering into God's work will find ourselves reaching into our own pockets to see the tasks fulfilled. If we totally rely on the "budget" before us, or on the money contributed by others, we will find that eventually it will not reach far enough. We will also become day laborers hired for a price rather than co-laborers with the Lord in His Kingdom. God loves when we give selflessly and willingly. His mission will require us to freely give and to pool our resources. Remember, God's gift cost Him personally; it was not a budget line item.

People also contributed their time and talents to the service of the Lord. They gave what they could offer. We accomplish a lot when many shoulder the task together and take responsibility to see the task through to completion.

Who Will Work With You?

Peoples relocated 183 years earlier by the Assyrian Empire offered Zerubbabel and his leadership team a willing hand to help rebuild the Temple of God (4:1-2). This was a critical point of discernment for those sent by Cyrus, King of Persia, for the task of rebuilding the Temple. Were these willing laborers "one with them in purpose and heart"? Would the offer become a "Trojan Horse," inviting confusion into their midst and undermining the God-given task? One key in understanding this request is recalling that the inhabitants of the northern cities ". . . worshiped the LORD, but they also served their own gods in accordance with the customs of the nations from which they had been brought" (2 Ki. 17:33).

Reflection

Is all help offered in order to fulfill the vision from God? Does some help come with strings attached which will ultimately harm the work?

Example: Children's Bible Funding

We had the privilege of working with the development of a Children's Bible in the language of the nation in which we worked. Editors in four nations worked together to produce a readable text for the entire region. Funds were difficult to raise for the preparation, typesetting, and editing. It is often easier to raise funds for this type of project after the printing is complete or for subsequent reprints. One church organization offered to contribute a large sum of money to the production phase with the condition that we place the name of their organization in the front of the book. The offer was tempting, but we declined. We realized that it was an offer whose intent was to purchase advertising, and this would have likely limited our distribution to only those who were inclined to work with this particular group.

Keeping Focused

> When the enemies of Judah and Benjamin heard that the exiles were building a temple for the LORD, the God of Israel, they came to Zerubbabel and to the heads of the families and said, "Let us help you build because, like you, we seek your God and have been sacrificing to Him since the time of Esarhaddon King of Assyria, who brought us here." But Zerubbabel, Jeshua and the rest of the heads of the families of Israel answered, "You have no part with us in building a temple to our God. We alone will build it for the LORD, the God of Israel, as King Cyrus, the king of Persia, commanded us" (Ezr. 4:1-3).

The word "You have no part with us in building a temple to our God" was not an exclusion to workers who were not completely Hebrew in bloodline. This was discernment regarding the enemies of Israel. Cyrus, King of Persia, and the governors of regions were all very involved with the repatriation and the rebuilding of the Temple. Their financial help was not refused. The true deception of those offering to help revealed itself in the text.

Missiological Implication

The church must be built by believers. The leadership team must be dedicated to Christ. Eager workers need to be fully committed to God and to His people before they are released in positions of spiritual authority.

A Good Offer Sours

Did Ezra make the right character assessment? The people who offered to help became his enemies. The real agenda of their hearts came forth. They discouraged the building (Ezr. 4:4) and even hired counselors to frustrate the reconstruction of the Temple (4:5). The true intent of their hearts showed that the offer to help to rebuild was deceptive.

The discouragement and threats turned to written lies in a letter sent to King Artaxerxes. They falsely accused the inhabitants of Jerusalem with rebuilding the city. The lies sent to King Artaxerxes were gratefully received and enemies were placed in positions of leadership. The order was issued to stop the construction of the Temple. The project stagnated for eighteen years. The opposition we may face as God's workers must not end with one discouraging word.

Handling Opposition

1. Listen to and obey the right voice.

Some opposed this project and tried to discourage those who were helping. It is important that we know whom God is calling to be a part of our team, regardless of the type of project in which we are engaging. Trusting in God, even when hardships come our way, is the key to success. Making everyone happy is not a principle of God's Kingdom.

2. Carry through with the will of God.

The rebuilding of God's house was stopped until others later followed through with God's will. They obeyed God even when they were not granted permission to do so. At times, fighting legal battles can sort out truth from error. At other times, facts are twisted and justice is lost in legal matters. In the Book of Acts, preaching the Gospel did not wait for legal permission. The disciples obeyed God rather than men, a decision we will sometimes also face. Man's desires cannot overpower God's will. When He calls us into service, we must obey.

3. Change hardened hearts through faith.

Sometimes it takes stepping out in faith into an unknown place in order to receive the blessings. Zerubbabel restarted the work after the words of two prophets, Haggai and Zechariah, encouraged the work. This was not a legal decree overriding the letter of Artaxerxes but an act of faith. This act of obedience led to clarification of the legal document written many years earlier.

4. Thank God.

The completion of the Temple inspired a joyful celebration to honor God. When God helps us or answers our prayers, we often forget to thank Him. Do not become so caught up in the moment that you forget to recognize the reason for your success.

Temple Construction Revived

Introduction

God uses prophetic voices in the community of His people. Both Haggai and Zechariah had prophetic roles that revitalized the stagnant work (Ezr. 5:1). Obedience is a challenge. God's will can be clearly understood, yet civil laws or popular opinion can extinguish the internal drive required to complete the call. The following messages pinpoint several areas we must consider in times of frustration and waning vision.

Prophetic Messages of Haggai

1. You have lost your God-given vision (Hag. 1:1-3).

God's vision is not subject to the world's opinion. His moral absolutes cannot be subject to "modern" human cravings; neither should His plans to build the church be tabled through unbelief or stopped by civil schemes. Moses could have resigned after his first encounter with Pharaoh. Expect opposition, but refuse to lose God's vision. Your loss of priorities will result in a sense of defeat and dishonor. On the other hand, God promises to honor us as we fulfill His calling on our lives (1:8). God's vision is also lost when our focus becomes self-centered. The people were very intent to look after their own houses and ignore God's house (1:9). Fear for personal finances and lifestyle will quickly eclipse the central theme of ministry.

2. You have lost faith in your work (Hag. 2:3-4).

The loss of confidence in your ministry is almost synonymous with discouragement. The people who knew what the former Temple looked like compared it with their unfinished business. They were discouraged to remember how the Temple once stood, and they compared that image with its current, inconsequential state. At times, God will ask us about the progress of our vision, "Does it not seem to you like nothing" (Hag. 2:3)? Face reality. Allow Him to revive His vision in your heart. Some who are anxious for great results in ministry can be discouraged when they wrongly compare results in their location with results from other areas of the world. God is good to renew our vision and strengthen our weak human frames that carry the direction of Almighty God. He is also able to use what we deem to be of little value for a great purpose. When a project or ministry stagnates, go back to God who renews vision.

3. "Holy Ministry" can deceive (Hag. 2:10-19).

Deception comes into the lives of God's servants when they presume that their lives are holy because of association to their daily ministry activities. Some have called this 'Christian professionalism,' which is defined as working at a ministry without a personal passion for God and His work. The Lord spoke through Haggai using the illustration of what causes something or someone to be consecrated or defiled. A consecrated object does not cause other objects to become consecrated by simply touching them. A defiled object, on the other hand, defiles any object with which it comes into contact. The meaning is this: holy work does not change your life. A defiled life, however, will ruin any holy work it touches. Blight, mildew, and hail ruined the harvest of the returned captives. God's blessing was withheld because of their sin-sick lives. Building the Temple was not sufficient to turn God's eye from their lives. Is God honored in your ministry? Is there strife within your church that withholds blessing? Though your ministry is flourishing, are areas of sin withholding blessing in your personal life?

Some have wrongly concluded that professionalism is a result of education. They would conclude that little or no training can insure that a work will not go stagnant. Lack of preparation is not an approach to freshness. A daily walk with God, short accounts with others, and a passion for personal and corporate purity keeps us fresh in Him. A passion for learning more of God and for how we are to minister is needed in each missionary's life.

4. Grace begins now (Hag. 2:18-19).

How do you get started again with God's calling? Remember that God desires to pour His blessing and His anointing on your life each day in a fresh way. He is not placing you on a three month trial and conditionally bringing the blessing if you respond correctly. In this passage, God was pouring encouragement upon the people of Jerusalem with the understanding that they needed to return to His call on their lives.

Zechariah's prophetic words began two months after Haggai began to prophesy. (Compare Haggai 1:1 and Zechariah 1:1.) His prophetic surgery was also directed to the leadership of Jerusalem, stirring them to return to God's direction in order to complete the Temple.

Prophetic Messages of Zechariah

1. Don't lose your vision (Zec. 1:8 - 2:13).

The Lord wants a "measuring line" raised up (Zec. 1:16) that brings a distinction between the people of His kingdom and the nations of the world. He wants His house restored, which is symbolic of His presence with His people. Their security while still living in darkness was unrealistic. The measuring line He wants to bring to His people is also to have an effect on the nations living in false security. God's measuring line requires that we live according to His standard and not to the standard of a new, tolerant world order.

One reason the people lost vision was that their leaders no longer challenged them with God's vision (1:18-21). The angel showed Zechariah four horns that scattered Judah, Israel, and Jerusalem. The people were not unified in their pursuit of God's heart. The four horns described were unleashed by God to scatter the people to the four winds. Future hope was immediately offered in the vision by allowing Zechariah to see four craftsmen.

> . . . the craftsmen have come to terrify them and throw down
> these horns of the nations who lifted up their horns against the
> land of Judah to scatter its people (Zec. 1:21).

God can overturn a nation or send the "craftsmen" who are able to repair any type of damage and confusion the nation has faced. This is very important to remember in our time. We must not put our trust in those we consider to be good, or even great, politicians. Our hope is in the Lord and in His ability to "craft" the peace and prosperity for which people yearn. The people described in this vision could not raise their heads. They had neither hope nor purpose (1:21). The gift of leadership would raise the heads of the people, which meant giving them purpose and dignity.

Jerusalem's inhabitants could only see the present roadblock to rebuilding the Temple. The real question was much greater than the Temple; it was ushering in the fullness of God's hope for the nations. God's vision for the nation, given through Zechariah, was the same two-fold vision given to Abraham. God's desire was to bless His people and to make them a blessing to the nations.

1. "I am coming and I will live among you" (Zec. 2:10).

2. "Many nations will be joined with the Lord in that day and will become my
   people" (Zec. 2:11).

This is the vision that raises our heads when opposition seems relentless. It is the knowledge that God lives with us, and that His desire is to gather the nations to Himself.

2. Refute Satanic Accusation (Zec. 3).

Joshua the High Priest was not able to lead in God's vision. His personal failures were overwhelming. Satan stood at his right side to make sure Joshua could not resume leadership. This was the first direct reference to the halting of the construction of the Temple because of a spiritual battle. Understanding Satan's involvement sheds light on the "crafted lies" sent to Artaxerxes to stop the building project. God expects us to understand the enemy's tactics and overcome them. Was there hope for Joshua? Is there hope for the missionary who is unable to lift his or her head due to moral failure? The Enemy is always ready to accuse, point out your faults, and attempt to keep you in a wasteland devoid of ministry for the Lord.

God Himself made provision through the angel to cleanse Joshua. Our minds and hearts must know victory. In faith, we must step out of the filth we sense clinging to our ministry, represented by Joshua's priestly garments. Zechariah, as intercessor, stepped into the vision God gave and ordered a clean turban for the high priest (3:5).

Two important truths impact us from this vision:

- Servants of God are refreshed through our intercession.

- When a servant of God stumbles, he must pray for restoration. Then his ministry is able to continue.

Satan is the accuser of the brethren (Rev. 12:10). Never succumb to Satan's corrupt character qualities. Bringing accusation against any of God's people will bring your life in line with Satan's servants. Matthew 18 gives us an outline to follow when confronting moral failure.

- Go to the individual privately (Mt. 18:15).

- Take one or two others along as witnesses (18:16).

- Bring the matter before the church (18:17).

- Treat the person as an unbeliever (18:17).

The last step means that we start over as we would with a pagan. The Gospel must be preached to those outside the church. Moral failure is not something we carelessly approach with gossip or accusations. Neither is an unrepentant sinner in the church treated as a believer.

In a vision, Zechariah heard a reference to the Branch, the servant of God (Zec. 3:8). The miracle of removing sin is God's business. He is the only one capable of paying the price to cleanse us from sin. He promises to remove the sin of the land in a single day (3:9), which is an enormous claim. References to the Branch, redemption, and single day cleansing are in the context of the high priest's condemnation. Sin will stop God's vision from continuing through your life. Redemption and cleansing allow us to lift our heads and get back to the work of fulfilling God's purposes.

3. Remember: "Not by might nor by power, but by my Spirit, says the Lord" (Zec. 4:6).

This was God's word to Zerubbabel, and it is also His word to you. God's work in your own strength is a recipe for failure. It was reasonable for Zerubbabel to stop the project. The picture given to Zechariah was of the golden lampstand which represented the presence of the Spirit of God. The lampstand had been present in the Temple since the days of Solomon. In the vision given to Zechariah, this particular lampstand was fed through " . . . seven channels to the lights" (4:2). The lampstand was fed by two olive trees: one on the right and one on the left. In other words, the lamp is eternally burning with an endless source of oil that flows through the channels to the lampstand. Your own strength is far from sufficient, but God wants your life to have an uninterrupted flow of His Spirit in order to accomplish His work.

4. Be Hungry for God (Zec. 7)!

God challenged both the fasting and the feasting of the people of Judah. Was the fasting truly unto the Lord or merely a custom? Did they feast to the Lord or enjoy a big meal? The primary focus of life is either God and His Kingdom or self. Christian ministry must come back to Paul's confession that he dies daily (1 Co. 15:31). The lifeless gears of ministry can turn, years after the Spirit has departed. Make sure that whether you fast or feast, preach or disciple, that you do it all unto the Lord. The fruit God expects from a consecrated life is abundant. He promises that when His people are fully given over to His work, the nations will come to know Him.

> This is what the LORD Almighty says: "Many peoples and the inhabitants of many cities will yet come, and the inhabitants of one city will go to another and say, `Let us go at once to entreat the LORD and seek the LORD Almighty. I myself am going.' And

many peoples and powerful nations will come to Jerusalem to seek the LORD Almighty and to entreat Him."
This is what the LORD Almighty says: "In those days ten men from all languages and nations will take firm hold of one Jew by the hem of his robe and say, `Let us go with you, because we have heard that God is with you' " (Zec. 8:20-23).

The fruit is both multi-ethnic and from many languages. God is disappointed when His people have no heart for the nations. But do remember: His joy is overflowing when our lives are available to fulfill the longing of His heart to bring the nations as a gift before Him. He loves the people of the world He has created, and He wants to enter into covenant with them.

Entreat The God of Heaven.

King Darius was pulled into the process when the governor of Trans-Euphrates questioned the validity of building the Temple (Ezr. 5:6-7). Darius responded to the governor by referring to the "God of heaven" (6:9, 10). This was a much broader term than the "God of Israel." Darius knew that this was not a localized god of a territory, as it had been reported to the king of Assyria (2 Ki. 17:26). The God of heaven was the God over all creation. This God could be entreated by people of the whole earth, including Darius himself. ". . . so that they may offer sacrifices pleasing to the God of heaven and pray for the well-being of the king and his sons" (Ezr. 6:10). This Gentile king saw the benefit of pleasing the God of heaven. Darius entreated the God of heaven at a time when the armies of Persia were threatened by Greece. Daniel's mission to the kings of Babylon and Persia was greatly blessed by God (Da. 2:47; 6:25-27).

Include All People In The Passover.

The Passover was celebrated after the dedication of the Temple. We are told that the Israelites who returned from exile in Babylon ate the Passover ". . . together with all who had separated themselves from the unclean practices of their Gentile neighbors in order to seek the LORD, the God of Israel" (Ezr. 6:21). God included all people, but there were conditions. His work with Israel and Judah had come with conditions. He turned away no one who set aside unclean practices and sought after Him. This is still true today. Seeking God and putting aside evil practices go together.

Chapter 13 - Esther: Life and Mission in Persia

Introduction

The book of Esther covers the years 483-473 B.C. Her story fits approximately after Chapter 6 in the book of Ezra. Esther became queen in 478 B.C. A miraculous series of events led this Hebrew orphan girl to become the most influential woman in the Persian society of her day. In some ways, quite similar to Daniel, Esther needed to draw on her faith in the one true God in order to overcome certain death for both her people and herself. This woman was chosen by God for a task only she could fulfill. Likewise, your purpose is unique. It is wrong to let God raise up other people to fulfill the ministry to which you are called.

We read that Xerxes "ruled over 127 provinces stretching from India to Cush" (Est. 1:1). A view of the world map, focusing from India to Ethiopia (ancient Cush), quickly conveys that this king had influence in many lands and in many languages.

The story of Esther coming to power contains many elements of a Middle Eastern story. The king gave a banquet lasting seven days (v. 5) which is not understandable in a western world in the twenty-first century. "Queen Vashti also gave a banquet for the women in the royal palace of King Xerxes" (v. 9). Separating men and women at separate banquets is also curious to a modern western audience. It is in this context that a drunken king sends for his queen to parade her in front of drunken male guests.

> On the seventh day, when King Xerxes was in high spirits from wine, he commanded the seven eunuchs who served him—Mehuman, Biztha, Harbona, Bigtha, Abagtha, Zethar and Karkas—to bring before him Queen Vashti, wearing her royal crown, in order to display her beauty to the people and nobles, for she was lovely to look at. But when the attendants delivered the king's command, Queen Vashti refused to come (Est. 1:10-12).

His vast power, however, could be undermined by instability! Queen Vashti refused the king's request. This refusal of a foolish request was the basis for searching for a new queen and discovering an orphaned Jewess.

The following points from the book of Esther describe how God reached beyond His people to extend grace. Applying this understanding to mission today will strengthen our resolve to obey and to firm up our trust in a God who never fails us, no matter the nation or city where we find ourselves.

Seven Principles For Cross-Cultural Ministry

The following seven principles from the book of Esther apply to our lives in cross-cultural ministry:

1. Take time to prepare for service.

> Before a girl's turn came to go in to King Xerxes, she had to complete twelve months of beauty treatments prescribed for the women, six months with oil of myrrh and six with perfumes and cosmetics (Est. 2:12).

Months of preparation were necessary for her chosen position. Esther had to be Persian in every way--in language, in beauty, and in customs.

Each of us knows a sense of belonging in the land of our birth and within the context of our family. We may also experience the challenge of learning how to "fit in" with another group of people. What type of preparation will take us into the very ministries our King requests? Many desire to enter into their ministry quickly, believing preparation would delay the call of God on their lives. Esther, beautiful as she naturally was, needed to learn how to become the queen of a nation.

2. Be adaptable to the culture but steadfast in your moral standards.

Mordecai forbade Esther to reveal her identity as a Jewess, which tells us that her ability to speak the Persian language was flawless. Mordecai was a Jew and thoroughly committed to his 'foreignness' while living in Persia; yet he denied his niece the option to walk the same path.

How do we identify with the Kingdom of God in any nation where we find ourselves? How "English," or "Korean" or "North American" are we as missionaries in lands other than those of our national heritage? Mordecai refused to bow to Haman (3:2). In many situations, each of us will need to discern whether our actions are acceptable to, or in violation of, our conscience before God. Without the freedom to adapt to cultural identity, workers likely become stiff and ineffective. However, a missionary who adapts to every situation, regardless of moral consequences, will blend like a chameleon, unnoticed and ineffective. Daniel was not flexible in his moral standard, but adapted fully into Babylonian life and his work within the government.

3. Trust God's sovereign ability.

They cast the pur, or the lot, in Haman's presence to decide a day and month to destroy the Jews (Est. 3:7). The pur would be similar to the rolling of dice in order to make a decision. Haman was looking for his "lucky day!" The word pur is the source of its plural in Hebrew, Purim, which was the name given to the Jewish festival that Mordecai established to commemorate God's deliverance of His people from genocide.

Never see yourself as a victim of either chance or predetermined fate. Rather, trust in God's sovereign ability to turn any circumstance around for good. God does grant people a free will and, at the same time, decides the course of history.

The lot is cast into the lap, but its every decision is from the Lord (Pr. 16:33).

4. Allow God to open doors for His purposes to work through you.

Several factors would seem to make Esther an unlikely candidate to save her people from destruction. She was a girl in a Middle Eastern setting. Orphan children needed to clearly prove their family history in order to avoid being accused of illegitimacy. Yet the principle of God stands:

> But God chose the foolish things of the world to shame the wise;
> God chose the weak things of the world to shame the strong. He
> chose the lowly things of this world and the despised things—
> and the things that are not—to nullify the things that are, so
> that no one may boast before Him (1 Co. 1:27-29).

How does this apply to your life? Is there a difference between preparation for service and confessing weakness before God, needing His strength? This is a point of discernment in the life of a missionary. You prepare and yet you know your inadequacies. God is the One who open doors for His purposes to work through our lives.

Esther, the orphan girl, saved a nation. A people group would have been wiped out without her intervention. Some greatly fear expulsion from their nation of calling and tone down their witness as a reaction to that fear. One challenge we face is to decide whether we represent our ministry or the Kingdom of God. Ministry is a risk in the world's eyes, but it is obedience before the Lord. Our need is to look at the larger picture and not become focused on our personal comfort.

5. Remember that God does not forget.

Mordecai was recorded in a king's journal. The miracle of God was both the recording of Mordecai's act of patriotism and bringing it to the king's attention at a later date. God does not forget any part of our lives...neither our acts of kindness nor our actions of faith. Live with the knowledge that God's goodness is not hidden or withheld from your life.

6. Understand the importance of your involvement in mission.

There are similarities between the "salvation" of the Jews from destruction and the salvation of any people from life without God. The end of this story is one of feasting, joy, and redemption for a people. In a similar way, the angels rejoice over one sinner who repents. The joy of redemption must shake us free from personal pleasure or fear of personal loss. Esther laid her life on the line to help her people. God calls us to also lay our lives, reputations, and personal comforts on the line for the salvation of people.

God's direction to His people has never changed. Modern times and personal pleasures always need to be overcome by the believer.

> For if you remain silent at this time, relief and deliverance for the Jews will arise from another place, but you and your father's family will perish. And who knows but that you have come to royal position for such a time as this (Est. 4:14)?

Mordecai's word to Esther needs to be applied to unreached people who, in a similar way, have no voice of their own for deliverance. You may have been raised up for this very purpose.

7. Welcome mentors into your life.

A mentor in the faith will have the God-given annointing to speak direction into your ministry. Do you have "uncles" or "mentors" in the faith? Is there someone to coach you in the ways of God? Humility is required to receive counsel from others and to resist the temptation to proudly believe you are self-sufficient. Pray for people to come into your life who can speak words of exhortation and help. Esther remained open to the input of her uncle.

> . . .for she continued to follow Mordecai's instructions as she
> had done when he was bringing her up (Est. 2:19).

We, too, need to remain open to the input of the people God sends to us, and humbly realize that we can always benefit from the advice and counsel of mentors, not only when we are physically or spiritually young.

Chapter 14 - Ezra: The Exiles Return

Ezra Sent to Jerusalem

Artaxerxes

Artaxerxes, King of Persia, sent Ezra to Jerusalem to rebuild the Temple during the seventh year of his reign in 457 B. C., twenty-one years after Esther became Queen of Persia. Esther influenced the Persian empire under his father, and no doubt had significant influence on this king. In his letter to Ezra, Artaxerxes refers to God as "The God of Heaven" (Ezr. 7:12, 21, 23), "Your God" (7:14, 19, 25, 26), "The God of Israel" (7:15), and "The God of Jerusalem" (7:19).

Artaxerxes is expressing something of God which is much deeper than referring to Ezra's religion or to the gods of another land. To speak of this God, Artaxerxes pinpoints the God of Jerusalem as both the God of Ezra the priest and the God of Heaven.

King Artaxerxes had a heart that was moved by an unseen hand of conviction. He committed himself to two very brave actions during a time when Persia was threatened by Greece:

1. He allowed any Israelite to return to his native Israel (v. 13). This act of kindness to the people of Israel acknowledged the Lord's sovereignty.

2. He and his advisors gave gold and silver to the Lord (v. 15). This was an act of worship by a Gentile king to the one true God.

Chronology of Babylonian and Persian Kings

The numerous references to the kings of Babylon and Persia can become confusing, especially when names are mentioned in several books of the Bible. Babylon was formerly the southern province of the Assyrian Empire. The Assyrian Empire was a vast region that encompassed five major areas of the Middle East from 2500 BC to 605 BC. The five regions included (1) Babylon, or southern Iraq, with major cities including Babylon, Susa, and Ur, which was Abram's former home; (2) Assyria, with major cities being Assur and Nineveh; (3) The Mitanni Province, further to the northeast in areas we call Kurdistan today; (4) The Hittite Kingdom that engulfs what we call central and eastern Turkey today; and (5) Assyria, which had also captured the area of Samaria (2 Kings 15:19, 29), which included the costal areas down to and including parts of Egypt. Babylon became prominent for approximately seventy years until the Persians to the east engulfed the entire Babylonian Empire. The following is a list of kings who had influence over Judah, its captivity, and its people scattered to the east--with the approximate years of their respective reigns.

1. Nebuchadnezzar was ruler of Babylon for approximately 44 years, from 605 B.C. until 562 BC. Under his rule Daniel and others were taken captive to Babylon.

2. Nabonidus, son of Nebuchadnazzar, ruled Babylon from 556 B.C. to 539 B.C. The six-year gap from Nebuchadnazzar's death to Nabonidus' rule is unclear.

3. Belshazzar ruled for only three years from 541 B.C. to 539 B.C. It seems he was placed in charge while his father, Nabonidus, was on a military campaign in Arabia (New Bible Dictionary pg. 129). Belshazzar is referred to as "son of Nebuchadnezzar" (Da. 5:11), a common practice when referring to a great king. Similar references can be made to Judah's kings who were referred to as "son of David."

4. Darius the Mede was 62 years old when he took over the Babylonian Kingdom (Da. 5:31). The Kingdom of Media was already absorbed by the Persian Empire, so this change of rule takes us to Persia. Darius the Mede was most likely ruling as govenor under Cyrus II, King of Persia. Daniel was placed in the lions' den during the days of Darius.

5. Cyrus II ruled Persia from 559 B.C. to 530 B.C. There needs to be no overlap of dates from Darius to Cyrus II because they are in different realms. Cyrus II was also called Cyrus the Great, and honored as ruler of Media and Elam, showing the expansion of the Persian Empire (New Bible Dictonary pg. 258). Zerubbabel's return to rebuild the Temple (538 B.C.) was during Cyrus II's reign.

6. Cambyses, son of Cyrus II ruled from 530 B.C. to 522 B.C. Cambyses is not mentioned in the biblical record. His reign is mentioned for continuity in dating the reign of Persian kings.

7. Bardiya, also a son of Cyrus II, ruled during the one year of 522 B.C.

8. Darius I ruled Persia from 522 B.C. to 486 B.C.

9. Xerxes I (or Ahasuerus) reigned from 486 B.C. to 465 B.C. It was during his reign that Zerubbabel was ordered to stop construction on the Temple. Esther

became queen of Persia during the reign of Xerxes.

10. Artaxerxes ruled after his father from 465 B.C. to 424 B.C. Under his rule, Ezra returned in 457 B.C. and Nehemia returned to rebuild Jerusalem in 444 B.C. This is ninty-five years after Zerubbabel had returned to begin work on the Temple.

11. Darius II, son of Artaxerxes and grandson of Xerxes I, ruled Persia from 424 B.C. to 404 B.C. He is mentioned in Daniel 9:1 in the time frame of Daniel's final visions.

Fasting In Preparation

Ezra proclaimed a fast in preparation for the long journey from Persia (Babylon) back to Jerusalem. He and the people humbled themselves and prayed for a safe journey (Ezr. 8:21-23). The king had personally given financially to the God of Israel. Ezra desired to impress upon the king the miraculous nature of God's protection. In mission we must obey the prompting of the Holy Spirit who will place our reputation, and even our lives, into the hands of God. God will not fail us or fail to fulfill His promises. This is not in His character and is simply not possible. Additionally, if we presume upon Him and do not receive the answer we expect, we are not living as His people. This requires that we hear His voice and know His leading.

Fasting is an important spiritual discipline. We, like Ezra, must do all we can to know the will of God as we move through situations requiring blessing and anointing. Routine events also need the fresh anointing of God. We clearly can do nothing without Him.

Intermarriage

Ezra was informed by some of the leaders that the people of Israel--including priests, Levites, and leaders--had intermarried with the people of the land.

> The people of Israel, including the priests and the Levites, have
> not kept themselves separate from the neighboring peoples
> with their detestable practices . . . (Ezr. 9:1).

This situation crushed Ezra's spirit. But God is not a racist; He created all people. So then, how are we to understand this passage? The book of Ruth highlights a Gentile woman of Moabite descent. The Exodus includes ". . . many other people

. . ." (Ex. 12:38). Rahab and her family, included with Israel, are most likely from a Canaanite or Amorite background.

What distinguishes this account in Ezra from the other accounts are the number of intermarriages, the wholesale acceptance of the ways and practices of the nations by the returning captives, and the intermarriage of leaders--the priests, (Ezr. 10:18-22) and the Levites (10:23-24).

The number of intermarriages listed was one hundred twelve (Chapter 10). Many listed in this account were priests and Levites. Leadership always becomes a standard to which others aspire or digress. Jerusalem and the Temple were filled with idols prior to captivity. The challenge was that those serving in the "Temple" with the holiest of assignments had lowered their standards. The Temple became only symbolic if those serving were not consecrated to the ways of God. Our churches and missions today, in a similar way, become only symbolic of our past if those serving are not dedicated to the ways and the holiness of God.

Ezra's prayer highlighted the following:

1. The land was corrupted by the corruption of its people (9:11).

2. Because of the level of sin, they were not to intermarry with them (Ex. 34:16; Ezr. 9:12).

3. They were not to seek a treaty of friendship with the people of the land (Ex. 34:15; Ezr. 9:12).

Examples of low standards

A European missionary woman in the Middle East met a Muslim man and married him. The mission and the sending church in her nation of origin were grieved with her decision and loss of testimony. Marrying a believer of another background and faith has many challenges. Marrying a person who does not share your faith is not of God (2 Co. 6:14).

A "mission" in the Muslim world signed a contract with the government, promising to never share the Gospel, deciding that their humanitarian work would be enough and not offensive to the people or to the government. Later, the "mission" became aware of others who were sharing their faith in Christ and they became nervous and judgmental, feeling that this might reflect poorly on them, as they, members of a Christian mission, had promised never to share the Gospel .

Ezra's advisors told him that the people of Israel, including the priests and Levites, " . . . have mingled the holy race with the peoples around them" (Ezr. 9:2). It is very important that we define the use of the phrase "holy race," and the context in which it is used. Israel was "holy, to the Lord," which meant set aside for the purposes of God, rather than holy by their own virtue.

The Passover was celebrated with the completion of the Temple and prior to Ezra's return. Those who ate of the Passover were the returning exiles, " . . . together with all who had separated themselves from the unclean practices of their Gentile neighbors . . ." (Ezr. 6:21). It appears from this passage in Ezra that the people were welcomed to eat the Passover on the condition that they had separated themselves from the practices of the nations. Therefore, the dividing line was separation unto the Lord rather than purity of race.

A point that must be noted is that Ezra received authority to rebuild the Temple under Artaxerxes, King of Persia. Those overseeing the future of Temple authority had the prerequisite of receiving their legal permission through a head of state. Refer to page 218 for more discussion of the rise of the Sadducees.

Chapter 15 - Nehemiah and the Unprotected City

Introduction

Nehemiah left Persia for Jerusalem thirteen years after Ezra arrived in that city. The book of Nehemiah describes a man sent by God with a message and a purpose. Nehemiah's drive to rebuild the city of Jerusalem was unquenchable. The focus in this book is on rebuilding the walls of Jerusalem. It is a great handbook for us as mission people in God's call.

Some of this book's themes include how we are sent; how God provides; the rebuilding of the walls; and God's desire that we remain dedicated, set aside for Him.

We also gain insight into God's people working with zeal, even though they (and we) feel unqualified for the task.

Nehemiah Hears the Call

Nehemiah heard a report of the state of Jerusalem in the month of Kislev, which is late November or early December. The walls that were broken down and the gates that were burned are symbolic of protection. Mission is an intense search for the hearts and minds of a people to come under the protection of God. People without moral foundations are unprotected. Any teaching can drift freely through the post-modern "city," inflicting silent destruction on its populace. Islamic walls and gates allow the wrong kind of information to enter while they block out the truth. Hindu worldview creates a system that "walls out" the idea of a Creator who is personal.

Nehemiah, the Intercessor

Nehemiah was an intercessor. Intercession is the ministry of identifying with the people for whom one prays. Nehemiah confessed the sins "we Israelites . . . have committed against you" (Ne. 1:6). Intercession is not the confession of another people's problems, nor is it blame focused upon an individual or group. Nehemiah identified with the sins of his people. Mission requires intercession, identifying with the people to whom you are called. The prayer of blame is only listed in the New Testament in the context of the Pharisee praying and not being heard (Lk. 18:11)! Nehemiah, on the other hand, humbled himself with mourning, fasting, and prayer. He identified with the sins of his people in Jerusalem.

> Let your ear be attentive and your eyes open to hear the prayer your servant is praying before you day and night for your servants, the people of Israel. I confess the sins we Israelites, including myself and my father's house, have committed against you. We have acted very wickedly toward you. We have not obeyed the commands, decrees and laws you gave your servant Moses.

> Remember the instruction you gave your servant Moses, saying, "If you are unfaithful, I will scatter you among the nations, but if you return to me and obey my commands, then even if your exiled people are at the farthest horizon, I will gather them from there and bring them to the place I have chosen as a dwelling for my Name" (Ne. 1:6-9).

Strategy

When Do You Speak the Vision?

God teaches us to be careful with timing. When do we share the vision? Many words that people have received from the Lord have been prematurely spoken without knowing how God wanted to bring them to fulfillment. Nehemiah mourned and fasted, yet without anyone around him aware of his struggle! It was illegal to be sad in the presence of the Persian king. Sadness indicated a lack of approval of the king's government or the disapproval of the king himself. Sadness in the king's presence could have cost one his or her life. Nehemiah was careful to patiently wait for God's timing. Prematurely sharing what we believe to be God's vision can be a form of pride.

The strength of the vision to be carried out will either depend upon human personality or upon God, who has rooted the plan in prayer.

Which do you prefer to lead your ministry: God's plan or your personal strengths? Moses began with human force and forty years later received God's direction. King Saul began as God's anointed and ended as one making a monument to himself.

Nehemiah waited until the month of Nisan to let the king see something of his heart (2:1). This was a four month wait, in prayer with God, before he allowed the king to know that something was desperately wrong. The king asked, "What is it you want" (2:4)? By this time, Nehemiah had a plan to see Jerusalem transformed. He was ready and described his vision to the king. "When will you get back" (2:6)? This was a reasonable request from an employer, the Persian government.

Nehemiah's Request

Nehemiah asked for permission to rebuild Jerusalem, his father's city. He gave the king a time frame for his leave of absence. This demonstrated that a plan was in place. He asked for letters from the king to provide for safe passage, protection that Ezra did not want (Ezr. 8:21-23). (The Bible gives us examples of many ways people lived out their faith in context.) He asked for a letter from the king to the keeper of the king's forest, requesting building materials. God granted all that Nehemiah had requested of the king.

Nehemiah's Sending Agency

Nehemiah was on God's mission. The Persian government was Nehemiah's sending base and financial base. In this case, God's mission was backed by a human institution. Nehemiah did not take a collection from the Jews in captivity, nor did he simply pray for his own protection. Like Esther, Nehemiah was in a position that only God could have orchestrated. His God-given position was used to fulfill God's plans.

Pray for laborers to be sent to the harvest; pray also for God's people to be sent to strategic posts of influence. Daniel, Nehemiah, and Esther entered positions that carried political influence. Zerubbabel and Ezra were priests who had a vision spoken to them by God for His people. Both groups were greatly used of God. Your ministry may have many possible expressions and should not be limited to one example of "holy" work.

Starting a Ministry

To begin one's ministry without the proper root system will only grant shallow growth. When Nehemiah entered the city of Jerusalem, he surveyed the damage to the walls before telling anyone about his plan (Ne. 2:11-12). With whom do you trust sensitive information or plans?

The officials did not know where I had gone or what I was doing, because as yet I had said nothing to the Jews or the priests
or nobles or officials or any others who would be doing the
work (2:16).

The "Jews, priests, nobles and officials" of your teams could be frightened off
by a partially prepared plan, one requiring uncertain commitment and offering
unclear goals. Nehemiah's meeting with those involved laid out both his plan and
the backing of the King of Persia (refer to 2:17-18).

The Ways of the Enemy

The enemy can destroy a vision from the Lord if it is shared before the proper
time. Some speak too quickly of a direction in ministry just to gain recognition or
to secure a place in leadership. The wrong people privy to sensitive information
can be used to squelch the plans of God. Talk to God before you talk to people.
Take time to listen to the Lord about His plan. By the time you are ready and are
released to speak, you will have both the direction and the plan to approach a
solution. Understanding timing is a mark of maturity.

Hearing of potential good for God's people disturbs the enemy (2:10).
The enemy uses lies, rather than truth, to achieve his purposes. "Are you rebel-
ling against the king?" is a threat of death (2:19). The challenge to stop a work,
or to quit before it even begins, is a tactic of the enemy. Know that you are called
by God, and know also that your calling will be challenged.

Ridicule
Ridicule is the next level of attack (4:1-2). The attack here was leveled at the poor
ability of the workers to carry out their orders, claiming the weight of a fox would
bring down their wall. Ridiculing the work of God, or the feeble people carrying
out the work, is very serious. Nehemiah took the threats seriously and organized
a prayer chain. He also kept an eye on these enemies.

Threats to Harm
Threatening to kill is another level of attack (4:11). Nehemiah organized the
workers with half of them working on the walls and the other half holding weapons in order to defend the work. Expect that Satan will want your work stopped.

He even sees the potential for God's strength in someone's life and will attempt to destroy that life before it reaches maturity.

Usurp Authority

The enemy will attempt to usurp authority in order to gain access to leadership or to the project (6:1-9). The tactic was the same in Zerubbabel's day. The project was nearly completed and those opposing it were discredited. They attempted to lure Nehemiah into receiving their counsel on rebuilding the city.

When all else failed, fear and doubt were used to slow the completion of the work (6:6-7; 6:10-14). Remember, God has not called you to deliver a half-completed city to Him. He wants all of His workers to remain faithful to their callings.

Missiological Implications in Hostile Environments

- Always take threats seriously. Some seasons require more vigilance, some less. When threats do come, discern what is a response in faith, fear, or presumption. This will most likely require praying with others.

- Never give up. It is God's work, not your work.

- Trouble will not go away and seldom will it diminish. Get used to fighting; but remember that your battle is with Satan, not with people. This is especially true in team conflict.

- Mission is not the easy road, but it is the heart of God.

- Build "the city" and the enemy will find out! This is true when fellowship and believers' community are established as well.

God's Qualifications

Examples from Nehemiah

Nehemiah was neither a city planner nor a general contractor in stone work. The crew he recruited to rebuild a broken city wall were hardly stone cutters and masons. When God calls you to a work, respond. This portion of Scripture testifies to God's ability to use ordinary people to perform extraordinary feats. The people rebuilding the walls of Jerusalem were as ill-fitted for the task as were the fishermen and the tax collector called to build the New Testament Church.

- Be very cautious not to disqualify yourself or others because of a seeming lack of abilities. Rather, learn what is required to accomplish God's task.

- Rejoice when you find someone who is qualified. Never look down on someone with professional training who could be a godsend. On the other hand, don't move into areas that are beyond you just because you sense God's anointing. This could be the lure of pride.

- Never tell people that prior experience or education is meaningless.

Who Built the Walls of Jerusalem?

1. Unlikely people with difficulties built and repaired the walls:

- Eliashib the high priest and his fellow priests (3:1)

- Uzziel the goldsmith and Hananiah the perfume maker (3:8)

- Rephaiah, ruler of a half-district of Jerusalem (3:9)

- Shallum, ruler of a half-district of Jerusalem, and his daughters (3:12)

- Levites (3:17)

- Temple servants (3:26)

- Goldsmiths and merchants (3:31)

2. Likely people with difficulties built and repaired the walls:

- The men of Jericho (3:2)

- The men of Tekoa... but their nobles would not put their shoulders to the work under their supervisors (3:5). Unfortunately, the men of Tekoa did not have their leaders bless or encourage the work they did for Jerusalem.

This Isn't My Responsibility!

Embrace An Integrated Vision.

Mission people must daily view their work as God's work, resisting the narrow vision of finishing only one task. Missionaries sent to India to preach the gospel have also rescued little girls from prostitution. While establishing churches, orphanages have been established. Clean water has often accompanied the Gospel. Schools have been built by missionaries. None of us can afford to miss the opportunities God brings to us. None of us knows the scope of our calling in the early years of our ministry. It unfolds as we obey our Heavenly Father in service.

Provide Justice for the Oppressed.

Nehemiah discovered that the people in Jerusalem and its vicinity were groaning under the taxation mandated by the wealthier class (Ne. 5). Sons and daughters were enslaved by fellow countrymen. Nehemiah fought for the rights and protection of the newly discovered poor within the city. You, too, will find new avenues of ministry of which you were previously unaware.

Confront Evil.

Twelve years into Nehemiah's mission, and after a time spent in Persia, he returned to follow through on the work of building the city. Nehemiah was a man with purpose, not given to quitting. He discovered that during his absence, Tobiah the Ammonite had moved into the city and was living in a storeroom for grain offerings and Temple articles (13:4-5)! Remember, house cleaning does not happen once. Battling the enemy is not finished after one victory. Get troublesome people off your payroll and away from positions of influence. Nehemiah threw Tobiah's personal effects into the street. Don't give up when the same problem presents itself again.

Stay Focused.

Sometimes leaders change priorities without having God's Kingdom in mind. A leader must revisit the general priorities of his people, drawing them back to God's command. Nehemiah returned to find that those who were called and anointed to take care of the Temple operation were nowhere to be found. They had gone home to provide for their families because the daily provision for the Levites had not been given to them (13:10-13). Notice in this case, people stopped giving when the purpose of the tithes was no longer relevant. Nehemiah found trustworthy men to oversee the storehouses and distribute provisions to the Levites. Problem solving is part of your mission calling. Don't give up.

Apply Tough Love.

Again, twelve years into his ministry, Nehemiah encountered people breaking the Sabbath (i.e. those who worked on the Sabbath) (13:15). He also encountered outsiders who entered the city in order to make sales on the Sabbath (13:6). He offered the threat of "laying hands on them" if they continued (13:21), which is not remotely close to the New Testament blessing! This tough leadership was required from a man in his position. He realized that God's judgment would return if people forsook His laws. We are sent to "teach them to obey" (Mt. 28:20). Few items run as counter to our enlightened western thinking as obedience to God's laws. Jesus told us:

> Anyone who breaks one of the least of these commandments and teaches others to do the same will be called least in the kingdom of heaven, but whoever practices and teaches these commands will be called great in the kingdom of heaven. For I tell you that unless your righteousness surpasses that of the Pharisees and the teachers of the law, you will certainly not enter the kingdom of heaven (Mt. 5:19-20).

Tolerance comes from poor leadership and reduces the moral standard. Compassion and forgiveness, however, do not change the moral standard.

Demonstrate A Passion for Holiness.

The next hurdle that Nehemiah faced was mixed marriages. "Half of their children spoke the language of Ashdod or the language of one of the other peoples, and did not know how to speak the language of Judah" (Ne. 13:24). Nehemiah was furious. He is recorded as rebuking the men, calling curses down upon them, beating some, and pulling out their hair. The frightening thing for Nehemiah was to see the people of Israel return to the very state for which God had judged them. The key in understanding this passage is that the children could not speak the language of Judah. This meant that the children of a Hebrew father and a Moabite mother would not have learned the ways of God in the community.

They would most likely have learned the religious practices taught by their mother in her language and in the context of her culture. Light to the nations cannot be realized while darkness from the ways of the people grows unhindered in the lives of the children. Syncretism, which is the only possible outcome from mixing people, languages, and faiths, is not a worthy goal. The values of any believer must be firmly rooted and growing before he or she is sent to another people.

Engage in Translation Projects

"The Levites (Jeshua, Bani, Sherebiah, Jamin, Akkub, Shabbethai, Hodiah, Maaseiah, Kelita, Azariah, Jozabad, Hanan and Pelaiah) instructed the people in the Law while the people were standing there. "They read from the Book of the Law of God, making it clear and giving the meaning so that the people could understand what was being read" (8:7-8).

- The Book of the Law of God was read in *Hebrew*.
- The meaning was made clear in *Hebrew*.
- Changes in language over the course of 1,100 years are significant.

Reinstate the Feasts and Life

We know that the Feast of Tabernacles was celebrated in the seventh month. Ezra opened the Book of the Law in the seventh month to instruct the people (8:1). When they heard of the Feast of Tabernacles, and that it was to be remembered in the seventh month, they reinstituted their calendar (8:13-18). The noteworthy point here is the great joy the people experienced. They sensed they were back on target with an awesome God.

God was not satisfied with the people of Jerusalem to simply have gates, walls, and a feast. Repentance from their sins and changing their ways were next on God's list. The scope of Nehemiah's ministry went far beyond building walls within which people would safely live. The safety within the city was as important as the safety from elements outside the city. The people not only repented from their pasts, but they signed a covenant that placed boundaries around their lifestyles (9:38). Their action of commitment is similar to starting a fellowship today. Faithful commitment is required by the community, not simply by its leader.

Conclusion

Nehemiah was a "sent one" with a purpose and a message. He was sent by the King of Persia with the authority of the Persian Empire to rebuild the city. Nehemiah's life found many expressions of ministry, firming up the walls both in a physical and a moral realm. The wall was completed in fifty-two days. His ministry continued for many years. Physical walls are much easier to maintain than moral boundaries. Nehemiah dealt with the deception of enemies and remained unwaveringly firm to his calling. By example, He teaches us about the firm resolve required to be a missionary and a leader.

Chapter 16 - Malachi

Introduction

Malachi means "my messenger" in Hebrew. The name may be a shortened version of Malachiah which means "the messenger of the Lord." The book of Malachi quickly draws our attention to God's heart for the nations for two reasons. The first reason is that we, who are privileged to live in New Testament times, are aware of the approaching approximate 400 year silence between Malachi and John the Baptist. This directs our attention to the last prophetic Word that God gave to His people before entering the period of silence. The second reason is that his very name, "my messenger," signals our attention to a sent one, or one with a mission message.

Malachi prophesied during a ten year ministry in the years 430-420 B. C., making him a contemporary of Nehemiah. This time period places both prophets speaking to a post-exile audience after the Temple was rebuilt and the sacrifices and festivals were reinstated.

Is That an Offering?

Malachi rebuked the priests, those set aside for full-time service to the Lord, for showing contempt for God's name (Mal. 1:6). This theme is carried throughout the book and is demonstrated by six specific, detestable practices. We must remember Malachi's words and heed his message regarding these six practices.

1. Placing Defiled Food on God's Altar (Mal. 1:7-9)

Always give God your best. This is a principle about which His people need to be reminded in order to avoid heartless, routine activities. The practice of offering " ... blind animals . . . crippled or diseased animals . . ." seemed good enough to the leaders of the second Temple (1:8). This attitude came from their desire to seek man's favor rather than God's blessing through obedience. Remember, what you live will be taught to the nations. You cannot hide a hypocritical practice and expect the nations you are trying to reach to walk with integrity. Live your message. Reproduce your life. Reflect Paul's words: "Follow my example, as I follow the example of Christ" (1 Co. 11:1).

2. Placing Useless Fire on God's Altar (1:10-11)

The Lord regards fire on His altar as useless from leaders whose hearts are not with Him! This means that our Christian activities are meaningless when our hearts are not pure. Our sacrifices are, therefore, unacceptable. God's vision is for the nations to come to Him with pure hearts. This cry comes out in the prophetic words given to Malachi.

> My name will be great among the nations, from the rising to the setting of the sun. In every place incense and pure offerings will be brought to my name, because my name will be great among the nations, says the LORD Almighty (Mal. 1:11).

The contrast is unavoidable. The jealousy stirred in the hearts of the leaders in Jerusalem was intentional. The coldhearted and begrudged sacrifices given on God's altar were not the standard for the nations. This reference to the nations is not dropped in by accident. The future hope of the Lord is for all nations to know Him. He is not pacified with half-hearted activities. Do the nations praising the Lord with pure offerings, from the rising of the sun to its setting, fill our hearts to overflowing? Does this vision grip us with purpose as the very reason we live?

The fallacy of the leaders in Malachi's day was twofold: living in one particular location and observing religious rituals as though these activities brought fulfillment of the Kingdom of God. God's eyes are on the unreached. Our activities in worship and sacrifice are to be reproducible. Our hearts must be stirred with the very things that stir God's heart. God says, ". . .In every place incense and pure offerings will be brought to my name . . . ." This tells us that He is not looking to be honored in only one location, but rather that He will be known and honored in every location. Incense and pure offerings speak of the prayers of God's people (Rev. 5:8). He longs for people in all locations to know Him through prayer and through offering their pure lives to His service. The vision of God is for "every tribe and language and people and nation . . . to be a kingdom of priests to serve our God" (Rev. 5:9-10), correlating with the prophetic words of Malachi.

3. Cheating on Your Pledges (Mal. 1:14)

When you make a vow to the Lord, fulfill your vow. Your promise is not a human expression of hope, neither is it contingent upon whether or not it is convenient to keep it. We do not make pledges in Christian conferences in order to please each other. Malachi pronounces a curse on those who do not fulfill their vows. It is necessary for us to remember that initial nudge of the Holy Spirit to give, and not later try to convince ourselves in a dozen ways to lessen the amount, or even to renege on giving altogether.

Once again, note that the nations are tied into the practice of fulfilling one's vows. God does not want cheating on vows to be reproduced. Is your life in Christ a life that can be reproduced among the nations? If you are not paying your tithes, you will not make a good missionary.

4. Breaking the Covenant of Marriage (2:10-16)

God hates divorce (2:16). He always hates broken covenant or broken promises. The men in Malachi's day were divorcing their Hebrew wives and ". . . marrying the daughters of a foreign god . . . " (2:11). Both divorce and marriage to people outside of covenant commitment stand out in this verse. These were not the "Ruths" or "Rahabs" of covenant promise. The people lost their God-given vision to be light to the nations and found vision for personal pleasure, which is idolatry. Selfishness of unmeasured proportions is frequently the alternative when we lose God's pure boundaries in our lives.

5. Robbing God (3:8-12)

Robbing God goes beyond cheating on your pledges or substituting a diseased animal for a healthy sacrifice. The Word of God clearly states that the people brought a curse upon themselves by paying partial tithes. It is the entire nation, not just the individual, that suffers from robbing God. The result of withholding one's tithes is lack of fruitfulness and watching one's crops (income) eaten by pests. We invite God's righteous reprimand when our tithes are fluctuating with our whims. Today, some go so far as to claim that tithing is an old covenant system that no longer affects the life of the Christian. It is the joy of giving, not the legal requirement to give, that frees us from self-focus. Giving reflects the heart of God, and it is He who encourages our generosity (Ps. 37:26). All that we have is either a gift, or it is borrowed from God. Taking possession of anything God loans to us leads to poverty and eventually to death.

> The wicked borrow and do not repay,
>   but the righteous give generously;
> those the LORD blesses will inherit the land,
>   but those he curses will be destroyed (Ps. 37:21-22).

The Kingdom of God, expressed both in church and mission, needs the financial tithes of believers in order to function.

What are the benefits of bringing the tithes into God's storehouse?

> Then all the nations will call you blessed, for yours will be a delightful land, says the LORD Almighty (Mal. 3:12).

It is important to recognize that "God's storehouse" is a symbolic term for the Kingdom of God. Tithing needs to be tied into blessing the nations with the light of the Gospel. Giving dutifully to a group that is not interested in "light to the nations" will not reap the benefit of the nations rejoicing. God's heart is for the nations to know Him. Rather than giving merely out of habit, our challenge is to find ways that our tithes and gifts can help in fulfilling God's vision for the nations.

The nations are affected by our actions on a daily basis. They either learn of God's grace, or they remain in darkness. They will benefit by knowing God through the message of those sent to them. Paul states that faith comes through hearing, hearing through preaching, and preaching through being sent (Ro. 10:14). Sending is not a budget item in the "optional" category.

Reflection

How will missionaries sent to the nations be provided for in their ministries?

6. Taming Your Tongue (Mal. 3:13-18)

We know the tongue is difficult to tame (Jas. 1:26). The people spoke against God and against the futility of serving Him. God hears your thoughts. He knows your heart. He also desires to reward those who speak properly with the fear of the Lord on their tongue (Mal. 3:16). Be careful how you speak to God and to people. He takes no delight in the slandering of leaders or fellow workers. He delights in purity and in the taming of a snappy, sharp tongue.

It is imperative that we learn to focus our words on that which builds up and encourages others in their walk with Christ. Paul wrote,

> . . . whatever is true, whatever is noble, whatever is right, whatever is pure, whatever is lovely, whatever is admirable—if anything is excellent or praiseworthy—think about such things (Php. 4:8).

Taming the tongue will require learning new habits that bring pleasure to God. Speaking about things that are right, pure, lovely, admirable and praiseworthy will also bring a transformation to the one speaking.

Four Messengers Sent

Messenger I

We know from the opening of the book of Malachi that he is a "sent one." This messenger is preparing our hearts through his writings to look expectantly for three more messengers to come, sent by God, with specific missions.

Messenger II

The "messenger who will prepare the way before me" is a reference to John the Baptist (Mal. 3:1). John is the one sent from God to testify to the light (Jn. 1:6). He was the one called to prepare the way for the Messiah. Malachi was a man moved by the Holy Spirit to prophesy about the coming one: completely human, yet filled with the Holy Spirit from his mother's womb (Lk. 1:41). We also fulfill this prophetic word when we prepare the way for Jesus to enter the hearts of people. Filling in voids in thinking (filling valleys) and pulling down false hopes (removing mountains) is part of the call of God on believers.

Messenger III

The messenger who prepares the way will announce the messenger of the covenant (Mal. 3:1). Malachi is preparing the reader for the coming of the Messiah who will usher in a new covenant. There would be no need for a messenger to prepare the way for the Messenger who would simply reintroduce the old covenant. So, what will the messenger of the new covenant, the Messiah, fulfill? He will bring real righteousness. The image of a refiner's fire or a launderer's soap is not an instant image. It is an image of one who will not give up with meager results, but will take the time in relationship to purify steadily. He will not be satisfied with a quick cleaning that leaves behind wrong attitudes or motives. His work will be thorough.

Messenger IV

The fourth messenger to be sent is Elijah. This reference to his preceding ". . . that great and dreadful day of the Lord" seems to refer to the second coming of Christ and to the day of judgment (4:5). What is the duty of this fourth messenger? His mission is to turn families back to working together. God's will is for fathers and children to be molded back into the family structure with love and harmony flowing between them. We live in days that find families fragmented. This is not God's will. Your duty as a believer must include restoration of families so that the Gospel of the Lord Jesus has its full effect. The homeless fathers need to return to their families. The street children of the world need to find a father. Mission will require living out God's heart as a father or as a son to families who have experienced the pain of separation. Your mission is to bring life to the regions living in death. God is calling you to be light to those still sitting in darkness.

Chapter 17 - Intertestamental Period

Introduction

We now enter the period of time between the prophesy of Malachi and the advent of Jesus, frequently referred to as the "silent years." These years were, in fact, very noisy with activity. Judah was controlled by numerous conquering nations, and there were assorted attempts to revolt from oppressive rule. Some of the Apocryphal or deuterocanonical books were authored during this period of time. The deuterocanonical books are regarded by the Catholic Church as the "second canon" of Scripture and are equal in authority to the previous canon. These books will be listed below with approximate times of authorship.

We know that many of the captives from Judah stayed behind in the former Babylonian, now Persian, Empire. Some Israelites in intertestamental times were assimilated into Assyrian groups in the Northern Kingdom of Samaria; other pockets of Jews from the Southern Kingdom lived in communities both in Judea and in Persia/Babylon. Some of the sectarian people we meet in the New Testament were not present in the Old Testament, bringing us to conclude that philosophies and assimilation formed people into new groups.

The Synagogue

Synagogues were formed during the intertestamental period. With the loss of the Temple in Jerusalem, and its accompanying organized religious ceremonies, the captives placed their religious energy into community centers. The synagogues were centers of religious ceremonies, Jewish culture, and the Hebrew language. References to synagogues in the New Testament are numerous, with locations mentioned in Galilee (Mt. 4:23), Capernaum (Mk. 1:21), Nazareth (Mt. 13:54; Lk. 4:16), Damascus (Ac. 9:2), Pisidian Antioch (Ac. 13:14), Iconium (Ac. 14:1), Thessalonica (Ac. 17:1), Athens (Ac. 17:16), Corinth (Ac. 18:4), and Ephesus (Ac. 18:26; 19:8). This tells us that the concept of local synagogues, which were formed in Babylon, was planted throughout Palestine, Syria, Greece and Turkey. The synagogue followed post-captive Jews to the locations they came to settle.

The synagogue was a great pattern for community life, encouraging the expression of faith in the one true God to establish a community-centered focus. Paul's initial missionary ventures took him to synagogues, and from there on to the Gentiles in those regions. Nestorian Christian missionaries of the East also initially followed the lines of synagogues, preaching Christ as Messiah to the Jews who remained in the regions of the former Persian Empire.

Questions

- Could synagogues have been used in Babylon to invite the local population into Jewish religious life?
- Could synagogues have been moved into Babylonian homes?
- How do existing churches receive non-Christians?

Persian Rule

The Persian rule was very encouraging to the Jews. It gave liberty to the Jews and to their religious leaders taken captive under the Babylonian Empire. Cyrus gave permission, as previously stated, for Zerubbabel to lead former captives back to Jerusalem and to rebuild the Temple. King Darius issued a decree to complete the rebuilding of the Temple after an eighteen-year stagnation of the project. For approximately one hundred and fifty years after Nehemiah's time, the Jews were able to carry out their religious observances without hindrance. The patterns of Zerubbabel and Ezra, sent as priests to oversee the rebuilding of the Temple and eventually Jerusalem, developed into governance by a Jewish high priestly office under Persian rule. The succession of power held by the high priests over Israel brought trouble as these priests vied for political authority. It was during this period of rivalry and strife that the Samaritan temple on Mount Gerizim was built (Open Bible, "Between the Testaments": 881). John Hyrcanus, the Hasmonean ruler (134-104 B.C.), later destroyed this temple.

The Old Testament historical writings are silent regarding the Persian attempts to conquer the kingdom of Greece. The Persians made two unsuccessful military attempts, events which overlap into the time of Queen Esther. This lack of success encouraged other kingdoms, such as the Egyptians and renegade Jewish clusters, to throw off Persian rule.

Greek Rule

Alexander of Macedon, also known as Alexander the Great, brought an end to Persian rule in the region. His armies swept from modern Lebanon, southward and eastward, changing the ruling structure of the region of Palestine. He built the city of Alexandria in Egypt (331 B.C.) and offered the Jews living there privileges similar to those of the Greek residents. His armies continued eastward, conquering Babylonian and Persian cities as far as the Punjab in India. His legacy was the introduction of Greek dress, language, gymnasiums, amphitheaters, and government. Schools and libraries were established in numerous locations. Some Jews took Greek names. Some fused the wisdom of Greek writers with their faith in the God of Abraham. Others refused to become polluted by Greek culture, retreating to intense studies of the Law of Moses.

After Alexander's death, the region was divided and ruled by four of his former generals. The district of Israel was ruled from the Greek power base in Alexandria. Under Ptolemy II, the third Greek general to rule Palestine, seventy-two men from Judea translated the Old Testament Scriptures into the Greek language. This translation became known as "The Seventy," or the Septuagint. Local governance during the days of Greek rule was still in the hands of the Jewish priests.

The Seleucids

Alexander's fragmented empire in the northern area of Syria was led by Seleucus I. His successors waged a series of battles with the leadership in Alexandria. Palestine's rule shifted yet again in 199 B.C. when the Seleucids gained the upper hand. Former rulers, from the Persians to the Alexandrian Greeks, allowed the Jews to enjoy a relative amount of religious freedom. The Seleucids were bent, however, on enforcing Greek culture. Rival Jews paid large sums to Antiochus IV of Syria, purchasing their governing seat. This practice outraged the orthodox Jews, especially with non-Levitical Jews ascending to power. Orthodoxy was outlawed. "The Jews were forbidden, under penalty of death, to practice circumcision, Sabbath observance, or the celebration of the Feasts of the Jewish calendar" (op. cit. 883). The new government ordered the sacred books of the Jews to be destroyed. In part, this could be the reason that fragments of the Old Testament have been unearthed in areas of Alexandria and the regions of the Dead Sea.

The Maccabean Response

An aged priest named Mattathias exploded with rage when a capitulated Jew offered a sacrifice at a pagan Greek shrine. The old priest killed both the Jew and the emissary from Syria. He and his five sons went on to destroy the pagan altar. Orthodox Jews now faced the military force of the Seleucids. Unwillingness to fight on the Sabbath brought many swift deaths. Mattathias countered that defending oneself on the Sabbath was permissible. New warfare tactics of the Jewish people emerged to take back their land from oppressors. Mattathias died and his followers chose his son Judas to be their leader. He became known as the Maccabee or "the hammer." Under the leadership of Judas the Maccabee, Syrian armies were routed. Judas attacked the Temple area and cleaned out the pagan symbols of worship. An altar to the Lord was set up in their place. Peace was short-lived after the return of the Syrian armies. Jonathan, a brother of Judas, led the Jewish armies for a season and became the new ruling high priest.

Simon succeeded his brother Judas as high priest, securing a loose independence from Syrian rule. He was placed as high priest for life, or until a faithful prophet would arise to replace him. This ruling office was termed the Hasmonaean rule, a term picked up from Asmonaeus, an ancestor of their family. His son, John Hyrcanus, succeeded his father as leader of the Hasmonaean state. Under his zealous rule, the temple in Gerizim was destroyed. The Hasmonaeans had consolidated power over much of Palestine by the time of John's death in 104 B.C.

Power changed hands through the following years. The land was ruled at times by a king and at other times and by a high priest. This thirst for power in Jewish circles is evident in the opening pages of the New Testament with the naming of Herod as King of Judea (Lk. 1:5).

The Sadducees

In the inter-testamental period the party of the Sadducees looked to the Hellenistic authorities to validate their influence (Dictionary of New Testament Theology, Vol. 3, pg. 440). This brings us to understand how those ruling over the Temple were void of belief in spirits, miracles, or the resurrection. They had complied with the ruling authorities understanding of spirituallity. Greek customs were widely dropped by many of the inhabitants of Palestine. Those who kept Greek philosophy alive did so because of the authority and influence they derived from association with ruling powers. Although Jewish in background, they denied the spiritual nature of the created world, the existence of spirits, angels, and the afterlife. Their lifestyle in the days of Jesus was characterized by wealth and honor, yet with a surprising lack of spirituality. Their material wealth gave them position in Jerusalem's aristocracy. Their affinity with Greek thought formed their bond with the high priesthood legacy of rulers. Initially, the combination of Temple oversight and denial of the spiritual world (cf. Lk. 20:27, Ac. 23:8) seemed ill-fitted. Yet it must be remembered that their affinity with the Temple was based on power and control over society. (Refer to page 197 for more discussion on Temple authority.)

The Pharisees

The orthodox of the Maccabean times continued to despise foreign rule in any form. Those who believed that both the strict adherence to the Law of Moses and the rejection of foreign influence were necessary for life became the party of the Parisees. Their name means "separated one," referring to the separation from Greek influence. Although closely following the Law, the Pharisees were later characterized by harshness and lack of compassion toward those outside of their circle. Their "separation" from other elements of society led them to their refusal to enter the homes of outsiders and to accept food from them. These strict practices influenced the lives of people in the New Testament. Jesus' sharp words for their hypocrisy came frequently.

The Pharisees began as a sect that interpreted the law. However, they considered their additional rules and traditions to be equal to the law itself. Some of the more noteworthy Pharisees of the New Testament were Nicodemus, Joseph of Arimathea, Gamaliel and Saul of Tarsus, who later became Paul the Apostle.

The Zealots

The party of the Pharisees had various outgrowths and expressions. Two of the more notable teachers were Hillel and Shammai. The former was more flexible, caring for the needs of the underprivileged and willing to find Roman rule compatible with his Jewish orthodoxy. The latter was strict in his teaching, rejecting Roman rule in every form. This strict form of teaching formed the Zealots who hated the Roman presence in Jewish land. Simon, one of Jesus' disciples, came from the band of the Zealots (Mt. 10:4). The antagonism of the Zealots eventually brought the crushing Roman blow that destroyed the Temple in 70 A. D.

The Essenes

The Essenes, like the Pharisees, adhered strictly to the Mosaic Law and separation from defiling elements of society. The Pharisees entered into Temple worship, though the party of the Sadducees controlled it. The Essenes, on the other hand, separated themselves from the defiling influence of society more strictly than did the Pharisees. They wrote, for example, that if one's animal fell into a ditch on the Sabbath, it was not to be pulled out. This was clearly beyond the rules laid out by the Pharisees. The Essenes are remembered today for their withdrawal into secluded societies like the Qumran community. They represented a believing community that was dedicated to Scripture and to purity. The negative factor, however, must also be mentioned. Their community did allow converts to join but cocooned itself from the defilement of society. They pictured themselves as a "clean" group rather than a cleansing light in society. This meant that one was required to become Essene in every sense in order to be acceptable. The danger we must avoid today is to view our communites as "separated and saved" as opposed to a saving and welcoming community. The Essenes were known for their hard work and study of the Scriptures. In some ways, they resembled a modern-day kibbutz.

The Herodians

The Herodians were a party of Jewish background that was quite at peace with Roman rule. They appear to have gotten their name by supporting Herod and the regime for which he stood. Because of their support of Roman rule, they were in sharp conflict with the Pharisees and the Zealots of the day. The time that the Herodians and Pharisees came together to question Jesus did not demonstrate their consensus, but rather their mutual distrust of Him (Mt. 22:15-16). The Herodians wanted taxes paid to Caesar and asked Jesus if He was on their side. The Pharisees denounced Rome and wanted to know where Jesus stood politically. Jesus' answer affirmed the Kingdom of God and the futility of living for wealth. Both Pharisee and Herodian were amazed and yet frustrated by His answer.

The Rule of Rome

Roman rule extended beyond the crumbling Greek hand. Pompey besieged Jerusalem for three months, crushing the rule of Seleucid oversight in the region. Temple worship was allowed to continue, but all signs of Jewish independence were erased. Herod was placed into power and agreed to remain loyal to Rome and pay taxes extracted from the population. His rule covered the years from 37 B.C. to 4 B.C., and he is well known for the murder of all infant boys in Bethlehem after the birth of Jesus. Anthony, the succeeding Caesar, named Herod the "King of the Jews." This gives us understanding of his response to the Magi who asked, "Where is the one who has been born king of the Jews? We saw his star in the east and have come to worship him." When King Herod heard this he was disturbed, and all Jerusalem with him (Mt. 2:2-3). His cruelty to all who opposed his power was well known. His wives and sons were brutally removed from him when they opposed his commands. Little wonder for his order to kill children when a new king was announced. "All Jerusalem with him . . ." would be fearful, knowing of the cruel reaction to follow.

Herod began the rebuilding of the Temple in Jerusalem in 20 B.C. It was not completed until 64 A.D., or 68 years after his death. The third Temple lasted only a few years, being destroyed by the armies of Titus in 70 A.D.

Conclusion

The intertestamental period included conflict from many sides. This conflict was fueled as much by lust for power and wealth, as it was by religious zeal. Conquered by Babylon, Persia, Greek factions, and now Rome, the cry for deliverance and salvation was acute. The deliverance and salvation sought after was illusively confused with human demands for freedom. The state of the Jewish people after captivity was still marred by willful rebellion against Yahweh. Their hunger for a strong prophetic voice to lead them was evident in the intertestamental period. Who was qualified other than God Himself to step into the confusion of life in Palestine and sort out the true goals of righteousness? How was it possible for the multiple parties present in Israel to hear a message that reintroduced God and His sovereign work to the lives of humankind? In our quest to understand God's heart and mandate for mission, will He include the nations in His kingdom, or will they be segregated from the lives of the Chosen People?

Chapter 18 - John the Baptist

Introduction

There is an amazing advantage we possess as believers today. We understand the continuation of the story begun in the Old Testament. It is necessary to grasp the link between the Old and New Testaments in order to keep us from a segmented view of God's work in human history. John's ministry marks the dividing line between these two great periods of God's work.

Elijah Has Come!

Malachi prophesied the coming of " . . . my messenger, who will prepare the way before me" (Mal. 3:1). Jesus told John's listeners that he was indeed the "Elijah" sent to prepare the way of the Lord.

> As John's disciples were leaving, Jesus began to speak to the crowd about John: "What did you go out into the desert to see? A reed swayed by the wind? If not, what did you go out to see? A man dressed in fine clothes? No, those who wear fine clothes are in kings' palaces. Then what did you go out to see? A prophet? Yes, I tell you, and more than a prophet. This is the one about whom it is written:
>
> I will send my messenger ahead of you, who will prepare your way before you. I tell you the truth: Among those born of women there has not risen anyone greater than John the Baptist; yet he who is least in the kingdom of heaven is greater than he. From the days of John the Baptist until now, the kingdom of heaven has been forcefully advancing, and forceful men lay hold of it. For all the Prophets and the Law prophesied until John. And if you are willing to accept it, he is the Elijah who was to come. He who has ears, let him hear" (Mt. 11:7-15).

Jesus is telling us that the end of an age has come. He tells us about all that the Prophets and Law prophesied until John. John was in the line of the Old Testament prophets, proclaiming righteousness and the necessity of repentance from the evil of the generation in which they found themselves. The Law also was predictive in that it spoke of a righteousness to come (Eze. 36:25-27) and God's ability to remove sin in a single day (Zec. 3:9). John prophetically addressed both needs by proclaiming the Messiah, Jesus, to be a sacrificial lamb sent to remove the sin of the world.

> The next day John saw Jesus coming toward him and said, "Look, the Lamb of God, who takes away the sin of the world! This is the one I meant when I said, `A man who comes after me has surpassed me because he was before me.' I myself did not know him, but the reason I came baptizing with water was that he might be revealed to Israel" (Jn. 1:29-31).

The importance of John's statement to us in mission is very significant. Jesus was the long awaited Messiah. Jesus would remove the sin of the world, not simply that of the orthodox Jewish nation. God's plan of redemption by the blood of Jesus would be sufficient to cleanse every tribe, language, people, and nation (Rev. 5:9). In this one statement, John also set God's agenda over the agenda of multiple Jewish factions. Jesus did not come to rid the land of Rome or favor the Pharisees' orthodoxy over the Sadducees' politics. The focus was rather the restoration of the created with their Creator.

John called for national repentance in every segment of society. He denounced the Pharisees and Sadducees, comparing them to venomous snakes (Mt. 3:7-9). He spoke powerfully without preference for wealth or political power. His rebuke of King Herod for incest eventually brought his ministry to a close (Mt. 14:3-5).

His words were unavoidable. The Jews of his day were so powerfully shaken that many followed his ministry and some became close disciples.

God's Plan Set In Motion

John emphasized repentance from sin, as did other prophets before him. The distinction of John's words highlighted that "the kingdom of heaven is at hand" (Mt. 3:2). His message was declaring that the order of God was now being set in place. Repentance was necessary to enter into that new, sharpened order of the Lord. His words came with the impact of an ax, cutting away dependency on human traditions in favor of the rule of God. He clarified that being a blood descendant of Abraham was not enough to insure insider relationship (Mt. 3:9). He spoke of the impending judgment on the nation of Israel, including every faction of Jewish sectarian life (Mt. 3:10).

John's baptism sealed the vow of repentant people (3:11). He promised that the coming of the baptism of the Holy Spirit was soon to be released (3:11). God's plan also calls for judgment to come, separating the righteous from the unrighteous as the farmer separates the valuable wheat from the unusable chaff.

The prophetic ministry of John gathered a faithful remnant of Israel around him as disciples (Mk. 1:4-6). We know that John welcomed disciples and spent his time in the wilderness of Judea (Lk. 3:2); not in the cities with the associated comforts. The desert is where God seems to build his people in preparation for ministry. Solitude and facing the reality of God's Kingdom come more readily in seclusion. The same was true for Moses in the region of the Sinai and for Jesus fasting in the desert for forty days.

The order of God's rule included John, yet this prophetic voice knew his place. He was a witness to the light to come (Jn. 1:7), but he was not the light himself. He understood his ministry to be the forerunner of the Lord's (Jn. 1:23), setting things in place so that the Messiah could be highlighted. He openly confessed he was not the Christ (Jn. 3:28) and was unworthy to untie the sandals of the Anointed One to come (Jn. 1:21-26).

John used the language of the bride and the bridegroom (Jn. 3:29-30). He called himself the friend of the bridegroom and acknowledged the importance of the honor going to the bridegroom. He was not called to gather disciples to himself, but rather to turn over his disciples as the bride is given to the groom. His declaration, "He must become greater; I must become less," is also ours. The supremacy of Jesus the Christ cannot be misunderstood. Jesus came from Heaven. We, like John the Baptist, were born into this world. Jesus is above all because He came from Heaven (Jn. 3:31).

John's ministry ended with his beheading at Herod's command. Tradition has this beheading taking place at Herod's summer palace near Madaba in Jordan. Tradition also tells us that his head was encased in the sarcophagus of Saint John the Baptist Greek Orthodox Church of Damascus. This church was made into a mosque in the early centuries of Islamic rule in Syria.

Conclusion

Several prophets of the Old Testament predicted John's ministry. John completed the line of Old Testament prophets, living and ministering before the offering of the sacrifice of the Lamb of God. He spoke of the salvation of the world, the baptism of the Holy Spirit, and the judgment to come. John linked all of these events with Christ, while stepping back to give the honor to Him. Unlike the inconclusive ending of the Old Testament, John's ministry ended with the light to the world appearing and with the path of repentance laid for the coming Kingdom.

Part 3:

The Ministry of Jesus in the Four Gospels

He said to them, "How foolish
you are, and how slow to believe all that the prophets have
spoken! Did not the Messiah
have to suffer these things and
then enter his glory?"

Part 3: The Ministry of Jesus in the Four Gospels

Introduction

Our journey through the Old Testament confronted us with several reinforced themes. The New Testament underlines some of the clearer Old Testament themes, and it also highlights the themes which remain in an inconclusive state. Old Testament background is necessary for our understanding of the New Testament. The knowledge of God and the framework He developed with His people form our understanding of the Messiah, His ministry, and life with His people. The following themes stand out from our Old Testament understanding of the Kingdom and Mission of God:

1. **God is the Sovereign Ruler over all kingdoms.** He is the Creator and Sustainer of the universe (Ps. 145:13; 1 Ch. 29:11). No other spirit or being is credited with creating, with sustaining life, and with giving order to His creation. We are commanded to have ". . . no other gods . . . " (Ex. 20:3; Dt. 5:7). His sovereign rule will include judgment on a world that loves evil and hates the Lord (opposite of Ps. 97:10).

2. **The Lord reveals His character.** He reigns in complete moral purity (Ex. 3:5-6; Ps. 15). His hatred of sin and its corrupting effects on people is evident. His moral order is not given as "advice"; it is a life and death directive. It is evident from His character that there is no excuse for moral complacency.

3. **There is community obligation on the lives of His people.** This comes in the form of God's commitment to the community of His people, and the commitment that His people should shoulder toward their community. This flows out of the merciful and compassionate character of God. Living with the knowledge of God draws His people to care compassionately for each other. There is an obligation to help keep the members living righteous lives.

4. **Light to the Nations and the expanding Kingdom is part of the Messianic reign.** This Kingdom, as we understand it, is eternal and is not the work of human hands (Isa. 9:6-7; Da. 2:44). It also encompasses the entire earth and is not isolated to one

ethnic group. The community obligation is to extend beyond Israel to the entire human community. Herein we find the Kingdom of God encompassing the world.

5. **A fifth theme calls His people to represent that "light to the nations."** We enter into His works, bringing a knowledge of the Lord to the nations (Ps. 67; Jer. 24:5-7). His obligation becomes ours. His desire is not for an isolated nation, but for all nations to serve their Creator.

6. **Persecution, suffering, and future hope are clearly a part of a life dedicated to serving God.** Laughing at Noah's life and his building project and at Jeremiah's experience in the mud of a well are examples of the persecution of the righteous. The hope we derive is not from our temporal surroundings but from the promise that His Kingdom is eternal, and we are a part of that Kingdom.

The first two themes (the sovereignty of God and the revelation of His character) are abundantly clear and are repeated frequently throughout the Old Testament. The people struggled with their commitment to their own community, showing the third theme to be fragmented, necessitating prophetic rebukes. The fourth (light to the nations) and fifth themes (obligation imposed upon His people) remain elusive and, for the most part, unrealized at the close of the Old Testament. The eternal God spoke into the lives of people in fragile human kingdoms. David's kingdom was divided, shattered, and struggled under surrogate leadership. His people had some involvement with the nations of the earth but recorded few examples of bringing "light to the nations."

The New Testament begins with a dramatic shift in content from the inconclusive ending of the Old Testament. The remarkable words of Jesus tell us in the first chapter of Mark that the Kingdom is near.

> The time has come, he said. The kingdom of God is near. Repent
> and believe the good news (Mk. 1:15).

Mark records these words after Jesus' temptation in the wilderness and after John was put into prison. There must be a fundamental difference between the sovereign rule of God described in the Old Testament and the coming Kingdom. This message of the newness of the Kingdom grabs our attention and promises fulfillment of the older mandates that were left unfulfilled. Jesus announced,

> When you enter a town and are welcomed, eat what is set before
> you. Heal the sick who are there and tell them, 'The kingdom of
> God is near you' (Lk. 10:8-9).

Paul carries this theme into action and into a demonstration of the Kingdom of God. The Kingdom among us invites the participation of God's people and promises His involvement with the Kingdom.

> For the kingdom of God is not a matter of talk but of power
> (1 Co. 4:20).

In our examination of the New Testament, the following six themes will be highlighted and take on added meaning "in the day of Messiah":

- God's sovereignty will take on new meaning through Christ and His Lordship. Judgment will come to the world "in that day," referring to the Second Coming of Christ.

- The revelation of God's holy character will culminate in redemption and forgiveness for all who call upon His name.

- God's covenant with His people will be highlighted through the blood of Jesus. His commitment to His people will take on new meaning through His sacrifice on behalf of all who receive Him. His anger, justice, and mercy are all satisfied in Jesus.

- The expanding Kingdom of God is evidenced through moral regeneration of those that follow the Messiah. The Kingdom also expands into the lives of Samaritans and Gentiles from many backgrounds.

- His people will be called to mission--the proclamation of the Kingdom of God to the nations. The community of the King will become a called out group of those dedicated to ushering in the Kingdom.

- Persecution, suffering, and future hope will follow those who bring the good news of the Kingdom. Jesus promised suffering to His followers. He also promised eternal life without suffering or tears. We as His people must embrace both the suffering set in front of us while we carry out His will and the promise that all tears will pass away.

Summary

The New Testament will bring fullness and understanding to the Old Testament themes. We who read the pages of the Bible must see ourselves stepping out into the challenges and anointings God has for us. We are the ones who will carry out God's vision of "light to the nations." The Bible is, above all books, meant to be applied to our lives. Take hold of His direction. Become a co-laborer with God in His desire for the nations.

Chapter 19 - Introduction to The Gospel Narratives and Acts

Who wrote the four gospels?

Mark, the oldest of the Gospels (A. D. 55), throws the reader into "The beginning of the gospel about Jesus Christ, the Son of God" (Mk. 1:1). After a brief quote from Isaiah of the one to prepare the way for the Messiah, Mark takes us into the ministry of John the Baptist.

Matthew wrote in about A. D. 60 from a strongly Jewish framework and quoted frequently from the prophets to verify what he saw, heard, and believed. His words, ". . . this took place to fulfill what the Lord had said through the prophet . . ." (Mt. 1:23) or ". . . spoken of through the prophet Isaiah . . ." (Mt. 3:3), transport the reader into the foundation of the Old Testament. Matthew gives us a window into the infant Jesus with the questions Joseph faced as a man engaged to a pregnant woman in a Middle Eastern Jewish context. He then tells us that the first group of people to "seek the King" were the Magi. This first people to recognize the royal nature of Jesus were Gentiles from the East. Matthew sets the tone for his finale of the Great Commission. This Gospel will affect the nations!

Luke wrote a two-volume work he called "Acts I and II." Volume one we know as the Gospel of Luke. Volume two we call Acts. Luke, our only Gentile author in the entire Bible, wrote slightly later than Matthew, which was approximately A. D. 60 – 63. The very fact that a Gentile's writings are included in the canon of Scripture tells us of God's inclusive heart for the world. Luke fills in important pieces to our understanding of the life of Christ, relating stories of women (Mary's song and story), Samaritans (the parable of the Good Samaritan), and lepers. Luke is the sole voice who tells of the birth of Jesus in a stable (Lk. 2:7). This brings the royalty of the Most High to the level of the most common of people. In Luke's writings, the first people to seek after Christ were simple shepherds. Angelic revelation was not withheld from these most common of people.

Volume two, or Acts, describes the coming of the promised Holy Spirit and His effect upon the nations. The message of Acts also follows the Pharisee Saul who became Paul, Apostle to the Gentiles. Luke describes the clumsy nature of the Jerusalem Council in dealing with the question of Gentile believers, and he contrasts this with the miracles and fruit among the Gentiles recorded in several nations. Between Luke, the Gentile author, and Paul, Apostle to the Gentiles, three-quarters of the

New Testament were written! This in itself is a broad and clear message that this Gospel is for the entire human race.

John wrote much later, at about 90 A. D. His purpose in writing his gospel was "that you may believe that Jesus is the Christ, the Son of God, and that by believing you may have life in his name" (Jn. 20:31). John introduces us to the Son from all eternity who became flesh. John begins with the incarnation of deity into human form. John the Baptist, our link from the Old Testament, bears witness to Jesus being the sacrificial Lamb of God for the salvation of the world. Worldwide salvation, as God's plan for the ages, came straight from John the Baptist's mouth and is carefully recorded by John the Evangelist.

The Genealogy of Jesus

The New Testament will be examined by initially looking at the four gospel narratives. The four authors provide unique information to the reader as well as complementary information that verifies the accuracy of each of the other writers. Two of these writers supply us with the genealogy of Jesus: Matthew and Luke. Matthew begins by tracing Jesus back to Abraham.

Matthew listed five women in the genealogy of Jesus. A study of God's heart in mission would be incomplete without understanding the lives of these women and the problems associated with them.

Tamar had twin boys, Perez and Zerah, through an incestuous relationship with her father-in-law (Ge. 38). The heart of God the Father reaches out to hurting, decimated families. He restores broken lives and includes them in His family. All of us are sin-ridden and ashamed. He brings us into the fellowship of His son Jesus and includes us in His family.

The next two women, Rahab and Ruth played a pivotal role with a man named Boaz. Rahab was a Canaanite prostitute. She was redeemed from her life of sin, and she truly exemplifies one who once sat in darkness and now is in the light. God incorporated this woman into the genealogy of Jesus. She and her husband Salmon had a son named Boaz. The Scripture is silent as to why Boaz, a land owner (Ru. 2:3), was willing to marry a Moabitess. It is possible that the son of a Canaanite and a former prostitute may not have been appealing to some of the good families in Bethlehem. We do know that Boaz was willing to extend his life and protection over Ruth. God is in the business of redeeming the destitute, restoring the outcast, and including them in His family.

David and Bathsheba had a son, Solomon. Matthew tells us that "David was the father of Solomon, whose mother had been Uriah's wife" (Mt. 1:6). Sin was not whitewashed from the people of God or from the family line of Jesus. Sin is not whitewashed from our lives. We are set free, yet we know the depths from which God has redeemed our lives unto Himself forever.

Mary was an engaged virgin. Few circumstances in a Middle Eastern setting, then and now, could be more difficult than a young, unmarried woman expecting a child. For the sake of his family honor, the groom-to-be would expose the woman and her pregnancy to her family. Her family would need to deal with the shame, either by stoning the woman or by sending her far away. What some people understand as shame, God calls joy and blessing. Relating to a holy God and His Kingdom is often regarded as shame in the world. Mary's experience is, to some extent, felt by all believers.

Luke takes us from Jesus back to Adam. Both Luke and Matthew speak of Joseph. Matthew calls Joseph ". . . the husband of Mary, of whom was born Jesus, who is called Christ" (Mt. 1:16). Luke tells us that "He was the son, or so it was thought, of Joseph . . ." (Lk. 3:23).

Questions

- How do people of Muslim backgrounds understand the following text in Luke: "He was the son, or so it was thought, of Joseph . . ."
- What is adoption in an Islamic society?

Visitations of Angels

The angel Gabriel announced the coming changes to God's administration and work among His people. Luke recorded God's declaration through two angelic visits, clarifying the anointing and ministry of John the Baptist and the incarnation of the Son of God.

The first visitation was to Zechariah. Both Zechariah the priest and his wife Elizabeth were descendants of Aaron. The story unfolds like an Old Testament record: Elizabeth was barren like Sarah (Ge. 16:1), Rachel (Ge. 29:31), and Hannah (1 Sa. 1:5).

The presence of spiritual beings is not an every day occurrence. Gabriel's first words to Zechariah were, "Do not be afraid . . ." (Lk. 1:13). Neither God nor His messengers are interested in frightening the people of God. Gabriel knew of Zechariah's prayer for his wife Elizabeth to have a child. This gives some insight into God telling the angels what we are praying for and their awareness of God's answers and timing. Gabriel knew more than Zechariah's personal case; he knew God's overall plan. The son to be born to this elderly couple was to have a God-picked name (v. 13), specific diet, and was to be filled with the Holy Spirit from his birth (v. 15).

The particulars of Gabriel's announcement of the birth of John the Baptist have some similarities with the birth of Samson (c.f. angelic visit, Jdg. 13:3, 9-20; special diet, consecration to God, 13:7, and born with foreign oppression, 13:5). The life and purpose of Samson, however, was vastly different to that of the life and purpose of John. Samson was raised up when Israel cried out to God as a result of its oppressive rulers. John lived in another epoch on God's timetable. John was to turn the hearts of Israel back to the Lord in preparation for the Messiah, ". . . to make ready a people for the Lord" (Lk. 1:17).

The second visitation was to Mary. God sent the angel Gabriel in the sixth month of Elizabeth's pregnancy to Mary (Lk. 1:26-27). The miraculous plan of God was revealed to Mary. She would have a son and was to name Him Jesus. God named His Son. We know from Gabriel's announcement that Jesus

1. was the Son of the Most High,

2. would reign as King in David's line,

3. would reign over the house of Jacob forever, and

4. His kingdom would be eternal.

Question

How did Jesus become a part of David's family?

> Even Elizabeth your relative is going to have a child in her old age, and she who was said to be barren is in her sixth month. For nothing is impossible with God (Lk. 1:36-37).

Mary was not isolated; her relative Elizabeth was also experiencing the miracles of God. Mary was a virgin in the Middle East and soon to be expecting a child. To whom could she turn who would understand her--and believe her? It is likely her parents were too culturally overridden with shame to rejoice in this miracle. It was the angel who told Mary of a person who would listen.

Mary traveled more than fifty miles from Nazerath to the "hill country of Judea" (1:39) to meet someone who would understand what God was doing in her life.

Reflections

To whom do you go when you want to share the direction of God's leading?

Are you able to listen to the telling of the miracles that God is doing in the life of a younger person?

Be careful to share your vision and direction with someone who can understand. Also, be careful to listen to the vision and/or the burden of a young person, remembering the direction God gave to your life.

Most likely, Mary traveled to Judea soon after the angel's announcement. In a matter of days she entered Elizabeth's home. The fetus inside of Elizabeth at six months was referred to as "the baby." This unborn child leaped inside of Elizabeth at the sound of Mary's greeting. At this point, Jesus was possibly a blastocyte--an embryo newly attached to the uterine wall. He was already called Lord by Elizabeth while still an early embryo. An elderly aunt and her six month fetus rejoiced in the miracle of the incarnation.

The third visitation of an angel was in Joseph's dream, recorded in the book of Matthew (1:20). After nearly 400 years of silence, God was speaking through dramatic encounters with angels. Their messages were all taken very seriously.

Adoption

How did Jesus become "David's son"? His lineage is traced back through Joseph, though Joseph had no blood relation to Jesus. Hence, Jesus was adopted into the lineage of Joseph. Adoption is a requirement to enter the family of God. Jesus' entry into the biblical lineage is not by natural birth. The mystery of Psalm 110:1 becomes understandable. Jesus is in the lineage of David and is, therefore, his "son." He is the Incarnate One and is, therefore, his Lord.

Never forget that you were adopted into the family of God. Paul understood the mystery of adoption. The reality is that the Kingdom of God is not here in its fullness, which makes our adoption realized by faith rather than by experience. All of us eagerly wait for our fullness in God to be realized.

> Not only so, but we ourselves, who have the first fruits of the Spirit, groan inwardly as we wait eagerly for our adoption as sons, the redemption of our bodies. For in this hope we were saved. But hope that is seen is no hope at all. Who hopes for what he already has? But if we hope for what we do not yet have, we wait for it patiently (Ro. 8:23-25).

Paul did not say that the Jews were natural children and the Gentiles were adopted. The adoption process that was already available to the Jewish people was now available to all.

> For I could wish that I myself were cursed and cut off from Christ for the sake of my brothers, those of my own race, the people of Israel. Theirs is the adoption as sons; theirs the divine glory, the covenants, the receiving of the law, the temple worship and the promises. Theirs are the patriarchs, and from them is traced the human ancestry of Christ, who is God over all, forever praised! Amen (Ro. 9:3-5).

He later wrote to the Gentiles at the Church in Ephesus that their adoptions were the plan of God from the ages and not an afterthought.

> For he chose us in him before the creation of the world to be holy and blameless in his sight. In love he predestined us to be adopted as his sons through Jesus Christ, in accordance with his pleasure and will— to the praise of his glorious grace, which he has freely given us in the One he loves (Eph. 1:4-5).

- None of us has a natural heritage that will merit salvation.

- Adoption is required to enter God's family and to serve Him.

- This is Good News for all the people to whom we bring the Gospel: *We are all adopted.*

The Infancy Narratives

Matthew tells us that Mary was found to be with child "by the Holy Spirit" (1:18) while engaged to Joseph. This former tax collector for Rome is convinced of the incarnation, the miraculous nature of a virgin expecting a baby by the breath of God. Never before has this happened; never again will this event be repeated. Matthew gives us a window into the struggle of a Middle Eastern Jewish man who discovers that his fiancée is already expecting.

Question

Why is the word divorce used to end an engagement?

Matthew brings his theology into his context. He is faced with the words spoken by "an angel of the Lord" and with the prophecy of Isaiah.

1. The angel directed Joseph to give to the child the name Joshua (Jesus).

2. Isaiah prophetically wrote that this son would be called Immanuel.

Isaiah 7:14 tells us, "Therefore the Lord himself will give you a sign: the virgin will be with child and will give birth to a son, and will call him Immanuel." The writer of the gospel defines the name "Immanuel" as "God with us" (Mt. 1:23). This is an interpretation of the prophesy of Isaiah, revealing the incarnation of God living with us through the title Immanuel. The title is not given to anyone else. The name chosen by God, and spoken through the angel, is Joshua. The Hebrew language offers only one name, Yeshua, which means "He will save His people from their sins." Jesus is a derivation of the Greek form of the Hebrew name. Salvation from your sin requires transformation. This is the refiner's fire and the launderer's soap referred to in Malachi.

> But who can endure the day of his coming? Who can stand when he appears? For he will be like a refiner's fire or a launderer's soap. He will sit as a refiner and purifier of silver; he will purify the Levites and refine them like gold and silver (Mal. 3:2-3).

Yeshua does not save His people because they are in His club or because He is indifferent to their sin. This salvation from sin requires a new heart and a renewed mind. Transformation of life is quite different from joining a group based on a common confession.

The Birth of Jesus

Welcome to Bethlehem

The incarnation presents us with the reality that God relates to our humanity; He came to us in the lowliest form of a baby. Luke tells us that Joseph was required to register in Bethlehem, the city from which his relatives traced their ancestry. Joseph probably had relatives whom he knew living in that town. Luke then tells us that he traveled "with Mary, who was pledged to be married to him and was expecting a child" (Lk. 2:5). The Middle East is a friendly place and one which protects mother and newborn. All of those conditions radically change when shame is involved. Shame turns the Middle East into an unfriendly place. The shame of pregnancy outside of marriage will slam shut the doors of relatives' homes. Joseph's continuing with Mary, who was pregnant but not by him, brought a heavy social burden. Luke tells us simply that there was no room for them in the inn (v. 7). Why wouldn't any mother or grandmother come to Mary's aid? *Shame*. Why wouldn't any father quickly give his room to help? *Disgust*. The incarnation would not be put on hold until society would work out their theology. The incarnation would take place in a stable.

Reflection

The "smaller incarnation" of missionary lives in a new land cannot be delayed until society is ready for the message.

The Shepherds and the Angels

One's job often defines one's social status. The religious elite held great social status. In the first century, shepherds were very lowly people and had no status. They were not immoral, however, as were the prostitutes, or unacceptable as were the Samaritans or the Romans. Shepherds in Bethlehem were Jewish but considered unclean.

The status of shepherds in Israel changed over the centuries. The Levites had sacred duties to perform in connection with the Tent of Meeting and later with the Temple in Jerusalem. They had no land as inheritance, but they were granted "...

towns to live in with pasturelands for our livestock" (Jos. 21:2). The Levites were shepherds and needed to be ceremonially cleansed to perform their priestly duties. The status of shepherds changed after the Babylonian exile. The Pharisees insisted on "clean" people to observe strict purification rites that were only binding to the priests while performing their duties. Jobs considered to be defiling took on new meaning. Shepherds were also suspected of dishonesty as a result of their poor pay (Dictionary of New Testament Theology, Vol. 3, pg. 556). They were not trusted as members of society and were classified with the tax collectors. The once-honored profession of Moses and David was reversed to one of the most despised in the first century. It is in this context that God breaks through, cutting to pieces religious shame and elevating the lowly heads of the outcasts. We must enter into the story and ask ourselves which people in our society we consider to be contemptuous. Do we wrongly look upon some with prejudice?

And there were shepherds living out in the fields nearby... (Lk. 2:8).

Now that we understand the status of shepherds, three spectacular parts of this story speak to us clearly. The first illumination in our quest to understand God's heart for mission is that the shepherds were the first to hear of the Messiah's birth! These descendants of David's profession, in David's town, were the Father's first pick for the birth announcement. An angel in brilliant light (Lk. 2:9) told them how to find the Messiah in a stable. The "heavenly host" (v. 13) was not a chosen choir; it was heaven's army. The awesome appearance was that of a singing army, aware of the birth in a stable and sent with orders from the Father to communicate with shepherds. It must be noted that the army did not sing for Herod or for the Sanhedrin.

The second part of our story's surprise is that none would be more welcomed in the stable than the shepherds. Jesus was on their level. This gave them solid proof that God's concern for them went to the foundation of their social standing. God did not reject them; He included them in His story.

Our third surprise is that the first evangelists in the New Testament were shepherds. Happy, angel-struck, wide-eyed shepherds told their story and announced the Messiah's birth.

The Lord broke through to humanity with the incarnation. He cut past societal chains by using shepherds. He confirmed Isaiah's writings that His ways are not our ways, and that His thoughts are not our thoughts (Isa. 55:8-9).

The Magi from the East

Prophesies abound in the Old Testament that spoke of the nations being drawn to learn of the ways of the Lord.

> In the last days the mountain of the LORD's temple will be established as chief among the mountains; it will be raised above the hills, and all nations will stream to it. Many peoples will come and say, "Come, let us go up to the mountain of the LORD, to the house of the God of Jacob. He will teach us his ways (Isa. 2:2-3).

Scripture is quiet as to the prophetic insight these visitors from the East had that drew them to Jerusalem in search of the King of the Jews. They are mysterious visitors from a non-Jewish context. Some have speculated that they came from Oman where frankincense was abundant. Others place them as Kurds or Persian Magicians. They were outsiders to the traditions of Israel, yet they believed the new King was to be worshiped (Mt. 2:2) and given gifts (v. 11).

What part of their background drew them to follow a star? What made them connect a star in the East with "His star"? Why did this star direct them to the birth of the King of the Jews? These answers are not found in Scripture. Matthew simply records that their understanding of the star, with the help of the chief priests and teachers of the law (Mt. 2:4), led them to Jerusalem, and eventually to Bethlehem. We must conclude that God works among peoples of the world to prepare them for their Savior and Lord. God has placed within the hearts of many people a story that opens a doorway for them to receive the good news of the Messiah.

Reflection

We cannot assume that all people have a correct story or that all story lines have validity. It is important that we take the time to hear the stories of the people to whom God sends us, and seek to make plain to them the God whom they have only known from a distance.

In Matthew's account, the Magi were the first seekers of the new born King. The vision of the nations rallying to the Root of Jesse was becoming a reality (Isa. 11:10). The mission of God in drawing people to seek His Son was, and remains, unavoidable.

The gifts offered by the Magi may seem odd, both for an ordinary child and even for a king. The gold, exchanged among the wealthy, would be welcomed by this needy family who would soon be forced to flee Bethlehem. Gold was the standard gift given to kings. Frankincense was normally used in a priestly function during religious obligations. Jewish kings were not to preform priestly duties (2 Ch. 26:16-20). They gave the child the frankincense; they did not burn the frankincense to Him in their worship. The third gift, the embalming substance with spice, pointed to death. Although we understand the gifts and the symbolism behind each one, we do not have record of why the Magi chose these gifts, nor their insight into this gifted, anointed life.

King Herod "The Great" was called "King of the Jews" by Caesar Augustas. When Herod heard the news of the Magi looking for the new king, he was disturbed and all Jerusalem with him (Mt. 2:3). Herod was threatened, and Jerusalem was afraid for good reason. It was said of Herod that it was better to be his dog than his son, for several of his sons had been brutally murdered when he suspected their disloyalty (New Bible Dictionary, pg. 478). Innocent children died because of Herod's rage. Our world is not indifferent; it is evil. Pain, torture, and death are all around us. Followers of the Messiah die every day because of the evil in this world.

The Magi were warned in a dream not to return through Jerusalem. They were in tune with the moving of God enough to obey the dream.

Question

Why were they not warned in a dream to avoid Jerusalem en route to Bethlehem?

Herod died in 4 B. C. after Joseph, Mary, and Jesus were in Egypt.

Dedication in the Temple

Luke describes the events surrounding the dedication of Jesus in the Temple after "the time of their purification" (Lk. 2:22). This most likely was forty days after the birth of Jesus, fulfilling the law of Moses.

Simeon knew through the Holy Spirit that this child was the Lord's Messiah. He had received the promise of God to see this child before his death. Now Simeon held Him in his arms. The flood of fulfillment that Simeon experienced was beyond description. His words prophetically announced the Messiah's presence and purpose:

> Sovereign Lord, as you have promised,
> you now dismiss your servant in peace.
> For my eyes have seen your salvation,
> which you have prepared in the sight of all people,
> a light for revelation to the Gentiles
> and for glory to your people Israel" (Lk. 2:29-32).

1. Simeon's knowledge of the Scripture and of the Messiah were evident. He knew that Jesus was the instrument through whom salvation would come.

2. The Messiah was the Light who would bring fullness/glory to the Gentiles. Simeon uttered this in the Temple, the House of Prayer, for all nations. He tied Isaiah's theme of "light to the nations" into the life of a forty-day-old boy who would one day bless the entire world.

3. Jesus was also the fullness of Israel. Israel would not have its fullness/glory without this Messiah.

The specifics of an evangelistic mandate to the nations were forming; and all were forming around a baby. We do not know if Simeon asked if Jesus was born in Bethlehem or if He was of the house of David. We do know that Simeon's revelation was sufficient to overcome human questions and receive God's gift. He also prophesied that this child would change the status quo; some people would be raised up, and others would be lowered. Conviction would come through the revelation of people's thoughts, and Mary would suffer in her soul as a result of Jesus.

Anna, a very old prophetess who was a widow and who worshiped God at the Temple night and day, arrived at the very moment Simeon was holding the child. She prophesied that this child would be linked to the redemption of Jerusalem. It was not revealed that His death would offer redemption to the people of that city as well as to all people of the earth.

The Boy Jesus

Jesus was drawn to his Father's house. He understood His heavenly Father as His source of belonging. All believers should come to the point of relating to their heavenly Father more closely than to their earthly fathers. Earthly fathers are guides--tutors to help us in this life. Our real roots of belonging, however, are linked to the Creator Himself. Earthly fathers and mothers are to be honored, which is one of God's commandments. Yet, if any followers of God the Father fail to look beyond their earthly parents, the vision of God's call and of His greatness will be diluted.

Extra-biblical Infancy Narratives

The biblical account of Christ The Anointed One is clearly divided into time frames. The prophetic accounts of the Old Testament described the anointing, ministry and eternal nature of the Messiah. New Testament accounts told of a miraculous conception and of angelic proclamations before and during His birth. The ministry of Jesus as an adult began after His baptism and temptation. No miracles in the biblical record were attributed to the child or boy Jesus. To do so would have high-lighted an invincible life of an untested son. Jesus had to pass through physical, social, and spiritual growth en route to maturity. This process, Luke tells us, took about thirty years (Lk. 3:23). Without this maturity, Jesus would not have been ready for a ministry in the public arena.

The Qur'an, on the other hand, tells us that Jesus preached to men from His cradle (3:45) and made clay birds come to life (5:110). Other extra-biblical material points to the miracles of the infant Jesus (Gospel of Thomas Ch. 2). Infant miracles place a different light on the character of God and of Jesus as well. Infant miracles de-pict Jesus as magical or gifted. The biblical account calls him the Anointed One. The difference between gifted and anointed is dramatic. The former tells us that somone has been given a gifting for a particular period of time. The gifting, which is attributed to God, does not allow us to see Jesus but simply look past Him. The anointing (*messah*), on the other hand, brings us to the characteristics of the Anointed One; it brings us to the incarnation (Isa. 49:5) and also to His sacrifice for our lives (53:4-6). The sacrifice of a gifted person is meaningless. The sacrifice of the Incarnate One pierces our souls and brings transformation.

Missiological Implications

The Messiah's genealogy demonstrates to us the Kingdom of God, His forgiveness of sin, and His acceptance of human frailty into His family. His geneology also tells us that the Kingdom of God welcomes all to be adopted into God's family. God, the Creator and Sustainer of human existence, broke into the physical realm through angelic visitations. He also invaded human life through the incarnation. The promise of forgiveness of sins is affirmed through Yeshua, the One who will save His people from their sins.

Both lowly Jewish shepherds and Gentiles were led to the infant Messiah. We conclude that the gift of the Messiah is an invitation for all people to experience transformation and become a part of God's Kingdom.

Some people will have dreams or visions that lead them to the Messiah. We must be open to help them find the true Messiah without rejecting the source of their revelation. We are not constrained to find a Bible reference that templates all revelation into the call of God to Messiah. The chronicle of the visitors from the East who were led to the Messiah is an example of this principle.

John was born to aged parents. No doubt, running and playing games with Zechariah and Elizabeth were limited. On the other hand, Jesus was born to parents who were completely on the other end of the spectrum. His mother was a young virgin. God's miracles were performed within the bodies of both the elderly woman and the young, unwed woman. Our faith must not be limited; God is able to work miracles in any arena.

The births of John and Jesus also lead us to understand the eclipsed nature of the Old Covenant and the miraculous invasion of the New Covenant.

The Ministry of Jesus in the Four Gospels

An overview of chapters 20 to 27

The transition from the Old Covenant to the New Covenant is a major theme in biblical theology. The significance of this transition is important to missiology because we are challenged with the scope and direction that the Kingdom of God will now take. The initial presentation in Chapter 20, *Jesus Inaugurates the Kingdom*, will look at the years of Jesus' life in large brush strokes. The message of His inaugurating the Kingdom will be applicable to mission personnel in both message and identification.

The presence of Jesus brought reactions from several faltering kingdoms. Today, we face the same faltering kingdoms in several forms as the Kingdom of God advances into new realms. The restoration of God's purposes brings a swift reaction from both satanic powers and human institutions that feel threatened. Missionaries need to understand *The Kingdom and Restoration* presented in Chapter 21 in order to conceptualize the battles before them in service to Jesus.

Mission requires action, and action requires disciplined lives to carry out God's will. Any church that allows the power of the gospel to slip into the realm of a good philosophy will find mission waning. It is a necessity to understand discipleship.

Chapter 22, *Discipleship in the Kingdom of God*, is a theme that must be studied, applied, and lived for the rest of your life. Discipleship brings freedom from the tyranny of harsh task masters.

The Kingdom of God extends a treaty to all inhabitants of the world which is based upon the death and resurrection of Jesus. The treaty offers forgiveness to everyone who turns to the Lord. Forgiveness is a hallmark of the Kingdom and is foreign to human systems. This seminal message of forgiveness must be poured out to the nations by missionaries sent to proclaim it. We who have tasted of God's forgiveness are qualified to take this news to others. Chapter 23 focuses on several aspects of forgiveness.

Chapter 24, *Jesus Teaches on the Kingdom*, will confront us with the style, methods, and content of the Master's teachings. Missionaries must understand the content of Jesus' teachings and then find ways to describe the Kingdom of God within the cultural settings they find themselves. The methods He utilized in the first century should not be viewed as outdated just because we live in the twenty-first century.

It is critical that we understand the nature of Jesus as the fulfillment of Old Testament prophetic voices. Chapter 25, *The Ministry of Jesus*, will examine several aspects of His nature that are evident throughout His ministry. Many of His characteristics are clearly forms familiar to us through the Old Testament. Some of His characteristics are specific to the New Covenant, and they present new forms of ministry. How do missionaries pick up the call of God and fit their giftings into the ministries to which they have been called?

The overarching biblical theme of the *Kingdom and the Nations* comes through very clearly in the gospels, and this is the focus of Chapter 26. The Kingdom of God is not limited to any earthly sect or cultural expression. The Kingdom is extended to Jews, Samaritans, Greeks, Phoenicians, and Romans. How Jesus navigates in the midst of the complexities of Jewish projected superiority will inspire each cross-cultural worker to break loose from old bigotries and extend the love of God to all. His mandate to carry the gospel of the Kingdom to regions beyond must stir us to action today, laboring with Him to complete the task.

What will *The Coming Kingdom* look like? What words does Jesus give us that describe the nature and scope of the life to come? Chapter 27 takes us to a brief look at the life to come, which is promised to us and to those who accept our message.

Chapter 20 - Jesus Inaugurates the Kingdom

The Kingdom of God appears in short glimpses throughout the Old Testament, intersecting and challenging human need. Dramatic events in the opening pages of the New Testament speak of the unseen Creator clearly declaring that the Kingdom of God is moving forward.

Four segments of Christ's ministry on earth can be noted from the Gospels:

1. Renewal movements

   Two renewal movements intersected each other. John and his disciples brought a renewal that affected many people, stirring righteousness within a stagnant religious system. This movement pointed the way to a second movement--that of Jesus and His disciples. The second movement ushered in the Kingdom of God and allowed it to grow into all regions. These renewal movements threatened the established Jewish political and religious powers.

2. The growing popularity of Jesus

3. Opposition to Jesus and His teaching

4. The crucifixion and resurrection of Jesus

The writers of the Gospels linked Jesus to the history of Israel. Matthew did so through genealogy. He also used the prophetic words of Isaiah in Chapter 7 to describe the virgin birth. Mark told us that John the Baptist was the forerunner about whom Isaiah had spoken, preparing the way for the Messiah.

Luke was the one writer who recorded the angel's foretelling of the birth of John who would prepare the way for the Lord. Jesus' birth was also foretold by an angel and linked to John's imminent coming. Luke told of Jesus' birth in Bethlehem, the city of David, and that angels announced His birth. The genealogy listed in Luke links Jesus to the past. He immediately moved Jesus into His ministry and pre-eminence by His association with the Holy Spirit who was present during Jesus' baptism.

John connected Jesus to the beginning, to creation itself. John declares that Jesus is the author of all creation and is the Word of God. He is the creator and the light in darkness. Jesus is the Incarnate One from eternity. Jesus is called the Lamb of God and the Son of God by John the Baptist in the first chapter.

John's Baptism and The Kingdom

Jesus began His public ministry when He was about thirty years old (Lk. 3:23). John the Baptist's life and ministry were the connecting links between the prophesies of the coming Messiah and the inauguration of the Messianic Kingdom. John stood with one foot on the promises of the Lord to come and the other foot on their fulfillment. John knew the stories his parents had told him about the angelic proclamation and his miraculous birth. He knew about the word his mother Elizabeth had spoken in Mary's presence. Neither of these stories, nor the stories his father had told, were enough to direct John's life and ministry. He needed to hear from the God who anointed him before his birth and sent him to baptize (Jn. 1:33).

Reflection

John the Baptist needed to hear from God personally. Hearing from his parents and listening to their stories was a help but not enough to sustain his ministry. In the same way, each of us needs to know the call of God on our lives. We need to know the anointing God has for us individually and corporately. Where is God directing you to serve His Kingdom?

John's ministry was not easy. Flattening mountains to prepare for the Messiah required denouncing human religious establishments (Mt. 3:7-10) and rebuking the current political leader (Mk. 6:17-18). Filling valleys gave ordinary people hope--through the forgiveness of their sins--and encouragement to live for God (Lk. 3:10-14). We have a similar responsibility to carry the news of the Messiah to an unreached world.

John's God-ordained ministry was to prepare the way for the Messenger of the New Covenant. Luke records:

> . . . the word of God came to John son of Zechariah in the desert. He went into all the country around the Jordan, preaching a baptism of repentance for the forgiveness of sins. As is written in the book of the words of Isaiah the prophet:

A voice of one calling in the desert,
'Prepare the way for the Lord,
make straight paths for him.
Every valley shall be filled in,
every mountain and hill made low.
The crooked roads shall become straight,
the rough ways smooth.
And all mankind will see God's salvation' (Lk. 3:3-6).

The Kingdom message of John was for all to repent of sin and to be baptized as a public sign of that repentance. The cutting word, "You brood of vipers!" (Lk. 3:7), was spoken to those who failed to show the fruit of repentance. Baptism is not a magical ritual that closes God's eyes to injustice. It is not a rite of entry to a Christian club. It is a public declaration of conviction and sorrow for past sin, and it is a commitment to righteousness in community.

Matthew also recorded, "The ax is already at the root of the trees . . ." (Mt. 3:10). This abrupt message announced that change was now taking place. This was not a word for the future; it was for that moment. Change had arrived. This dramatic word drew people from many backgrounds to follow John. His statement, "The Kingdom of Heaven is at hand" (Mt. 3:2), was also a word of new beginning for that exact moment in time.

The Paradox of the Kingdom

The first paradox of the Kingdom is that **it exists in some locations, but has not yet been proclaimed in all locations**. Confusion in mission happens when people believe that the Kingdom of God began with John's baptism, continued with Jesus' ministry, and naturally spread throughout the world. The confusion lies in the misunderstanding of how the Kingdom of God comes to new regions. John's proclamation was to a mainly Jewish audience in his location. The change with the arrival of the Kingdom in Israel had not yet begun in Persia nor in China. Many areas of the world still wait today for the proclamation of the Kingdom of God.

The second paradox was present in John's day and in his location: **the Kingdom is here and now, yet things seem to be like they were yesterday**. We still live in this paradox today. The Kingdom is now within us and yet expanding in both breadth and depth throughout the world. We, too, see the expressions of evil throughout the world where the Kingdom of God has not yet come or has not yet fully arrived.

The specifics of the "Kingdom is now" come at the announcement of "the Lamb of God who takes away the sins of the world" (Jn. 1:29). The inauguration of the Kingdom proclaims forgiveness, requires commitment and sacrifice, promises a baptism of the Holy Spirit, and opens the floodgates of God's grace--right now. The day of the Lord has begun. The paradox remains that we see each of these in part, and only in some locations of our world.

A New Society

The clarity and power of John's ministry were evident. Jews convicted of their sin flocked to John, confessed their sins, and received John's baptism as a sign of their public repentance. Note that Temple renewal was not part of John's ministry, nor was reforming the parties of the Pharisees and the Sadducees. Additionally, there was not a solicitation for human approval. God must be God and not asked to submit to human approval or affirmation. His ways do not ask for human, democratic acceptance.

Reflection

Never make decisions with the presupposition that the Kingdom of God requires you in order to function. It is an honor to serve the King. All of us are needed in service, yet the Kingdom does not revolve around our lives.

John's anointing started a new society. John confronted the Pharisees and Sadducees, calling them a brood of vipers and making them children of the serpent. John told the Pharisees and Sadducees that their claim to Abraham's lineage as proof of Kingdom inheritance was pointless: "I tell you that out of these stones God can raise up children for Abraham" (Mt. 3:9). John knew that God had the ability to create and to transform. He also did away with the idea that bloodlines made people more or less worthy of the Kingdom of God.

His message was not one of seclusion as was so common in his day (i.e. the Essenes), but it was a message of a transformed life lived within the greater community. His message included the sharing of clothing and food (Lk. 3:11) with those in need. It should be noted that no mention was made of focusing their sharing only with those in a believer's community. There was a greater sense of the Kingdom of God expressed to the world rather than to a closed community.

All Are Welcome, All Must Repent

John told the tax collectors, "Don't collect any more than you are required to" (Lk. 3:13). To the soldiers he responded, "Don't extort money and don't accuse people falsely—be content with your pay" (Lk. 3:14). John did not tell the tax collector to look for another job--one that did not support an occupying power or corrupt temple system. He did not tell the soldiers to leave their potentially violent profession. It was possible to be a baptized soldier in Herod's army, or even in Caesar's army. Today, we understand that it is possible to be a baptized, believing lawyer, used car salesperson, or fighter pilot. God's righteous standard is more important than the expected peer pressure to abuse your position for personal gain.

Most professions are redeemable! Jesus' words to the woman caught in adultery, "Go now and leave your life of sin" (Jn. 8:11), must be applied to 1) the leaving of evil professions (i.e. marketing stolen cars, selling illegal drugs, lying to pervert the legal system) and 2) walking in righteousness in all redeemable professions.

National pride or priorities are misplaced if used as a filter to select people worthy for knowledge of the Kingdom. A baptized believing soldier in Caesar's army was just as welcome as a believing soldier in Alexander the Great's army or today in the Russian army. It is important we hear John's message and not expect to convert people's political persuasion to qualify them for the Kingdom. This message must impact our faith in the Son of God to make His people "one flock with one shepherd" (Jn. 10:16). The kingdom of God is far too broad and too encompassing to scrutinize nationalities.

Questions

Does a communist need to leave his/her political understanding to enter the Kingdom?

Is a Palestinian required to accept Israel before he/she can enter the Kingdom?

Renewal requires "coming out" from routine

John called people to the other side of the Jordan where he baptized. This was the same river--the same side of the river--their fathers had failed to cross because of unbelief (Nu. 14:29-33). John baptized "on the other side of the Jordan" (Jn. 1:28) which, in a sense, called the people back to the wilderness and back to the place of renewal. It reminds us of the conditional promise of the land coming with faith in God and repentance from sin. It also reminds us of Joshua calling for the people to be circumcised as they crossed into the land of promise (Jos. 5:1-8). Now John, from beyond the Jordan, called for the circumcision of the heart as the faithful entered not a land, but a Kingdom. John's baptism required people making the effort to put aside their routines. It required action, not just a simple acknowledgment of John the Baptist's teachings.

Look, The Lamb of God!

John announced, "Look, the Lamb of God, who takes away the sin of the world!" (Jn.1:29), identifying Jesus as the sacrifice of the Father. John was not the only one identifying the Messiah. He testified that the "one" who told him to baptize said that "The man on whom you see the Spirit come down and remain is he who will baptize with the Holy Spirit" (Jn. 1:33). The third testimony was the "voice from heaven" (Mt. 3:17) identifying Jesus as the loved Son. The timing was right. John the Baptist recognized the sign of the Spirit, and the Father spoke from heaven. There was no mistaking the identity of that person.

John was not certain of the identity of Jesus before the baptism. He was, however, very clear after the event. We have no idea of the thoughts running through the mind of Jesus prior to His baptism. Certainly it took faith to be baptized and to fulfill all righteousness. By this statement we infer that Jesus knew His identity but was not to announce Himself prematurely. In fact, others were to make the announcement. The clear words of John the Baptist, the sign of the Spirit, and the voice of the Father were now permanent marks in Jesus' mind. The time had come.

Revealing Jesus as the Messiah Through the Temptation (Matthew 4)

Satan was understood to be a personality in the book of Job. His influence destroyed the garden of God and the harmony between God and man in Genesis 3. The Gospel writers bring our attention to the focus of this evil personality on Jesus, Messiah of God. "Then the Holy Spirit led Jesus into the desert to be tempted by the Devil" (v. 1). The announcement of the Messiah was picked up by dark, evil powers. The Holy Spirit, filled with wisdom, led Jesus into a confrontation with the Devil himself.

The Holy Spirit knew exactly what bait would attract the Evil One. The announcement by John, the appearance of the Holy Spirit as a dove, and a voice from heaven all pointed to the very Incarnate One of God among the human race. As Jesus daily fasted and prayed, Satan had his eye on Him. After Jesus had fasted forty days and nights, when He was very tired and hungry, Satan made his move.

Satan was not accustomed to tempting people and facing defeat. He seemed to be unchallenged in his ability to ruin God's creation. This encounter was of another magnitude, yet the enemy came with precise bargaining pieces that he thought would be impossible to refuse.

Part of God's mission is to defeat the works of Satan (Heb. 2:14). Jesus' ministry began by confronting His adversary. Jesus faced three temptations; Satan faced three defeats. Jesus did not use His powers to satisfy Himself. He refused to tempt God, as Satan so enticed Him to do. Jesus refused to worship Satan to regain the world.

Miracle in Cana

The first miracle of Jesus took place at a wedding in Cana in the district of Galilee. An understanding of chemistry tells us that only the Creator can transform one molecule into another and change elements into other elements. It is just as complex (humanly impossible) as changing stones into bread. The difference between the temptation of bread and the miracle of Cana is that Jesus did not use his Creator's power to satisfy Himself. This was for someone else's need, that of an embarrassed wedding host.

Jesus is the Bridegroom and we as His people are the Bride. This miracle early on in the ministry of Jesus reminds us of the marriage supper of the Lamb that will one day gather believers from all nations, peoples, and languages. His wedding feast will go on as planned. Jesus worked in obedience to the Father. We conclude that the Father's desire to speak of new wine, created better than the old, points to the new Kingdom.

The miracle in Cana was significant because it revealed to the newly called disciples that Jesus had power, and it confirmed to His disciples His Messianic place.

> ". . . and his disciples put their faith in him" (Jn. 2:11).

Proclamation of the Kingdom in Nazareth

Jesus announced Himself in His hometown of Nazareth. He did not fit into the mind set of the Jewish scribes. In their minds, Messiah would cleanse the nation from foreign impurities and establish a kingdom which would honor the scribes and teachers of the law. Jesus read from Isaiah, proclaiming Himself to be Messiah.

> He went to Nazareth, where he had been brought up, and on the
> Sabbath day he went into the synagogue, as was his custom. And

he stood up to read. The scroll of the prophet Isaiah was handed
to him. Unrolling it, he found the place where it is written:

The Spirit of the Lord is on me,
because he has anointed me
to preach good news to the poor.
He has sent me to proclaim freedom for the prisoners
and recovery of sight for the blind,
to release the oppressed,
to proclaim the year of the Lord's favor.

Then he rolled up the scroll, gave it back to the attendant and
sat down. The eyes of everyone in the synagogue were fastened
on him, and he began by saying to them, "Today this scripture
is fulfilled in your hearing" (Lk. 4:16-21).

Fulfillment of this Scripture meant the presence of Messiah. The reference to
Isaiah 61 validated the sound nature of Scripture and the necessity of faith in God
aligning with His Word. He did not read the next verse from Isaiah 61:2, "and the
day of vengeance of our God." That day is coming but not yet fulfilled. The other
verses confirmed His presence and proclaimed His ministry.

Jesus gave a description of the Kingdom of God. We who are heirs and ambas-
sadors of the Kingdom must focus on the directives which Jesus highlighted in
this passage. We are to

1. be filled with the Spirit of God,

2. preach the good news to the poor,

3. proclaim freedom for prisoners,

4. heal the sick (blind), and

5. break the bondages of the oppressed.

These five areas are part of the anointing on the Body of Christ. We can follow
Jesus into each area He described in Nazareth. We are not called to initiate judgment on the earth; that is reserved for the return of Christ. Those in the Body of
Christ declaring judgment and taking the role of judge are out of line with God's
call upon His disciples. Neither Crusades nor Inquisition are part of our calling.
Islam turns the Nazareth proclamation on its head. Judgment is the message
dealt to the non-Islamic world. "Conformity or death" is the aberration imposed

to bring people into submission.

The announcement that "today" the Kingdom of Messiah is fulfilled is not a vague reference to the future. The utterance of the Nazerene signified that He was the Messiah and that He was openly proclaiming that His Kingdom had begun.

As Jesus read this portion of Scripture, He knew that anger was building in the people. He quickly referred to the grace of God shown to non-Jews in providing for a Gentile woman of Sidon and healing a Syrian army commander from leprosy. His message was plain and clear. The Kingdom of God would come to those who acknowledged their unworthiness, to those hungry to receive the kingdom, or to those who humbly obeyed. This brought swift opposition as members of the synagogue attempted to destroy Jesus.

The proclamation of Jesus in Nazareth clashed with the Jewish religious leaders in several ways. Jesus had not been trained in the strict line of Pharisee school. His message did not align with their expectations. He proclaimed Himself as Messiah, shocking those hearing His words. Jesus pushed His exclusive Jewish crowd to bigoted anger by mentioning these two Gentiles who were loved and cared for by God. These two stories, in combination with His proclamation of being the Messiah, were likely what triggered the short fuses of the religious scholars. The preconceived notion of many Jews that Messiah would restore Israel to strength and dignity and remove corrupting Gentile elements was challenged in this synagogue setting. How could a Messiah be valid while mentioning help for Gentiles? How dare He refer to these Gentiles as ones for whom God cared, looking past the needs of a native born Israelite?

Growing Popularity of Messiah

Those following Jesus grew steadily from a few disciples to enormous crowds. The following Scriptures tell us of this fact:

- The "whole town" came out to Jesus for healing and deliverance from demonic powers (Mk. 1:32-34).

- He fed and taught five thousand men, plus women and children (Mk. 6:30-44; Mt. 14:13-21; Jn. 6:1-13; Lk. 9:10-17).

- The four thousand were fed along the Sea of Galilee (Mt. 15:20-31; Mk. 7:31-37).

- A crowd of many thousands had gathered, so that they were trampling on one another (Lk. 12:1).

The attraction to Jesus was overwhelming. He taught as one with authority, not as the religious elite. He also healed all who were brought to Him on different occasions (Mt. 8:16; 12:15). He had compassion for the crowds, which is evident from His provision of food. We, too, are challenged to provide for people's needs and allow our hearts to be moved with compassion.

The popularity of being with Jesus was not always out of the purist of motives. This is still true today. God knows we begin our understanding through the lenses of our own worldview, moving toward seeing Jesus for who He really is. This takes time. Sometimes, people are drawn readily to the Jesus they understand; others are driven away, unwilling to make him Lord of their lives.

His healings and miracles attested to His being Messiah. The blessings that came to people's lives were a sign that the Messianic Kingdom was already among them. When asked by John's disciples if He was the one for whom they had waited, Jesus answered by making reference to Scripture--Isaiah 35 and 61--and its fulfillment. He did not simply tell of His miracles or teaching. On the surface the difference was minor, yet Jesus made clear the fulfillment of what had previously been written so that all would firmly believe. There would never be a need to extrapolate His life to mystic writings, or to force His story into a poorly fit reference. He was the Messiah long prophesied to come.

The thousands who were drawn to the Messiah were often those looking to benefit from Jesus in some way. Jesus did not come simply to perform healing miracles or to provide food service to the hungry. He did not come as a secular humanitarian aid worker. Jesus came to transform lives. The Kingdom of Messiah was not present only to bring comfort to the human race, but to set the order and rule of God in its proper place. The contrast is clear between making Jesus our King to bless and validate our human existence, and recognizing Him as King and submitting to His rule.

> Jesus, knowing that they intended to come and make him a king by force, withdrew again to a mountain by himself (Jn. 6:15).

> Jesus answered, "I tell you the truth, you are looking for me, not because you saw miraculous signs but because you ate the loaves and had your fill. Do not work for food that spoils, but for food that endures to eternal life, which the Son of Man will give you. On him God the Father has placed his seal of approval" (Jn. 6:26-27).

People love the benefits of one who can multiply bread. Healing all diseases is a great relief to people in all time periods and in every nation. Jesus referred to "food that spoils" which is true for stomachs that are full today and will be hungry tomorrow. This is also true for human bodies healed today that will still die "tomorrow." Improving physical life in a fallen world is good, but it is not the fullness of the Kingdom of God. It is not possible to remain in the old ways of your life--the only difference being a full stomach--and, at the same time, grasp the newness of the Kingdom of God. One must rule; the other fades into the past. His desire is that we come to Him for ". . . food that endures to eternal life . . ." (Jn. 6:27).

Jesus' popularity should draw people into discipleship with Jesus as the one and only Lord. Yes, we do want Him to be with us in the struggles of life, but as the one to whom we submit rather than the one who gives us relief for a short time or who obeys us and does our bidding. This truth brings clarity to our message in all time periods: Jesus is Lord and requires our complete life.

The question arises: How does the Body of Christ express love to a physically hungry or needy community? This is a delicate question that requires both insight and a response. The good news of the gospel is that God cares about us. Understanding the love of God compels us to love our neighbors and to care about their needs. James tells us that true faith will do something about the physical needs of people.

> Suppose a brother or sister is without clothes and daily food.
> If one of you says to him, "Go, I wish you well; keep warm and
> well fed," but does nothing about his physical needs, what good
> is it (Jas. 2:15-16)?

We can be misunderstood at times just as Jesus was misunderstood as the best choice for king. Food and clothing do not represent the whole gospel and should never be used to bribe people to desire the Kingdom. The term "rice Christian" is a reference to the Chinese who "converted" in order to receive the benefits the missionaries brought to their region. Physical blessings must be available to all living in a region in order to prevent the appearance of faith being bought.

James also tells us that providing justice for the needy and shelter for those without family are priorities of the Kingdom of God.

> Religion that God our Father accepts as pure and faultless is this:
> to look after orphans and widows in their distress and to keep
> oneself from being polluted by the world (Jas. 1:27).

Looking after people in their distress will require social action and standing firmly in the face of cruelty for those who have no voice or power in society. The mission of God is to view the world and all its inhabitants as people He desires to bless and transform, a people He longs to call His own.

The Rejection of Messiah

The Messiah was the Incarnate One of God. Jesus, in taking on human form, came into a world made up of a variety of people. The nations were still in darkness, except for a few brief encounters with God (i.e. Jonah in Assyria, Daniel in Babylon and Persia, and Esther in Persia), and held many different worldviews. Hinduism had begun nearly sixteen hundred years before the incarnation of Christ, and the advent of Buddhism was about five hundred years before Christ, or two generations after Nehemiah's time. Jesus came to a people who had background with the God of creation. We know that He came to His own people--the Jewish nation--but for the most part they "did not receive him" (Jn. 1:11). Some did receive Him and had the power to become sons and daughters of the Creator (v. 12).

Jesus was rejected for three major reasons. First, people who love the world and the things of the world will never be drawn to the rule and authority of God (1 Jn. 2:15-17). Love for the world and for the power and wealth found therein will always be at odds with the Creator. Second, the ways of Satan are always at war with the ways of God, with His people, and with His creation. The thief's ways are to steal, kill and destroy (Jn. 10:10). The third reason that rejection was inevitable was because of the controlling nature of the Jewish religious system. The political and financial systems of the Pharisees, Sadducees, and teachers of the law of Moses were not willing for the Kingdom of God to set priorities straight. These three areas are not easy to isolate as only one cause. At times, the ways of the world and the ways of the enemy are synonymous. Some religious establishments flow very smoothly with the ways of the world and in opposition to the ways of God's Kingdom. We will explore these three areas of rejection, understanding the difficulty of separating them completely from each another.

Rejection from the World

The teaching of Jesus was not physically enticing. When potential disciples promised loyalty, Jesus promised no housing package (Mt. 8:20; Lk. 9:58). Retirement benefits, from the world's point of view, were also not part of His promise. People who believe the story of Jesus are sometimes fearful of the cost of being a disciple or the shame associated with someone not competing to impress the world.

The Kingdom of God does not come and "one-up" the prevailing wages in a community. This underscores the necessity to understand the economy of a particular city or nation when mission enters a new people group. Hiring locals at a "fair" wage could be beyond the local standards and, therefore, undermine the realities of the Kingdom and halt further mission. Jesus does promise that God knows our needs before we ask (Mt. 6:8, 32; Lk. 12:30). The question comes down to trusting in God for today's bread and not storing up our own riches for future needs when the world is hungry today.

Jesus was rejected by some because he ate at the home of Zaccheaus. This tax collector was obviously wealthy, and he was detested by the lower class people in Jericho. Tax collectors were also despised by the Pharisees who viewed them as people working for the foreign occupation forces. Tax collectors were normally hired from the native population as subordinates under the foreign administration (The New International Dictionary of New Testament Theology, Vol 3, pg. 757).

> All the people saw this and began to mutter, "He has gone to be the guest of a 'sinner' (Lk. 19:7).

Going to the home of a tax collector brought complaints from onlookers. Part of the rejection of the Messiah was demonstrating--in a visual and practical way--the call of God to those hated and rejected by society. Can we, for Christ's sake, enter the home of a politician known for corruption? What will people say? This is where knowing the difference between the praises of God and the praises of people becomes critical. The praises of people will normally take us into pleasing the majority or giving people what they want to hear and see. The praises of God are in obedience to His voice. Only those who listen to God will affirm your obedience to His call. Those listening to the world and its desires will complain of your actions and reject the direction of God.

The Enemy's Hatred

The desire of Satan was to defeat the Incarnate Son of God. Blatant confrontation in the wilderness took place when no other person was present. The three confrontations with Satan in the wilderness questioned Jesus' rightful place as Creator, Lord, and the only one to be worshipped.

The normal ways of the Enemy take place through people to whom God has given the ability to make decisions. Human decisions can have the fingerprints of Satan, desiring to influence society against the will of God.

Popular shift away from Jesus was far more sinister than not liking His message or His style. The shift against Jesus brought a desire to kill Him, a sign of the Thief.

> Every day he was teaching at the temple. But the chief priests, the teachers of the law and the leaders among the people were trying to kill him. Yet they could not find any way to do it, because all the people hung on his words (Lk. 19:47-48).

This rejection by the religious elite, combined with the Enemy's desire to destroy Jesus, was contrasted here with the people desiring to hear the Master's words.

Rejection by the Jewish Religious System

The advent of John the Baptist ended a four hundred year period of God's silence. The last word spoken by God before this period of silence was through the prophet Malachi.

- In this prophetic word, God rebuked the religious leaders for bringing crippled or diseased animals to His altar (Mal. 1:5-8).

- God spoke against the religious elite for not having a heart to honor His name (2:1-9).

- God hated that the religious leaders were divorcing their wives to marry younger, foreign women (2:10-16; Ezr. 9; Ne. 13:23ff).

- God rebuked the entire nation for not paying their tithes (Mal. 3:8-12).

- He promised a curse upon them if the children's hearts did not turn to their fathers, and if the fathers' hearts did not turn to their children (4:6).

God's former discussion with the religious leaders through Malachi seamlessly picks up with the Incarnate Jesus. It was inevitable that the coming of Jesus would bring the rejection of the Jewish religious elite. The Pharisees desired to hold on to their self-serving system at all cost.

The following are the reasons for the rejection of Jesus by the Jewish religious leaders:

1. When Jesus grew in popularity with the masses, the Pharisees accused the people of having a curse upon themselves (Jn. 7:49). Jealousy of Jesus was not the only problem the religious leaders had. Jesus cut through their religious norms in search of honest human hearts.

2. The religious leaders rejected Jesus when He forgave the sins of the paralytic (Mk. 2:6-7; Lk. 5:21). They were unable to look beyond Jesus' human form. They were also unable to encourage people with mercy or describe a transformed life. To the Pharisees, people fit into social categories: the sinners, the ignorant, or those within their own inner circle. Flowing between these social categories was not an option.

3. The Pharisees avoided the touch of people categorized as sinful. Jesus allowed a woman with a dark past to touch Him and then released her of her guilt. This drew the disdain of Simon the Pharisee (Lk. 7:39). Simon equated his own aversion to "sinful people" with the purity of the prophets. Jesus' love and acceptance for all people went against the grain of Jewish separatist thinking. Their misunderstanding of the prophets' holiness was challenged by Jesus at the Nazareth Synagogue, describing two Gentiles whom God cared for during Israel's time of need.

4. The Sabbath was governed by numerous rules of the religious elite. Jesus incurred their anger repeatedly by healing on the Sabbath (Mt. 12:10; Lk. 6:7; Lk. 14:3). Their hearts were too hard to hear Jesus explain God's love for people being expressed on the Sabbath. Even though they would help a son or a donkey that fell into a well on the Sabbath, they opposed Jesus healing people and gaining popularity. In their frustration to understand how a man born blind could be healed, they called Jesus a sinner who did not keep the Sabbath (Jn. 9:16).

Missiological Implication

Mission requires us to understand the cultural setting of people, yet fulfill the will of God which must cut against some of the traditions of people. A difference between the ministry of Jesus in Israel and ministry to an unreached people is the amount of time needed to address issues. The taboo nature of the "men's house," fear of sacred trees thought to contain spirits, or a society's violence must be addressed--not in a scathing rebuke that expects them to know better, but in the broader scope of teaching and discipling people in the ways of the Kingdom of God.

5. The Pharisees rejected Jesus casting out an evil spirit. Although what Jesus did was good, freeing a person from an evil spirit, they needed to find fault, at all cost,

to keep themselves from agreeing with Jesus.

> But when the Pharisees heard this, they said, "It is only by Beel-zebub, the prince of demons, that this fellow drives out demons" (Mt. 9:34; Mk. 3:22; Lk. 11:15).

To agree with Jesus would be to follow Him as a disciple. Following as a disciple would necessitate the dismantling of their social system, their pay scale, and their control over people.

Missiological Implication

Mission requires that Jesus becomes greater and that we become less. Our position in life, our pay scale, and any sense of authority must be lost in the quest for God's Kingdom to be manifest among us.

---

6. Jesus crossed the traditions of the Jews that wrongly made the common, holy (Lev 10:10). Washing hands before eating does not make one spiritually clean.

> Why do your disciples break the tradition of the elders? They don't wash their hands before they eat (Mt. 15:2; Mk. 7:1-4; Lk. 11:8).

Purity of the heart is not obtained by bathing in the Ganges River (Hinduism) or by ceremonial washing before prayer (Islam). The true question for the Pharisees was whether Jesus would honor them through their rules.

7. The chief priests, the teachers of the law, and the elders challenged the authority of Jesus while He taught in the temple courts. His response clearly challenged their authority and brought their swift rejection.

> Jesus entered the temple courts, and, while he was teaching, the chief priests and the elders of the people came to him. "By what authority are you doing these things?" they asked. "And who gave you this authority" (Mt. 21:23; Lk. 20:1-8)?

"Where did you get this authority?" is still a stumbling point for many people. No church or mission has spiritual authority over a geographic region or over the people in a region. This point brought great misunderstanding to the Pharisees. People belonging to a religio-political system can look suspiciously at people of

another "affiliation." The question, "Who is your covering?" can be asked to validate or refute someone's flow of anointing. None of God's people own a ministry.
God is free to replace errant disciples or entire ministries. Eli's role as priest (1 Sa.
2:30-36; 3:11-14), Saul's position as king (1 Sa. 13:13-14), and Elijah's prophetic
ministry (1 Ki. 19:14-18) were all replaced. Eli and Saul lost touch with the leading of God. Elijah and Jeremiah listened to God's voice, directing them away from
self-centeredness (1 Ki. 19:19-20; Jer. 15:15-21).

Jesus pressed the point of God's ultimate ownership and ultimate authority in the
parable of the tenants. He began the story by telling of a man who had planted
a vineyard (Lk. 20:9-19; Mt. 21:33-46). The vineyard was Israel (Isa. 5:1-7). The
one who planted or established Israel was God. The "farmers" were those given
leadership to cultivate Israel in the ways of God. One possible understanding of
the man going "away for a long time" could refer to the four hundred years of
silence between Nehemiah / Malachi and the advent of the Messiah.

The tenants took possession of the vineyard, seeing themselves as more than farmers responsible for someone else's property. They repeatedly refused to produce
fruit for the owner which demonstrated that their position was more important to
them than God's reason for having placed them there. Not producing fruit for God
is also a clever fit into the hands of Satan. Satan's delight is to spoil God's garden,
the health and prosperity of God's people, and ultimately God's planned redemption of the entire world. The death of the "son" in this parable brings the sinister
hope of ruin to God's master plan. God, the owner and Lord of all things, has no
problem removing leadership and setting others in place. God will not allow any
one to steal His vineyard, nor will He tolerate their personal plans for His vineyard.
To tolerate others' plans for His vineyard means cowering to human leadership, or
even submission to satanic leadership. It must be remembered that God removes
evil and establishes His kingdom on the foundation of righteousness (Isa. 9:7).

After hearing this parable, the reaction of the teachers of the law and of the chief
priests was the immediate rejection of Jesus (Lk. 20:19). Their desire to arrest Jesus
fit them neatly into the very parable that had angered them.

John's Gospel

The problem with Jesus' authority was compounded by His declaration that He
was the Bread of Life (Jn. 6:35). This challenged the Jews on two points. First, Jesus was preeminent to Moses and his ministry. The Jews held Moses in such high
regard that they lost sight of his human nature. Second, Jesus claimed to be from
heaven. Jesus corrected the faulty thinking of the Jewish crowd by declaring that

the manna given in the wilderness had been from God and not from Moses. For Jesus to be "bread from heaven" meant that He was the gift of God to nourish souls. Jesus further confused them by declaring that He was the true "manna" from heaven and would grant eternal life to all who would eat of Him, or "ingest" Him into their lives.

Discipling of the nations is not simply encouraging people believe the story of Jesus; it is to help them "ingest" the Messiah and to be transformed. The complexity of His words were a stumbling block to those looking to find fault with His message. Jesus even pressed the issue further by declaring that all needed to eat His flesh and drink His blood (Jn. 6:54). The repulsion of the Jews was predictably in line with the command of God to avoid eating blood (Lev. 17:10-14). They could not understand the meaning of the atonement wrapped up in the words of Jesus.

> For the life of a creature is in the blood, and I have given it to you to make atonement for yourselves on the altar; it is the blood that makes atonement for one's life (Lev. 17:11).

8. The Pharisees rejected Jesus' declaration that "You cannot serve both God and Money" (Lk. 16:13). Money is to be used to glorify God, not to glorify self. Within this command is a mandate to help the needy, which means giving up the desires of the flesh to live an increasingly better life. This relates to the rebuke recorded in Malachi for those who did not honor the Lord and only gave begrudgingly to fulfill the minimum requirement. Turning a blind eye to the poor dishonors the Lord and places the hard-hearted with those "goats" that failed to recognize the hungry, the thirsty, the stranger, those needing clothing, the sick, and the prisoner (Lk. 16:31-46).

The truth of the gospel compels us to love people in need, even if like the prisoner, they are reaping what they have sowed. For example, we love the aids patient, even if errant lifestyle brought on the illness. A list of needy people must be viewed in light of Jesus loving the woman caught in adultery and the "sinful" woman who anointed His feet. Love does not require perfection before it is expressed.

Missiological Implication

Obedience to God in ministry will bring rejection from the world, hatred from Satan, and denunciation from controlling religious powers. Living for Christ will precipitate persecution. God is our source for direction and affirmation. Expect the Enemy to find scathing words to discourage both you and your ministry.

On the Other Hand

Jesus' rejection by the religious leaders was a result of obedience to the Father in inaugurating the Kingdom of God. Rejection is not to be flippantly applied to all situations to validate one's "suffering for Jesus." Both true and false prophets and sincere and misguided disciples face persecution. Rejection is not a verification that someone is living for the Kingdom of God.

Joseph Smith, founder of the Church of Jesus Christ of Latter Day Saints, viewed his imprisonment as unjust before God and as a potential sacrifice for people.

> "God is my friend," wrote Joseph Smith to his wife in 1832. "In him I shall find comfort. I have given my life into his hands. I am prepared to go at his call. I desire to be with Christ. I count not my life dear to me, only to do his will." Days before his death in 1844, the Prophet reiterated: "I am ready to be offered a sacrifice for this people" (History of the Church 6:500).

No one but Christ is a sacrifice for people. Some take on a "Christ figure" mentality when rejected, but the root of their rejection is the errant pathway they offer. Marginal "prophetic" people drifting through churches and missions equate their rejection by the religious elite to that suffered by Jesus. Be very clear on this point: Marginalization of self-seeking individuals cannot be equated with the Son of God invading the world to redeem it for God. Self-seeking individuals should be handled with love, yet without apology. We are obligated to protect others from their errant teaching. Self-seeking people desire subservient attention and honor from others. Jesus requires that all of us grant God His rightful place in our lives. Jesus must become greater, and we must become less.

The Arrest and Crucifixion of Jesus

Jesus was born to die as the sacrifice for the sin of all humankind. John the Baptist announced Him as the Lamb of God. When the Pharisees told Him to leave because Herod sought to kill Him, He replied:

> Go tell that fox, `I will drive out demons and heal people today and tomorrow, and on the third day I will reach my goal.' In any case, I must keep going today and tomorrow and the next day—for surely no prophet can die outside Jerusalem (Lk. 13:32-33; See also Mark 8:31)!

Jesus was not about to flee from Herod. He would be the one to choose the time of the sacrifice; it would neither be a human nor a dark power.

The surrender of Jesus on the cross to the will of His Father broke through the old ways that only led to death. The Kingdom of God, as expressed in redemptive cleansing, was set in motion through the cross. God accepted the sacrifice of Jesus as a substitution for the death required by the law for each soul. God's law was not to be broken, but God found a way for it to be satisfied.

The future of believers of God in Christ rests upon the death of Jesus on the cross. There, His ministry on earth reached a climactic point. All of salvation history, about which the prophets had spoken, came to a dramatic conclusion through His death. Another epoch began with His rising from the dead. His death was a major watershed for all of history and the point to which we look, by faith, for the cleansing forgiveness offered by the Creator.

The Necessity of Christ's Death

God's mission through Jesus was to open a new covenant through His sacrificial death. Jesus came to restore covenant between God and humankind. He came to die--to offer His life as a sacrifice for us (Mt. 20: 19, 28; Mk. 10:45; Lk. 9:22; Jn. 10:10-11).

The cup of the New Covenant was the blood He was about to shed (Lk. 22:20). The redemption of humankind depended upon Jesus following through with the plan of God. Many still wanted Jesus to perform miracles in order to establish a kingdom based on power. God was establishing a Kingdom based on righteousness, one which would last forever. At any moment, God's power could have rid the earth of the Roman legions in order to establish a people of power. His desire, however, was to change the hearts of Jews and non-Jews alike. This required the mission of Christ in righteous suffering.

The Resurrection, Real Proof

The Necessity of the Resurrection

All Gospel accounts speak of the resurrection of Jesus. God's mission included more than a perfect sacrifice for the forgiveness of sins. His plan was to open access to the tree of life and restore fellowship eternally with resurrected people.

This plan could include not only the righteous living in Christ's day, but the saints of old before the eternal covenant was finalized.

The disciples saw the empty tomb, the discarded grave clothes, the moved stone, and the absence of official guards at the grave. Putting together the meaning of what had happened took them some time.

Paul writes that Jesus humbled himself to death on the cross. This was the reason God had given Jesus a name above all other names (Php. 2:5-11). Paul tells us that our attitude should be the same as that of Christ Jesus.

Jesus as Resurrected Lord

The resurrection was simply the surprise of God. Only faith in the Creator and understanding His Word would bring understanding to this surprise. Followers of Jesus were left with their mouths hanging open at His appearance. All other religious systems would strive to explain the absence of Jesus' body and to dilute His resurrection into common spiritual manifestations.

In the aftermath of Jesus' death, He appeared to His disciples in intervals over a forty-day period of time (Ac. 1:3). Each Gospel writer tells of the instructions and ministry of Jesus over these days. The appearance of Jesus brings us understanding of His Kingdom. He did not appear to the Pharisees and Sadducees in order to prove that His words were true regarding the rebuilding of His temple. He did not come to the eleven to set up the new corporation. He did not provide the finances on His resurrection day to start the movement. The surprise of His resurrection was followed by the surprise of His appearances.

Jesus in Jerusalem

Matthew tells us that the women who went to the tomb early Sunday morning were the first to see Jesus and to hear His greeting (Mt. 28:9-10). The resurrected Christ gave instructions to the women regarding the coming meeting place in Galilee. The resurrected Christ was not a detached spirit, but rather a living, speaking, and very tender leader of the believers. Expect Him to come into situations today to calm questioning hearts. Frequently we hear of reports of His appearance throughout the unreached world, often "dressed in white!"

The instructions Jesus gave in Galilee to the eleven disciples brought focus to their next steps and life mission. We are told that He began by speaking of God's authority in heaven and on earth. This authority had been bestowed upon Him. His command to the disciples, then and now, comes with the authority to accomplish His will. Any voice attempting to stop the world-wide expansion of the Kingdom of God is countering the authority and direction given by God. All nations are to be discipled in the ways of God in Christ. This is the will of God and His mandate to us. Obedience leads us to fulfilling His mission mandate.

Mark tells us that the women went to the tomb early Sunday morning, and that an angel in the tomb announced the resurrection of Jesus (Mk. 16:6-7). Only Mark gives us the specific word from the angel who singles out Peter's name in order to make sure that he will attend the Galilee meeting. Not only were the women the first to hear the news, but Mary Magdalene was the first to see the appearance of the resurrected Christ (16: 9-10). The significance is the appearance of Jesus to a hungry, needy soul. His first appearance was not to the apostles but to a lonely woman. His first appearance was to bless Mary's bewilderment and bring peace to her life. How could Mary ever forget His appearing to her?

Mark's final word regarding the resurrected Christ records His command to bring this good news to the entire world (16:15-18). The breadth of this command will not be grasped for some time. It would include regions far beyond the "two rivers" to the east and beyond Rome to the west. This command included languages yet unknown to the eleven disciples, and some which remain unknown to this day! It included regions that had their own belief systems that needed to be shaken by the truth of the resurrection. Jesus promises life to all who believe and judgment to those who reject the truth. Mark related the promise of Jesus' presence with us as did Matthew. However, Mark added that the miraculous powers of Jesus would also remain with us.

Luke confirms that the women were the first to the tomb and the ones who heard the angelic announcement that Jesus had risen from the dead (Lk 24:1-10). The surprise of Jesus came with His joining two men walking to Emmaus (13-35). These men were confused and having difficulty accepting the news of God's miraculous working. They knew Jesus had been dead for three days (v. 21) and yet the women were claiming that He was alive (vv. 22-24). Their natural minds could not comprehend this. It is here that Jesus appeared to them. The natural mind cannot conceptualize the creative power of God. Today, anyone who believes the resurrection story has also had God's intervention, placing an internal witness into his or her heart. It is the blessing of God to open Scripture and to interpret history and coming events through the eyes of the Creator. Human logic alone will misread the past and be afraid of the future. Current problems will overwhelm those looking to set ecological, economic, and political events in proper order. The mind of Christ is needed today to bring peace to our hearts in the confusion of life.

Luke tells us of a meeting prior to the Galilee gathering that took place resurrection Sunday evening in Jerusalem. Jesus arrived on the heels of the testimony given by the two returning from Emmaus. The text helps us to look into the eyes of the awe-struck disciples.

> He said to them, "Why are you troubled, and why do doubts rise in your minds? Look at my hands and my feet. It is I myself! Touch me and see; a ghost does not have flesh and bones, as you see I have."
> When he had said this, he showed them his hands and feet. And while they still did not believe it because of joy and amazement, he asked them, "Do you have anything here to eat?" They gave him a piece of broiled fish, and he took it and ate it in their presence (Lk. 24: 38-42).

The resurrection of Christ will always grip the new believer and bring a challenge to live in faith beyond what eyes can see.

The disciples were blessed with the "opening of their minds" to understand Scripture (v. 45). The blessing given to the two en route to Emmaus was now given to the eleven also. Opening the mind to understand Scripture is an act of the Spirit of God. It is to be enormously sought after and prized as one of the treasures of the Kingdom. Without an understanding of Scripture, the disciple is left with only glimpses into the working of God. Mission requires a mind opened by the Spirit to understand Scripture.

Luke highlighted the words of Jesus at this Sunday meeting:

> ...repentance and forgiveness of sins will be preached in his name to all nations, beginning at Jerusalem (v. 47).

The message of repentance and forgiveness is a message to be granted to the entire world. Luke agrees with the other synoptic writers that this message is to bless all nations. He adds a particular word that will lead us into his second volume, Acts. Jesus commands His disciples to remain in Jerusalem waiting for the promise of the Father. Our attempts to bring the news of the resurrected Christ to the nations must be anointed by the Holy Spirit. Mission requires the promise of the Father to fulfill the work assigned to us.

John takes us to the ministry of the resurrected Christ at different times. We understand the details of Peter and John running to the tomb after hearing Mary Magdalene's story of the missing body (Jn. 20:1-5). John also tells us that the problem of understanding the resurrection lies in not understanding Scripture (v. 9). This reiteration of the necessity of understanding Scripture calls us to a lifelong quest to grow in understanding, and then to disciple the nations regarding the purposes of God.

Mary Magdalene was the first believer to see the risen Jesus. His appearance to Mary brought calm to her broken heart (20:15-17). The Shepherd was also seen coming to the one lonely doubter, Thomas (vv. 24-29). The joy Jesus takes in ministering to a struggle in a believer's heart cannot be overlooked. He cares for each individual. Our pain, loneliness, doubts, and fears are all ministered to by the resurrected Jesus.

John tells us of the disciples' encounter with Jesus on the evening of His resurrection. Jesus entered the room whose doors were locked out of fear (20:19). Fear was a real factor in the lives of the disciples. The power of God to overcome fear came with the blessing of the Holy Spirit which John recorded. Luke relates that their minds were opened to understand Scripture. (Compare John 20:22 and Luke 24:45.)

Jesus sent His disciples as the Father had sent Him (Jn. 20:21). This verse requires our grasping the full extent of the anointing and authority placed on our lives to complete the mission of God. The Father's burden is our burden. His sacrifice of Jesus in order to accomplish the task of world-wide forgiveness is taken on as our sacrifice to carry the message to all people.

Jesus in Galilee

Seven of the eleven disciples were present when the 153 fish were caught (21:1-3; 11). This scene is reminiscent of the catch of fish after some of the disciples-to-be labored fruitlessly all night (Lk. 5:4-11). His message at the time of the first catch was, ". . . from now on you will catch men" (Lk. 5:10). Some today rebuke the disciples for fishing as though they were pulled in by the world. Jesus gives no such rebuke. Fishing was the livelihood of several of the Galilean disciples. Most likely it was also an enjoyable pastime. Paul was not rebuked for working. Neither should we equate disobedience to the activities of the early disciples.

Jesus ate with the disciples. He spent time together with them as He had done before. The book of John ends with Jesus speaking alone with Peter. Peter was specifically invited, along with the general invitation to the other ten disciples, to be in Galilee (Mk. 16:7). This was the solitary opportunity for Peter, who had denied Jesus three times, to come face to face with Jesus and His asking three times: do you love me? Jesus forgave Peter. This is clear through the call of God reiterated to Peter to feed the lambs and sheep of God. The unforgiven are not called to represent God or minister to others for Him. Peter's anointing had not been lost or lessened. When we as servants of God find fear or selfishness in our lives, we also need to turn to the hope Jesus gave to Peter to press on in ministry. The tendency we will have is to take on a worldly sorrow and disqualify ourselves for service. Jesus calls us back to our place of ministry.

Missiological Implication

Jesus' appearances to His disciples brought peace in the midst of sadness and confusion. Understanding the resurrection will require understanding Scripture. Presenting the good news of the Kingdom of God and the resurrection of Jesus will also necessitate the promise of the Father and the power of the Holy Spirit in our lives. Jesus meets with us. He builds our lives, forgives us in our weakness, and encourages us to continue with the anointing we have received.

Chapter 21 - The Kingdom and Restoration

Introduction

Jesus came to bring restoration to a corrupted world and its inhabitants. His Kingdom comes with creative power to restore. Bodies are healed, though only temporarily, because death does face us all. Lives are restored permanently in our continued walk with the Lord. The heart of the Creator is to redeem the world rather than to annihilate it, but restoration will require more than a surface cleaning. Jesus enters into battles to free people from both human institutions and spiritual prisons. Darkness has made its presence felt through disease and the mutation of God's creation. The cry to "Let my people go, so that they may worship me" (Ex. 7:16) is still very relevant.

The Kingdom of God will utterly destroy any kingdom, earthly or Satanic, that opposes its advent. Daniel prophetically saw the destruction of at least five kingdoms, four of which had not yet been established. Understanding the restoration of the Kingdom of God requires patience on our part and faithful work affirming its expansion.

> While you were watching, a rock was cut out, but not by human hands. It struck the statue on its feet of iron and clay and smashed them. Then the iron, the clay, the bronze, the silver and the gold were broken to pieces at the same time and became like chaff on a threshing floor in the summer. The wind swept them away without leaving a trace. But the rock that struck the statue became a huge mountain and filled the whole earth (Da. 2:34-35).

Each of the following themes will come to light repeatedly throughout the Gospels:

(1) Jesus will confront evil spiritual powers that dig in for the battle to claim both the world and its people as theirs.

(2) Hardened human elements in religious communities work for their systems and, therefore, against the Kingdom of God.

(3) Battle clashes are unavoidable with misguided human institutions that have created systems fighting against the will of God.

(4) Disease that has crippled so much of humanity will be confronted by the Creator. This will be addressed in chapter 25.

Kingdom Battles with the Enemy

Much later, John wrote in his first epistle that "The reason that the Son of God appeared was to destroy the devil's work" (1 Jn. 3:8). He wrote this approximately sixty years after the earthly life of his beloved friend and Lord, which gave him time to reflect on the importance of the Messiah's work. By necessity, the entrance of the Son of God to establish God's Kingdom required facing the enemy and his dark systems and bringing ultimate destruction to the ways of darkness. This preeminent factor in Jesus' ministry brings every missionary face-to-face with the same task: destruction of the devil's work.

Reflection

What are some ways you will face and destroy Satan's work in the nation to which you are called?

Satan heard the declaration from the mouth of John the Baptist that Jesus was the Messiah. He saw the Spirit of God descend upon Jesus in bodily form and heard the Father declare that Jesus was His beloved Son. The battle lines were set on God's terms. This time the battle was not with a servant like Job who felt he needed to convince God of justice. Neither was the battle with David who, in a moment of weakness, lived out a wicked moral standard. This battle was with Jesus, who knew His mission and His place before God. The Incarnate Son had entered the arena.

> Then Jesus was led by the Spirit into the desert to be tempted by the devil. After fasting forty days and forty nights, he was hungry. The tempter came to him (Mt. 4:1-3).

Read from a strictly human standpoint, being led into the desert to be tempted by the Devil sounds ominous. None desire to meet the prince of demons and be tempted by him. But the context is not simply a human plan that leads a person into a confrontation with the Evil One. The context is the Holy Spirit leading the Son into the desert. It has the appearance of bait put before the enemy in order to draw a line in the sand which will ultimately bring defeat. God does not tempt us with evil (Jas. 1:13). The Father would not have tempted the Son with evil; nor would the Holy Spirit tempt Jesus or any human with evil. It was the humanness of Jesus--in a weakened state after fasting--that brought an enemy looking for an easy kill. **What followed the baptism of Jesus was the unfolding of God's plan to defeat the Devil rather than testing Jesus to see if His heart was in tune with God.**

Jesus entering the desert is reminiscent of the prophets of old, like Moses, who had times of solitude in order to improve their vision and knowledge of the Lord. Being led into the desert shares the language of Leviticus 16 in conjunction with the scapegoat, the goat on which the sins of Israel were imputed by the priest and then released into the wilderness. The scapegoat would be easy prey for a variety of animals and would never return to Israel proper. Jesus was led into the wilderness by the Spirit, yet He returned after facing and defeating the devourer.

1. **The Bread** – Jesus is enticed to prove He is the Son of God by feeding His hungry body.

    The tempter came to him and said, "If you are the Son of God, tell these stones to become bread" (Mt. 4:3).

The Devil is the father of lies who desires to inject doubt and destroy faith. "Prove who you are and feed yourself" is the stealthy word. Who except the Creator could change a rock into usable food? This confrontation could not be taken as an isolated challenge. John told the Pharisees and Sadducees that their claim to Abraham's lineage was pointless: "I tell you that out of these stones God can raise up children for Abraham" (Mt. 3:9). John knew that God creates and transforms. The same thought seemed to now challenge Jesus. The response Jesus gave, "Man does not live by bread alone, but on every word that comes from the mouth of God" (4: 4), defeated the challenge to: (a) prove Himself, (b) create from the stones, and (c) feed Himself through His power.

The challenge to prove ourselves and eventually feed ourselves with the power derived from religious position will always confront us. We, too, must overcome the same temptations in order to remain approved of God.

2. **The Temple** – The wilderness where Jesus fasted was far from Jerusalem. How Jesus strode uphill to Jerusalem, and how long it took Him, is unclear. We read:

    The Devil took Him up to the holy city and had Him stand on the highest point of the temple, "If you are the Son of God," he said, "Throw yourself down" (4:5-6).

The Spirit of God led Jesus into this encounter. We must conclude that the Spirit of God led Jesus to the Temple and later to the "very high mountain." This present temptation was for Jesus to overcome potential self-destruction with something dramatic. The lure was for Jesus to prove Himself to the religious leaders of Israel. "Jesus, if they recognize your blessing and power, certainly all Israel will be in your hand," Satan reasoned. Jesus defeated the temptation by quoting, "Do not put the Lord your God to the test" (4:7). The priority for Jesus was to honor God, and His words smashed against Satan's foundation of religious pride. We, too, will be lured with the temptation to prove ourselves before an errant religious community. In a moment of weakness, we must not confuse a desire to prove ourselves or our ministry with a power encounter with a false religious system. Discerning the motive of our next actions will either place the focus upon us or upon the God who restores people to Himself.

3.   **The Mountain** – This temptation was substantial. Jesus did not bite on the stones or fall to mesmerize Israel. This great temptation was to regain the lost world as His own. The Enemy knows God's desire to redeem the whole world, but Jesus knows there is no shortcut to world evangelism and discipleship. In this temptation, Satan did not question, "If you are the Son of God," as he did with previous temptations.

Payment for the world with His life was not too heavy a cost; worshipping Satan would have been the wrong payment. Satan's desire for worship was very subtle, yet evident. Jesus' response, "Away from me, Satan," was razor sharp. None of us can bend God's rules to obtain personal gain. Winning His people's hearts cannot come by means of putting God to the test. World redemption will never be accomplished by changing the order of leadership from God to anyone else. Today, we rejoice greatly because Jesus did not submit the planet to Satan in order to regain the nations. Each of the three temptations will surely be repeated in the lives of disciples like us sent to do the will of the Father.

Missiological Reflections

Missionaries must remember the types of temptations placed before Jesus, knowing that the same, or very similar, temptations will be encountered in their ministries.

Location	Temptation	Your Response?
The Wilderness	Prove yourself to yourself Use your position for your own purposes (money, sex, power)	
The Temple	Prove yourself to the religious community Prove you are more anointed than their leaders - false power encounter	
The Mountain	Take a "shortcut" to do God's will Bend rules of righteousness to obtain a righteous goal The goal overshadows the path of God to get there	

Other Battles with Satanic Thought

Jesus battled Satan's wisdom and fine-sounding direction when He predicted His coming death to His disciples. The reaction of Peter at this announcement received a stiff rebuke:

> Peter took him aside and began to rebuke him. But when Jesus turned and looked at his disciples, he rebuked Peter. "Get behind me, Satan!" he said. "You do not have in mind the things of God, but the things of men" (Mk. 8:32-33).

Satan enters into the seeming wisdom of human beings which is actually contrary to the will of God. Hearing and obeying the voice of God is required of all disciples. Straightening Jesus out, as Peter attempted to do, is in the same vein of thought as a wise relative telling someone called of God to reconsider that call in light of danger, financial questions, possible diseases, or even possible rejection. How very important it is that we understand the mind of our Lord before giving "advice" to one of God's people. Advice can sound like words of wisdom but, in actuality, might be the words of Satan redirecting the servant of God--causing this servant to miss the power and intent of his or her mission.

Another battle with Satan came in the Garden of Gethsemane. We know Jesus was in agony, and that His sweat was like drops of blood. That level of intensity was crushing. Something was pressing Jesus beyond what we see with our eyes in the Garden.

> Every day I was with you in the temple courts, and you did not
> lay a hand on me. But this is your hour--when darkness reigns
> (Lk. 22:53).

Satan's trap was set to destroy Jesus and His rightful place as the Creator and owner of all things. Satan entered into Judas to carry out this treachery (Lk. 22:3). He used the institutions of Judaism, the Roman government, and a close friendship to destroy the Incarnate Messiah both physically and emotionally. Do we personally expect any other treatment from the one who hates our Lord?

The next words of satanic derision came during a time more intense than Jesus' forty days of fasting. The words of darkness and ridicule came during His crucifixion.

> The people stood watching, and the rulers even sneered at him.
> They said, "He saved others; let him save himself if he is the
> Christ of God, the Chosen One."
> The soldiers also came up and mocked him. They offered him
> wine vinegar and said, "If you are the king of the Jews, save
> yourself."
> There was a written notice above him, which read: THIS IS THE
> KING OF THE JEWS.
> One of the criminals who hung there hurled insults at him:
> "Aren't you the Christ? Save yourself and us" (Lk. 23:35-39)!

The same language used by Satan during the wilderness experience came out several times during the crucifixion. The sneering question, "If you are the Son of God," came from the Jewish rulers, the Roman soldiers, and even a criminal also facing death. The hammering blows of rejection from every direction remind us of the prophetic words of the Psalmist:

> Do not be far from me,
> for trouble is near
> and there is no one to help.
> Many bulls surround me;
> strong bulls of Bashan encircle me.
> Roaring lions tearing their prey
> open their mouths wide against me.
>
> I am poured out like water,
> and all my bones are out of joint.
>
> My heart has turned to wax;
> it has melted away within me (Ps. 22:12-14).

Jesus was overcome by human rejection; His heart was melting away in sorrow. The crucifixion should not be viewed only as a time of Jesus' victorious joy in serving the Father and redeeming humanity. It cost Jesus tremendous suffering and rejection that crushed His heart. Satan comes in times of intense frustration and rejection. He attacks us in times of pain and sorrow. But as Jesus called out, so we must echo, "Do not be far from me, for trouble is near and there is not one to help."

The sign written by Pilate was also a scornful word: THIS IS THE KING OF THE JEWS. The Incarnate King was brutalized, scourged, and naked before all. The sign is a crushing reminder of the depths to which Jesus' humiliation was carried for us.

The culmination of Satan's plans fell into the plan of God to resurrect Jesus from the dead. Ironically, Satan was defeated with a death blow that came through the death of Jesus. The resurrection of Jesus from the dead is eternal and bitter humiliation for Satan.

Missiological Insights

How important it is for the servant of Christ to trust when all seems overwhelming and in the hands of the enemy. Nothing is impossible for God. He loves the challenge of the impossible. He delights in blessing His children. Our need is to trust Him in the middle of the storms of life, even as death comes to our door. He is the resurrection and the life.

Clashes with Demonic Spirits

Jesus confronted dark spirits routinely in His ministry. Mark tells us that Jesus' first confrontation with an evil spirit after His baptism occurred in His home town of Capernaum.

> Just then a man in their synagogue who was possessed by an evil spirit cried out, "What do you want with us, Jesus of Naza- reth? Have you come to destroy us? I know who you are—the Holy One of God!"
> "Be quiet!" said Jesus sternly. "Come out of him!" The evil spirit shook the man violently and came out of him with a shriek (Mk. 1:23-26).

We learn several things from this passage.

1. In this context, darkness reacted to the presence of light. Darkness, at times, seems to hide and does not want to be identified. In this case, the clash of kingdoms was very clear.

2. Demonic spirits know that they will be destroyed by Jesus. This means that He has tremendous power over this dark spiritual realm.

3. The dark spirit identified Jesus as the "Holy one of God" (Mk. 1:24; 3:11-12). At that point, Jesus silenced the spirit. Publicity by an evil source would have been counterproductive. The Kingdom of God was announced by Jesus and His disciples, not by darkness and its envoys. Evil spirits never possess good insight and are, therefore, never worthy of our listening.

4. A major point of this story can be missed if we focus too closely on details. Jesus does not want spirits possessing, oppressing, or influencing human beings created in His image! The clash of kingdoms takes place because Jesus came to set the captives free. "Get out of this person!" is not to be spoken lightly or given a length of time in which to consider it. Jesus wants people free--now! Demonic manifestations should not be limited in our minds only to multiple voices and personalities. Demons are capable of making people deaf (Mk. 9:25), mute (Mt. 9:32-33; Lk. 11:14), and blind and mute (Mt. 12:22). They can also create seizures (Mt. 17:18; Lk. 9:42) which may be related to tumors. With this in mind, it is important that we pray for the sick, discerning if darkness is at the root of the malady.

Kingdom Clash with Religious and Political Institutions

Battles with religious systems are bound to happen during the course of a missionary's experience. It is important that we understand the difference between a disagreement between believers and a battle with unbelieving religious powers. The former are fellow servants of Christ whom we continue to bless, even in disagreement. When Jesus addressed His disciples, He commanded them to love each other (Jn. 15:12). Factions and infighting are not part of the righteous call of God on our lives. The weapons of our warfare must be left at the doorway of the community of Jesus. The latter represents institutions opposed to the reign of Christ as Lord. And yes, there are times a clear line of distinction is not evident.

Jesus clashed with the Pharisees, the teachers of the law, the Sadducees, and the Herodians. The first three were religions entities and the fourth was a political body. He disagreed with the ultra religious Essenes and the nationalistic Zealots. His clash with the religious (Mt. 23) over their blatant hypocrisy highlights the kingdom they solidified in opposition to the Kingdom of God. The problem with their darkness and opposition is that they made entry into God's Kingdom nearly impossible.

> Woe to you, teachers of the law and Pharisees, you hypocrites!
> You shut the kingdom of heaven in men's faces. You yourselves
> do not enter, nor will you let those enter who are trying to (Mt.
> 23:13).

Each Jewish religious group thought it best represented the Kingdom of God. Each mistook its activity for the Kingdom. The Pharisees and the teachers of the law believed people needed to follow them and conform to their rules which, in fact, blinded both them and their followers to the truth. They became a closed wall of opposition to the Kingdom of God.

In a similar way, political parties like the Herodians and the Zealots looked through mutually exclusive lenses and valued their personal standards much higher than God's redemption for all people. The Herodians loved their power and taxation to keep the system running. The Zealots wanted all non-Jewish elements cleansed from the land. Their goals opposed the coming of the Kingdom and the ways of Jesus. Similar political groups throughout the ages have opposed the generous salvation of the Messiah. Corporations that focus on trade can be blind to the needs of the people they exploit. Others that fight for ethnic or religious cleansing also find themselves opposed to the One who created all in His image.

The Pharisees and The Sabbath

Who is in charge? The Pharisees understood themselves to be the righteous keepers of the true faith. Any work for God had to be either their initiative or sanctioned by them. They expanded the rules that governed the Sabbath and expected to run Israel by these rules. People doing good of any kind were expected to fit within the rules of the Pharisees in order to avoid confrontation. The Pharisees also controlled the synagogues. Violation of rules would mean dismissal from the synagogue community and taking on a near "untouchable" or shunned status. They used their power to control people rather than to defend the weak.

Jesus, led of the Father, came into the synagogue of His home town and encountered the religious elite.

> Another time he went into the synagogue, and a man with a shriveled hand was there. Some of them were looking for a reason to accuse Jesus, so they watched him closely to see if he would heal him on the Sabbath. Jesus said to the man with the shriveled hand, "Stand up in front of everyone."
>
> Then Jesus asked them, "Which is lawful on the Sabbath: to do good or to do evil, to save life or to kill?" But they remained silent.
> He looked around at them in anger and, deeply distressed at their stubborn hearts, said to the man, "Stretch out your hand." He stretched it out, and his hand was completely restored. Then the Pharisees went out and began to plot with the Herodians how they might kill Jesus (Mk. 3:1-6).

Healing the man with the shriveled hand to the Pharisees was far less important than coming under the Sabbath rule. How do we examine ourselves to see if we are concerned for God's priorities or for our own?

The Pharisees clashed with Jesus on the Sabbath on several occasions:

Picking grain on the Sabbath	Mt. 12:1-8; Mk. 2:23-28; Lk. 6:1-5
Healing a shriveled hand	Mt. 12:9-14; Mk. 3:2-4; Lk. 6:6-11
Healing a crippled woman	Lk. 13:10-17

Healing a man with dropsy	Lk. 14:1-6
Healing a paralytic	Jn. 5:1-17
Healing a man born blind	Jn. 9:1-34
Highlighting the work of God among Gentiles	Lk. 4:16-30

The Pharisees could neither see nor understand the work of God through Jesus because He did not live under their rule. Once again, they saw themselves as the Kingdom of God, and violators could not be tolerated. Jesus, on the other hand, pointed to God and His Kingdom by healing on the Sabbath. The message heard by those healed was that God personally cared about them.

The Pharisees and Forgiveness of Sins

Jesus clashed with the Pharisees when He forgave the sins of a paralytic in His hometown (Mk. 2:1-12). He also drew questions from onlookers when He forgave a woman of poor reputation in Simon the Pharisee's home (Lk. 7:48-50). His Kingdom came with forgiveness and naturally came against those standing in the way who were unwilling and unable to offer forgiveness. Their inability to grant forgiveness came by holding an exact copy of the law against others' lives. Their anger with what they considered to be blasphemy blinded them to the miracle of a paralyzed man now walking, or a woman set free from her past. To the Pharisees, miracles did not validate Jesus as sent from God; they concluded that He healed through another power. The difficulty for the religious elite was that Jesus was living out the work of God while not under their system. Forgiveness is an expression of the Kingdom of God, and those offering forgiveness through Jesus are doing the work of the Kingdom. Expect opposition from those who feel they have something to lose when you offer people forgiveness in the name of Jesus.

Reactions to the Announced Son of God

Jesus inaugurated a Kingdom, yet the Kingdom was not in its fullness. As we have stated, His grand introduction squarely clashed with opposing kingdoms. Isaiah's prophetic word echoed by Habakkuk, "... for the earth will be full of the knowledge of the LORD as the waters cover the sea" (Isa. 11:9; c.f. Hab. 2:14), had not yet become a reality.

A violent reaction to the coming King and Messiah existed in Jesus' day, and still exists today. Some kingdoms reacted to the coming of Jesus by virtue of His position. The coming of Messiah (the anointed Incarnate One, or Christ (χριστου) in Greek) challenged kingdoms opposed to the reign of the Lord. The announcement disturbed Herod ". . . and all Jerusalem with him" (Mt. 2:3). Herod's earthly kingdom had no room for another system of leadership. Brutal reactions, like the slaughter of the innocent in Bethlehem (2:16-18), are not uncommon by kingdoms threatened by another king. Ancient thrones of Rome and Communist systems of the modern age have despised the freedom offered by the Son.

Rejection by the local synagogue, or social isolation, was experienced by Jewish believers in the Messiah. One rejected by the synagogue became nearly on the level of a Samaritan, someone ceremonially unclean and without connectivity to be able to engage in life's daily necessities.

> . . . they were afraid of the Jews, for already the Jews had decided
> that anyone who acknowledged that Jesus was the Christ would
> be put out of the synagogue (Jn. 9:22).

Make no mistake, the miracle of a man born blind and now seeing did not touch the hearts of the religious powers threatened by a higher Kingdom. Do not be surprised by a similar reaction by those afraid to lose their control over society.

The Jews attempted to kill Jesus for His claim that God was His Father--which amounted to Jesus being the Son (Jn. 10:33) or the Incarnate One. This reaction is picked up by Islam, claiming that the greatest sin is association by anyone with God. This sin is unforgivable (Surat In-Nisa': 48). The misconception is that of the association or the elevation of humans to a level with God, rather than God Himself coming into our form.

Few challenges could be as severe to the kingdom of the Pharisees and teachers of the law as the advent of the Messiah, the anointed Son of God, who refused to validate them or their system. Jesus' answer to their question, "I charge you under oath by the living God: Tell us if you are the Christ, the Son of God" (Mt. 26:63), sealed His predetermined, sacrificial death. Similar reactions through the ages have been given by systems that hate those who confess a new King (Lk. 23:2).

Conclusion

The Kingdom of God enters into our world and confronts errant kingdoms. Its entrance into regions controlled by satanic powers, religious systems, or human institutions challenges and overcomes their authority. Our mission is to bring the knowledge of the Son of God to a world still in darkness, which also requires facing the same three opposing kingdoms. Jesus will be victorious over all as His eternal Kingdom expands to encompass the whole earth.

The kingdoms of the enemy, of human institutions, and of opposing religious systems will, at times, react violently to the coming of Jesus. Their opposition is to the freeing, forgiving work of Christ that denies their control and oppression on the world's inhabitants. Our prayerful, consistent witness is required in the face of opposition.

Chapter 22 - Discipleship in the Kingdom of God

The Calling of the First Disciples

How did twelve men in the first century come to be known as the disciples of Jesus? At what point did they leave everything to follow Him? These questions compel us to examine the four gospel records and piece together the events that led to the Master's call upon their lives.

Andrew's Heart for God

John baptized with water so that Jesus would be revealed. John's disciples knew of His revelation and anticipated the coming Messiah. They expected the Messiah's arrival at any moment and heard John point to Jesus as the Lamb of God (Jn. 1:29). Andrew was not only a fisherman, but a disciple of John the Baptist. Andrew recognized Jesus as the Messiah largely because of John the Baptist's testimony (Jn. 1:31-40). Andrew followed Jesus to his house, eager to learn more of the one to whom John the Baptist pointed (v. 40).

Simon and others follow Jesus

John's gospel account relates the introduction of Jesus to Simon through his brother Andrew. Simon and partners had caught nothing during a whole night of fishing. After many hours of failure, he obeyed the command of Jesus to try again (Lk. 5:5). He personally witnessed Jesus' power and authority over the physical world and also knew Jesus to be the Holy One of God. This miracle of fish engulfed Simon's partners in another boat. Two boats were on the verge of sinking with the enormous amount of fish (v. 7). Luke tells us that these four men left everything and followed Jesus.

It must be noted that neither Simon nor Andrew, nor the sons of Zebedee--James and John--saw Jesus as their personal magician to aid them in fishing (Mt. 4:18). None of the four are recorded as asking Jesus to remain and help them with their business. All four left the boats and the nets to follow Jesus. This is to be contrasted with those who ate the bread at the feeding of the five thousand, to whom Jesus said, "You are looking for me because you ate bread" (Jn. 6:26). Disciples follow the Kingdom of God rather than look for their own fulfillment.

It is key to note that Simon was overwhelmed by the awareness of his sin in light of the holiness of Jesus. Simon sensed the presence of one with authority in many areas (Lk. 5:8). What events led these men to leave everything and follow Jesus?

The sequence of events most likely was:

1.   John the Baptist baptized Jesus (Mk. 1:9-11)

2.   The Wilderness Experience (Mk. 1:12)

3.   John the Baptist's testimony to Jesus the Messiah (Jn. 1:35-36)

4.   Andrew followed Jesus to his house (Jn. 1:37-40)

5.   Andrew brought his brother Simon (Jn. 1:41)

6.   Jesus called Philip, who then brought Nathanael (Jn. 1:45)

7.   Proclamation in Nazareth (Lk. 4:16)

8.   Simon's mother-in-law healed (Lk. 4:38-39)

9.   Catch of fish (Lk. 5:1-9)

10. Repairing nets and contemplation (Mt. 4:21)

11. Calling of four disciples (Mt. 4:18-20; Lk. 5:11)

The significance of multiple events is that the disciples were not called to follow someone whom they had only briefly met. The four accounts give us pictures painted from different viewpoints. Jesus called men who knew of John the Baptist's testimony concerning Him. They saw His healing power, His authority over nature with the catch of fish, and they heard Him teach in Nazareth about Himself-the Messiah. People need to understand who Jesus is in their lives before they are challenged to leave all and follow Him. In a similar way throughout the ages, people were called to follow Jesus after they had had exposure to His ways and tasted of His life. It is unrealistic to require people who are only superficially acquainted with His ways to follow Jesus into a mission ministry.

The Cost of Discipleship

Each of Jesus' disciples, then and now, leave everything to follow Him. Discipleship costs everything we have, many times over. Jesus laid out the cost of discipleship after being confronted by Peter's rebuke to the plan of God. The plan of God was for Jesus to suffer, die, and on the third day be raised to life. The clear call to discipleship seems to be in the context of understanding the plan of God for the nations:

> Then he called the crowd to him along with his disciples and said: "If anyone would come after me, he must deny himself and take up his cross and follow me. For whoever wants to save his life will lose it, but whoever loses his life for me and for the gospel will save it. What good is it for a man to gain the whole world, yet forfeit his soul? Or what can a man give in exchange for his soul? If anyone is ashamed of me and my words in this adulterous and sinful generation, the Son of Man will be ashamed of him when he comes in his Father's glory with the holy angels" (Mk. 8:34-38).

Discipleship requires that we listen carefully to the words of the Lord and obey Him. We lose the dynamic of His call when we second guess the intent of His direction or tone down His words based on the world's norms. His words must form us, as opposed to our attempts to reform His words.

Self denial is required of a disciple. It is not possible to live for yourself and still call yourself a disciple. A disciple loses his or her rights as a member of society, loses rights to control finances, and loses any demand to live in one particular place--as family members may have for generations. Disciples become members of a new Kingdom that honors commitment and sacrifice without the promise of the rewards that the world offers. Overtime in the Kingdom of God does not mean greater cash flow. Sacrifice for Jesus is not followed by a year-end bonus. It is necessary for disciples to keep God's blessings in perspective--His goodness and the eternity He has granted. His blessings are not a repayment plan for services rendered.

Jesus does not only tell us that we may lose all when we follow Him, but He promises that we will find true meaning in life as we forsake all for His sake (Mk. 8:35). The distinction is very important. It tells us that our fullness, or the wages paid, are on a different scale, and that the world will not understand our "pay stubs." Bonhoeffer wrote,

> As we embark upon discipleship we surrender ourselves to Christ in union with his death--we give over our lives to death.

Thus it begins; the cross is not the terrible end to an otherwise godfearing and happy life, but it meets us at the beginning of our communion with Christ" (1963:99).

Discipleship that brings fullness of joy meets Jesus at the cross, not only at the beginning of one's walk with Him, but also at many junctures throughout life.

Levi left everything to follow Jesus, including his lucrative income (Lk. 5:27-32). However, his following the Master did not bring disdain for former friends. Rather, he invited his friends, along with Jesus, to a banquet at his home. This expression of the Kingdom of God deeply touches our souls. All of one's friends and business partners will have the opportunity to see and hear the testimony of on-going transformation. All new disciples have contacts with friends in the world who must be introduced to Jesus.

Jesus as our example ". . . made himself nothing, taking the very nature of a servant" (Php. 2:7). As true as this statement is, we must not give this message in isolation from the abundant life offered in Christ. Saints of God are dressed in white, reflecting their purity (Rev. 3:4), rather than dressed in black, mourning the life to which they have died. We welcome the work of Jesus to align us with the values of the Kingdom which will not pass away.

The world we release from our grip is passing into oblivion. Never forget this fact: Escape from a sinking wreck and co-ownership on a new ship are fabulous opportunities. We join a system marked by God that "gave him a name that is above every name" (Php. 2:9).

Jesus addresses shame as it relates to Himself and His words (Mk. 8:38). Every culture has the values of shame and honor, though the way they are expressed may be quite different. Each culture will also have different reasons to experience shame and honor. The shame about which Jesus speaks relates to any person desiring to be liked or respected by society. The value of His Kingdom must be taken so seriously that love of reputation is sacrificed. Why is this? It is the difference between what a society holds valuable and what the Kingdom of God does not. All societies reflect the fallen state of the human race. Some societies promote deception which the Kingdom rejects. Other societies value sexual lure and honor those who push extremes; the Kingdom of God calls these sin. Materialism is a value that ranks very highly worldwide, but this craving for self-satisfaction causes one to refuse to look at the cries of the needy. Jesus is opposed to self indulgence and commands us to give to those in need (Mt. 6:3-4). Love for God and love for money cannot coexist in one's heart (v. 24). Discipleship demands that we refuse, not embrace, the corruption of this world.

Jesus' command to His disciples was "follow me" (Mk. 1:17; Lk. 9:23). There is no option to believe in Jesus without following Him. The option many are given today to "simply accept Jesus" does not appear in the New Testament. The story of the young man who wanted to inherit eternal life without sacrifice depicts Jesus' demand for discipleship and obedience (Mt. 19:16-23). Each of us will find something difficult to relinquish as did this man with his wealth. The joy of discipleship comes when we continue to say "yes" to His bidding, knowing we are part of a higher calling than this world can offer.

Faith may begin with a short prayer to receive Jesus, but it certainly requires more. Some, without an understanding of discipleship, have asked people only to "believe" the story of Jesus, including His death and resurrection. Many hold to this story from a distance without personally experiencing life with Jesus. Mission is illusive because they have not tasted of discipleship. Faith is wrongly defined as a mental agreement with historical facts; it is, rather, a change in lifestyle. It is a frustrating work to preach world mission and sacrifice to those unprepared to take the "risks and loss" involved with following the Savior.

Disciples are called ". . . the salt of the earth" and "the light of the world" (Mt. 5:13-14). This means that our presence brings change to the worldview of those around us. We are not just regional salt and light; we are to bless, enrich, and transform the whole earth. Discipleship affirms the worldwide mandate to change the lives of people through Jesus.

Question

How does salt lose its saltiness?

Disciples Called Apostles

Disciples followed their master with a daily focus on becoming more like their example. The designation of "apostle" was given to the inner circle of twelve.

> Jesus went up on a mountainside and called to him those he wanted, and they came to him. He appointed twelve—designating them apostles—that they might be with him and that he might send them out to preach and to have authority to drive out demons (Mk. 3:13-15).

Matthew tells us that the apostles also had authority to heal the sick (Mt. 10:1).

Apostles are

1. chosen to be sent out,

2. sent to represent the Master,

3. anointed to further the Kingdom of God, and

4. will suffer for Jesus (Mt.10:24-25).

An apostle is a "sent one." It is a function of expanding the Kingdom; it is not a positional title of administrative leadership. Missionaries are sent ones with a mandate to communicate the news of Jesus along with a demonstration of the power of the Kingdom. They are not sent to gather people or movements under their administrative and foreign authority.

Apostles need an environment in which it is safe to grow. While learning to minister, the nurturing relationship of Jesus with the circle of twelve brought them into contact with people of many backgrounds. Some who have not moved out of their location may misunderstand the apostolic drive to regions beyond. It is important that apostolic movements continue to honor and bless church communities, some very static, that fail to grasp their calling. None of us is to play the role of the Holy Spirit. His children, with many different callings, must be free to follow Him rather than a particular movement or way of building community.

This is not Discipleship!

Both the world and religious systems form disciples and create subtly dangerous expressions that must not be copied by God's people. Imitating disciples of the world or of religious systems will bring misunderstanding in form and in meaning to the true disciple's life. Motives will be twisted for selfish gain, and the vision of the Kingdom of God will morph to a desire for a personal kingdom or personal honor.

> "Be careful," Jesus warned them. "Watch out for the yeast of
> the Pharisees and that of Herod" (Mk. 8:15).

Jesus made reference to the Pharisees and to Herod in order to warn His disciples to stay clear of forms of discipline that lead to darkness.

The Pharisees and teachers of the law raised an accusation against Jesus and His disciples (Mk. 7:5). Mark tells us that their traditions required ceremonial washing after being in the market and the special handling and cleansing of cups, pitchers, and kettles (v. 4). In the days of Jesus, the ultra-religious had rigid traditions to keep them within the "community of purity." Jesus called their community "hypocritical" (v. 6) and their rules "taught by men" (v. 7). They set the fence--the boundaries--in place and then judged others by their human religious standards. It is very important that we guard ourselves, and those with whom we work, from human traditions that bring bondage and establish an insider/outsider mentality. Discipleship of the nations is a far cry from forcing our cultural ways upon a people.

The false discipleship of the Pharisees established rules for the Sabbath which bound people rather than add value to their lives (Lk. 6:1-5). Jesus valued His disciples over the rules of a community. Eating, for example, was more important than protecting rules.

Discipleship will honor father and mother, obeying the commandment of God. The Pharisees, on the other hand, emphasized the importance of subservience to their group over any benefit parents could have given or received (Mk. 7:9-13). How do we understand these verses in light of Jesus' words to enter discipleship?

> If anyone comes to me and does not hate his father and mother,
> his wife and children, his brothers and sisters—yes, even his
> own life—he cannot be my disciple. And anyone who does not
> carry his cross and follow me cannot be my disciple (Lk. 14:26).

The words of Jesus were shocking in a world that hid behind the traditions of family and community. Jesus was not advocating the snubbing of parents. The difference was attitude. The attitude of the Pharisees developed converts who were children of hell (Mt. 23:15). This contrasted to Jesus' disciples who were salt and light in the world. The Pharisees developed people who learned to separate people living under a set of rules from those without rules. Jesus taught us to love our neighbors, even the Samaritans who experienced daily rejection.

Look at your life. Do you reflect the rules of a religious society or the spontaneous life of the Kingdom of God? The Master's touch will develop those who love God rather than the self righteousness of rules. Disciples know their weaknesses, but they also know the Master who can help them in their struggles.

Missiological Implications

The disciples needed Jesus' renewed definition of both cleanliness and defilement to enable them to move among the Gentiles and the Samaritans, and to travel to far regions without fear their lives would be defiled and unpleasing to God. Granted, it took time to implement this freeing word. There was now no religious conflict between bringing the Kingdom to the entire world and remaining within the safety of ceremonial purity. Jesus spoke, "You have a fine way of setting aside the commands of God in order to observe your own traditions" (Mk. 7:9)! He tore down the wall of human tradition that imprisoned the knowledge of God and kept it from the rest of the world.

The disciples were about to implement this freeing lesson. They heard Jesus defend their eating to the Pharisees and to the teachers of the law. Could they make use of this knowledge to propel them in their ministry? Could they eat with those considered "unclean" by the Pharisees for the sake of the Kingdom? They were about to come face to face with the deeper meaning of clean vs. unclean and of worthy vs. unworthy.

Discipleship and the Nations

The disciples heard clear instruction on what defiled a person. They heard that what is inside one's heart and unseen is far greater than the traditions of outward purity. The context of the word is, at times, as instructive as the words spoken. After confronting the Pharisees with what was clean and unclean, Jesus traveled north: "Jesus left that place and went to the vicinity of Tyre" (Mk. 7:24).

Some have misunderstood Jesus' words in the context of meeting a Syrian Phoenician woman as desiring preferential treatment for the house of Israel. Is this woman a dog? Is her demon possessed daughter an animal? The Pharisees they had just left would have claimed both the woman and her daughter to be beneath them and their hearts too hard to help. Jesus traveled to Tyre to continue with the Father's work and to complete the lesson of what was pure or defiled for His disciples. This woman was as important to the Father as the widow of Zaraphath was in the days of Elijah (1 Ki. 17:7). The bigotry of the Pharisees was far more defiling than national origin.

Jesus left directly after the demon was cast out. The mission the Father had given Him was accomplished! He traveled with His disciples and they were exposed to more questions about the clean and the unclean. They went further north to Sidon, which is farther from their homeland. They continued on to Galilee and then to the ten cities of the Decapolis (Mk. 7:31). The Decapolis were cities that rejected Jewish rule and were considered unclean areas by the Pharisees (New Bible Dictionary, pg. 276. Also see the discussion on the Decapolis in Chapter 26, "Jesus, The Kingdom and the Nations.").

Questions

- Do you know of an example of someone who obeyed God against religious tradition?

- Can you apply God's instructions to broader areas of your life, going beyond the direct lesson?

Discipleship Requires a Fresh Start

The Pharisees and teachers of the law found Jesus to be very strange. He certainly did not represent or model their standards at all. On one occasion they disagreed with Jesus on three points: the forgiving of sins (Lk. 5:22), eating and drinking with tax collectors and sinners (v. 30), and Jesus' disciples not fasting as they did (v. 33).

Jesus responded by telling them:

> No one tears a patch from a new garment and sews it on an old one. If he does, he will have torn the new garment, and the patch from the new will not match the old. And no one pours new wine into old wineskins. If he does, the new wine will burst the skins, the wine will run out and the wineskins will be ruined. No, new wine must be poured into new wineskins. And no one after drinking old wine wants the new, for he says, `The old is better' (Lk. 5:36-39).

Jesus clearly was describing for His disciples a new way of thinking and living in a new Kingdom. New garments made poor patches. The truth that Jesus was conveying was that the new expression of the Kingdom of God was not meant to support the old system. It was the Kingdom that was central, not the system that attempted to house the Kingdom. Forgiving sins and mixing freely with tax collectors and sinners did not mesh with the old religious system. Detailed rules regarding the keeping of the Sabbath and fasting within a hierarchy had no meaning in the New Kingdom. The mistake made by religious leaders living in many time periods throughout history was one of supporting their system while losing sight of the Kingdom.

The difference between aged wine and new wine represents the ever-changing expression of the Kingdom of God. This comparison challenges all of us to value the newness of the Kingdom--which we do not fully know--and to be willing to leave behind the old ways--which we do know. Older wine with age tastes better; it is more "polished." But that refinement is not the taste of the Kingdom, but that of a well oiled human system.

Jesus was interested in redeeming the world, feeding the hungry, healing the sick, and restoring the leper, regardless of their backgrounds. The Kingdom of God must honor God and all created in His image. The freshness of the New Kingdom is not represented by a system like Islam that moves rigidly from culture to culture with laws imposed on the world.

Are rules important to God's people? Are they of any value to us? Laws and rules are very important. The law of love, toward God and toward your neighbor as yourself, guides and overrides the complications (and conflicting nature) of a rule book. Can I help a stranger fix a flat tire when I am en route to a Sunday morning service? Do I attend the midweek prayer meeting when God is prompting me to knock on my neighbor's door and live the life of Jesus? The heart of the Pharisee sees the rule and the comfort of the routine it creates. The heart of a disciple sees people, regardless of their backgrounds. The Pharisee would have been satisfied had he made it to the service on time and had he attended the Wednesday prayer meeting. Disciples have the Kingdom oozing from their lives--always salty, always giving, always looking to bless.

Discipleship and All Professions

Discipleship is not for a select few professions. Not all have understood this message in their walk with Jesus. As a child in school I asked, "How can I serve the Lord?" I was told that there were two options: to become a pastor or teach in a Christian school. Neither option drew me. The Kingdom of God calls all to discipleship and labor. Granted, not all professions are redeemable. Jesus' words to "go now, and leave your life of sin" (Jn. 8:11) can be applied to good professions with an evil twist as well as to an evil profession like marketing children. Professions that are not redeemable need to be left behind. The Lord wants to make use of all our background to advance His Kingdom. How important that we have believing senators, mechanics, and entrepreneurs. How important that the missionary and the supporting team find fullness in advancing the Kingdom of God.

The Vision of Disciples

All four gospel writers present the command of Jesus to carry the news of His life-giving freedom to the entire world. They concur with Isaiah's writings that the age of Messiah will bring "light to the nations" (Isa. 51:4).

- **Matthew** tells us that Jesus met His disciples in Galilee according to plan (Mt. 28:16). He charged His disciples:

  > Therefore go and make disciples of all nations, baptizing them
  > in the name of the Father and of the Son and of the Holy Spirit,
  > and teaching them to obey everything I have commanded you.
  > And surely I am with you always, to the very end of the age
  > (Mt. 28:19-20).

He commanded His disciples to go and make disciples. He was not simply telling them to go and tell a story. His words were clear that the work of God was to include every tribe on the planet. This took the disciples time to understand, and it required the empowerment of the Holy Spirit.

- **Mark** tells us that Jesus commissioned the disciples to preach the gospel of the Kingdom to all creation (Mk. 16:15-16). Mark goes on to describe the powers of the Kingdom which are released to disciples who obey the Lord's command.

- **Luke** tells us of two men on the road to Emmaus who met a stranger. The stranger listened as the two disheartened disciples told of the news of the day and of their confusion (Lk. 24:13-24). Luke goes on to tell us that Jesus opened the Scriptures to describe all that had to take place with His suffering and death. They recognized Jesus later as He broke the bread.

Later, with the other disciples, He ". . . opened their minds so they could understand the Scriptures" (24:45). Luke found it important that the story of Christ be clearly tied to the Scriptures. He also verified the necessity of God's working in a believer's life to illumine the Scriptures.

Jesus gave two important instructions on this subject:

1. Repentance and forgiveness of sins will be preached in Jesus' name to all nations.

2. You must be clothed with power from on high before you go to accomplish the mission of God.

- **John** tells us that Jesus appeared to the eleven the evening of His resurrection, passing through locked doors to be with them (Jn. 20:19-23). He proved it was indeed Him and charged His disciples:

> As the Father has sent me, I am sending you. And with that he breathed on them and said, "Receive the Holy Spirit" (Jn. 20:22).

His calling is our calling. His anointing from the Father is ours too. We are to carry the "Light to the Nations." Much is involved in understanding our being sent as Jesus was sent from the Father. Some of these areas include:

- The Power of the Holy Spirit

- Representing the Kingdom of God

- Turning the other cheek

- Laying down our life

- Praying to the Father

- Going to the entire world

- Searching for tribes of other sheep

- Speaking as the Father speaks

- Doing the works that the Father reveals

- Teaching the masses

- Rebuking the proud

- Reshaping the hearts and minds of people

He breathed on them a deposit of the Holy Spirit that would come in fullness during their lives. We must be filled with the Holy Spirit to accomplish the work of God on earth. His life is necessary in us in order to bring the news of salvation to the nations. Neither the work of the gospel nor the infilling of the Holy Spirit is optional.

Jesus' special appearance to Thomas was tender and personal, but sobering (Jn. 20:24-31). Jesus showed himself to Thomas and, as a result, the others received an encouraging second appearance by the Master. All of the disciples saw Jesus once again. His words, ". . . blessed are those who have not seen and yet have believed" (20:29), were for all who were not present with the eleven. The world would believe in the death and resurrection of Christ on their word. We need not ask for a special appearance of Jesus to confirm our faith. The nations will hear the testimony of Spirit-filled disciples and will believe.

Jesus appeared to disciples in Galilee (Jn. 21). The Lord seems to mentor us without giving direct commands at every juncture in life. He wants us to put together the words He has previously spoken and make life decisions in faith. This appearance was personal with John and Peter. Jesus desires to also meet with us privately, always encouraging us to remain faithful to Him and to the Kingdom of God.

Conclusion

Becoming a true disciple is tremendously freeing and comes through dying to ourselves and to worldly pleasures. We will naturally be misunderstood by people around us who miss the significance of Jesus transforming a life into a new creation.

The world is to be reached by disciples. Nothing short of true discipleship will have an impact on this needy, twisted world. The message we speak will be backed by the life we live. We are "sent ones" with the anointing, the power, and the message needed to bring others into discipleship.

Chapter 23 - The Kingdom and Forgiveness

Introduction

Forgiveness is a mark of the Kingdom of God and its subjects. Forgiveness must be initiated by the Creator and then understood by the creation. This order is important from a biblical perspective in order to avoid errant, humanistic aberrations that fail to lead us to peace with God. And who can be the source of forgiveness other than God? No other name under heaven offers the forgiveness of sins. Understanding the nature of forgiveness empowers us as the disciples of Jesus. Forgiveness is a gift from God that is to be offered to the world by those who have tasted its fruit.

What is the condition on which heaven offers forgiveness? The conditional nature of forgiveness is the dividing line between world religions. Christ was the sacrifice that the Father offered for our forgiveness. His sacrificial death met the conditions needed in order to provide forgiveness.

Reflection

- Buddhism tells its followers to become better through freedom from personal desire.

- Islam expects forgiveness as a payment for good services rendered.

The Old Testament is filled with the words "forgiven," "forgive," and "forgiveness."

Examples are rich from the story of Joseph interacting with his brothers.

> Your father left these instructions before he died: `This is what you are to say to Joseph: I ask you to forgive your brothers the sins and the wrongs they committed in treating you so badly' (Ge. 50:16-17).

Examples of forgiveness are given at the dedication of the Temple when King Solomon repeatedly asked God to remember His mercy and forgive the sins of

Israel when they confessed their faults (1 Ki. 8). The cleansed Naaman asked if he would be forgiven in the future, knowing he was to enter the temple of a false god (2 Ki. 5:17-19). The prophets gave warning to those who would be forgiven if they repented, and the fearful judgment that would come to the unforgiven (Isa. 22; Jer. 4:1-2).

The New Testament grabs our attention by offering forgiveness on a colossal scale. This understanding of forgiveness offered in the gospels will transform the lives of honest listeners who apply this power to their lives. Transformation takes place because the chains of past condemnation are broken. Jesus truly does set prisoners free. We begin by examining the record of Luke as he predates the birth of the Messiah with the story of Zechariah and Elizabeth.

> His father Zechariah was filled with the Holy Spirit and proph-
> esied:
>
> Praise be to the Lord, the God of Israel,
> because he has come and has redeemed his people.
> He has raised up a horn of salvation for us
> in the house of his servant David
> (as he said through his holy prophets of long ago),
> salvation from our enemies
> and from the hand of all who hate us—
> to show mercy to our fathers
> and to remember his holy covenant,
> the oath he swore to our father Abraham:
> to rescue us from the hand of our enemies,
> and to enable us to serve him without fear
> in holiness and righteousness before him all our days.
>
> And you, my child, will be called a prophet of the Most High;
> for you will go on before the Lord to prepare the way for him,
> to give his people the knowledge of salvation
> through the forgiveness of their sins,
> because of the tender mercy of our God,
> by which the rising sun will come to us from heaven
> to shine on those living in darkness
> and in the shadow of death,
> to guide our feet into the path of peace (Lk. 1:67-79).

The words and phrases used to describe forgiveness in Zechariah's prophecy enter into many aspects of life. The concepts of "forgiven" or "set free" are much broader in his prophecy than only personal transgression. Zechariah also understood communal restoration with God that accompanied purity on both the individual and corporate levels. Note the words and phrases from Zechariah's prophesy and the type of forgiveness offered:

- Redeemed

- Horn of salvation

- Salvation from our enemies

- The hand of all who hate us

- Mercy to our fathers

- Remember his holy covenant

- Enable us to serve him without fear

- In holiness and righteousness before him all our days

- Give his people the knowledge of salvation

- Through the forgiveness of their sins

- Because of the tender mercy of our God

- The rising sun will come to us from heaven to shine on those living in darkness and in the shadow of death

The news of "a people prepared for the Lord" had been given inside the curtain (Lk. 1:17). John's message was to prepare people to trust in the Messiah and to live with the knowledge that the curtain had been removed.

Forgiveness and redemption were presented through the message of Mary's song at her meeting the expectant Elizabeth. She sang of help to Israel and of mercy to Abraham and to his descendants forever. (Lk. 1:54-55). The coming of the Messiah would mean eternal mercy for Abraham and his descendants. God's gift of mercy was wrapped in the Messiah. God's mercy would be shown through the atonement. God's mercy was tied into His bringing forth the Messiah. His mercy was not shown by His changing the rules or ignoring His previously spoken word.

Favoritism shown to a select group, which is mercy without atonement, is opposed to the character of God.

Zechariah affirmed the coming redemption of the people of God (1:67-75). His song began by emphasizing the salvation that would come through the House of David. His song focused on the redemption through the Messiah who was from the line of David. Both Zechariah and Elizabeth were of the line of Aaron. His specific words, "… to enable us to serve him without fear in holiness and righteousness before him all our days," clearly spoke of the New Covenant. Serving God without fear, and in righteousness, speaks of a transformed life. We can contrast this with a priest entering the most holy place with fear. Complete forgiveness, redemption, and transformation are offered in the New Covenant. This is Messiah's role.

Zechariah's prophetic voice turned to his son John whose role was to point to the coming Messiah and prepare His way. John could not offer forgiveness of sins on his own, but rather only in light of the atonement of the coming Messiah. John did not come with his own message from God; his message and ministry through baptism were intricately tied to Messiah.

John preached a "baptism of repentance for the forgiveness of sins" (Lk. 3:3). His call to repentance was in light of the New Kingdom. The forgiveness offered was real; it was not a hope for the future. It was closely linked with the One to come. John's message included "And all mankind will see God's salvation" (Lk. 3:6). God's generous mercy and His gift of redemption are for the entire world.

Questions

What is a baptism of repentance?

Is a baptism of repentance just an action?

Does it bring a deep level of transformation?

Aspects of Forgiveness in the New Covenant

1. Forgiveness Requires the Blood of Jesus

The covenant is "cut" with blood. The New Covenant is different from the Old Covenant. The Old Covenant required blood for the atonement of sin; the New Covenant supplies the blood. The Old Covenant promised judgment for every infraction. The New Covenant, though it does not overlook the seriousness of sin, promises forgiveness. He offered Himself as the atonement for the requirements of the law.

> Then he took the cup, gave thanks and offered it to them, saying, 'Drink from it, all of you. This is my blood of the covenant, which is poured out for many for the forgiveness of sins' (Mt. 26:27-28).

We are forgiven on the basis of the blood of the Messiah. Forgiveness that is offered without the life blood of Jesus is an empty promise without transforming power. Living in righteousness based upon works develops a self-focused life steeped in religious pride. Living in the atonement for forgiveness paid by another should mold a broken life into a transformed life, and a self-righteous life into a humbled life. The New Covenant is meant to change us from within rather than simply meet legal requirements.

Jesus gave His disciples a cup of wine to share. He described the wine as His blood, the blood of the covenant poured out for many. The covenant between God and man is the contractual ability to walk together. The covenant is the necessary agreement to bring humankind back into relationship with a Holy Creator.

Jesus was telling His disciples that His blood would be given as the requirement to reinstate the human race into fellowship with God. The alternative, not recognizing the blood of Jesus nor His death, maintains separation from God. God offers His covenant for the New Kingdom.

Human-made covenants are worthless novelties which expect God to meet us on our selfish, twisted level. No human based covenant could represent all human expressions. The created cannot lay out contractual requirements upon which the Creator must agree. The order is nonsensical. This means that people who give reasons as to why they think they are acceptable to God reverse the Creator/

created order. Their reasoning, outside of complete acceptance of His covenant, is baseless and futile.

The blood of Jesus was offered inside the Temple once for all as the atonement for our sin. "The curtain of the temple was torn in two from top to bottom" (Mt. 27:51). The Temple curtain separated the inner court, or the holy place, from the most holy place. The curtain was entered once per year by a chosen member of the priesthood (Lk. 1:8-10, 1 Ch. 24:19, Ex. 30:10). Atonement was made inside the most holy area. No one had the authority to enter this most holy place before God except to make atonement for sin. This special place was God's design to bring forgiveness to the people. The significance of this temple curtain torn at the time of Jesus' death must be grasped. The most holy place no longer was separated from the inner court. A torn temple curtain could not have been repaired, nor should it have been. The atonement through the sacrifice of the Messiah would not be repeated. The atonement for sin was complete.

The physical place of the most holy place has moved. Our hearts are now the dwelling place of God. Atonement and forgiveness are complete. We are completely forgiven through the blood of Jesus. All must be invited to enter this realm of the forgiven and the justified. The redeemed have access to the Father. This is a major message of the Kingdom of God.

Building walls of "Christian isolation" works against the torn curtain of the Kingdom of God. We are compelled to live in a world needing to experience complete forgiveness. Christian expressions that establish a safe house mentality seek to define themselves as an inner "sacred community" rather than an open "saving community." The former finds peace through separation. The latter finds fullness in proclaiming the peace of God through Christ. One affirms the need for the curtain; the other lives in fullness because the curtain has been removed.

2. Repentance

The work of God is to offer forgiveness with the intent to rebuild our lives into those which will also offer forgiveness to others. A life which has accepted forgiveness, and lives in that state of forgiveness, is transformed into a humble, gracious life. The significance of John's baptism for the forgiveness of sins is that it is a single, one-time event.

> And so John came, baptizing in the desert region and preaching
> a baptism of repentance for the forgiveness of sins (Mk. 1:4).

Periodic animal sacrifices were stopped through a single event. Through the solitary action of John's baptism, the mountains and valleys were flattened. The way was prepared for the blood of the New Covenant which was another solitary event for all humankind.

Jesus picks up the message of repentance for the forgiveness of sins in the initial stages of His ministry. The message Jesus preached was simple and clear:

1. The time is right now – not some future epoch.

2. The Kingdom of God is coming in fullness.

3. Change your ways; allow God's goodness to have its effect on your life! (1:15)

God does not call the human race into repentance without offering hope. Repentance is our first step to acknowledging the rightness of the Kingdom of God. Repentance is not a single solitary act. Both the revelation of our need and the beauty of the Kingdom of God draw us into increasing states of repentance. Paul recognized this growth and labeled its fruit "love for others." He writes, ". . . your faith is growing more and more, and the love every one of you has for each other is increasing" (2 Th. 1:3). The purpose of God is for our transformation from our acceptance of the world to our acceptance of the Kingdom and its citizens. We are in the world but not part of it in increasing stages.

Matthew tells us that Jesus ministered in Capernaum and thus fulfilled the prophecy to remember the Gentiles living in darkness (Mt. 4:13-16). Repentance became part of Jesus' normal speech. "From that time on Jesus began to preach, 'Repent, for the kingdom of heaven is near'" (Mt. 4:17). There is a continuance in Matthew's record that suggests part of Jesus' message was always directed toward repentance. Repentance as a command always brings with it the understanding of hope--and that hope is the forgiveness of sins.

3. Reconciliation with other people

Reconciliation with people is required if we desire to walk with God. Jesus tells us to leave our offering at the altar and be reconciled. This means that we are to break with our religious ceremony and take care of the conviction we hear from our renewed conscience (Mt. 5:23-24). Our gift to God, and even to our religious ceremony, is defiled if we know of a broken relationship and allow it to remain broken. Our gift to God is not meaningful if bitterness, a grievance, or a problem are allowed to go unchecked!

Power and weakness in prayer are also addressed by Jesus as they relate to reconciliation with others (Mk. 11:25-26). Jesus addressed the broad question of spiritual authority in relation to the withered fig tree (11:20). His response was not focused on the tree, but rather on the power released to those who bring their requests to the Father in faith. This power of God is promised to those subjects of the Kingdom of God who pray in faith. The focus of Jesus' instruction quickly changes. God, He promises, will speak to us in prayer. God will speak to us in many ways when we approach Him in prayer with our requests. He will bring to our minds people who have sinned against us.

> And when you stand praying, if you hold anything against anyone, forgive him, so that your Father in heaven may forgive you your sins (Mk. 11:25).

When we pray and people who have wronged us come to mind, we have three choices:

- Battle with the thought that appears to be unrelated to our prayer time.
- Take the people and events of our memory "to the Lord" and pray for justice.
- Commit the people, events, and hurts to God as we forgive everyone who has sinned against us.

Only the third choice is in accord with the words of Jesus. Only forgiving others brings assurance that we are able to be forgiven before God. If the same people or events return to our minds in subsequent prayer times, we can forgive again, and again. It may also be healthy to simply recall that these people are forgiven and release them. Forgiveness is an expression of the power of the Kingdom of God. This force is so powerful that it breaks the chains of depression and of addictive, recurring sins.

An unforgiving person is not promised the power of God in prayer. Jesus links the power of answered prayer to a forgiven, cleansed disciple. This is a disciple who knows how to forgive.

4. Generosity Rather than Being Exacting

Jesus removed any thought that "an eye for an eye" was a response encouraged by God. Righting a wrong by demanding equal, vindictive payment was never a command. It was a safeguard to keep people from seeking overpayment for a wrong suffered. Jesus tells us not to demand our rights if we are wronged. This word denounces punitive law suits that "send a message" to the doctor, to the factory, or to the coffee vendor. "An eye for an eye" was the safeguard to keep destructive reciprocity from undoing a society. But Jesus went far beyond this safeguard. He told His followers not to resist an evil person. How weak this appears in a self-centered society--no revenge, no fighting back, no harboring hatred. He went on to say:

> If someone strikes you on the right cheek, turn to him the other also (Mt. 5:38).

This word sends uncomfortable waves of conviction down the spines of unbelievers. "It is impossible to live this way," they reason. Turning the other cheek requires Christ within us. The intent of our new response is focused on the King and His Kingdom, not on our individual honor. Our true honor is found through identification with the Messiah, not by defending ourselves.

The world would be so much better off with people trusting God for their honor rather than a law suit. When wronged in this life, and because we follow the Master, we must express our supreme confidence in both the prevailing justice of God and in the coming Kingdom of Heaven which is open to us. Jesus told us to go two miles with the one who forces us to go one mile. Roman soldiers were allowed to press civilians to carry their armor and equipment the distance of one mile. Occupying soldiers could press local Jews into this service. Jesus tells us to go double the distance of the legal requirement of serving oppressive regimes. The Kingdom of God develops disciples who not only forgive, but who serve the oppressive.

> You have heard that it was said, 'Love your neighbor and hate your enemy.' But I tell you: Love your enemies and pray for those who persecute you, that you may be sons of your Father in heaven (Mt. 5:43-44).

Shahdi - Case Study

Shahdi was a former member of the PLO. He had learned to hate his oppressors. Thoughts of his former Gaza home brought the awful memories of his mother's death when a high caliber Israeli machine gun bullet penetrated the walls of their home and her body. Loss of life, land, and dignity forged rage within him. His anger turned toward revenge.

In Shahdi's search for answers, he miraculously came upon a Bible and began reading the Gospel of Matthew. The words "love your enemies" came out of the page as a revolutionary new concept. He had learned to hate. Now he was struck by the powerful words of Jesus to love his enemies.

A vision immediately followed. In the vision which God gave Shahdi, he saw a lion with the body of a lamb. He also saw people in his vision who were dressed in white, who welcomed him without reservation.

The words he read and his strange vision eventually led this former PLO member to believers and to a personal relationship with his Messiah. Today he knows both the Lion of Judah and the Lamb of God who takes away the sins of the world as one person in Jesus. His former hatred has melted away. The peace he has with Jesus can only be described as the true revolution.

5. Forgiveness Received and Given

We receive forgiveness as we forgive. The Bible is clear that our forgiveness can only be granted as we learn to forgive others.

> Forgive us our debts, as we also have forgiven our debtors (Mt. 6: 12).

Forgiveness is not automatic, nor is it endlessly flowing without conditions. Forgiveness should flow to the transformed and then on to those who have wronged them, whether they are fellow believers or unbelievers. When forgiveness for past sin becomes cloudy, you may have a besetting, nagging problem. Guilt and shame tell us to get before our God and allow Him to bring to mind any sin requiring repentance, including the sin of unforgiveness.

Forgive anyone who comes to your mind. This act of forgiveness may need to happen repeatedly. Some hurts take time to heal. The tenderness of a healing wound should not be mistaken as unforgiveness. Forgiveness encourages the healing process. Forgive and remain in a state of forgiving.

6. Do not Judge

Jesus takes the concept of forgiving others to a deeper level. He commands us not to judge others (Mt. 7:1-2). Judging others is the critical attitude, or critical spirit, that is focused on people's ministries, characters, lifestyles, or even word choices. A person with a judgmental demeanor will find something positive to say about someone, but quickly add qualifications that fail his or her standard, or even a biblical reason that places the person in a bad light. Passing judgment on others has the same result on our lives as not forgiving them. Both bring us into the place of judgment. We are healthy people when we remember that there is one judge and lawgiver, God Himself. Placing ourselves into the seat of the judge always results in judgment coming back our way.

There is room, however, to help someone grow. Correcting someone, rebuking their sin, or mentoring the person into a deeper walk with God are not to be avoided. Jesus tells us to be very careful to go through self examination and remove the big problems before attempting to work on the smaller details in our brother's or sister's life (7:3-5).

7. Forgiveness and the Welcome Mat

The character of God actively searches for those who have corrupted their own lives, wooing them to purity. If He simply set His standard, none of us would find the path to life. Grace is extended by God as the path leading to the truth and leading away from death. His grace, if received and followed, leads to life in Christ.

Luke described the grace of God in Chapter 15. Tax collectors and sinners wanted to hear Jesus speak. The Pharisees did not have the carpet of grace rolled out for anyone. This is a challenge for our lives: Do we have standards to be met, or do we extend grace to love people into Kingdom living?

Reflection

When do people without Christ want to listen to you?

Grace is expressed as the legs and feet that carry forgiveness to those who need it. What an honor to have it said of us: "That man welcomes sinners and eats with them" (Lk. 15:2). This is an expression of the legs and feet of forgiveness.

The three parables that follow describe the legs moving and searching. The lost sheep, the lost coin, and the lost son express the searching, longing heart of God for the one who is lost. The Pharisee, with self-defined high standards, had no stairway to descend to meet the needy. To the Pharisee, a lost sheep was welcomed when it found its way back to the sheep pen. The lost coin was useful if it rolled uphill to a pocket. The lost son was more complicated and utterly unfindable. He had no means by which to clean himself or dress properly. The lost son had no room in which to sleep. Legally he had no field to work, no stall to fill, and no seat at the dining table. Some will think "And how do we know that granting another chance won't cost us more and, once again, be squandered?" The father in this parable used his legs of grace to run and meet his younger son. He also used the same legs to leave the party and meet the older son. Forgiveness must be offered; it is not a required standard to be met. The parables of Jesus point out God's intervention in our lives, which is absent in works-based belief systems.

Forgiveness requires God extending grace. Forgiveness is meaningless without conviction of sin. Conviction of a wrong done is also a gift of the Holy Spirit. Jesus promised that the Holy Spirit, the Counselor, would bring conviction of sin (Jn. 16:8). The Father extends grace, the Son offers salvation, and the Holy Spirit brings the conviction of sin to move our hearts in God's direction. Forgiveness is an act of the whole Godhead, the Trinity, in our lives.

8. Forgiveness of Sins and Healing

Physical healing came to the paralytic at the Bethesda pool. Jesus later told the man to "stop sinning" (Jn. 5:14). The order in which Jesus offered forgiveness and physical healing is noteworthy, but not a pattern. He certainly got the man's attention. The message we carry needs to contain both physical and spiritual wholeness.

Matthew and Mark tell us that Jesus was in His hometown of Capernaum (Mt. 9:1; Mk. 2:1). Luke fills in an important detail. He tells us that the Pharisees and teachers of the law came together while Jesus taught. These religious leaders came from every village of Galilee and from Judea and Jerusalem (Lk. 5:17). The house was packed with many types of people, from curious neighbors to trained religious thinkers. The scene was set for a spectacular encounter. Jesus used the opportunity to free the man from his past sin. The paralytic had two needs. People, including the religious elite, saw only one need: his body needed healing.

Question

If you are teaching the Kingdom of heaven and a broken body or mind is brought to you, what do you see? What do you have to offer?

Jesus declared forgiveness to the paralyzed man and then asked which was easier, forgiveness or healing? Jesus forgave sins knowing the crowd would be shaken. These three gospel writers tell us that the teachers of the law had thoughts which opposed those of Jesus. They called Him a blasphemer. In this example of the coming Kingdom, Jesus knew their thoughts. An expression of the Kingdom of God is for hearts to be laid bare. The fact that Jesus answered their thoughts was proof that the Kingdom of God had arrived. Jesus was revealing that an expression of the Kingdom was forgiveness of sin.

Jesus offered forgiveness to the paralytic without confession of sin or any sign of repentance. Normally we see ourselves as evangelists or teachers, proclaiming the story of Christ's death and resurrection. We normally tell the story and "instruct" people to find forgiveness through faith in the story they heard, read, or saw. The appropriation of grace and forgiveness is left to the listener. Is it possible in our story telling to offer forgiveness of sins through the blood of Jesus? Is it possible to declare that all who acknowledge Him are forgiven? Certainly there are times when people grasp the theoretical and are unable to move to the obvious application. Proclaiming forgiveness moves the hearer into the rest and fruit of the Kingdom. Discipleship in the way of God will take years. It seems reasonable to declare forgiveness that is offered in Jesus and disciple people into its meaning. Is it wise to take months or years of discipleship before offering forgiveness? Entering His rest is a key to experiencing the Kingdom of God. Entering His Sabbath rest by proclamation is a fabulous gift.

Reflection

We need faith for forgiveness offered to our audience. We need faith for healing and restored lives. God calls us to more than just religious teaching. People need to taste the fruit of the Kingdom of God.

9. Forgiveness and Compassion

Forgiveness is linked to mercy and compassion (Mt. 9:12-13). Forgiveness is not rewarded to the perfect, but to those who need help. Jesus was anointed by a woman considered to be immoral (Lk. 7:36-50). Forgiveness set her free and did not contain stiff words of public embarrassment.

On another occasion Jesus met a woman caught in adultery.

Then neither do I condemn you, Jesus declared. Go now and leave your life of sin (Jn. 8:11).

The guilty know they are caught. It takes the heart of the Father to set His children free from sin's bondage. The question of justice can come up, especially for disciples caught in sin. How do we restore disciples or open a new door of freedom for those moved to repentance? Jesus used a welcome mat, words of acceptance, with the needy. Only the self-righteous religious authorities were chided. The community of believers should be a place of safety, because everyone there knows the forgiveness they have received from the Father and from other people. On the other hand, when the humility of confession is covered over by the outward appearance of perfection, a place of safety can become a place of cruel judgment.

Questions

How have you experienced forgiveness?

How are you at freeing others from their sins against you?

How do you express forgiveness to those closest to you?

10. Continuous Forgiveness

Jesus entered the discussion about forgiveness after being prompted by Peter's question about the amount of forgiveness to be granted in one day (Mt. 18:21-35). The question was one of law and of legal limit--was forgiving seven times enough? The response of Jesus was in two stages. The first stage addressed the legal requirements by moving the "fence line" from seven to four hundred ninety offenses. Most of us can keep a running account of five, seven, or ten offenses. To keep a running account of three hundred or four hundred offenses would require a ledger. Keeping track of offenses runs counter to the very principles of forgiveness. The slate is to be wiped clean.

The second view of forgiveness came in a story form. There was a man who owed an enormous debt. This man represents all humans in debt to God. Who can possibly pay the crushing debt of sin which is beyond our comprehension? A talent of silver in New Testament weights was approximately 41 kilograms. Ten thousand talents of silver would have required approximately 23 truck loads to transport. The price of this quantity of silver on the current world market was meant to tell us that this servant's debt could not have been repaid. His position before God represents our position as well. The debt we owe God cannot be covered by our own abilities. The forgiven slave quickly forgot the size of the debt he was forgiven and turned with judgment on a fellow slave.

The Kingdom of God is a Kingdom of forgiveness. It is a Kingdom of the forgiving and the generous. This translates into looking past the faults and the debts of others and examining our own lives. The sins of others are like droplets of water; forgiving those is nothing compared to the ocean of forgiveness we have received from God. Harboring any grudge, for any reason, places us alongside the wicked, unforgiving servant.

Forgiveness as a clean record does not mean an inability to help a person see error in his or her life. Jesus told us, "If your brother sins against you, go and show him his fault, just between the two of you" (Mt. 18:15). Forgiveness carries the attitude of release. Vengeance and bitterness must not be part of a believer's life.

> So watch yourselves. If your brother sins, rebuke him, and if he repents, forgive him. If he sins against you seven times in a day, and seven times comes back to you and says, `I repent,' forgive him (Lk. 17:3-4).

God promised Cain His vengeance upon anyone who killed him. Lamech twisted those words to avenge himself of any who did him wrong. He vowed to kill anyone for wounding him. In a similar way the Qur'an tells Muslims to take revenge. The contrast between The Bible and The Qur'an is dramatic.

Bible	**Qur'an**
[The Lord speaking] It is mine to avenge, I will repay (Dt. 32:35).	He who commits aggression upon you, you are to commit aggression against him as he committed against you. (Sura Al-Baqara 2:194)

The character of God teaches His followers to release grievances against others. The Prince of Peace never encourages us to "get even."

11. Forgiveness and the Nations

Through revelation from God, John the Baptist understood the extent of forgiveness offered by Jesus, the sacrificial Lamb. His confession came very early on in the ministry of Jesus and not as a deduction from the life of Jesus.

> The next day John saw Jesus coming toward him and said, "Look, the Lamb of God, who takes away the sin of the world" (Jn. 1:29, 36)!

John understood well the message of the Father's forgiveness of sin through the sacrifice of the Messiah-Lamb. John's revelation from the Father would not be equaled by the disciples until Pentecost, or even later in the writings of Paul. John the Baptist had already made the transition from blood covenant through repetitious animal sacrifice to the single, one-time sacrifice of God's Messiah-Lamb. The Holy Spirit in John's life from birth (Lk. 1:15) testified to Jesus: His life, His atoning death, and the redemption offered for the whole world. Each of these concepts fights against human nature which is fallen and hiding from God. Human intellect does not lead us to the understanding of Jesus and the fullness He offers believers. These areas of revelation are a ministry of the Holy Spirit. Revelation of God's redemption offered to all peoples is also a word of the Holy Spirit. The disciples learned a great deal from their Master, Jesus. Yet it was not until they were filled with the Holy Spirit that the confusing story and tragic ending to Jesus' life unfolded into a clear plan of the Father. For them, and for us, the death of Jesus and His resurrection become a story of unsurpassed victory.

Reflections

How important is the fullness of the Holy Spirit in your life?

For people to understand the story of Jesus, they need both teaching and the revelation of the Holy Spirit.

How often do you pray for others to be filled with the Holy Spirit?

A fullness of the Holy Spirit and His revelation will point to the following: Jesus as the Messiah, His role as the sacrifice for sin, and the necessity that the message of forgiveness be carried to the whole world.

Jesus was known to be the Messiah from the beginning of Luke's record (Lk.1:41, 44, 49). It took years, however, for them to understand that their Messiah would suffer as the sacrifice for sin (Lk. 24:25-26). More revelation was needed to carry this message as a priority to the Gentiles (Ac. 8:1;10;15).

Some believers only have part of this revelation. To them, Jesus is Messiah and He died for their sin. However, the Spirit desires revelation in all believers that propels them to share this news with others. The proof of this revelation is found in lifestyle and in actions based on faith.

The resurrected Christ came to the disciples, "the eleven and those with them" (Lk. 24:33). In the midst of the excitement shared by two disciples who met Jesus on the Emmaus road, Jesus brought important words that would never leave their bewildered minds. The story brings us into the closed room with frightened disciples, joining them in examining His hands and feet (v. 39) and watching Him eat (vv. 41-42). His desire to help them understand that He had been resurrected, and was not just Spirit, was also revealed.

His message is to impact us as deeply as it did His disciples gathered on the day of His resurrection. His words at that important first gathering tell us: "repentance and forgiveness of sins will be preached in his name to all nations..." (v. 47).

All nations are to hear the message of repentance and forgiveness of sins. The welcome mat of God's forgiveness is the mission mandate. It is to be "rolled out" to every tribe, every language, and every people group. The character of God seen through Jesus' words is generous, forgiving, and extending to those who yet know nothing of His story. The welcome mat of forgiveness cannot be a random word to ease the conscience of people living in darkness. It must be the clear, accurate story of God, of His creation, of our rebellion, and of His sacrificial gift to offer forgiveness. Any other offering of forgiveness misses the eternal significance of salvation. Other forms of forgiveness--humanistic comfort or meeting the requirements of other religious systems--at best range from superficial to deeply confusing and deceptive.

12. The Unforgiven and the Hard Hearted

Forgiveness is a generosity of heart that is seen in compassion. Jesus told the Pharisees, "I desire mercy, not sacrifice" (Mt. 12:7; Hos. 6:6). The two examples that Jesus gave to this accusing, condemning group were (1) David and his men eating the consecrated bread of the priests, and (2) priests working on the Sabbath. Jesus was not overlooking the law of God, but using common sense. People are important. Forgiveness, mercy, and compassion go together. They keep us from exacting legalism and self-righteousness. The Pharisees and teachers of the law, who often lacked these qualities, looked for infractions to accuse people. Their hard, unforgiving hearts led them to plot the death of the One who was Lord of the Sabbath (Mt. 12:14).

Confronted with Jesus' healing a demon possessed man, the Pharisees accused Jesus of healing by the power of the Prince of demons (Mt. 12:22-32; Mk. 3:20-30; Lk. 11:14-23). They mistook the power of the Holy Spirit for the power of Satan. Jesus responded by telling the crowd about what was forgivable and what was unforgivable. Speaking against the Holy Spirit is sin with eternal consequences. This word must be taken to heart today. Healings, prophetic utterances, speaking in tongues, and youth believing God against all odds may well be expressions of the Holy Spirit. Teaching or correction must be pointed toward glorifying God, not defending a theology or a cultural system.

Conclusion

Forgiveness is not a human concept; it comes from another realm. God carefully brought understanding of forgiveness to His people throughout the ages. Blood and death were always required to bring us back into harmony with the Creator. God offers forgiveness to restore relationships: human to human and human to God. Both are necessary for us to walk in freedom.

The message we bring to the nations is a message we have personally received and one by which we live. It is also a message that is filled with reconciliation between humans and their Creator. The message also brings teaching on how to live out the life of forgiveness with others, transforming old grudges into renewed friendships.

The message of forgiveness will require some to lay down their lives in order to impact the hearts of onlookers. A life given to God's forgiveness will speak volumes and will penetrate hardened societies in a way that mere words could never express.

24. Jesus Teaches on the Kingdom

Introduction

Jesus taught wherever He went. He taught the crowds about the Kingdom of God. He taught His disciples about practical faith in the Father. He also taught His disciples how to go and to teach others. Simply sitting at the feet of the Master was not (and is not) an option. Jesus clearly lived what He taught and never took the posture of a sterile guru in meditative disconnect from humanity.

The four gospels are filled with the teachings of Jesus. Volumes have been written on Jesus and His teaching ministry. The endeavor of this study of the gospels is to understand mission and the Kingdom of God through the teachings of Jesus. How Jesus taught, what He taught, and the implications of following His teachings will change our lives (Mt. 7:24).

How did Jesus Teach?

The hallmark of Jesus' teaching was empowering His disciples to carry out the ministry. For example, Jesus did not baptize, but He delegated this activity to His disciples (Jn. 4:2). Teaching passes on authority and releases others into service. In this passage, we understand that Jesus' disciples were capable of instructing people in the ways of righteousness and baptizing them. There was no need to wait until Jesus was in the vicinity to perform baptisms. Jesus also empowered the twelve to drive out demons, cure diseases, heal the sick, and preach the Kingdom of God (Lk. 9:1-2).

Questions

What types of teaching are not empowering to others?

Do you teach to fulfill a ministry or to empower others and release them into Kingdom ministries?

It must be noted that "driving out demons," "curing diseases," and "healing the sick" are three separate activities. 1) As disciples, we have the power and authority over the evil spirits that haunt, oppress, and invade human lives. 2) We have the clear mandate to find cures for diseases so that polio and cholera, for example, cease to cripple and destroy lives. 3) We have the power and authority to pray for the sick to be healed. Praying for those who need a touch from God is part of our task.

All three of these activities are needed and are not in conflict with each other. All three must be centered around the preaching of the Kingdom of God, which should bring a wholesomeness to a community. Healing the sick is often that for which many disciples long, because miraculous healing demonstrates the power of God. His miraculous power is also displayed through the casting out of demons. While there is truth that God's power is displayed in healing and driving out demons, we must concentrate on asking God for help in long-term study in order to cure diseases.

Medical research, and the years of intense study needed to prepare to do this research, are in complete harmony with prayer for the sick. The study and practice of psychology and the driving out of demons are not in conflict as long as the Kingdom of God is central. The mistrust between the physical and spiritual worlds arose when, during the Enlightenment, science looked through the lens of evolution and disdained the spiritual which was labeled as "non-empirical." At times, the Body of Christ reacted with scepticism toward the empirical world of scientific study and wrongly distanced itself from the secular. The world God created must be studied from many points of view in order to be properly understood.

Prayer for individuals and their community brings us to the conclusion that God wants the blessing of positive change. Clean drinking water, healthy farming methods, and factory processes that bless the workers all express Kingdom values. There is no limit to the creative ways God can bless a community in its own context. We do not press for one earthly political system to replace or dominate all others, committing other systems to a refuse pile. Communities in Afghanistan do not need Swiss housing standards imposed upon them in order for foreign Christian workers to acknowledge that the Kingdom of God is present. However, replacing the poppy cash crop with agriculture that feeds a population is a holistic expression of the Gospel. Kingdom values bring quality of life into any culture.

In His instruction to the twelve in this particular outreach (Lk. 9), Jesus told them to go to the Jewish population. They were instructed not to go to the Gentiles or to the Samaritans. This outreach was clearly not a fund-raising event, but a fresh expression of the arrival of the Kingdom of God in Jewish communities. Jesus instructed His disciples to receive provision--food and lodging--as it was offered (Mt. 10:11-13). Blessings will come to those who provide for Christ's disciples. Provision as basic as a cup of cold water will not be overlooked (v. 42).

This is where the disciples started. It was not a formula for all outreaches. A time would shortly come for the disciples to reach out to Samaritans (Jn. 4) and to Gentiles (Mt. 8). A time will come to pack a bag and take young believers in Christ to new lands. But as mission develops, we must not become so self-sufficient that we refuse the hospitality of a community or no longer look for people of peace. Each community approached with the gospel needs to feel they have something to offer, and that they have intrinsic worth.

Reflection

Some missionaries find it uncomfortable to come to a new people with needs for personal provision. The Celts and the Moravians went with needs. Is there value in our being uncomfortable for the sake of the gospel?

Kingdom Teaching - The Sermon on the Mount

This set of teachings was given to the disciples after spending approximately 1½ years with Jesus. This should not be considered advanced teaching for the newly appointed apostles (Lk. 6:12-49), but rather fundamental to Kingdom life and Kingdom values, understandable by people from many backgrounds. Luke tells us,

> A large crowd of his disciples was there and a great number of
> people from all over Judea, from Jerusalem, and from the coastal
> region around Tyre and Sidon, who had come to hear him and
> to be healed of their diseases (vv. 17-18).

The crowd was made up of disciples, curious Jews, and Gentiles. One cannot look to mission in the New Testament without understanding the values Jesus gave in the Sermon on the Mount and applying them to how we, as disciples, live our lives.

1. Holding on to God, despite pain in life (Mt. 5:3-12)

Jesus tells us that the following people are blessed:
- the poor in spirit
- those who mourn
- the meek
- those who hunger and thirst for righteousness
- the merciful
- the pure in heart

- the peacemakers
- those who are persecuted because of righteousness
- those who are insulted, persecuted, and falsely accused

Two sides of the blessing exist. We know God blesses people of the covenant, and He promises to make people of the covenant a blessing to the nations (Ge. 12). The first side to the blessing is that, when in covenant relationship with the Lord, we will have the Kingdom, be comforted, inherit the earth, be filled, receive mercy, see God, be called sons of God, be glad, and rejoice. This means that the Kingdom values for God's children supercede the pain of this life. Kingdom values do not, however, eradicate the pain of life which will always exist. In fulfilling the purposes of the Kingdom, one must expect the insults and persecution thrust upon Christ-followers.

The second side of this blessing is "to enter into life" with those to whom we carry the good news of the gospel. We will identify with the poor in spirit, those mourning, those hungry for righteousness, and the persecuted because they, too, identify with Christ. Our life is found in becoming a blessing to the people of the nations who struggle in this life. We are called to identify with the needy of this world.

2. You are Salt and Light (Mt. 5:14-16)

Jesus compares His people to two images, both of which can significantly impact their surroundings, even if only in very small amounts. Salt preserves and keeps out decay, both in meat and in a society. Salt cleanses and yet stings. It brings out the flavor and allows people to live abundantly in a new-found fullness. Unused salt can have its effectiveness leached out and become worthless.

Light can be both centralized, exemplified by a stationary lighthouse, and dispersed, exemplified by a lantern carried to dark areas. Light in the Kingdom of God is also both central (the church) and mobile (mission). Light is necessary in dark areas. The power of light is soothing and revealing to dark areas. Remember that your light is more visible at night than it is during the day.

3. Jesus points the way for true holiness (Mt. 5:17-48)

Holiness is part of the Kingdom because it is an attribute of the King. Jesus clarifies that He is not about to abolish the law; yet fulfilling the law is not enough in the Kingdom.

> For I tell you that unless your righteousness surpasses that of
> the Pharisees and the teachers of the law, you will certainly not

enter the kingdom of heaven (5:20).

This verse could sound overwhelming, knowing the extent to which the Pharisees and the teachers of the law adhered to their rules. God requires honest obedience, purity of heart, and more than merely squeaking by the basic requirements of the law. He longs for our heart attitude to be as His Father's heart is in heaven-- burning with zeal to do what is right. Be perfect, therefore, as your heavenly Father is perfect (5:48) is the call of the Shepherd to a life of freedom.

4. Live for God rather than for yourself (Mt. 6:1-34)

Jesus tells us to give to the poor, to pray, to fast, and to live a life filled with doing good. But He commands us to do these things so that all honor goes to our heavenly Father. We can certainly do acts of righteousness in order to gain approval and to be noticed, but Jesus tells us to give and to fast in secret. He tells us to pray behind closed doors. In the teaching on prayer, Jesus teaches us to pray to the Father in faith, with the emphasis on the Kingdom of God. He cares about our daily needs and is not forced through "modern" economic trends to cover our cravings.

Trusting God is the opposite of worrying. We must be careful not to pray about a difficult situation and then continue to worry as though God does not exist. The example of how God cares for the birds demonstrates to us how God cares about the seemingly insignificant little things of life. Of how much more value to Him are we who enter the Kingdom of God?

Worry is synonymous with the pagans--those who really have no God to take care of them. Modern pagans include those who say they have no god, as well as the religious of any background who live as though God is not personally interested in their daily lives. Pagans worry about food, drink, and clothing. Jesus tells us to focus on His Kingdom and on His righteousness; the rest will be supplied.

5. Warnings from Jesus (Mt. 7:1-6)

Jesus warns us that judging others is a deadly trap that opens the door for judgment to return upon us as His people. Conflicts between believers will arise, but we are commanded not to judge or disparage others, believer and nonbeliever alike. Each of us struggles, and the "plank" in our own eye is often more obvious to all but ourselves. Stay alert! Learn to forgive and then go the second mile. This is not just advice, but it is essential to life in the Kingdom. Pray for others and encourage them. These are the fruits of the Kingdom which testify to the Sprit of God living in a believer.

6. Faith in the Kingdom (Mt. 7:7-12)

Ask, seek, and knock are commands for those who desire faith to open new doors. A believer cannot live a life of faith while believing only for the natural to be released. Jesus knows the faith required to accomplish His will. He is giving us tools to accomplish more than what we see on the surface. Mission requires the penetration of the gospel into new regions. Ask, seek, and knock are mandatory tools in our expression of faith.

7. Test for those claiming to be believers (Mt. 7:13-20)

These tests in the Kingdom are for our benefit as we interact with those who call themselves believers. They are also a standard by which our lives will be checked frequently. The broad way and the narrow way exist. There are sheep and there are wolves. Grapes come from grapevines and figs from fig trees. Thorn bushes and thistles do not produce good fruit. A bad tree cannot produce good fruit. If the fruit is good, the tree must be good. Jesus is telling us to look at the fruit. It will be evident where people's hearts are in this life.

The fruit of darkness is revenge, bitterness, unforgiveness, and manipulation. Those producing the fruit of darkness, even when they speak of their commitment to a religious form, need the light of Christ.

The Parables

Introduction

Jesus only taught what the Father had already spoken to Him (Jn. 8:26, 28, 38, 40). This meant that Jesus listened to His Father's instruction and then placed the teaching into the context of first century Jewish and Palestinian thought. Each of us has the mandate to take what God has entrusted to us and place it into the context of the people and setting in which we are living and ministering. Missing this very important point will lock the communicator into talking to his or her own believing peers rather than to the lost, or out of time and/or cultural relevancy.

A necessity for our study is to keep to the topic of the Kingdom of God and mission. This is especially true in light of the avenues we could take in the teaching presented in the gospels. Jesus taught using many different styles. He varied these styles according to His audiences. The central message He brought gave insight into the

Kingdom of God. The parables paint a picture of the many aspects of the Kingdom.

1. Parables came as obscure teachings to the disciples, but with the advantage of private interpretation. To the crowds, the teachings were hard to understand.

> The knowledge of the secrets of the kingdom of heaven has been given to you, but not to them. Whoever has will be given more, and he will have an abundance. Whoever does not have, even what he has will be taken from him. This is why I speak to them in parables:
>
> Though seeing, they do not see;
> though hearing, they do not hear
> or understand. (Mt. 13:11-13; Dt. 29:4)

2. To those with open hearts and a hunger to understand, His teachings were increasingly clear and revealed the Messiahship of Jesus. To those who took offense at Jesus healing on the Sabbath or His seeming lack of connectivity with the local religious leaders, the parables became simply "hard sayings" (Jn. 6:60). Their disgust for Jesus grew more intense as they listened to Him teach (Lk. 20:19; Mt. 21:45-46). Expect that teaching people about the Kingdom of God will bring a similar response to that which Jesus received.

3. The parables Jesus spoke were placed in a religiously hostile context. If Jesus had spoken in complete openness, the force of His message and the speed of the message would have overwhelmed the audience. Parables allow a "soak in" property to the teaching. The worldview of a people is a very deeply held value that will often be defended. Parables come with "time-released abilities" that bring undeniable truth in very simple form that breaches the walls of worldview castles.

The NEW Parabolic Formula!
Special time-release prescription for those-hard to-reach worldviews

Questions

What does storytelling mean to you?

Is storytelling a relevant tool to convey the gospel today?

The Parables of Jesus

Parable	Mark	Matthew	Luke
New cloth on old garment	2:21	9:16	5:36
New wine in old wineskins	2:22	9:17	5:37-38
Sower and the soils	4:3-8, 14-20	13:3-8, 18-23	8:5-8, 11-15
Lamp under a bowl (or hidden)	4:21-22	5:14-15	8:16; 11:33
Growing seed	4:26-29		
Mustard seed	4:30-32	13:31-32	13:18-19
Tenants	12:1-11	21:33-44	20:9-18
Faithful and wise servant	12:42-48	24:45-51	
Fig tree	13:28-29	24:32-35	21:29-31
Watchful servants	13:35-37		12:35-40
Wise and foolish builders		7:24-27	6:47-49
Weeds		13:24-30, 36-43	
Yeast		13:33	13:20-21
Hidden treasure		13:44	
Valuable pearl		13:45-46	
Net		13:47-50	
House owner		13:52	
Lost sheep		18:12-14	15:4-7
Unmerciful servant		18:23-34	
Workers in the vineyard		20:1-16	

Parable (continued)	Mark	Matthew	Luke
Two sons		21:28-32	
Wedding banquet		22:2-14	
Ten virgins		25:1-13	
Talents		25:14-30	19:12-27
Sheep and goats		25:31-46	
Money lender			7:41-43
Good Samaritan			10:30-37
Friend in need			11:5-8
Rich fool			12:16-21
Unfruitful fig tree			13:6-9
Humble place at feast			14:7-14
Great banquet			14:16-24
Cost of discipleship			14:28-33
Lost coin			15:8-10
Lost son			15:11-32
Shrewd manager			16:1-8
Rich man and Lazarus			16:19-31
Master and his servants			17:7-10
Persistent widow			18:2-8
The Pharisee and the Tax Collector			18:9-14

4. The parables were usually told in order to convey one simple truth; Jesus teaching did not cover the fifty most urgent topics of the day. In our zeal to speak to people, especially to unreached people with hardened worldviews, we must learn the art of speaking about one single truth at a time. It is an instructional fallacy to teach people volumes, confusing and frustrating them so that they are unable to apply anything. Jesus wanted people to act upon what they heard (Mt. 7:26).

5. The parables are contained in Matthew, Mark, and Luke. A student of the Word must note the context in which the parables were given. Examination of similar parables from another gospel writer will shed light on their meaning. Mark's writings, thought to be the oldest, record early on the parables of Jesus. Matthew and Luke record several additional parables. Insight into Kingdom and mission is unavoidable as we examine the parables.

The Parables of the New Cloth and New Wine

Jesus addressed the question of why the Pharisees and the disciples of John fasted and why His disciples did not have the same outward tradition. Jesus did not inaugurate a fullness of the Kingdom by adding some finishing touches to the present work of the Pharisees. His two examples explained how new cloth on an old garment and new wine in old wineskins brought ruin. New wine, like the newness of the Kingdom, needs to be preserved. Placing this newness into an old form will bring an explosion and eventual loss. He clarified that the Kingdom of God must be understood as something new, not built into the human structure of the old. Jesus did not reject the prophets of old, but rather the human structures that would strangle the new life of the Kingdom. Questions of wineskins will become very important when Kingdom and mission confront non-biblical prophets and animistic systems.

The Kingdom must be built on its own foundation. The uniqueness of Jesus and the exclusiveness of the Son of God will be lost if He becomes another Hindu avatar, or just another great teacher in Buddhism.

Questions

Missiologists speak of categories of change for new believers. Some are part of a church community that speaks a foreign language, like a Pakistani believer in Jesus entering an English speaking church in Karachi. This is called a C-1 experience. C-2 could be using the local language, but with many foreign forms. This scale goes to a C-5 expression, where a person is a believer in his or her heart, but still totally affiliated with all former religious expressions, with no outward sign of change. What are the implications of new wine skins in light of C-5 contextual teaching?

What relation do new wine skins have with insider movements? Do wine skins need to be changed for any believer?

The Parable of the Sower and the Soils

In this parable we note how Jesus adjusted His teaching style to His audience. Matthew recorded two very important facts that give us a parameter from which we look at the parables. (1) He wrote that Jesus "... went out of the house and sat by the lake" (Mt. 13:1). The subsequent parables were therefore taught to the crowds, the general public who watched Jesus from a distance and who needed general teaching. (2) Matthew also wrote, "Then he left the crowd and went into the house. His disciples came . . . " (13:36). That next set of parables can be taken as teaching to an inner circle who needed a specific message.

Jesus called the parable of the sower and the soils (Mt.13:1-9; Mk. 4:1-9; Lk. 8:4-8) the key to understanding all of the other parables (Mk. 4:13). In this parable Jesus described four types of soil:

1.   Path—where Satan steals the seed

2.   Rocky—with no depth of root, quitters

3.   Thorny—representing the cares and worries of life which choke the seed

4.   Good soil—producing one hundred, or sixty, or thirty fold

These four types of soil represent the varieties of ways the good seed of the Word of God is either squandered or received. Some people have such familiarity with the ways of Satan that the seed never has the chance to root. Others are less resistant to Satan and overwhelmed with the cares of life. Some are very receptive and affect others with their newly transformed lives.

This parable describes our mission in the Kingdom. The Word of God must go out to all people. This is the will of a loving God. The response of individuals will only be known in time. Neither crops nor people can bear fruit instantly. The Spirit brings the growth (1 Co. 3:6). A people or nation should never be labeled with one of the four types of soil. For example, labeling a nation as stony soil because it "lacks depth" would be a serious missiological blunder. The parable is meant to give hope to Kingdom co-workers as we carry our inevitable burden for the many who will not respond. All types of people represented in this parable will be found in all locations!

Fruitfulness that comes from good soil will produce more grain for more sowing of the seed of the Word. This parable links the good soil to the harvest which is useful in developing more workers. Fruitful believers are naturally called to expand the Kingdom. Reproducing the seed of the Kingdom is a natural by-product of faith.

All believers must take the parable of the sower and the soils to a deeper level. Each disciple must be good soil--*perpetually* receiving, understanding, and sharing his or her faith. All of us must allow the paths that are hard packed, the rocks of shallowness, and the thorns of desires to be worked on and transformed by the Holy Spirit. This is not a one-time event or simply a sorting station without future hope. Our challenge is to remain good soil, to listen to the Master's voice, and to continue to bear fruit into our old age. Our response to the words spoken to us by God will reveal our hearts. His desire is to help us with our goal to remain fruitful.

The Hidden Lamp

A lamp does no good under a bowl or under a bed (Mk. 4:21). In a similar way, truth is useless unless given as a guide to those in darkness. Truth is not to be stored in a warehouse or used to judge the ignorance of the unguided. Truth must be proclaimed. Those given the light of God must be involved in dispersing that light to others. Disciples are to remain neither hidden nor quiet. This is not meant to judge the timing or style of proclamation used by a new people group. The danger is to wrongly believe that remaining silent in order to protect ourselves is sanctioned by God.

The Parable of the Tenants

Jesus spoke this parable against the Jewish religious system that usurped the authority of God over Israel and its true purpose (Mk. 12:12). Israel was no longer the servant of the Lord, obeying His bidding. The Jewish leaders ran their kingdom at will and rejected God's intervention. The reference to the vineyard owner giving the vineyard to others (Lk. 20:16) tells us that people from the nations will take up leadership positions in the Kingdom of God. This triggered a quick response from the crowd: When the people heard this, they said, "May this never be" (Lk. 20:16c)!

Mission always requires that we don't hold on to our work too tightly, remembering that the Holy Spirit is free to expand the work or raise up new leadership far more capable than our initial efforts. It is the Kingdom of God, not a kingdom of which we are in charge.

The Parable of the Wise and Foolish Builders

Jesus must be taken seriously. His teaching is to be applied to daily life (Mt. 7:24-27; Lk. 6:47-49). When hearing the words of Jesus, the common Arabic response is "kalaam saliim" or "really nice words." This parable speaks of lordship because it directs the hearer to action. Simply hearing the Word is a recipe for disaster. The call of God on our lives will beckon us to help people to live out the life of Jesus, not simply listen to His words. Mission requires implementation, not just proclamation.

We must allow time for people to understand the word of the Lord and to act upon that word. Expecting too many changes in a short amount of time leaves both the missionary and the listener frustrated. Growth requires the steady acceptance of the claims of God and subsequent change.

Parable of the Yeast

Yeast affects dough. There is a living, organic reaction in the right conditions. The Kingdom of God will spread; there is no stopping its advance (Mt. 13:33). The Kingdom does not change us immediately, but in time we should resemble Jesus. The life of Jesus introduced to a community will begin a process that brings transformation.

Yeast comes in many forms. Jesus told His disciples to "Be on your guard against the yeast of the Pharisees and Sadducees" (Mt. 16:6). This means that His disciples, including us, need to be on guard against influences that begin small but then permeate our lives with transforming power. Both the hunger for power and wealth we saw in the Sadducees, and the control and coldness we saw demonstrated by the Pharisees, will ruin our lives if we allow them to enter. Be on your guard! Types of music, fashion, and movies can also shape the way we live. Old influences, or old yeast types, need to be removed from our lives (Ex. 23:15). The ways of "Egypt," which were our former ways of living, need to give way to the freshness of the Spirit of God.

Yeast permeates the dough. Some believe they are God's children, though other forms of yeast are present and active in their lives. The question is heard, "What is wrong with living with my girlfriend?" Our lives do not have isolated compartments that shield one type of influence from another. Your behavior, when no one else is present, will describe the dominant working yeast in your life. It will describe your purpose in life and your morality before God.

Reflection

What types of "yeast" or influences does God want out of my life?
How can I be a better example of the Kingdom when questions of influence arise?

The Hidden Treasure and the Pearl

The parables of the treasure hidden in a field and the pearl of great price speak of the value of the Kingdom of heaven (Mt. 13:44-45). Two men sold all they had in order to obtain the treasure. The value of the Kingdom cannot be compared to any other treasure, relationship, or citizenship. These parables are precious to us in the Kingdom for two particular reasons:

* Believers need to be reminded that when life for the sake of the Kingdom becomes difficult, they still own the treasure. Paul knew of the Kingdom's value: ". . . having nothing, yet possessing everything" (2 Co. 6:10).

* Unreached people who hear the invitation to the Kingdom will need to count the cost. Our joy is to remind them of the words of Jesus that they will gain far more then they lose.

When you experience momentary frustrations, never lose your zeal to identify with the Creator and Sustainer of all things.

The House Owner

> Therefore every teacher of the law who has been instructed about the kingdom of heaven is like the owner of a house who brings out of his storeroom new treasures as well as old (Mt. 13:52).

Some translators render this passage: "All teachers of the law who become disciples of the kingdom . . .". The question arises as to whether teachers of the law in Jesus' day were trained in the life of the Kingdom and, conversely, if modern day disciples need a foundation in the Old Testament. The parable of the house owner challenges us to value all that God has spoken. Jesus is telling us that the knowledge of the Kingdom places a high value on the beauty of the Old Testament and a disciple's understanding of Kingdom values. Our message is solid when we bring treasures that burn within us today and confirm the words that our Creator spoke thousands of years ago. The true knowledge of the Kingdom brings awareness of what God is doing directly through the Son of God today. The Word of God is timeless and is never stale. It is very important that we understand the Bible to be God's compilation of one long story; it is not a set of rules only relevant for one period in time.

This parable also teaches us that His words are not contradictory. God does not speak a word that does away with former words. Jesus did not come to do away with former things as though God's word needed to be improved upon.

> Do not think that I have come to abolish the Law or the Prophets;
> I have not come to abolish them but to fulfill them. I tell you the
> truth, until heaven and earth disappear, not the smallest letter,
> not the least stroke of a pen, will by any means disappear from
> the Law until everything is accomplished. Anyone who breaks
> one of the least of these commandments and teaches others to
> do the same will be called least in the kingdom of heaven, but
> whoever practices and teaches these commands will be called
> great in the kingdom of heaven (Mt. 5:17-19).

Jesus is very clear that the truth of God and His ways are eternal. In contrast, the Qur'an teaches that God spoke in time periods, overriding what he previously had spoken with something of equal or greater worth (The Cow 2:106).

The Lost Sheep, Coin, and, Son

Luke gives a series of parables (Lk.15) that must be understood in light of mission. The parable of the lost sheep (Mt. 18:12-14) was given to the Pharisees who did not like the company Jesus was keeping with the tax collectors and the prostitutes. Jesus saw them as people who needed the Shepherd. The emphasis is on repentance that opens the door to be "found." God's mission is salvation. Search for the lost sheep brought the shepherd to leave the ninety-nine "in the open country" (Lk. 15:4) and to work hard to retrieve one that was lost. Never should the heart of the shepherd be scorned by those looking after the "ninety-nine" who are well taken care of. Care for church activities is not meant to overrun the shepherd's calling to seek for the lost.

In a similar way, the lost coin describes the untiring search for the one lost coin. Once again, the emphasis is on the sinner who repents. Both the sheep that was found and the coin that was found brought such excitement to the one searching; even friends and neighbors were called upon to join the party. We are told that heaven is having a party over the lost one brought home. This tells us that human joy is shallow if only looking at the present ingathering. Contrast this to God's yearning for the billions of unreached to be brought home.

The parable of the lost son is actually a story of a lost son and a hardened son. The older son was hardened in his own self-righteousness. The younger son was lost through leaving his father--his source and his protection. This parable gives us an understanding of God's heart that desires to bring His children home to purity and to safety. God seeks the lost and lets them know they are welcome. He also reasons with the hardened to understand His heart in order to see life with much greater mercy.

This parable was spoken to the Pharisees, members of the religious elite who were unconcerned for the needy sinners to come home to the Father. Can we care about the work of God's house and actually remain unconcerned for the lost? Is mission lost in religious duties? Do we know the pain in which people live who are separated from the Father?

The parables of Jesus should never be applied only to the Pharisees, while we attempt to avoid eye contact with the one speaking. We must hear Jesus' words that remind us that care for the present vineyard is not enough if the lost are absent from the Father.

The Parable of the Two Sons

The Kingdom of God is not comprised of those who know what is right. A major challenge is to bring people to do what is right before God and fellow humans. The parable of the two sons (Mt. 21:28-32) was a word spoken against the religious leaders who outwardly committed themselves to God but who inwardly were self-seeking. Jesus pointed out that ". . . tax collectors and the prostitutes are entering the Kingdom of God ahead of you" (v. 31). Those who openly did not intend to follow God are turning around and serving Him today. God looks for a life of action rather than of religious words. This brings us to question: "What is conversion?" God is not requiring a verbal confession that is not backed by a life of service. His mandate is to live for Him and call others to do the same. Therefore, we are not called to bring people only to the point of confession. A prayer to God for help in living for Him has value, as does confession of His Lordship. Yet the verbalization of faith is not a substitute for obedience in the Kingdom. Confusing these points will develop people who know the right answers but lack heart motivation to love God and their neighbor in practical ways.

Banquet Parables

Several mission points are noteworthy in the banquet parables. These points relate to the way people are invited, the type of individuals who are invited, and those who actually attend.

1. The parable of the **wedding banquet** in Matthew 22 speaks of both the coming marriage supper of the Lamb and the present life in the Kingdom of God. The invitation by the king in the parable to the banquet was not one to be refused. The neutral position for "invited but not accepting" was not an option. They faced the fate of the king's anger and total destruction. People invited into the family of the king made a mistake of eternal consequences by refusing his kindness.

This story gives us understanding regarding the future banquet in heaven and the gathering of people formerly thought unfit for the presence of the king during a lavish feast. The inclusion of unlikely guests is the joy for all who know the King. None are truly worthy of His invitation. The servants brought ". . . both good and bad, and the wedding hall was filled with guests" (v. 10). This challenges our concepts in mission because it is not only the good who come to the banquet, but rather all those who respond to the King's invitation. Our job is to invite and to welcome all to His banquet. This is clearly an aspect of our call in mission. We welcome all and allow God to be the one who changes them.

2. Note that Jesus did not teach in a random fashion. Jesus ate at the house of a well-known Pharisee on a Sabbath. The scene is set in a tense atmosphere where ". . . he was carefully watched" (Lk. 14:1). In this banquet setting, Jesus took the opportunity to minister healing to a man. He also observed the behavior of people in the Pharisee's house, watching how they looked for seats of honor. Mission requires that we listen to the Father and obey His direction. Rather than fitting in with the common behavior and culture, we need to take time to observe people and to pray for healing when asked to do so. It is in this context that Jesus told a

story about seeking a **humble seat at a wedding**. His principles of the Kingdom came through in each situation. The lessons for us are to be applied.

3. Within the same context of the banquet in the Pharisee's home, Jesus continued on with the parable of the **great banquet**. He delivered His stories in a framework that gripped people's hearts. This parable gives us the reasons why those originally invited to the banquet had refused to come (Lk. 14:16-24). The excuses given were those of purchasing property, improving their businesses, or getting married. Obeying the King, rather than tending to personal affairs, is demanded of all. Luke adds, ". . . not one of those men who were invited will get a taste of my banquet" (v. 24). Jesus gave a message that showed God's invitation to be commonplace to some. Many of the Jewish leaders were self-centered rather than Kingdom-centered.

God wants the banquet hall filled. The requirement of us as servants is to be about the Master's business, which is inviting people to the banquet. The life we live for God today will certainly prepare us for meeting the King. The poor, the crippled, the blind, and the lame are society's rejects. This reference contrasts those who considered themselves worthy with those considered unworthy. Those whom the religious community considered less than worthy were the underprivileged of their own society and people of Samaritan and Gentile backgrounds. Although not clearly stated as Samaritans or Gentiles, the contrast of those initially invited and those invited later is very clear.

4. The parable of the **ten virgins** describes the long wait for the bridegroom to arrive for the wedding banquet. This was not a separation between the people of God and the people of the world. All ten virgins were waiting for the return of the bridegroom, and all ten fell asleep. The extra supply of oil carried by the five wise attendants speaks of the anointing of the Spirit that can carry us through difficult times. Consistency in prayer, a disciplined life of service, and keeping short accounts with sin invites the Spirit of God rather than grieves Him. The fullness of the Spirit, and an extra portion as well, are required to truly meet the bridegroom. This fullness is to be ours today because it describes the reality of the Kingdom. All the virgins had a fullness of the Spirit described as a burning lamp. Only five of them planned to refill their lamps. A fullness of the Holy Spirit does not mean crossing the finish line or entering a special membership club. The Spirit energizes our service, which means we need to give attention to His fullness in our lives.

Stewardship Parables

The **parable of the talents** speaks of properly handling that which is entrusted to us and the Master's reward to the faithful (Mt. 25:14-30). Matthew follows the parable of the ten virgins with a warning to invest the gift that God has given each of us. Any investment brings some type of return. Investing your time, your language abilities, your heart for the needy, your financial gifts to advance the Kingdom--all bring return for the investment God has in your life. Storing your gift in fear of the future, or simply resting in the fact you have an anointing, brings the crushing rebuke of the Master. Similar in meaning to the parable of the virgins, we are warned not to receive the gift of the Spirit without applying His gifts for return. Reminiscent of the five loaves and two fish, Jesus wants us to give what we have in order for Him to do what we cannot.

Luke takes us to Zacchaeus' home in Jericho where Jesus is en route to Jerusalem (Lk. 19:1-10). Jesus arrived at the sycamore tree that Zacchaeus had climbed in order to see Him. Jesus looked at Zacchaeus and called him by name, asking him to come down from the tree. Jesus wanted to spend the day at his house. Note the cultural context: Jesus invited himself to someone's house. This meant "quick thinking" hospitality on the part of the host. This Middle Eastern setting challenges western planning and desire for control. The guest honors a person by choosing him or her as the host. Tribal conflicts can be defused when a prominent person asks a member of the opposing tribe to host him. Receiving hospitality is honorable, but humbling. Granting hospitality is a privilege that bestows honor upon the host.

Jesus honored Zacchaeus. We read, "All the people saw this and began to mutter, 'He has gone to be the guest of a "sinner"'" (v. 7). The entire crowd murmured at the honor showed to the local rich and despised tax collector. The equivalent in our thinking would be if Jesus passed through and visited a wealthy yet question-able lawyer or a dirty politician. "Why visit that scum?" We wrongly expect Jesus to gravitate to the homes of good people rather than offer salvation to the lives of the spiritually needy. Jesus was focused on granting life to people rather than guarding His reputation before the self-righteous. This must guide our direction as we express the Kingdom of God.

The **parable of the minas** was told by Jesus directly after His encounter with the repentant Zacchaeus for several reasons. Luke tells us that some expected the Kingdom to arrive with Jesus entering Jerusalem (Lk. 19:11). This parable tells us that the noble was going away for a long time. Jesus, like the noble, was to be pronounced King from a higher power, not by the local authorities.

The noble distributed about three months wages into the hands of ten servants (Lk. 19:11-27; The Full Life Study Bible, pg. 1564). He commanded them to put their minas to work. The message is to invest your life with that which God has given you. Neither parable hints at faithful servants investing their God-given resources and losing them. Neither will our investment in the Kingdom, for Jesus' sake, ever be able to be lost. Loss is only possible when we do not purposefully work with the Kingdom in mind. The reward given by the returning King hints at our ruling and reigning with Him in the coming Kingdom.

Separation Parables

The Weeds

The Word of God produces fruit. The seed of the enemy also produces fruit (Mt. 13:24-30). Bad fruit is the result of starting with the wrong seed or corrupting the truth of the Word of God with human philosophies. The owner's servants were amazed that weeds had come up in a field containing good seed (v. 27). There was surprise in the servants' voices, wondering how the work of the enemy had taken place unnoticed. The Spirit desires to use our lives to spread the good seed of the gospel. It is possible that our lives could be misunderstood and bring forth fruit we were not expecting. The challenge is before us to 1) preach the purity of the whole Word of God, 2) allow ourselves to be transformed by the Lord and not be a negative excuse for anyone's lifestyle of sin, and 3) not blame ourselves for weeds or corrupted philosophies that come up in people's lives.

The Net

The parable of the net has a similar message (Mt. 13:47-50). Separating the weeds from the grain and the good fish from the bad is a job left to higher powers. It is not for us to sort through all of the motives, nor set all records straight. The mission worker must take encouragement from God's ultimate authority. Our task is to continue spreading the "seed" or the "net" so that a harvest takes place.

Question

What can I get from the story of Zacchaeus?

(1) Jesus knows us by name – even the less honorable.
(2) He searches for the lost.
(3) Jesus bestows honor on our lives.
(4) We visit people and bestow honor on them in Jesus' name (Mt. 20, traveling from Jerusalem to Jericho). This is mission "along the way" in our daily lives.

The Sheep and the Goats

This parable vividly describes the sorting at the time of judgment, between the people of God who lived for Him and those who knew of the Lord yet lived for themselves (Mt. 25:31-46). The sheep separated on His right blessed the hungry, the thirsty, the new person in town, the naked, the sick, and the prisoner. We need to get this picture clearly in our hearts: The sheep are involved in blessing people wherever they find them--which is an instant correlation to the mission of the Kingdom. The sheep of God actually did something for other people. They were called the righteous and were awarded eternal life. Matthew places this parable after the parable of the ten virgins (one filling of oil is not sufficient) and the parable of the talents (make use of your anointing). The context of these three parables highlights what the Master needs to see in our lives.

The Word of God must be taken as a whole. Paul writes,

> That if you confess with your mouth, "Jesus is Lord," and believe
> in your heart that God raised him from the dead, you will be
> saved (Ro. 10:9).

Too often this encouragement toward faith is taken to push people toward a confession or knowledge of a creed. Jesus urges us to get involved with people and their needs. A sign of salvation is renewed awareness of needs and appropriate action. A heart in tune with God will see Jesus in need, rather than just another needy person.

Eternal judgment was given to those who saw the needy and did nothing. It appears from this text that they called Jesus, Lord, but to no avail. A cold, uninvolved heart does not represent God's Kingdom.

The Good Samaritan

The parable of the Good Samaritan was told in the context of a Jewish lawyer asking Jesus how one inherits eternal life (Lk. 10:25). This parable clearly states that loving one's neighbor is not conditional on being part of the correct religious community. Priests and Levities were unquestionably part of the religious system, most likely ceremonially clean, and yet avoiding human need. Samaritans were considered ceremonially unclean, cultists, and unpatriotic to the Jewish cause. The definite hero in this story was the Samaritan who was an outcast to Jewish society. It cost the Samaritan time and finances to help the robbed and beaten individual back to life.

The mission of God calls us to serve the human need we find before us. We, like the Samaritan, will find inconvenience, financial pressure, and stains on our car seats when we help those in need. The needs of people do not come at convenient times in life. Their financial needs often come when we are already challenged to make ends meet. The image of the Samaritan helping someone in great need must remain in our minds.

Kingdom Values and Worldly Values – Luke

Honor before men--putting on a good front--has the marks of that which is detestable before God (Lk. 16:15). Impressing God is not going to be that which impresses the human heart which is so corrupted. Hollywood beauty and highly paid sports personalities do not draw God's attention. These examples will have their equivalent in every society and must be addressed by the advancing Kingdom. A heart after God will be drawn to that which interests God. A heart that loves God will serve God. His heart is inclined toward those who fear Him (Pr. 14:26). On the other hand, those who love the flesh and the world are at war with God (1 Jn. 2:15-17). The draw to possess things, the unbridled pull of extramarital sexual attraction, and the desire to "one-up" someone is from a corrupted world at odds with its Creator. Whoever claims to live in Him must walk as Jesus did (1 Jn. 2:6).

Created in the image of God is not to be confused with the present state of human nature. Our fulfillment comes through life in the freedom and boundaries given by the Creator. Returning to His values brings peace to our lives and to the community in which we live.

Conclusion

Jesus taught His disciples and the crowds in a variety of ways. He empowered His disciples to carry on His teaching ministry and His vision for the entire world in need of discipleship.

The teaching of Jesus cuts against the direction in which the world and dark spiritual powers have distorted the values of the Creator. His teachings establish a true foundation and bring life to those who hear and obey His message.

The Good News of the Kingdom of God has been proclaimed from the time of John the Baptist (Lk. 16:16-17). The Good News is not in conflict with the message of the law or any of the prophets.

Chapter 25 - The Ministry of Jesus

The ministry of Jesus fulfills several Old Testament themes. Aspects of His dynamic presence are foreseen in Old Testament personalities. The roles of prophet, priest, king, and servant, previously attributed to the Messiah to come, will find fulfillment in Jesus. We must be careful not to distort our vision of Him by relegating Him to one particular role. We need to examine all of the various aspects of Jesus' life and then ask ourselves how we can follow in His footsteps.

Old Testament Ministry Types

Jesus as Prophet, yet Greater

The ministry and life of Jesus reminds us of some of the prophets of old. The wandering of Abraham through a land he did not possess (Ge. 12:7) is similar to the life of Jesus who said, "Foxes have holes and birds of the air have nests, but the Son of Man has no place to lay his head" (Lk. 9:58). This value resonates with us as mission people, knowing that we have our inheritance with Him, yet remaining strangers and wanderers on this earth. We agree with the writer of the book of Hebrews that as people of faith we are "aliens and strangers on earth" (Heb. 11:13).

Reflection

Mission brings us into an "alien and stranger" mode that does not dissipate upon return to our birth nation. Pilgrimage with God, rather than travel abroad, sets our course for His Kingdom.

Abraham could never offer eternal life as Jesus did on numerous occasions (i.e. Jn. 8:51). This offer drew the Jews to question Jesus as to whether He thought He was greater than Abraham. To this Jesus replied, "Your father Abraham rejoiced at the thought of seeing my day; he saw it and was glad" (Jn. 8:56). These words set the tone for the greatness of Jesus to which Abraham looked forward with anticipation. Jesus went on to clearly reveal His identity in the same encounter: "I tell you the truth," Jesus answered, "before Abraham was born, I am" (Jn. 8:58)! In this Jesus stated His eternal nature and named Himself as the "I AM," or the one who now held the power of life within His being. He identified Himself as the one who spoke to Moses at the burning bush. This was more than they could stand to hear. We in mission are not greater than Abraham, but ***our message is greater*** in that its conclusions bring all nations into covenant with the I AM.

Moses was similar to Jesus in that he was hidden after his birth while boys around Him were murdered. Moses was a prophet who repeatedly spoke God's words to Pharaoh, "Let my people go" (Ex. 5:1; 7:16; 8:1; 8:20; 9:1; 9:13). Jesus also came to "proclaim freedom for the prisoners" (Lk. 4:18-19), all who are held captive to sin. But Jesus did not square off against a Gentile king, as Moses had faced Pharaoh. He faced the Jewish religious system that burdened people (Mt. 23:4). He also confronted the devil who degrades and enslaves people created in the image of God (Lk. 13:16).

Jesus is greater than Moses in several ways. First, Moses led people away from a geographic region of slavery and toward their promised land, though their hearts remained bent toward their own needs. Jesus leads people away from self-centered lives, regardless of location, into a promised Kingdom of sacrifice and commitment to God. God gave the law through Moses that was designed to expose the errors of our hearts, but Jesus fulfilled the following prophetic words:

- People would one day rely on the Lord (Isa. 10:20).

- The burden would lift from their shoulders (10:27).

- The Root of Jesse would stand as a banner for the people (11:10), which meant that Jesse's descendant would be the direction and hope of the people.

- God's anger would turn from us (12:1).

- We would give thanks to God for what He has done and make Him known in the nations (12:4).

- God would then give people a heart to know Him (Jer. 24:7).

One far greater than Moses leads us to daily find freedom from the slavery of sin and the lure of the world. One greater than Moses leads us to proclaim God's goodness among the nations.

Elijah traveled repeatedly throughout the land in a prophetic ministry similar to the ministry of Jesus. Elijah ministered to a widow in Zarephath, bringing provision and the resurrection of her son (I Ki. 17). This was similar to Jesus traveling to the region of Tyre and Sidon to heal a demon-possessed girl (Mt. 15:21-28). The resurrection of the Shunammite's son through Elisha's ministry (2 Ki. 4:18-36) took place two kilometers from where Jesus raised the widow's son in Nain (Lk.

7:11-17). Elisha brought healing to Naaman the leper (2 Ki. 5:14); Jesus healed ten lepers simultaneously (Lk.17:14). Elisha ordered ". . . twenty loaves of barley bread baked with the first ripe grain . . ." to be placed before one hundred men (2 Ki. 4:42-44). Jesus had a great crowd follow Him because they had seen the miraculous signs. Although each of the four Gospels presents the story, John gives us the details. "Here is a boy with five small barley loaves and two small fish" (Jn. 6:1-13). These overlapping similarities brought people to say: "A great prophet has appeared among us" (Lk. 7:16). They were correct in recognizing the places of miracles and types of people to whom Jesus ministered, yet they missed the much greater significance of Jesus, the Anointed One.

Some prophets came with specific words for kings, as did Elijah and Elisha. Some, like Isaiah and Jeremiah, had words for the nation of Israel. A ministry to political leaders, or to Israel, or to another nation like Jonah fulfilled, does not make one greater or lesser. Jesus claimed He was greater than Jonah (Mt. 12:41), which meant His position was not to be compared with another prophet on a human level. Jesus came as the fulfillment to the prophetic utterances, rather than a human prophet with a particular message. All that Jesus spoke must therefore be taken in the context of Jesus as the fulfillment of God's heart for the nations.

Jesus as Priest

A priest is one who officiates at the altar and mediates between God and the people. Priests were consecrated to serve in a specific capacity before God (Ex. 28:3), and they made sacrifice for their own sin before making atonement for the people (Lev. 9:7; 16:6).

The priest would pronounce a person clean or unclean in relation to infectious skin diseases. Jesus proclaimed a person healed, at times telling them to not sin again. We see this in the case of the paralytic at the Bethesda pool (Jn. 5:14). Other times He healed and told the people to show themselves to the priest, as in the case of lepers (Mt. 8:4; Lk. 17:12). His words did not conflict with the prescribed priestly duties, either by declaring the leper clean, sacrificing animals, the sprinkling of blood, or anointing with oil. Jesus was the high priest of the New Covenant and not in competition to take over the officiating of the Old Covenant. The introduction of the New Covenant made the Old obsolete.

Jesus as high priest of the New Covenant declared, "It is finished" (Jn. 19:30). By this He declared atonement to be complete for the sins of the entire world. We are declared clean before our Heavenly Father, before other believers, before the world, and before demonic powers. As high priest, He pronounces over us that we are clean, which is a declaration that allows us into the fellowship of God. Jesus is " . . . greater than the temple" (Mt. 12:6), which formerly stood as the one place for both atonement for sin and meetings between God and priests on behalf of the people. Jesus is greater than the Temple and greater than the sum of the Old Covenant because:

1. Through Him complete atonement has been made, once for all human kind.

2. He is the source of fellowship between God and all people. He is not limited, as is the Temple, to a geographic location.

Jesus prayed as priest of the New Covenant (Jn. 17:1-5). He did not confess His own sin, but rather declared the fullness of the completed work that the Father had given Him to accomplish. He prayed for His disciples to be protected, recognizing that both the world and the evil one hate His disciples. He prayed that His followers would be one as He and the Father were one, and for the future generations of believers to believe as the current disciples believed. As high priest of the New Covenant, He saw the expansion of the community of believers who would fulfill the vision of Habakkuk to cover the entire world (Hab. 2:14). We enter into the work of the Father and the priestly work of Jesus by praying and working for this expansion of the community of believers worldwide.

The high priest of the Old Covenant met the high priest of the New Covenant during the trial with the Sanhedrin (Mt. 26:57-68; Jn. 18:19-24). Those officiating for the Old Covenant declared the words of Jesus to be blasphemy and called for His elimination. **The two covenants are not simultaneously viable.** One covenant must rule while the other is declared obsolete by the One making the covenant, God Himself.

The high priest of the New Covenant addressed the central nature of meeting with God at the time of His death. Moses wrote of the solemn nature of the yearly atonement made on the tenth day of the seventh month (Lev. 16:29). The high priest of the Old Covenant made atonement for the sins of the people once a year, which in itself points to the temporary nature of that atonement. God commanded:

> Put the altar in front of the curtain that is before the ark of the Testimony—before the atonement cover that is over the Testimony—where I will meet with you. Aaron must burn fragrant incense on the altar every morning when he tends the lamps. He must burn incense again when he lights the lamps at twilight so incense will burn regularly before the LORD for the generations to come. Do not offer on this altar any other incense or any burnt offering or grain offering, and do not pour a drink

offering on it. Once a year Aaron shall make atonement on its horns. This annual atonement must be made with the blood of the atoning sin offering for the generations to come. It is most holy to the LORD (Ex. 30:6-10).

Jesus fulfilled the requirements of the Passover lamb and the atonement for the people in a single day, which fulfilled the prophecy that God would remove the sins of the people in one day (Zec. 3:9). He entered the holy of holies, opening the way for our fellowship with God at the mercy seat by tearing the Temple curtain in two from top to bottom (Mt. 27:51). This place "where I will meet with you" was now accessible to all by virtue of the sacrifice placed upon its altar.

Jesus the King

Moses rejoiced that "the Lord will reign for ever and ever" (Ex. 15:18), knowing that God is truly over all nations and kings of the earth. The specifics of this coming ruler are clearly seen from a variety of angles in Old Testament prophetic writings. Isaiah tells us that His rule will:

- Expand in both magnitude and in quality of peace

- Reign on David's throne

- Bring justice and righteousness and be upheld forever

- Be established by God Himself (Isa. 9:7)

Jeremiah wrote that the "righteous branch of David" would rule with wisdom and fairness throughout the land (Jer. 23:5). The angel Gabriel announced to Mary the incarnation and the eternal reign of Jesus.

> But the angel said to her, "Do not be afraid, Mary, you have found favor with God. You will be with child and give birth to a son, and you are to give him the name Jesus. He will be great and will be called the Son of the Most High. The Lord God will give him the throne of his father David, and he will reign over the house of Jacob forever; his kingdom will never end" (Lk. 1:30-33).

The anticipation of the coming King does not often help us see the time between the birth of the King, the sacrifice made by the King, the expanse of the realm and scope of the Kingdom, and the fullness of His kingly rule.

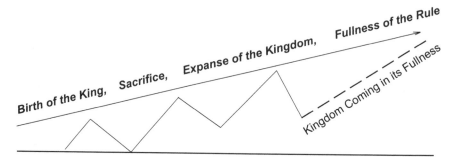

One of the mistakes of God's people has been taking an aspect of the prophetic promise and reading all events in light of the one promise. The surprise of the Messiah is that He combines so many aspects of God's work, opening doors of transformation while establishing an eternal Kingdom.

His rule as King was not like other kings before him. David's son, as was previously stated, was one with a heart for God's purposes. He was also the great shepherd, reflecting David's background and heart for the people. The Messiah was not Saul's son; one who was deaf to the commands of God and willing to erect a monument to himself. At the same time He was not simply a king in the line of David, because the magnitude of His Kingdom was not to be compared with any earthly kingdom.

> The Queen of the South will rise at the judgment with this generation and condemn it; for she came from the ends of the earth to listen to Solomon's wisdom, and now one greater than Solomon is here (Mt. 12:42; Lk. 11:31).

Jesus cannot be compared with any earthly king. "Greater than Solomon" clearly states that He is greater in wisdom, greater in majesty, and greater in understanding than the greatest king we are able to imagine.

Jesus as Servant King

The servanthood of Messiah and His ruling majesty are at times difficult to separate. God frequently referred to King David as His servant. The Lord's heart of compassion for the fading kingdoms of Israel and Jerusalem was because of "David my servant" (1 Ki. 11). God's protection over Jerusalem was also because of His memory of closeness to David (2 Ki. 19:34). God's compassion for us and for the nations is because of His Servant King Jesus. The Servant King is one who reflects the heart of God by having the same longings and aspirations. The reference to "David my servant" also brings us to the Chosen One who will establish the eternal Kingdom.

> You said, "I have made a covenant with my chosen one,
> I have sworn to David my servant,
> I will establish your line forever
> and make your throne firm through all generations" (Ps. 89:3-4).

David died and was buried in Jerusalem. His line lives on through the lives of those "holding to" the Messiah. The specific word of his throne established through all generations brings us to the significance of the eternal Kingdom. God, who is eternal, will Himself establish the throne of the Servant King.

The Servant King was referred to in prophecies as "David" because He was in the lineage of David through adoption. The references to "anointing" are references to the *messah*, the semitic term for the choosing and setting apart of one for the task. Different kings and prophets were anointed for their particular tasks, signifying God's choosing and His approval. The reference to The Anointed One, the Messiah, is reserved for One and One alone. There have been several anointed kings, but there is only one Messiah.

Further references in Psalm 89 speak of God sustaining the Anointed One, and that no enemy will subject Him to tribute. Followers of Jesus could easily have placed this in the immediate context of Messiah and mistakenly believed that His role as leader was to overthrow all foreign powers. Within this same passage was the promise that no one could oppress Him, and that God would strike down His enemies. The complexity of this prophecy is that it must be taken together in the broader context of other passages referring to the Suffering Servant and not simply to the Servant King.

> I have found David my servant;
> with my sacred oil I have anointed him.
> My hand will sustain him;
> surely my arm will strengthen him.
> No enemy will subject him to tribute;
> no wicked man will oppress him.
> I will crush his foes before him
> and strike down his adversaries.
> My faithful love will be with him,
> and through my name his horn will be exalted.
> I will set his hand over the sea,

his right hand over the rivers.
He will call out to me, 'You are my Father,
my God, the Rock my Savior.'
I will also appoint him my firstborn,
the most exalted of the kings of the earth.
I will maintain my love to him forever,
and my covenant with him will never fail.
I will establish his line forever,
his throne as long as the heavens endure (Ps. 89:20-29).

This reference is truly a description of the eternal, firmly established rule of the Messiah King who will one day come in fullness. Today we are subjects of the King to whom we offer our loyalty, yet we are still subjected to the powers and hatred of the world and the enemy of God. At times, we still suffer harsh tribute for His name and feel the sting of oppression set against the Church. The Kingdom of God is among us and, at the same time, its fullness is yet to come.

The titles King and Servant King leave us wondering when His Kingdom will be established. Jesus said that "one greater than Solomon is here (Mt. 12:42), which means now. It does not say "will one day come." With the current state of human affairs, the role of Jesus as King is presently more difficult to grasp than His role as priest. He reigns in our hearts as King and Lord, yet we do not see the fullness of the Kingdom. We join with His instruction to pray,

> ". . . your kingdom come, your will be done on earth as it is in heaven" (Mt. 6:10).

We are captivated by the reality that each attribute of the Incarnate Jesus must come in fullness. Just as He completely fulfilled the priestly role of making atonement for our sin, He will also one day completely fulfill the role of the eternal King whose Kingdom will have no end. Note that the Kingdom in its fullness will also require judgment in fullness. He in His mercy is not yet unleashing "the day of vengeance of our God" (Isa. 61:2). This part of the Isaiah 61 prophecy was not quoted by Jesus in His Nazareth address (Lk. 4:16-21) because He went on to say, "Today this scripture is fulfilled in your hearing" (v. 21). Each part of Isaiah's prophetic words will find fulfillment, but not at the same time. We can know with certainty that His day of vengeance is coming, just as the day of atonement and the days of healing have also come.

Isaiah

The Spirit of the Sovereign LORD is on me,
because the LORD has anointed me
to preach good news to the poor.
He has sent me to bind up the broken-hearted,
to proclaim freedom for the captives
and release from darkness for the prisoners,
to proclaim the year of the LORD's favor

Luke

The Spirit of the Lord is on me,

because he has anointed me
to preach good news to the poor.
He has sent me to proclaim freedom for the prisoners
and recovery of sight for the blind,
to release the oppressed,

to proclaim the year of the Lord's favor

Then he rolled up the scroll, gave it back to the attendant and sat down. The eyes of everyone in the synagogue were fastened on him, and he began by saying to them, **"Today this scripture is fulfilled in your hearing"** (Lk. 4:18-21, emphasis mine).

In another time

and the day of vengeance of our God (Isa. 61:1-2).

Jesus as Suffering Servant

The Suffering Servant brings a new set of attributes to our minds and humbles and affects us in ways that the titles 'King' and 'Servant King' are unable to do. Samuel was a type of suffering servant, hearing God speak and knowing the old system represented in Eli had been judged (1 Sa. 3:10-16). Jesus was the son in His Father's house who knew of the coming judgment on the house of Israel (Mt. 23:37). The Suffering Servant is pictured in David who was anointed, yet another would not recognize his anointing (1 Sa. 15:28; 18:8; 20:31). In a similar way, Jesus is the Anointed One, but His kingdom has not yet been fully realized. The anointed David fled with people cursing and mocking his sad state of life (2 Sa. 16:5-8). Jesus also endured mocking during His Sanhedrin trial (Mt. 26:67-68), His Roman judgment (27:27-31), and His execution (27:32-44). Although similarities exist between Jesus and Old Testament types, the Suffering Servant reaches a deeper level.

Isaiah spoke of a servant who should not be afraid because God would help him (Isa. 41:8-10). This word in Isaiah can be read with different emphases: (1) God is always victorious and will crush the servant's enemies, or (2) God will help the servant and bring victory through the shame, strife, and crushing blows. Both are actually true, but patience is required to understand both aspects of God's strength and victory.

Isaiah tells us that this Suffering Servant will be filled with the Holy Spirit and will bring justice to the nations (Isa. 42:1). The Suffering Servant will be set aside for major ministries, which Matthew picks up on and to which he makes reference (Mt. 12:18-21). Isaiah pushes the theme further and equates the Suffering Servant with the New Covenant.

> I, the LORD, have called you in righteousness;
> I will take hold of your hand.
> I will keep you and will make you
> to be a covenant for the people
> and a light for the Gentiles,
> to open eyes that are blind,
> to free captives from prison
> and to release from the dungeon those who sit in darkness
> (Isa. 42:6-7).

The Suffering Servant would be made a covenant for the people, including the Gentiles. This was a change in covenant coming by the hand of the Lord. The Old Covenant required the sacrifice of animals on a regular basis; the New Covenant was offering the Servant. Healing that restores the physical and spiritual sight of the blind would come through the Suffering Servant of the Covenant. Freedom for the captives who are prisoners of people, of psychological prisons, or of spiritual dungeons would be found in the Suffering Servant. The Servant and the Covenant were linked in the words of Jesus, "just as the Son of Man did not come to be served, but to serve, and to give his life as a ransom for many" (Mt. 20:28). He said that His service included giving His life as a ransom. The image of a ransom helps us understand the freedom we obtain through Him.

Isaiah continued with this theme, describing the servant who would be "lifted up" and whose "appearance was so disfigured beyond that of any man" (Isa. 52:13-14). The burden and pain of this servant is difficult to put together with the image of the victorious King. It is a description of the Messiah who will bring freedom to those living in darkness to the ends of the earth. This Servant was "crushed for our iniquities" and "by his wounds we are healed" (Isa. 53:4-5). The depiction of the cross and the image of the Servant who willingly endured pain on our behalf was prophetically laid out for our understanding. For us in mission, it is necessary to tie the historic Messiah of the gospels to numerous ancient prophetic records.

Jesus told us that greatness and servanthood are linked in His Kingdom (Mt. 20:26), which is not like the kingdoms of earth. Servants and rulers outside of His Kingdom on earth presently have very little in common. The greatness of His Kingdom must require a servanthood that is greater than any human servant. Just as He is greater than the Temple, He is also more deeply committed than any servant. Part of our calling in Jesus is to reflect the depth of servanthood that brings blessing to the nations. Jesus said that the greatest disciple is the one who serves (23:11). Nations need servants to sort out the multitude of problems associated with selfishness. Servants are needed in manufacturing, in agriculture, to study linguistics and cultural mores, to explore uses of natural resources, to seek justice for the oppressed--and they do so for the King.

Practical examples of service during Jesus' ministry were expressed in healing all who came to Him (Mt. 8:16; 12:15), and in even making sure that the wine for the wedding was sufficient (Jn. 2:1-11). All of us experience fatigue in ministry and set boundaries that protect us from burnout. Jesus seemed to throw Himself into any ministry made available by the Father. His service was expressed in washing the disciples' feet (Jn. 13:4-17). This gives us a visual for serving others through washing dishes, vacuuming carpets, and child care. The Kingdom of God is expressed through the humility of a tremendous servant; not simply by a great King or a priestly duty.

New Kingdom Ministries

Some aspects of Messiah that prophetically describe His appearance do not have Old Testament personalities which reflect His likeness. The presence of Jesus brought healing on a scale that no previous man or woman of God had known. Jesus also gathered a following like an evangelistic shepherd who had no counterpart in the Old Testament. His teaching ministry conveyed the truth of the Kingdom of God to the masses--outside of Temple grounds and on any day of the year. His teaching ministry also marked Him as 'sent from God' outside of the bounds of the Jewish traditions.

Messiah, Our Healer

The search to understand the healing ministry of the Messiah takes us back to Old Testament statements that describe His coming. Jesus Himself understood the necessity of His life in light of prophetic writings. He related the following message to the disciples of John, linking His ministry to the words of Isaiah 35. The signs, wonders, and spread of the good news of the Kingdom point to this being the Anointed One of God. Jesus was indeed the Messiah.

> When John heard in prison what Christ was doing, he sent his
> disciples to ask him, "Are you the one who was to come, or
> should we expect someone else?"
> Jesus replied, "Go back and report to John what you hear and
> see: The blind receive sight, the lame walk, those who have
> leprosy are cured, the deaf hear, the dead are raised, and the
> good news is preached to the poor. Blessed is the man who does
> not fall away on account of me" (Mt. 11:2-6).

The healing ministry of Messiah included every sickness, regardless of its progression. His healing ministry was far more pronounced than every example combined in the Old Testament. There was no escaping the fact that the Kingdom had come in new levels through Jesus' ministry. We, too, are called to pray for the sick (Mt. 10:1; Lk. 9:1). This must be part of the presentation of the Gospel among the people to whom we are called. We pray in faith, though we do not always experience the results for which we hope. Obedience is praying; the results are up to God. The excitement of healings, combined with the news of the Messiah's life given for ours, is transforming. Healings bring confirmation that Jesus and the Kingdom of God are among us.

With the order to "heal every disease and sickness" (Mt. 10:1), we can draw the conclusion that medical training and hospitals are a continuation of the blessing of God. Medical research to counteract and eradicate diseases is the will of God. Although Jesus did not concentrate on human level intelligence in bringing a cure for all diseases, He did tell us to expect to go beyond His ministry (Jn. 14:12). We should not miss the beauty of God's calling to all types of professions by wrongly believing that only miraculous healings through prayer are a sign of the Kingdom. Destroying the works of the Devil in the form of disease is the will of God. Simply praying against a particular disease or disorder will relegate the Church and Mission to a mystical level and will allow accusations of living apart from reality.

Jesus the Evangelistic Shepherd

The Lord was referred to as the Shepherd of Israel (Ps. 80:1). This brings to our minds the tender leadership attributes of gathering, protecting, and providing. These were evident throughout the course of Israel's existence when they were guided and rebuked by the unseen hand of the Shepherd. A human equivalent is difficult to find. David was a shepherd and later a king. Moses led the people, but in many instances they simply followed out of a lack of other choices.

Jesus spoke to multitudes of people. He had an attraction that drew people from many walks of life. Some of the attraction was the result of His ability to heal every disease. The scene was always very tender, with Jesus the Shepherd taking care of all who came to His care.

> Large crowds from Galilee, the Decapolis, Jerusalem, Judea and
> the region across the Jordan followed him (Mt. 4:25).

The attraction to the miracles was not always from a pure motive, or even out of curiosity. Jesus fed the five thousand men (and the women and children in the crowd) who were all there to witness His miraculous ministry (Jn. 6:1-13). The miracles and the bread drew people to crave such a King as this, who could always provide for both their physical and spiritual needs (v. 14).

The breadth of Jesus' ministry as an evangelist and shepherd spoke to entire cities like Korazin and Bethsaida (Mt. 11:21). These examples stretch our understanding from a personal or friendship evangelism to one of proclaiming a message to the masses. His bold pronouncements were plain for all to hear, especially the weak and the downcast who came en masse to hear His words. Jesus sowed very broadly, stating publicly that He would give rest to all who would come to Him--including the weak and those carrying heavy burdens (v. 28). This offer of rest for their souls or, in other words, eternal life to all who would listen and believe, did not require great previous biblical knowledge. We must share not only the message, but also the method Jesus used on a large scale to offer rest for souls.

Jesus as shepherd and evangelist was also able to reach out to the individual as He did at the well in Samaria, quickly offering the woman eternal life (Jn. 4:10). His attractiveness was the compassion He offered to both individuals and to groups of people, likening them to "sheep without a shepherd" (Mt. 9:36).

Peter spoke for the disciples in their commitment to follow Jesus because Jesus had the words of eternal life (Jn. 6:68). This is our challenge to also speak with words that offer life and healing in our day to people who are still harassed and wandering.

Jesus the Teacher

Jesus taught on a scale beyond any teacher in the Old Testament. Ezra's teaching ministry brought a rebuke to the gathered assembly at one point (Ez. 10:10-11). Jesus taught in boats, on land, in the northern regions of Galilee, and throughout Judea. His ministry engaged people with illustrations from farming methods (Mt.

3:3-23) to stories of hidden treasures (v. 44). He taught in the home of a disciple (Mt. 8:14), in the home of a tax collector (9:10), in His own home (Mk. 2:1-2), and in the Temple courts (Jn. 7:14). He taught in any place and on all occasions. His explanation of the Kingdom of God and of true righteousness shook the nation of Israel.

The teaching ministries we often think of today are within a set time frame and often within a building. Ministry based on a location misses the dynamic of the Kingdom of God. Jesus challenges us to take the message out to the people in any circumstance and in any location.

Jesus and His Ministry of Prayer

The picture of Jesus praying sets a new standard for us as disciples. Prophets like Elijah prayed and God answered their prayers (1 Ki. 18:20-39). Jesus brought us into a new realm of prayer, instructing us to call upon God as our own Father (Mt. 6:6) and helping us to learn to personally talk to God (6:9). The prayer ministry of Jesus took the illustration of the Old Testament prophet and placed it into the hearts of common people. We, too must offer those around us the freeing knowledge that God personally, as a father, listens to the requests of His children.

The intensity of Jesus in prayer is a model for us to follow. He withdrew from the crowds in order to pray (Mt. 14:23). This tells us of the importance of God replenishing our weary spirits after intense ministry. Ministry does not originate from our hearts, but from the heart of God. Therefore, we need the Spirit of God to renew our lives, both for our refreshing and for direction for future ministry. Jesus spent entire evenings before the Lord (Lk. 6:12-13). Our example leads us to times of intense prayer, during which we don't let go or casually ask for wisdom.

Missiological Conclusions

"Greater than Solomon" brings to mind that this King is over realms and systems beyond our imagination. "Greater than the prophet" gives us a glimpse of someone who is very close to God and able to be heard by Him in prayer. "Greater than the Temple" speaks of something of God beyond the sum total of the Old Covenant. Jesus was, and is, greater than the prophets, greater than the Temple, greater than any king, and more loyal than any servant. The ministry of Messiah brings a fullness we still fail to fully grasp. We look forward to His coming reign as King over all.

We are drawn to the ministry of Jesus, knowing that our lives are able to emulate many aspects of His ministry. We can boldly proclaim the truth of God on a large scale, and we are able to teach in any circumstance or location concerning the ways of God's Kingdom. We are also called to pray like Jesus, teaching whole communities to call upon God as their Heavenly Father, no longer distant or cowering in fear before Him.

Our understanding of mission draws us to honor Jesus in each aspect of His ministry. We are to be a reflection of His faith. We are to pray as He did for the sick. We are to stand firm against hypocrisy in any form. We are called to establish truth and justice in opposition to the devils fighting against His Kingdom. As sons and daughters of the great King, we smile at our present circumstances, knowing we will one day enter realms of righteousness, peace, and joy beyond any earthly expression or comprehension.

Chapter 26 - Jesus, The Kingdom, and the Nations

The Kingdom and the Nations - Matthew

Matthew's recording of the Great Commission (Mt. 28:16-20) is no doubt the most quoted mission passage in the entire Bible. Did Matthew have more to say about the Gentiles of the nations? Does his record of the Good News of Jesus build toward the final command, or is the final command an isolated comment?

Review:

We previously looked at the foundation Matthew established, confirming the Messiah's birth.

- The Genealogy of Jesus

- The Magi from the East

Matthew boldly addressed the theme of the Gentiles and the Kingdom of God. The first encounter we have with Jesus' attention on the nations in His adult ministry came during His temptation in the wilderness.

> Again, the devil took him to a very high mountain and showed him all the kingdoms of the world and their splendor. "All this I will give you," he said, "if you will bow down and worship me" (Mt. 4:8-9).

A major purpose of the Messiah was revealed through the dark eyes of the Enemy's trap. Satan enticed the Lord with something very valuable. Jesus desires to bring the world, all of the people groups, into His Kingdom. His plan of action to bring the nations back to Himself was not revealed in this setting. Matthew understood the necessity of Kingdom expansion to encompass all nations. Directly after the temptation narrative, he continued telling us that the area in which Jesus settled fulfilled the prophesy of Isaiah. Jesus came to live in an area known as "Galilee of the Gentiles" (Mt. 4:15; Isa. 9:1). The Light to the Nations prophesied by Isaiah (9:2) was physically present. Expansion of the Kingdom of God would need new expressions and new forms to outstrip an archaic system which had failed its mission.

The expansion of the Kingdom would certainly take place. The news of Jesus "... spread all over Syria" (Mt. 4:24) and brings us to realize early on that the news of Messiah was penetrating Gentile areas which were formerly seen by Jews as hostile, warlike kingdoms.

> Large crowds from Galilee, the Decapolis, Jerusalem, Judea and
> the region across the Jordan followed him (Mt. 4:25).

The Decapolis

The Roman leader Pompey liberated Hippos, Scythopolis and Pella from the Jews (New Bible Dictionary: 276). It appears that the cities reverted to their preferred Greek cultural roots in defiance of the Jewish system. These liberated cities were joined by others forming a union of ten cities, or Decapolis. It is a term that represented ten cities " . . .characterized by high Greek culture . . ." (Compton's Interactive NIV Bible). Nine of the ten cities were located east of the Jordan River. The Decapolis represented cities with customs that would have alienated the Pharisees, Essenes, and any other Jewish system fearful of religious defilement. These cites ". . . formed a league for trade and mutual defiance against Semitic tribes" (New Bible Dictionary: 276).

Cities of the Decapolis:

Scythopolis
Hippos
Pella
Gadara
Philadelphia (known in King David's time as Rebboth Ammon, later as
    Ammon, today as Amman)
Dion
Gerasa
Raphana
Kanatha
Damascus

Other cities were later added to the ten, forming a band of eighteen in the 2nd century A.D.

For further study, see coins of the Decapolis.

The crowd following Jesus included people of both Jewish and non-Jewish backgrounds. The beauty of this passage is that backgrounds fade when people follow the Messiah. No other event would naturally draw people from such antagonistic backgrounds.

Jesus healed "a man who was deaf and could hardly talk" in the region of the Decapolis (Mk. 7:32-37). The people were overwhelmed with amazement (v. 37), contrary to the reaction of the Pharisees. Unreached areas of the world will often welcome the refreshing presence of God. We should not wrongly imagine that the rejection of the ruling religious authorities is the only response from the nations.

The Beatitudes

Matthew transitions from the crowds following Jesus to The Beatitudes (Mt. 5). What was absent in this address was any reference to Israel, although references are made to the Sanhedrin (v. 22) and to the altar (v. 24), terms readily understood by the people in that entire region. The terms "salt of the earth" (v. 13) and "the light of the world" (v. 14) were spoken to all present. (The mental transformation that must take place in the believer's mind is colossal.) Every person in listening distance had the opportunity to follow Jesus and then to bring "salt and light" (transformation) to his or her world. Jesus was clear to the crowd that He did not come to abolish the Law or the Prophets but to fulfill them (v. 17). His presence with a multi-racial crowd was not to bring a blurring of lines, what modern terminology calls tolerance. His call to become sons of "your Father in heaven" (v. 45) was very clear.

Pagans are people without God. People without God have no one to ask for help in time of need. Jesus makes reference to pagans worrying about food, drink, and clothing (Mt. 6:31-33). Regardless of formal religious background or a background of animism, those who worry about the necessities of life reflect life without the Provider. Many highly structured religious cultures in the world seem to have "god awareness," yet they have intense struggles to cover daily needs. The presence of the two indicates the need to know the true character of God in Christ.

Jesus referred to "everyone" three times in Matthew Chapter 7. All are invited to do the will of the Father who is in heaven (v. 21). All must not only hear His words, but put them into practice (v. 24). This invitation was given without limits of background. Neither a background of Jewish ancestry nor one of Greek culture would have been able to save one from the great crash and impending destruction of God's judgement that comes to all (v. 26). The same applies to all people in all times.

The Roman Centurion

The centurion was a Roman military officer in charge of 100 men. This Gentile, Roman army officer came to Jesus with faith for his servant's healing. He understood the principle of authority. Authority doesn't require the one in charge to be present – his orders must be carried out. Jesus responded, "I tell you the truth, I have not found in Israel faith like this" (Mt. 8:10-12; Lk. 7:9-10). This was the first contrast Jesus gave between Israel and the nations. Jesus knew this centurion represented a faith that would later come from people of the nations. His speaking out that "many will come from the East and the West" (Mt. 8:11) helps us envision the nations that will come to know Him. The "East" brings instantly to mind the Babylonians, the Persians, the Medes, the Afghanis, the Pakistanis, the Indians, the Japanese, the regions we now know belong to the Chinese, and the islands of the South Pacific. The "West" encompasses the Greeks, the Romans (like the one to whom he was speaking) as well as regions of Spain, Ireland and beyond. Luke adds "and the North and the South" (Lk. 13:29-30), which encompasses the entire world. We must train ourselves to include all peoples, especially the unreached, the neglected, and those yearning for a life that will only be realized in Jesus as Lord.

Jesus went on to say:

> But the subjects of the kingdom will be thrown outside, into the darkness, where there will be weeping and gnashing of teeth (Mt. 8:12).

"Subjects of the kingdom" refers to Israel or the Jewish nation. Jews not responding to His invitation will be judged (Mt. 22:2-14). Controversies rage on the position of the Children of Israel today. Some strongly believe that the Jews are a favored people by virtue of blood line. This position points the finger of accusation of "replacement theology" at those not giving special preference to the Jews. Replacement theology is a belief that "the Church" has replaced Israel as the people of God. The confusion lies with the definition of both Church and outreach to Jewish people.

The biblical definition of ecclesia (what we call church) is the group of believers in Jesus the Messiah, called out from living according to the world's standards and daily renewing their commitment to the cross of Christ. The term Church loses its universal significance when isolated to an ethnic, cultural, or denominational framework. For many Jews and Muslims, the term "church" brings to mind the Crusades, the Inquisition, and similar oppressive political or military conquests.

Because of these dark marks on the history of those calling themselves "church," mission requires intense wisdom in inviting people to faith. We must learn to invite people to fellowship with Jesus the Messiah and with us. It requires learning the art of allowing faith in the Messiah to flow among all people without making their conscience feel they have joined a sect that requires rejection of their background and people. God is greater than culture.

Outreach to Jewish people must be encouraged, along with missional expressions to all peoples. The call of God on a person's life is to be honored and not assessed according to what an individual or a group feels is most important. Someone with the call of God to Pakistanis should not be made to feel that his or her calling is secondary to those called to the Jews, or vice versa. All need the saving work of the Messiah. None will survive the great crash of a life not built upon the foundation of obedience to Jesus (Mt. 7:26-27).

The Kingdom of God is much broader than seeing world evangelism through the eyes of Israel. Those coming from the east and from the west, who feast with Abraham, Isaac, and Jacob, will come from many cultural and ethnic backgrounds. Jacob (Israel) and the Persians are welcome at the feast on the basis of faith in the Messiah. Culture and bloodline do not allow alternative admission strategies. There is not a two-covenant redemption: one for Jews and another for Gentiles.

The Roman's request was granted. It brings to mind the prayer of Solomon, asking God to hear the prayer of the foreigner.

> As for the foreigner who does not belong to your people Israel but has come from a distant land because of your name—for men will hear of your great name and your mighty hand and your outstretched arm—when he comes and prays toward this temple, then hear from heaven, your dwelling place, and do whatever the foreigner asks of you, so that all the peoples of the earth may know your name and fear you, as do your own people Israel, and may know that this house I have built bears your Name (1 Ki. 8:41-43).

Jesus is that Temple, made without human hands. He hears and answers the prayers of all who come to Him. It is the heart of the Father for people of the earth to know and fear Him. A restored physical temple built with human hands is pointless and obsolete.

The Gadarene and Gergesa Demoniacs

The region of the Gadarenes is the setting for Jesus ministering to two demon-possessed men. Gadara is one of the cities of the Decapolis, those free cities that spurned Jewish rules and oversight. This is evident by the presence of a "herd of pigs" (Mt. 8:30). The background of the demoniacs is not clear, but we surmise that they are from a background that strict Jews would certainly avoid. The pigs would assure that the division was clearly marked.

Mark gives a similar account of a demon-possessed man further north in the region of Gergesa, which is another city of the Decapolis (Mk. 5:1-17). Both accounts record the possessed person or persons living among the tombs. Mark makes some distinctions in that the man in Gergesa was frequently bound by chains. Mark also tells us that the demons identified themselves by the name Legion. A legion is a term for a Roman army division of between 4,000 to 6,000 men (New Bible Dictionary: 692). Mark tells us that the herd size was about two thousand.

As Jesus had healed the blind on different occasions, He also healed the demon possessed on different occasions. These miracles were not one time occurrences. It is not strange to think that different cities of the Decapolis in the region of Galilee raised pigs to secure their borders. Both accounts have the people from the surrounding areas asking Jesus to leave their region. Mark tells us that they saw the man clothed and in his right mind, and they heard about what had happened to the pigs (Mk. 5:15-16).

The man in Mark's account begged to become a disciple and to follow Jesus. Jesus responded,

> Go home to your family and tell them how much the Lord has done for you. So the man went away and began to tell in the Decapolis how much Jesus had done for him (Mk. 5:19-20).

The man who was freed from demons became the first evangelist throughout the Decapolis. His natural line of communication was with his family and those culturally near to him. Ancient cities east of the Jordan River heard how Jesus alone had freed and healed a man possessed by demons. Light to the Gentiles was expanding.

Not to the Gentiles!

Jesus sent out the twelve disciples on their first solo ministry trip without Him (Mt. 10). Part of His instruction package stated,

> Do not go among the Gentiles or enter any town of the Samari-
> tans. Go rather to the lost sheep of Israel (vv. 5b-6).

At times, this command has been misunderstood to be a guiding statement, always giving preferential outreach to the house of Israel. This command was to be
taken at face value. It was the first outreach of the twelve. Jesus was using their
natural backgrounds and training them to be effective among their own people.
Encouraging young disciples to become effective among their own people is always a healthy and encouraging starting point. People who develop a ministry to
other people groups, without knowing how to relate to their own people, often
develop an unhealthy detachment from their natural cultural roots. The judgment
on the Jewish nation was soon coming; it would be destroyed in only forty years.
But Jesus did not stop with this point, even as He sent the twelve out in mission.
He instructed them that they " . . . will be brought before governors and kings
as witnesses to them and to the Gentiles" (v. 18). This initial focus on the Jewish
people was not a mandate in ministry, but rather a starting point for their particular
time. The nation of Israel still needed to hear the good news of the Kingdom. Jesus
told the story of the fig tree that did not produce fruit (Lk. 13:6-9), a reference
to unfruitful Israel. In this story, the owner was ready to cut the tree down, but
still willing to give it one more year of help (fertilizer) and wait for the outcome.

Jesus' ministry among the Samaritans and Gentiles also frees us to envision the
direction our lives must take in ministry.

Unrepentant Cities

Matthew records a word of judgment to three cities in northern Galilee: Korazin,
Bethsaida and Capernaum, his hometown (Mt. 11:21-24). The Gentile areas of
Tyre and Sidon would have a more bearable judgment than that of Korazin and
Bethsaida because they did not have the miracles performed in them that could
have brought faith. Sodom also perished without the signs and wonders that
were performed in Capernaum. Blessing does not come by association or because
Jesus was present. Blessing comes through the act of repentance from sin and
obedience to God.

We must take this reasoning to another level of understanding. Neither Sodom
nor Capernaum had the Bible as we do. The blessing is not ours by familiarity
with the stories of Jesus. Our blessing is in obedience to the words of Jesus and
fulfilling His call on our lives.

The Canaanite Woman

The Pharisees confronted Jesus over His disciples not washing their hands before eating (Mt. 15:1-10). Jesus told the crowd that it is what comes out of a person that defiles, not what they eat. Jesus took His disciples directly after this encounter to the Gentile region of Tyre and Sidon, and there He met a Canaanite woman. Why did He enter this Gentile region by choice for a retreat with His disciples? The first impression we have is that this woman was from the region to which Elijah was sent. Zarephath was between Tyre and Sidon. Jesus was nearly thrown from the cliff defending God's love for the Gentile woman in Elijah's story (Lk. 4:24-25). Here was a woman from the same region, asking for her demon-possessed daughter to be freed from that demon. Jesus appeared to snub her requests, calling her the name that most Jews used for the Gentiles—a dog (Mt. 15:26). To whom was Jesus speaking primarily? Was He addressing the woman or His disciples who still did not understand the work of God which was to be unleashed among the Gentiles?

The woman came back with an amazing reply: "Yes, Lord," she said, "but even the dogs eat the crumbs that fall from their masters' table" (Mt. 15:27; Mk. 7:28). How could a woman, called a dog by the Master, whose daughter was in desperate need, come back with such a quick response?

Two items must be pointed out from this story. The first is that Jesus healed her daughter. He responded to this woman just as He did to the centurion's request to heal his servant. He also noted her faith as He did with the centurion's. The second important item is that Jesus came to do the will of the Father who sent Him (Jn. 6:38, 7:16). This meant that Jesus would only heal the woman's daughter according to the will of the Father. The Father directed Jesus to Zarephath to heal the woman's daughter! His words were not drawing division between Himself and the Canaanite woman, but rather exposing prejudice in a self-serving Jewish system.

Cleansing of the Temple

Jesus drove out those who were buying and selling in the court of the Gentiles (Mt. 21:12-16; Mk. 11:15-18). Temple usage had degenerated from Solomon's day. Originally intended by God as a place for all nations to come in order to know Him, it was now an area strictly controlled by the Sadducees. Jesus' reference to the house of prayer is taken from Isaiah 56.

> And foreigners who bind themselves to the LORD to serve him,
> to love the name of the LORD, and to worship him, all who keep
> the Sabbath without desecrating it and who hold fast to my

covenant— these I will bring to my holy mountain and give them
joy in my house of prayer. Their burnt offerings and sacrifices
will be accepted on my altar; for my house will be called a house
of prayer for all nations (Isa. 56:6-7).

The size and design of the Temple changed from the one built in Solomon's day, to
the one built during the days of Cyrus under the leadership of Ezra (Ez. 3:11-13), to
the one built under Herod's authority, including an "inscription prohibiting the
entrance of a foreigner under threat of penalty of death" (Josephus, Ant. 15, 417,
quoted by the New International Dictionary of New Testament Theology, Vol. 3,
pg. 789). The purpose of God in the Temple was not to morph as a result of the
destruction and two subsequent rebuildings of the structure. Room changes and
usage were not to be according to modern Sadducee desires.

Jesus' reference to a den of robbers is not to be taken only as unfair scales in the
Temple market. We have no reference to Jesus overturning scales in the regular
market place. The heavy robbery of which they were accused was that of stealing
opportunities from foreigners to hear the Word of God, to seek healing, and to
sacrifice at the Temple of the Lord. God is robbed when foreigners are not brought
back to the Creator of all life.

The subsequent cursing of the fig tree reflects God's anger toward an unfruitful
people who failed to produce the fruit of the Kingdom of God (Mt. 21:18-22). These
two events, the confrontation of Temple theft and the cursing of fruitlessness,
are linked together in sequence and meaning. Kingdom values and the warning
against fruitlessness must be taken seriously.

The Signs of the End and the Nations

Jesus warned His disciples to carefully understand the signs that would precede
His return, which include wars, famines, and earthquakes. He commanded us,
however, not to be afraid of these signs (Lk. 21:9). Events may occur which may
not necessarily signal His return. The difference between recognizing signs of the
age and anticipating His return is sobering and must awaken the believers in our
present age! He told us to stand firm through hard times. What does standing
firm mean to the believer? Does standing firm mean that we do not reject our
faith in light of persecution? Does standing firm mean we pay tithes in financially
challenging times, or attend meetings when our schedule is tight? Standing firm
must include actively spreading of the gospel to all people.

Jesus told us what would signal the end of the age:

> And this gospel of the kingdom will be preached in the whole
> world as a testimony to all nations, and then the end will come
> (Mt. 24:14).

Mark records, "And the Gospel must first be preached to all nations" (Mk. 13:10). The nations hearing the good news of the Messiah and His forgiveness offered to all will precede the end of the age.

Some movements have missed the purpose of God by focusing on the signs of the times. Wars, famines, and natural disasters have brought some to believe that the end was so very close that their daily life and future planning were paralyzed. The "Y2K" phobias eclipsed the centrality of the gospel for some believers. Firearms were purchased to protect threatened food supplies, clearly missing the essence of the Kingdom of God. Jesus warned us to stay away from the fear of the future.

Others have become intently sidetracked with dates predicting the return of Christ. William Miller focused on the prophetic writings of Daniel, predicting exactly 2300 years from the fall of the Temple in Jerusalem to the second coming of Christ (Ahlstrom 1972:479). He arrived at the date of March 1843, which was revised to March 1844, and finally to October 22, 1844 . People who followed his teaching sold their homes in anticipation of the return of Jesus. Other similar movements have lived on credit, anticipating the return of Christ and the end of all systems as we know them. Enormous disappointment has resulted from false hopes of specific dates of Christ's return. The error is that Jesus did not tell us to spend our energy calculating the date of the end of time. He told us to take the gospel of the Kingdom to all people. The two theologies differ greatly on how one lives life daily.

New speculations are currently exploring the 7,000 year "complete" cycle of the earth. Because we are currently 6,000+ years from creation, some ask why Satan is still not bound for the final 1,000 years. Have we delayed the reign of Christ? Foolish questions keep believers from the real goal which is the spread of the gospel.

> No one knows about that day or hour, not even the angels in
> heaven, nor the Son, but only the Father. Be on guard! Be alert!
> You do not know when that time will come (Mk. 13:32-33).

Dates and sequences are clearly not our business. The return of the Messiah is in the Father's timing. Our duty is to be on guard and to stay alert. This is the message of Messiah to all peoples.

Great Commission - Matthew 28:16-20

The command of Jesus to make disciples of all nations was given while in Galilee, before His ascension to the Father on the Mount of Olives (Lk. 24:50). Matthew ends his recording of the life of Jesus with Jesus' final command rather than with the final glimpse of Him at His ascension. Matthew is describing more than a story line; he is giving direction to the believers around him and to those who will come after him. Our task is to disciple the nations. This is not a side point to another major theme. God requires us to bring the news of Jesus to the nations. Mark also ends his recording of the life of Jesus with the command to "Go into all the world and preach the good news to all creation" (Mk. 16:15).

Jesus said that all authority had been given to Him (Mt. 28:18). Because of His authority we are sent to the nations. We have been given full authority by Jesus for this task. You do not ask permission to bring the good news of Jesus; it is your obligation. Nations that publicly forbid the gospel are not to be avoided. We have a higher authority.

Working with others in mission is a joy that should not be circumvented, at least when this luxury exists. We affirm the principles of the Kingdom when we pass on to the next generation of believers the necessity to take this news to those still sitting in darkness. Jesus did not require that we place a certain structure in motion before the discipling of the nations could take place. It is important that believers from highly structured societies do not rob believers from "grass roots" organizations the joy of obeying His commands. We must all be about fulfilling the commands of Jesus. Different societies will learn principles of mission as they are directed by God and proceed. Mistakes will happen that will become opportunities for learning.

Jesus commanded us to baptize as the nations are discipled. The Church, building upon the command of Christ and the actions of the apostles, has held baptism as an important step for two millennia. Today, some still ask if it is a necessary part of the Christian life. Baptism is a rite by which the believer identifies with the death and resurrection of Christ. Baptism is an expression of spiritual death to one's former life and its resurrection to new spiritual life in Christ. Baptism also includes encouraging people to walk in obedience to the commands of Jesus. As with any of the Lord's commands, discussing which ones are now relevant and which ones have passed with time will only cloud our ability to walk in freedom. No one should take on the task of rewriting the New Testament.

In baptism the bondage of past sin is broken. Old habits do not die easily, though the spiritual dimension to these habits has been addressed. Because baptism testifies to the community of believers that death has come to one's old ways, it is important that the community helps the newly baptized person walk in newness of life and form new patterns. Baptism without discipleship is just a ritual. With discipleship, baptism is a powerful tool that allows us to work with the power of the Holy Spirit.

The Spirit of God within us testifies that we are God's children (Ro. 8:16). This internal witness is the mark of God upon the life of the believer. His internal witness tells us of the cessation of legal demands from the law. After baptism, we begin with a completely new and clean record. Yet we know that the enemy's accusations will still pursue the believer. It is an act of faith to testify publicly that the legal ties to sin are broken and that we are dead to our former way of life.

The resurrection of Christ becomes the pattern for our new freedom. The life that Jesus lived, He lived unto God (Ro. 6:10). Our resurrection from the waters of baptism is to include assimilation into the new community of believers. This is why it is so important for us to be baptized by the community of believers with whom we will live. A foreign pastor coming to baptize will not be there later to answer the questions of the new believer, to form a bond of friendship, or to help the new believer assimilate in the community. Baptism needs to take place on the local community level in order to be a resurrection into community life.

For further discussion on baptism, see Romans 7.

The Kingdom and the Nations – Luke

Luke, our Gentile author, contributed a major part of the New Testament with his two volume work called Acts I and Acts II, which we know as The Gospel of Luke and Acts. His attention to Jesus' life, given for all nations, will be very important to our understanding of Scripture. Luke wrote to Theophilus, someone with an obvious Greek name, to describe the news of the Messiah (Lk. 1:3; Acts 1:1).

Luke approached the Kingdom and the Gentiles carefully in his gospel recording. The groundwork he laid would expand to become one of the major themes in Acts. Luke began with the ministry of John the Baptist, quoting Isaiah 40:3-5. He applied the passage to this messenger, the Baptist, who prepared the pathway for the Messiah.

> A voice of one calling in the desert,
> 'Prepare the way for the Lord,
> make straight paths for him.
> Every valley shall be filled in,

> every mountain and hill made low.
> The crooked roads shall become straight,
> the rough ways smooth.
> And all mankind will see God's salvation' (Lk. 3:4-6).

While John's ministry was to focus on the Messiah and to prepare a people to receive the Messiah's message and Kingdom, Jesus' ministry was to encompass the entire world.

Gentiles of Distant Lands

Luke tells us that Jesus taught in the synagogues of Galilee, but he is silent on the content of Jesus' teaching (Lk. 4:14-15). He gives us a clear window into the message Jesus spoke in the synagogue of Nazareth, making reference to the widow of Zaraphath and Elijah's care for her needs (Lk. 4:24-25; 1 Ki. 17:1-16). Jesus went on to speak of Naaman, the captain of the Syrian army healed in Elisha's day (Lk. 4:27; 2 Ki. 5:1-14). These two examples of God's love for the Gentiles infuriated the residents of Nazareth. They attempted to kill Jesus for His comments (Lk. 4:28-30). The message "freedom for the prisoners and recovery of sight for the blind" (v. 18) seemed well enough received. However, several items became lit fuses for the people of Nazareth:

- Today this scripture is fulfilled in your hearing (v. 21).

- No prophet is accepted in his hometown (v. 24).

- He made references to God blessing Gentile people who were grateful (vv. 25-27).

Offense could have been taken at any one of the three comments. Combining the three, with a focus on God's grace for the Gentiles, triggered anger in Nazareth. It was too much for a known, hometown boy to claim He was the fulfillment of the ages. It was too much for Jesus to claim His anointed position in Nazareth. How dare He then tell the community, for whom He had once worked as a carpenter, that God longed to meet the needs of people whom Israel considered both unclean and their adversaries!

Jesus spoke about both the Ninevites who had repented after Jonah's preaching and the Queen of the South who had sought out the wisdom of Solomon (Lk. 11:29-32). The Queen of the South was a reference to the Queen of Sheba (1 Ki. 10:1) who was most likely from Ethiopia (Dictionary of New Testament Theology, Vol 2, pg. 381). Jesus compared the listening but unresponsive crowd to the positive response found in Nineveh and to the hunger of a woman who had traveled thousands of miles to hear the wisdom of Solomon. The power of His words struck deeply within the false kingdom mentality of the Jewish mind that allowed them to believe they were superior to others. Jesus proclaimed that others would hear and respond to the voice of God. He also clearly contrasted His fullness with Jonah and Solomon as vessels. Patience for Israel existed, but the time was soon coming for the news of the Messiah and His Kingdom to be given to people who would respond. The parable of the fruitless fig tree was a warning to all planted in God's vineyard (Lk. 13:6-9). Unresponsive lives will not be coddled forever. What fruit is God requiring of your life?

Samaritans

The Samaritans were ethnically different, culturally different, and religiously estranged from Jewish life. Jesus sent some of His disciples to a Samaritan village to prepare the way for His arrival. Luke writes that "the people there did not welcome him, because he was heading for Jerusalem" (Lk. 9:53). The Samaritans rejected His coming because He was headed to the political and religious center of their rejection. The cultural conflict within the Samaritan people of Jesus' day is present with many Middle Eastern people today. If one has clear ties with the Jewish system, building friendships with their enemies is very complex.

Jesus needed to go to Jerusalem to fulfill the mandate the Father had spoken through Moses and Elijah on the mountain (Lk. 9:30-31). Their belief that Jesus represented the old guard of Judaism was a cultural miscalculation on their part; it was not the direction in which Jesus was headed. This is important to grasp so that mission workers do not overreact to cultural tensions and become anti-Jerusalem, anti-Jewish, or even anti-Church. One does not need to reject a people to be accepted by another people. The disciples were ready for judgment to be dealt to the Samaritans:

> When the disciples James and John saw this, they asked, "Lord, do you want us to call fire down from heaven to destroy them?" But Jesus turned and rebuked them, and they went to another village (Lk. 9:54-56).

The only rebuke Jesus had in this situation was directed toward His disciples for their quick, judgmental attitude. His words, on the other hand, warned of the destruction in Korazin, Bethsaida, and Capernaum (Lk. 10:8-15)--cities in which His miracles had been performed. The three cities mentioned should have recognized the works of the Messiah and changed their evil ways. The amount of understanding present in these cites was contrasted with Tyre, Sidon, and Sodom--cities which faced massive destruction with far less understanding of the Kingdom of God. In a similar way, the Samaritan village needed patience rather than quick judgment. Luke brings a contrast to the reader between cities sitting in darkness and cities that have experienced light. We , too, must understand the responsibility of cities that have received truth and even revival. Western cities that have clearly heard the Word of God will also be judged by how they use the truth they have heard. Cities in the East in Iraq, Iran, and Pakistan have not experienced these levels of truth. They, too, will be judged, but not for their apathy to spread the truth which they have not heard.

Jesus continued with a dramatic contrast in the parable of the Good Samaritan (Lk. 10:25-37). He addressed the question presented by ". . . an expert in the law . . ." by speaking of three men faced with a need before them. The priest and the Levite were men with whom the expert could relate because they also knew well the Jewish law. The Samaritan was unfamiliar with the law and purposely steered clear of Jewish traditions which considered Samaritans to be perpetually defiled. Yet the heart of compassion rather than the knowledge of the law was clearly honored by Jesus.

> Which of these three do you think was a neighbor to the man
> who fell into the hands of robbers?
> The expert in the law replied, "The one who had mercy on him."
> Jesus told him, "Go and do likewise" (Lk. 10:36-37).

We must grasp the intent of the words of Jesus. He drives us to respond like a good neighbor who lives with compassion for people personally unknown to him or her. Jesus clearly was warning His disciples not to be experts in the law without compassion. Nor should we perform religious duties while blind to the needs in our cities--or even traveling between cities. Because of Jesus' words to "Go and do likewise" (v. 37), it is unthinkable that people fabricate institutions in His name that do the opposite by training religious teachers who are neither concerned for human suffering nor address it in practical ways.

The reason we love our neighbors is because of the work of God already in our hearts and lives. This is unlike humanism which helps the poor without any commitment to the Kingdom of God.

Jesus healed ten lepers as He traveled to the border between Samaria and Galilee. The significance of this story contains three major themes:

1. Jesus healed ten lepers.

The story is one of the power of God's healing offered instantly to many. There is no sense of limited power or a need to pray for people individually, which is normally the impression taken from an individualistic western viewpoint.

2. Only one of the ten returned to thank Jesus.

The story demonstrates a difficult reality, telling us that 90% of those healed in this setting did not bother to give thanks to the one who had granted their healing. It is a reminder of God's good hand extended to both the grateful and the ungrateful.

3. The thankful man was a Samaritan.

> One of them, when he saw he was healed, came back, praising God in a loud voice. He threw himself at Jesus' feet and thanked him—and he was a Samaritan.
> Jesus asked, "Were not all ten cleansed? Where are the other nine? Was no one found to return and give praise to God except this foreigner?" Then he said to him, "Rise and go; your faith has made you well" (Lk. 17:15-19).

Luke points out the ethnic background of the one thankful person. For Jewish readers, it points to the nature of the human soul that desires blessing but fails to come under the hand of the Creator. Jealousy within the Jewish community should be stirred up to also give thanks to God. For the Samaritan or Gentile reader, the message clearly spoke of healing offered to the nations and the necessity to give thanks to the One who included them.

The Gentiles and Jesus' Death

Jesus made reference to the Gentiles and to their involvement with His death. He told His disciples:

> He will be handed over to the Gentiles. They will mock him, insult him, spit on him, flog him and kill him. On the third day he will rise again (Lk. 18:32-33).

The reference of "will be handed over" described the Jewish nature of His arrest and the subsequent Gentile involvement in His further humiliation, torture, and execution. The Roman involvement in His death was a representation of all nations. All are responsible for the humiliation, torture, and death of the Messiah. Luke later tells us,

> . . . their shouts prevailed. So Pilate decided to grant their demand. . . . and surrendered Jesus to their will (Lk. 23:23b, 25b).

It is not possible to claim that another occupying power would have been more righteous than Rome or less prone to political pacification. Jew and Gentile alike stood speechless before God without excuse. All were guilty of turning away from the Righteous One, yet God's redemption would be offered to all people.

The angels reiterated this message to the woman at the tomb, reminding her that both Jew and Gentile would be involved with the rejection and death of Jesus.

> Remember how he told you, while he was still with you in Galilee: 'The Son of Man must be delivered into the hands of sinful men, be crucified and on the third day be raised again.' Then they remembered his words (Lk. 24:6-8).

It was clearly mentioned several times that Jews and Gentiles alike were party to the rejection, scorn, and death of the Messiah. The foreknowledge of God is beyond human comprehension. He understands human pride and also knows that He is the only solution for both Jew and Gentile. He is our source of transformation and peace, now and eternally.

The Road to Emmaus

Jesus surprised two disciples on the day of His resurrection. Jesus often surprises us by showing up when we really need His voice to speak to our hearts.

> ...but we had hoped that he was the one who was going to redeem Israel (Lk. 24:21).

The two on the road to Emmaus had something particular in mind when they expressed hope that Jesus would "redeem Israel." The redemption of Israel was the restoration of the Kingdom of David to prominence. This would necessitate the ousting of foreign conquering powers as well as the cleansing of the people from evil and their perverted lives. To them, redemption would mean Jesus ushering in a new age of Israel and His leading the nation.

This is not, however, what Jesus came to accomplish.

> He said to them, "How foolish you are, and how slow of heart to believe all that the prophets have spoken! Did not the Christ have to suffer these things and then enter his glory?" And beginning with Moses and all the Prophets, he explained to them what was said in all the Scriptures concerning himself.
>
> While they were still talking about this, Jesus himself stood among them and said to them, "Peace be with you."
>
> He told them, "This is what is written: The Christ will suffer and rise from the dead on the third day, and repentance and forgiveness of sins will be preached in his name to all nations, beginning at Jerusalem. You are witnesses of these things. I am going to send you what my Father has promised; but stay in the city until you have been clothed with power from on high" (Lk. 24:25-27; 36; 46-49).

Jesus made it very clear that He needed to suffer, die, and rise again. His Kingdom was not one set up on earth with the limited scope of bolstering the nation of Israel. That vision would be far too small in light of "all nations" mentioned in verse 47. Repentance and the forgiveness of sins must be offered to every nation. The message recorded for us to understand is that this Gospel is for all nations. This powerful word on the day of His resurrection breaks forth during the incredible surprise that He is alive. His appearance on the road to Emmaus instructed and transformed bewildered disciples into people of faith with vision for the nations.

The Kingdom and the Nations – John

Introduction

The Fourth Gospel approaches the story of Messiah quite differently than the synoptic gospel writers. John does not tell the story of Jesus' birth or of the angelic announcement. John takes us to "The Word became flesh and made his dwelling among us" (Jn. 1:14). He begins with the incarnation, then fills in the story line. He does not begin with the facts of Jesus' birth (Matthew and Luke) or the miraculous fast-paced nature of His ministry (Mark). All four writers, however, bring us to the same conclusion: Jesus is Incarnate of the Father, the Redeemer, and the Life-giver of all the world.

John moves quickly in the opening lines of his gospel, declaring Jesus to be the ful-fillment of the prophetic words of Isaiah concerning light to the nations--that grace would be extended to people not seeking after God, but marooned in darkness.

> . . . in the future he will honor Galilee of the Gentiles, by the
> way of the sea, along the Jordan—
> The people walking in darkness
> have seen a great light;
> on those living in the land of the shadow of death
> a light has dawned (Isa. 9:1b-2).

Isaiah envisioned the "light" coming to those in darkness; not the people in dark-ness fleeing their backgrounds and coming to the Kingdom of Light. To a degree, both are true. Grace is extended to those who have no hope, and the grace of God is affirmed by fleeing old ways of darkness.

Our New Testament missiology of Jesus must be formed by linking the eternal Messiah and His ministry to Old Testament prophetic insight. John declares Jesus as light for all people. God's desire is that this message enters every dark and sinful region of our world.

> In him was life, and that life was the light of men. The light
> shines in the darkness, but the darkness has not understood
> it (Jn. 1:4-5).

Darkness was found in both Jewish and Gentile regions. Isaiah's prophecy of light to the nations (Isa. 51:4), and his recording that the Messiah would be a light to the Gentiles (49:6), must influence our reading of John's gospel. Jesus is the author of life, He is the light of every person, and darkness does not understand the work of Messiah. Jesus reiterated that He is the "light of the world" (Jn. 8:12). His illuminating power offers the ability to transform an individual from one who once walked in darkness to one who will never again be in darkness! This power of transformation is a foreshadow of the resurrection.

John contrasts "his own" and "all who receive him" (1:11-12). He never excluded the Jewish people, but he did make it clear that receiving Jesus was the way of true life. What it means to receive Jesus must be clarified to keep a life transfor-mation from slipping into a theological sentence or simply a sinner's prayer. "His own" are the Jewish nation. Not all of the Jews rejected Jesus. John and the other disciples were from Jewish heritage. Use of the phrase "the Jews" often refers to the religious community rather than to the common people of Jewish ancestors. John wrestled to understand the Messiah and those who would benefit from the

Messiah's light. His conclusion of "all who receive him" solves for us the question of the scope of Messiah. He is for all people and all nations, and He brings life to all who receive Him. The evangelist recorded the words of John the Baptist, declaring Jesus to be the Lamb of God who takes away the sin of the world (1:29 -> See discussion on John the Baptist's ministry, Chapter 29, Jesus Inaugurates the Kingdom.). The theme of "whoever believes" will be reiterated in this gospel several times (Jn. 5:24-29).

The Father told John the Baptist how to identify the Messiah.

> I would not have known him, except that the one who sent me to baptize with water told me, 'The man on whom you see the Spirit come down and remain is he who will baptize with the Holy Spirit' (Jn. 1:33).

Jesus was the one who baptized with the Holy Spirit. Outpouring of the Spirit must be linked with the one who freely baptizes with the same Spirit. This word cannot be separated from the prophecy of Joel, promising an outpouring of the Spirit of God upon all people, not neglecting any group of people.

> And afterward,
> I will pour out my Spirit on all people.
> Your sons and daughters will prophesy,
> your old men will dream dreams,
> your young men will see visions.
> Even on my servants, both men and women,
> I will pour out my Spirit in those days (Joel 2:28-29).

The Spirit is promised to:

- All people

- Old and young

- Male and Female

First Cleansing of the Temple

During this early Passover in the ministry of Jesus, He traveled to Jerusalem with His disciples and made a whip to drive the offenders out of the temple courts (Jn. 2:15). Like Nehemiah, Jesus found that making a stand in leadership did not change the actions of people if their hearts had not been changed. Nehemiah had to confront the same people on more than one occasion (Ne. 4:7; 13:6-9). Jesus also made the same point early in His ministry, and even during the week of His crucifixion (Mt. 21:12-13).

John records a Jesus filled with zeal for the house of God (Jn. 2:17), quoting from the psalmist David:

> I am a stranger to my brothers,
> an alien to my own mother's sons;
> for zeal for your house consumes me,
> and the insults of those who insult you fall on me (Ps. 69:9).

The zeal that consumed Jesus over the house of God was specific. His anger was God's anger over the exclusion of the nations from seeking the Creator. Solomon prayed that the nations would come to the Temple and know the Lord, even as Israel was privileged to know Him (1 Ki. 8:43). Welcoming the nations to the Temple of God was echoed by Isaiah the prophet. Isaiah recorded the invitation of the Lord, including the foreigners in the Sabbath rest of God, the Temple courts, and communing with God in prayer. The foreigners were also encouraged to bring offerings to the altar of God, which in the minds of the Pharisees seemed to be sealed off and only reserved for Israel.

> And foreigners who bind themselves to the LORD
> to serve him,
> to love the name of the LORD,
> and to worship him,
> all who keep the Sabbath without desecrating it
> and who hold fast to my covenant—
> these I will bring to my holy mountain
> and give them joy in my house of prayer.
> Their burnt offerings and sacrifices
> will be accepted on my altar;
> for my house will be called
> a house of prayer for all nations" (Isa. 56:6-7).

It was in this setting that Jesus found the Temple courts used as a market with no heart for the nations. Jesus was not only light to the nations, but willing to fight for their acceptance before God and oppose those called the people of God. His zeal for the nations still consumes Him. We, too, must understand His zeal for the nations to know Him as we do, never resting in the satisfaction that we have completed enough, or that His work among us is somehow more important than His love for the unreached.

Message to Nicodemus

The conversation between Jesus and Nicodemus enlightens us to the idea of redemption through rebirth as a spiritual child of God. In this discussion, Jesus told Nicodemus the Pharisee that the love of God was for the entire world. We must take the words of Jesus literally when He speaks of the world, and not think about only the present people of God. Jesus described a God who was not seeking to condemn the Gentile nations, but rather One who desired to bring them under His grace and eternal redemption. This message for the nations should not be missed in our desire to understand the gift of salvation and regeneration.

> For God so loved the world that he gave his one and only Son, that whoever believes in him shall not perish but have eternal life. For God did not send his Son into the world to condemn the world, but to save the world through him (Jn. 3:16-17).

The Woman at the Well

Jesus' dialogue with a Samaritan woman gives us insight into His love for, and His ability to speak to, those considered to be outsiders or cultists.

The Samaritans were socially unacceptable to the Jews. Israel, the Northern Kingdom, had fallen to the Assyrians (733-721 BC). The Samaritans were deported to Assyria and never were accepted back into Judaism. "The anti-Samaritan stance of Judaism assumes a total deportation of the population of the Northern Kingdom; hence the equation of the Samaritans with the Cutheans" (New International Dictionary of New Testament Theology, Vol. 3, pg. 450). They returned in 400 B.C. as a mixture of Israelite and Assyrian and settled in Samaria.

The Samaritans were religiously unacceptable to the Jews. Their position as religious heretics was sealed when they established their own temple on Mount Gerizim "towards the end of the 4th cent. B.C." (Ibid. pg. 451). The Samaritans apparently built their temple as a reaction to their exclusion from the rebuilding the Temple in Jerusalem by Zerubbabel (Ezr. 4:1-3). Antiochus IV pressed for worship in Palestine to honor Zeus Hellenios, to which the Samaritans complied in order to avoid persecution (Ibid. 452). This added to first century Jewish disdain for the Samaritans, knowing the suffering their forefathers had received under former Greek and now Roman rule. In their fourth creed, they declared their temple on Mount Gerizim the only legitimate center of worship. By this, they declared Jerusalem as an invalid place of worship! At this point in time, the two people seemed more opposed to each other than did Israel with the other Gentile nations. Samaritan men were considered defiled, and Samaritan women were thought to be the equivalent of perpetually unclean. Jews would normally go to great lengths to avoid Samaritans.

The text tells us that Jesus "... had to go through Samaria" (Jn. 4:4). The question must be raised as to John's intent. Is the meaning one of being forced because there was no other possible direction but through Samaria? Or is the meaning one of delight, that Jesus needed to be with the Samaritans. The Greek εδει gives the meaning "to be necessary." Jesus gave us a clue to His intent by not running through the region, but rather by sitting down to rest at their well (v. 6).

The Samaritan woman came to the well at the sixth hour, which is high noon (v. 6). Women do not draw water in a Middle Eastern setting at noon. The well is normally a communal place with activity in the early hours of the day. The woman appeared without companion and seemed to be scorned for some reason within her village. Her mournful plea, "... so I won't . . . have to keep coming here to draw water" (v. 15), tells us that her life was one of weariness. Jesus words confirming that she had no husband and, "The fact is, you have had five husbands, and the man you now have is not your husband" (v. 18), bring most to conclude that she was a pre-Hollywood scandalous role model. Middle Eastern men would not marry a "loose woman" because it would bring shame to the extended family. One possible insight is that she was barren and thus scorned by other women with children who drew water early in the morning. It is possible that her present man, before entering marriage, wanted to know if she could bear children, as her five previous men had likely questioned. Living with a man who was not her husband, for whatever reason, was still sin.

Jesus asked for a drink (v. 7), breaking centuries of polarity between the two peoples. It must be understood that Jesus was willing to use her cup, place it to His lips, and express no fear of contamination. It is also important to note that He asked this woman for help.

Missiological Implications

1. Reaching out to a people necessitates our willingness to identify with them. Never can the worker expect a fruitful ministry while despising the people he/she is sent to reach. Eating and drinking with people brings a sense of acceptance.

> 2. At times, nationals can be robbed of the blessing that comes from supplying the needs of the foreign believer serving in their midst. Jesus was open with the woman about His need for a drink. Openness to receive help by a national (believer or otherwise) brings us to the same level. The foreign worker with no financial needs, no health needs, and no practical needs gives a false impression of self-sufficiency. Allow others to minister to you.

The woman said, "You are a Jew, and I am a Samaritan woman" (v. 9). She knew her place and found this conversation to be very much out of the ordinary. The response of Jesus was also out of the ordinary and challenges our understanding of salvation. He told her,

> If you knew the gift of God and who it is that asks you for a drink, you would have asked him and he would have given you living water (v. 10).

This was an offer of eternal life to a woman who had just met Jesus. We must conclude that eternal life is offered on the solitary basis of knowing Jesus and not by confessing theological points about Him. Living water and regeneration of the Spirit are offered freely to someone from a cultic background.

Points of Contention

Politics affect your evangelistic efforts. National heritage will often set up boundaries that frequently classify people as friend or enemy. This is also true in a religious sense. We hear people say, "You have your religion and I have mine." Boundary lines are drawn through culture and run deeply.

The woman had several points of contention with Jesus the Jew. Her distinctions stated:

> You are a Jew, and I am a Samaritan woman. How can you ask me for a drink (v. 9)?

> Are you greater than our father Jacob, who gave us the well and drank from it himself, as did also his sons and his flocks and his herds (v. 12)?

> Our fathers worshipped on this mountain, but you Jews claim that the place where we must worship is in Jerusalem (v 19).

Of course Jesus could have defended His proper heritage, His superiority to Jacob, and the legitimacy of the Temple in Jerusalem. But these points of controversy were relatively unimportant compared to the reality of Jesus the Messiah. Our communication with people must allow trivial arguments to be set aside in order to center our discussion on what is really important. Jesus' response to her third point of contention concerning the proper place of worship brings a powerful challenge to us to creatively think outside of religious confines. Jesus said,

> Believe me, woman, a time is coming when you will worship the Father neither on this mountain nor in Jerusalem. You Samaritans worship what you do not know; we worship what we do know, for salvation is from the Jews. Yet a time is coming and has now come when the true worshipers will worship the Father in spirit and truth, for they are the kind of worshipers the Father seeks. God is spirit, and his worshipers must worship in spirit and in truth (4:21-24).

The power of Jesus' words stirs us to examine our response to people whom we call "outsiders." How do we rethink the response to someone who says, "We pray in the mosque, you pray in the church"? It is vital that we overcome flat answers and learn the art of blessing people who desire to walk with God. Culturally, their walk with God may look different from ours. We must be open to know God's grace to the unreached in new ways.

Our other option is to attempt to form people into our own cultural context and make them just like we are. Evidently this is not a Kingdom value because Jesus did not invite the woman to Jerusalem, or to Jewish ceremonial washings, or to acknowledge the legitimate nature of the Temple in Jerusalem. Is it possible in our attempt to reach people of vastly different backgrounds that we, too, must learn the art of "passing over" controversial points in order to bring Jesus to them?

Reflection

What aspects of your cultural background are best left at the border of a new culture? Remember this when culture becomes a stumbling block.

What part of your witness is more religious than life giving?

Jesus did say that "salvation is from the Jews" (v. 22). He did not circumvent the foundation of His historical nature and God's salvation in order to make the message more compatible. We, too, must make certain that our message does not breathe heresy under a guise of contextual presentation of the gospel. Jesus is not an avatar of Hindu thought; He is not another Buddhist teacher. Heresy is born from quick answers that do not consider the ramifications that most likely will occur five or ten years later. Taking Jesus out of His context of "salvation is from the Jews" will mean that we are attempting to present Messiah without prophetic input as to the scope and nature of His ministry. The only safeguard we have against false prophets and false Messiahs is to remain within the context of Scripture, checking our motives while keeping our understanding of God's character fresh.

Many of the Samaritans believed in Jesus as the Messiah because of the testimony of the woman (v. 39). The response was overwhelming and reflected Jesus' stimulating word to the disciples to open their eyes and look at the fields (v. 35). The response was so tremendous because of the context of the village that had begun that morning with natural antagonism against the Jews and the thought of a Jewish Messiah. The Samaritans urged Jesus to stay with them, and He did (v. 40). This meant the disciples also stayed in Sychar, slept in Samaritan beds, ate food prepared by Samaritan women, and drank water from Samaritan cups. Their cultural challenge could not have been greater, yet their first experience was ushered in by Jesus. An incarnational message cannot be related without incarnational living.

The Samaritans understood the scope of Messiah when they told the woman, "... we know that this man really is the Savior of the world" (v. 42). Jesus was not a Jewish Messiah, but rather the Savior of the entire world, Samaritans included. They had personally experienced the breakthrough of the light to the nations. Jesus lived with them for a short time, forever removing the false foundation that the God of Israel was not interested in their lives. The enemy's dark foothold in this way was broken by personally meeting and hosting the Messiah. The disciples would still grapple with this truth for some time to come because their starting point as Jews would need to see Gentile people as a "white harvest" rather than their enemies, or worse yet, enemies of God.

The Jews later accused Jesus of demon possession and of being a Samaritan (8:48). Jesus emphatically stated that He was not demon possessed, but He did not address the question of His physical lineage. The Jews, no doubt, used the accusation of being a Samaritan as a slam against Jesus, but He did not respond by denying affiliation with a people He loved and with whom he had spent two days. Jesus was, is, and always will be one with every culture and nationality in the world. For Him to deny one group of people, He must deny all.

All are Invited

Jesus frequently spoke of the generous nature of God's grace given to all who believe. His words were for ". . . whoever hears his words" (Jn. 5:24-29), never specifying that a Jewish background was a prerequisite to receive life in His name.

Jesus entered a discourse with the Jews after the feeding of the five thousand in which he contrasted "no one" with "everyone" (6:44-45). When He said that "no one can come to me unless the Father who sent me draws him," He negated the notion that Judaism was able to save its followers. He also made it clear that the Father, not a religious system, draws people to Jesus. It is extremely important in our work among unreached people to remember that the Father, not our background, calls people to repentance in Christ. We enter into His work and co-labor with Him. Jesus contrasted this word with "Everyone who listens to the Father and learns from him comes to me." People of peace worldwide need the opportunity to hear from God the Father and to learn from Him. Jew and Gentile must be given the invitation to join the Prince of Peace at His wedding feast. All need the chance to find Jesus through obedience to the Father. The doors of heaven are open to "everyone" who finds Jesus. No door opens without Jesus.

One Shepherd for all Peoples

Jesus is the gate by which we enter the Kingdom of God (Jn. 10:7, 9). He is also the Good Shepherd who lays down His life for all His sheep (vv. 11, 14). The sheep here refer to those who have come under His care, those who are heirs of salvation and the Kingdom of God. John records Jesus saying, "whoever enters through me will be saved" (v. 9). The open invitation of "whoever" is without restrictions of community of origin or previous knowledge of God.

Jesus goes on to describe people of other backgrounds who will also listen to His voice, the voice of the Shepherd. His vision for the Kingdom is one of many peoples and many backgrounds, yet oneness through Him as the Shepherd. His description gives us a picture of the Church who will offer people of every tribe, language, and background one Savior and one Lord.

> I have other sheep that are not of this sheep pen. I must bring them also. They too will listen to my voice, and there shall be one flock and one shepherd (v. 16).

The words "one flock" tell us that ethnic backgrounds will fade away in the King-dom. Personal values will give way to Kingdom values.

Jesus prayed in His priestly prayer that His disciples would be protected from the evil one (17:15). The enemy will work through both the world of fashion in Paris and the austere world the of Buddhist life. The tolerance of India and the intolerance of Islam also need the Son to set them free. The material excesses of the West and the material deprivation of dictatorships must be addressed by the freeing hand of God.

When Jesus prayed for His disciples, He also prayed for the disciples who would come as a result of their message and their lives. He prayed that His followers would not just link with Him, but care for each other. The impact on the world will be through the unity of the worldwide Body of Christ.

> My prayer is not for them alone. I pray also for those who will believe in me through their message, that all of them may be one, Father, just as you are in me and I am in you. May they also be in us so that the world may believe that you have sent me. I have given them the glory that you gave me, that they may be one as we are one: I in them and you in me. May they be brought to complete unity to let the world know that you sent me and have loved them even as you have loved me (Jn. 17:20-23).

The Father's Timing

Jesus entered Jerusalem during His final week before the crucifixion. He had just been anointed at Bethany in preparation for burial (Jn. 12:7), and He had made His entry into Jerusalem, riding the young donkey according to the prophetic word (Zec. 9:9). Jesus was sparked by something that had happened in Jerusalem which made Him say, "The hour has come for the Son for Man to be glorified" (Jn. 12:22). That spark came as a result of Greeks in the city who wanted to see Him. His ministry was now touching people of other languages and cultural backgrounds. This request by the Greeks broke through the confines of a Savior in Israel on a new level. The vision of the Father to be a light for the Gentiles and to bring His salvation to the ends of the earth had begun (Isa. 49:6).

> Now there were some Greeks among those who went up to worship at the Feast. They came to Philip, who was from Beth-saida in Galilee, with a request. "Sir," they said, "we would like to see Jesus." Philip went to tell Andrew; Andrew and Philip in

turn told Jesus. Jesus replied, "The hour has come for the Son
of Man to be glorified (Jn. 12:20-23).

It was the signal by the Greeks asking to see Jesus that triggered the next events. The Father had spoken from heaven, which had only happened three times during Jesus' ministry: at His baptism, when He met with Moses and Elijah on the mountain, and in the final week before His death and resurrection.

The trigger point in Jerusalem drew out a rapid response from Jesus, the confirming voice of the Father, laying out three goals that God would accomplish through the death and resurrection of the Son.

1. Now is the time for judgment on this world.

2. Now the prince of this world will be driven out (12:31).

3. But I, when I am lifted up from the earth, will draw all men to myself (v. 32).

Jesus' death would bring a standard by which all systems in the world would be judged. None would escape the judgment of God when His Son had been held to public disgrace and murdered in innocence. Although judgment was not seen in its fullness, it will come with certainty as will other aspects of the Kingdom. Jesus told us that His suffering and triumph will drive out the prince of this world. Power to overcome both the world and the enemy will be released through Jesus, the fullness of which we eagerly await today. The suffering and death of Jesus, the innocent Lamb of God, will bring life and transformation that overcomes sin and bondage.

Jesus will draw all men, all people, all nations to Himself. Several key thoughts are important to remember, especially by mission workers who will soon be released to do His will with strength. Jesus must be lifted up on the cross and His story repeatedly told to honor Him before the nations. No other means will draw people to repentance than the cross of the Messiah. And finally, all men are to be drawn to Jesus. Never do we need to ask if God wants a people to be reached for His Kingdom. The answer is always and emphatically, yes! The scope is worldwide and the means is the cross.

Conclusion of Jesus and the Nations from the Gospels

All four gospel writers speak of the Kingdom of God offered to Gentile peoples living from Jerusalem to the ends of the earth. Each writer approached the subject in a different way but with the same result. Matthew boldly proclaimed that Jesus was the Savior of the world, beginning with the Magi and then introducing us to several Gentiles. He built toward the final words of Jesus, commanding us to go with the gospel of the Kingdom into the entire world. Mark picked selected stories showing Jesus' heart for the nations and concluded with the commission to take the message of salvation into the entire world. Luke began gently, drawing from genealogy, with the message of John the Baptist and with stories of the lives of selected Gentiles. He did this in order to make the point that Jesus was the fulfillment of the ages. Luke also records a powerful commissioning word on the Emmaus road. Luke's contribution would delve more deeply into the topic of Jesus and the Gentiles in his second work, Acts. John's message linked Jesus as light to the nations, confirming the words of several prophets of old. He also allowed us to see Jesus in Samaria, working with people left to rot by the Jewish community. John took us into the heart of the Father to help us to see the nations and God's yearning for their redemption.

Chapter 27 - The Coming Kingdom

The coming Kingdom, as we have previously stated, is already inaugurated among us. We seek to understand what this Kingdom will look like in its fullness when God has brought an end to all unrighteousness. This glimpse into God's coming reign takes us into a brief look at the signs that will accompany the transition from the earth, as we presently understand it, to a new world. The signs of the end of this world are not a description of the Kingdom of God, but of its necessary transition. It is the judgment of the King inflicted upon the devil and upon those who prefer darkness to the light of God. Our message will be incomplete if we lead people to hear about the "end times" without describing the coming of the beautiful reign of our God. Our message must always have future hope or it will lead people to react to scare tactics, which make a very poor foundation on which to train disciples.

Signs of the End

Jesus taught His disciples to understand the signs of the end times. In response to the disciples pointing out the splendor of the Temple and the buildings surrounding it, Jesus replied that not one stone would be left upon another (Mt. 24:1-3; Lk. 21:5-6). From this we conclude that the destruction of the Temple would be complete, which took place during the reign of Titus in 70 A. D. The following are the signs and instructions Jesus gave to His disciples two days before the Passover (Mt. 26:1). He knew they needed instruction to sustain them during the difficult days that would follow. We also need His words for the days in which we live. Our faith is renewed when we understand that He is indeed coming again. The world we presently see will not remain in its fallen state for all time.

Questions

- Do you know your job, your ministry to the Lord in these days?

- Are you living today for eternity and for God's values?

Notes and Reflections on Matthew 24:

1. Deception will come. Be careful you are not deceived.

2. Wars will come. Do not be frightened.

3. Famine and earthquakes will take place as signs of the beginning of birth pains.

4. You will be persecuted and killed because of the testimony of Jesus.

5. Your imprisonment will give you opportunity to bear witness to Jesus. The Holy Spirit will give you the words to speak.

6. People will turn away from the faith, hating other believers.

7. Most will grow cold because of the intensely wicked world in which they live.

8. **And this gospel of the kingdom will be preached in the whole world as a testimony to all nations, and then the end will come (v. 14).**

9. There will be a time to flee for your lives.

10. Pray that you do not have to flee in winter or on the Sabbath.

11. The days will be cut short or no one will remain faithful.

12. False Christs and false prophets will come and bring amazing signs and wonders.

13. Do not believe when people say that the Christ is here or there. When He comes, everyone will know He has arrived.

14. The sun will be darkened and the moon not give its light.

15. When Jesus returns, all nations will mourn.

16. Destruction will come like in the days of Noah. Life will carry on as normal, and no one will suspect that destruction will arrive.

17. A word to the servants of God: (1) Be a blessing to others and take care of them until Jesus comes. (2) You will be punished if you fight with others and live as though His return will never take place. (3) Always be prepared to stand before the Son of Man.

Connections between the above points are very complex because of the time variation between events. One scattering of God's people took place after the stoning of Stephen. Persecution of the people of God has taken place throughout the ages, both from peoples and political systems outside the Church, as well as from the organized Church itself. False prophets have always been with us; false

Christs are with us today. The nations presently hate the work of God and any hint of His leadership or moral standard in their lives.

But the nations do not yet mourn at His appearing. Destruction to the entire world has not happened, although destruction on catastrophic levels has occurred in isolated areas of the world.

Intense hatred exists between various peoples of the world. This is almost to be expected with those who do not know God or His transforming work in their lives. Believers also can enter this trap of hating others and growing cold because of the intense wickedness in the world. Are you free from hatred? We must draw upon our confidence in Christ's return and faith that the Lord will reign as judge. Our duty is to remain faithful witnesses to God's Kingdom, and not to place ourselves wrongly in the place of judge.

The coming Kingdom should not be viewed through a lens of coming destruction. A description of the coming Kingdom must paint the bright and beautiful picture of life forever with the Lord after the eradication of evil forces.

Jesus entrusted disciples with the work of carrying the gospel of the Kingdom to the whole world. Are you faithful with this charge given to all disciples?

> And he said to them, "I have eagerly desired to eat this Passover with you before I suffer. For I tell you, I will not eat it again until it finds fulfillment in the kingdom of God." For I tell you I will not drink again of the fruit of the vine until the kingdom of God comes" (Lk. 22:15-16, 18).

> And I confer on you a kingdom, just as my Father conferred one on me, so that you may eat and drink at my table in my kingdom and sit on thrones, judging the twelve tribes of Israel (Lk. 22:29-30).

The ministry of Jesus was a foretaste of the coming Kingdom in its fullness. Jesus opened the eyes of some blind men and some lame men walked. Yet the fullness of "the blind receive sight" is not totally with us. The most pronounced of His words yet to be fulfilled are ". . . the dead are raised," which points to a future fullness. We cannot satisfy the words of the Messiah by only having Jairus' daughter raised, the widow of Nain receiving back her son, and Lazarus' return from the dead.

> Jesus replied, "Go back and report to John what you hear and see: The blind receive sight, the lame walk, those who have leprosy are cured, the deaf hear, the dead are raised (Mt. 11:4-5).

The transfiguration of Jesus (Mt. 17) gives us a quick glimpse into a world of spiritually alive people. We consider Moses (~ 1500 B.C.) and Elijah (~ 870 B.C.) as long dead. God buried Moses, and Elijah was taken to heaven in a "chariot of fire." Both of these men are very much alive and able to speak the will of God to the Messiah.

The contrast between King Herod and King Jesus could not be more dramatic. Herod was furious that another king was in his realm (Mt. 2:3) and that an easy assassination eluded him (2:16). Jesus, on the other hand, is the Prince of Peace (Isa. 9:6). His Kingdom will last forever (9:7), which means it cannot be threatened.

The contrast of earthly kingdoms and the Kingdom of God brings us to a clear understanding of the oppression and violence of the former, and the peace and unity of the latter.

Purity and the Kingdom of God

John the Baptist's declaration, "Repent, for the kingdom of heaven is near" (Mt. 3:2), brings us to realize the purity required to enter and remain part of the Kingdom. Purity is not an entrance ticket that buys a person immoral privileges. The Kingdom is pure and stands in stark contrast to an Islamic image of God's Kingdom. The image of Islamic eternity appeals to the dark side, to lusts that have never surrendered to the purity of the Kingdom of God's light (1 Jn. 1:5). This appeal to Muslim males misrepresents God, who never condones evil.

John also spoke of ". . . gathering his wheat into the barn and burning up the chaff with unquenchable fire" (Mt. 3:12). The coming Kingdom will be a gathering of all who live like Jesus. The coming Kingdom will also oversee the complete and total destruction of the chaff, or those apart from Kingdom values and redemption. Eternal destruction in hell is a biblical value that may be scoffed at by greater numbers in the western world more than ever before. The opinions of finite people do not establish the values of the Kingdom. Humans in a fallen, distorted state are blinded by their desires. Those with imported, transcendent values of the Kingdom can see priorities and values clearly. The values of God must be imported because they do not originate from a corrupted world.

The Voice of God

God spoke at the baptism of Jesus (Mt. 3:17). The clarity of His voice on a few occasions is very special, but also rare. Believers listen intently to discern the inner "still, small voice" and trust they discern clearly. We expect to have God speaking more directly with us, as Adam and Eve once experienced.

The Kingdom in its fullness will be void of accusations and temptations to sin. The accuser of the brethren will not be present. Encounters with Satan, as Jesus had in the wilderness, will not be possible in that day (4:1-11).

The Kingdom of God will be void of disease--completely free. There will be no pain, no sickness, no hunger, and no demonic harassment of any kind (4:23). All who came to Jesus were healed (4:24), yet in the limited confines of this life. The power of the new Kingdom working through Messiah, and the resurrection power already at work within His being, restored the lives of large numbers of people within the confines of the limits of this world. Diseases, tumors, and demons were dealt with, and most were dealt with instantly. Eternal life will be realized when His voice calls us forth from the grave.

> Do not be amazed at this, for a time is coming when all who
> are in their graves will hear his voice and come out—those who
> have done good will rise to live, and those who have done evil
> will rise to be condemned (Jn. 5:28).

The vision He lays before us is one of eternal restoration--body, soul, and spirit.

Jesus promised that the coming Kingdom would have tremendous rewards. He promised mercy, not giving us what we rightfully deserve. He promised that we would be called the sons and daughters of God. He promised that the pure in heart would be blessed and that they would see God (Mt. 5:8).

This promise takes believers who are pure in heart past the encounter of Moses when he was allowed to only see God's hand and then God's back--but not His face (Ex. 33:19-23). But we shall see Him face to face.

Part 4:

The Formation and Expansion of the Church

As he neared Damascus on his journey, suddenly a light from heaven flashed around him. He fell to the ground and heard a voice say to him, "Saul, Saul, why do you persecute me?"

Part 4: The Formation and Expansion of the Church

Introduction

As we study the formation and expansion of the Church from Acts through the book of Revelation, we note many themes which help us interpret Scripture. Some Old Testament themes were clear, yet sometimes difficult to apply to the life of the community member in Israel. The gospel records highlight some of these themes that had elusive application or weak representation in the Old Testament. (Refer to page 229.) Themes highlighted in this section are meant to help us stand on the shoulders of the apostles, doing a greater and more expansive work in the Kingdom of God. We are also helped by acknowledging their struggles, knowing there is room for us to follow the Lord into uncharted territory.

Community obligation to the lives of God's people is highlighted as never before, with possessions becoming community property, "sharing everything they had" (Ac. 4:32). We are introduced to special provision for widows (Ch. 6), offerings for the poor (11:29-30), and churches providing for the spread of the gospel (Php. 4:15). Community obligation will also be highlighted throughout the Epistles. God cares that His people continue to walk in righteousness.

God's emphasis on **Light to the Nations** is given new strength, drawing His people into the joy of His works among many people groups. The young community of believers would face questions about how the Gentiles would be incorporated into the Church. Their wrestling with these issues is designed to propel us beyond their questions and into fruitful ministry.

The reality of **persecution and suffering** are presented in Acts, initially with beatings and imprisonment, and moving quickly to meeting the first martyr, Stephen. We understand **future hope** through both Stephen's gaze into heaven at the face of Jesus, and the culmination of the Body of Christ joined forever with the Lord in Revelation.

The Lord is Sovereign, the great King over heaven and earth. Judgment in the book of Acts will come to those who claim to follow Christ but who live in deception. Judgment will come to a ruler who equates himself with the divine (Ac. 12:21-23).

The Lord's sovereignty is evident in prison doors opening and in His martyrs who are welcomed home.

We are compelled to live our lives for the joy set before us in obedience to the Lord, neither clinging to this world nor to its possessions. The New Testament clearly portrays a life with God open to all, overcoming the problems faced in this world. This is not a record that encourages us to blend in with our cultural surroundings or reinterpret morality in light of society. Eternity must be in our souls from the time we begin our walk with Jesus, abandoning all for His sake.

The Acts of the Apostles

Introduction

Luke, "our dear friend . . . the doctor" (Col. 4:14), is the author of Acts. It is generally agreed that he wrote the book in approximately A.D. 63 upon completion of his gospel record. Luke was more than a historian. As a theologian and missiologist, he selectively puts before the reader historical facts that help us see the overall plan of God. The Gospel of Luke introduces the Messiah as the fulfillment of Scripture. The Book of Acts exposes us to a wide variety of people impacted by the news of Jesus. Luke presented us with dramatic shifts in the two works that he penned. **The first dramatic shift** was the contrast of the starting points in the two volumes. The first volume began with Zechariah the priest performing Temple duties and an angelic visitation announcing the birth of John, the forerunner of the Messiah. That starting point was the center of Jewish tradition dating back to Solomon and to the Temple, the very center of Jewish power. Acts, by contrast, brought us to a common upper room where the Holy Spirit had been poured out upon one hundred twenty ordinary disciples.

A second dramatic shift was between the early references to God's work among the Gentiles in Nazareth, work which had met with opposition (Lk. 4:24-27), and the nearly completed focus on the expansion of the Church into Gentile regions that we find in Acts. Both volumes showed those living under Jewish tradition struggling deeply with both the Samaritans and the Gentiles who were welcomed into the community of faith. As the spotlight shifts, we see the emphasis turn to proclaiming the Gospel of the Kingdom to the Gentile world. The theology of receiving "the nations" into the family of God is the daily topic found in Acts. God inspired this Gentile author to record the activities of the early Church. He takes us into 32 nations, 54 cities and 9 islands of the Mediterranean. Through his writings, we are introduced to government officials, sorcerers, miracles, and the effort required to carry the Gospel to regions beyond. The conclusion we must draw is the necessity for us to continue spreading the message of the Kingdom of God, despite the possibility of persecution that all believers face for the Name of Jesus.

A third dynamic shift was from highlighting the ministries of the early apostles to a transformed Pharisee named Saul. Acts was not written as a biography of the eleven - now twelve again. The life and ministry of Matthias takes only two sentences. In fact, most of the other eleven apostles are not mentioned outside of the meeting to choose Matthias (Ac. 1:13). More time is given to Stephen's anointed life, his death, and the repercussions following his death than to writing about a fraternity of twelve. Luke's story follows the anointed Philip to Samaria and to the desert road, rather than describing the faith of those working in Jerusalem.

A fourth pivotal point in Acts was the bridge into the letters of Paul, apostle to the Gentiles, who wrote much of the rest of the New Testament. Because of Luke's introduction of this "untimely born" apostle Paul, the letters to believers in seven cities and regions, and pastoral letters to three individuals, are meaningful to us today. Luke's historical record of Christ becoming real to many peoples through this apostle helps us to understand Paul's heart for "the glorious riches of this mystery, which is Christ in you, the hope of glory" (Col. 1:27).

A fifth noteworthy point in the Book of Acts was the continuation of a major theme from the Gospels, that of searching Scripture to understand the believers' present context. Look for believers to quote Scripture references that brought understanding to their changing world. The Old Testament became a living treasure chest of instruction and guidance. This is significant to our faith today. The early Church searched the Scripture to understand their times and formulate their faith. Those early believers turned the world upside down. We, too, must apply our faith in context rather than tolerating our depraved society. Tolerance of society produces an innocuous life that is unthreatening and has a false sense of peace.

Committees have a significant place in Acts. All leadership groups grapple with new challenges before them. It is important to understand both the place of committees and of individuals who listen to the Lord

Look for **significant individuals** in this book who listened to the voice of God and who responded with obedience. They set before us a powerful example. If they could listen and obey, so can we. Our world is not more dangerous, nor our circumstances more complex, to ignore the obvious call to bring the gospel to the entire world.

28. The Spirit and The Nations

Jesus' words before His ascent into heaven are recorded in Acts Chapter 1. He told His disciples to remain in Jerusalem until clothed with power from the Holy Spirit. The significance of His words must be taken directly for all of us desiring to follow as disciples.

> On one occasion, while he was eating with them, he gave them this command: "Do not leave Jerusalem, but wait for the gift my Father promised, which you have heard me speak about. For John baptized with water, but in a few days you will be baptized with the Holy Spirit" (Ac. 1:4-5).

The baptism of the Holy Spirit is the starting block for the book of Acts, similar to the starting block into which runners place their feet. Just as dramatic as the Kingdom Jesus inaugurated, so the start and the expansion of the Church through human lives began with the anointing of the Holy Spirit. This was the time of an enormous shift in the work of God among people. Emmanuel, God with us, took on an entirely new meaning as the Holy Spirit came to the life of each believer.

Reflection

What is the similarity or difference between Emmanuel, the baby in the feeding trough, and Emmanuel in the book of Acts?

Without the anointing of the Holy Spirit, our words will convey (in human strength) historical records that are nice, but still powerless to transform a life. God expects those who convey the truth of the gospel to move with the power of the Holy Spirit. It is the Spirit of God who brings life. Jesus said, "Flesh gives birth to flesh, but the Spirit gives birth to spirit" (Jn. 3:6). The Spirit of God longs to bring life to the hopeless inhabitants of the world. His desire is to speak through the disciple to impact the listener with the truth of the Word of God and the living stories of Jesus. It is a fruitless struggle to form a better society based upon better principles, yet lacking the internal drive of the Holy Spirit to transform a people. **Mission begins by waiting upon God, often collectively, to receive power from on high.**

Jesus encouraged His followers to ask for the Holy Spirit without fear (Lk. 11:9-13). He likened imperfect earthly fathers who give good gifts with His perfect Father who always gives good gifts. There is no fear for the believer to ask for the anointing of the Spirit of God. The issue is not pushing charismatic, pentecostal, or apostolic teaching. It is the gift of the Father offered to all those hungry to do His will.

The disciples' discussion in the context of Jesus teaching on the imminent coming of the Holy Spirit still centered on the Kingdom and Israel, showing their lack of conceptualizing the direction and call of God (Ac. 1:6). The work of the Holy Spirit is necessary for us to understand the priorities of God, as opposed to our preconceived or cultural priorities. Without the Spirit of God, we as believers in Jesus can remain locked in old arguments, battling on human terms, and looking for prominence on turf in a deviant kingdom which is opposed to God's Kingdom.

Once filled with the Holy Spirit, believers will need to grow into the scope and type of ministry to which they are personally called. This movement will be led by the Spirit of God rather than by a centralized, human-based planning commission in one geographic location.

> He said to them: "It is not for you to know the times or dates the Father has set by his own authority. But you will receive power when the Holy Spirit comes on you; and you will be my witnesses in Jerusalem, and in all Judea and Samaria, and to the ends of the earth."
> After he said this, he was taken up before their very eyes, and a cloud hid him from their sight (Ac. 1:7-9).

Jesus said that His people would be witnesses in several spheres **simultaneously.**

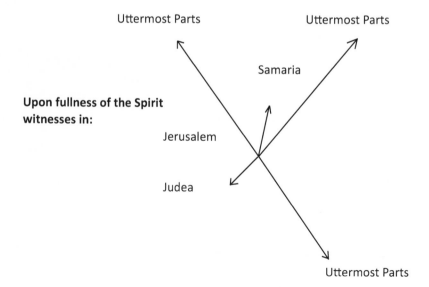

This was not a recipe for mission stages, completing Jerusalem before moving on to Judea, for example. Some mistake this directive for world mission as a set of sequential steps. There is nothing in the command of Jesus that would disqualify mission in any region or limit the preaching of the Kingdom of God in regions beyond until closer regions are covered. As we will discover in the pages of Acts, Gentile regions of Antioch were touched by the gospel before "saturation evangelism" covered Jerusalem and Judea. Likewise, Paul's ministry would touch numerous regions of Gentiles while unbelievers still persecuted believers in Jerusalem. Because of the significance of the Holy Spirit leading mission, it is important that we allow Him to lead, not qualifying one region as ultimately more important than another or one's calling as more important than another's. It is not our prerogative to downplay mission to "Judea" or to make one "uttermost part" a superior calling over another.

Question

Some leaders have stated, "We will first reach our Jerusalem!"
What are the implications of this statement?

The outpouring of the Holy Spirit on Pentecost began in Jerusalem. Today, the Spirit of God moves upon people in all locations, but we must ask why this work began in Jerusalem and not in Galilee, the region from which the disciples originated? The prophetic word through Isaiah described the centrality of Jerusalem, both in people coming to learn about God's ways as well as being sent forth from that city.

> Many peoples will come and say,
> "Come, let us go up to the mountain of the LORD,
> to the house of the God of Jacob.
> He will teach us his ways,
> so that we may walk in his paths."
> The law will go out from Zion,
> the word of the LORD from Jerusalem (Isa. 2:3).

Jesus was telling His disciples that they would be witnesses as they went out. His words propel us to seek lost communities and bring the Kingdom of God into their lives.

Centrifugal Mission

God's heart leads us outward into the world. We seek to understand the language, culture, and worldview of each people group in the world. For example, believers in Algeria and Brazil have a duty to take the gospel to regions beyond themselves, and they need to be informed of their God-given duty. The Spirit of God compels His people to continue the missionary task. We must trust the call of the Spirit in the lives of believers from numerous backgrounds, trusting that they will be led, as we are led, to carry the news of the risen Lord.

Pentecost and Mission

Pentecost (πεντηκοστησ) is the Greek term for the seven weeks[1] after Passover. The Old Testament feast, known today as Pentecost, is the Feast of First Fruits, The Feast of Harvest or The Feast of Weeks (Heb. shaw-boo'-ah for the seven weeks). This feast takes place at the beginning of the wheat harvest. This second feast of three focused on the beginning of the wheat harvest, looking with eyes of faith and believing that the entire harvest would come in fullness. We must make the inference that God is concerned for all nations to be brought into his "barn," which is more significant than annually believing for only an abundance of bread. The initial part of the wheat harvest symbolizes the Spirit entrusted to us, while the fullness of our lives is linked to the harvest of the nations that is to come. Israel was commanded not to reap to the edges of its fields or gather the gleanings, because both were for the poor and the alien living among them (Lev. 23:22). Mission with the anointing of the Holy Spirit will bring us to ask new questions including: How do we apply our initial fullness of the Spirit to work among the poor and refugees worldwide?

The disciples previously experienced a filling of the Holy Spirit on the day of the resurrection (Jn. 20:21-23). But this time, the coming of the Spirit was different. The Spirit came:

1.   With the sound of a "violent wind . . . from heaven"

2.   With flames that came to rest on each of the 120 gathered in the house

3.   With the speaking in languages of at least fifteen different people groups

The Spirit of God was poured out on believers in a common room, not in the Holy of Holies or even in the courts of the Temple. The Spirit of God would not

---

1   Seven weeks plus one day after Passover Sabbath (see Lev. 23:16)

have come like a rushing wind to that particular upper room had the one hundred twenty been meeting somewhere else. This means that God is looking for His people with whom He can both indwell and co-labor in Kingdom ministries. Jesus told the Samaritan woman that a time was coming when true worshipers would not be limited to geographic regions, but would be free to worship anywhere in spirit and in truth (Jn. 4:21-24). Although this initial outpouring of the Spirit came in Jerusalem, the time would come very soon for subsequent outpourings in Gentile regions. We as God's sent ones must be prepared for God to move on people in any location of His choosing. We must understand the significance of the group who received the Spirit of God on that first Pentecost and the religious groups who did not.

All of the disciples who gathered in the upper room were filled with the Holy Spirit at the same time, not just the upper leadership. This move of the Holy Spirit engulfed the body of believers without exception, anointing every one of them. Each was linked directly with God--and not through an anointed person. This is significant because of the need for each person to look to God for both anointing and calling. This has similarities and contrasts with the anointing shared by the seventy elders chosen to help Moses.

> So Moses went out and told the people what the LORD had said. He brought together seventy of their elders and had them stand around the tent. Then the LORD came down in the cloud and spoke with him, and he took some of the power of the Spirit that was on him and put it on the seventy elders. When the Spirit rested on them, they prophesied—but did not do so again. However, two men, whose names were Eldad and Medad, had remained in the camp. They were listed among the elders, but did not go out to the tent. Yet the Spirit also rested on them, and they prophesied in the camp. A young man ran and told Moses, "Eldad and Medad are prophesying in the camp" (Nu. 11:24-27).

One similarity is the common location in which a mass anointing took place. In this case, it was in a camp in the Sinai desert. A difference in the two anointings is that some of the anointing on Moses was taken and distributed to the elders. Moses, as a leader, was very much affirmed in this action. The anointing in Acts had everyone looking directly to the Lord. Another contrast is that the chosen leaders in the Sinai were anointed and prophesied. In Acts, all gathered believers received the gift of the Father that Jesus had promised. All were now set aside for service. All believers need the anointing of the Spirit of God.

Centripetal Mission

The gathering of God-fearers in Jerusalem was like a lighthouse. The Temple and worship of God in this particular city drew people. The "God-fearing Jews from every nation under heaven" (Ac. 2:5) heard the disciples declaring the wonders of God in their own native languages. We do not know if they heard words of worship or the message of Christ's death and resurrection proclaimed. We do know that they heard and understood in their own languages.

The gathering of God-fearing Jews in Jerusalem, hearing the message of forgiveness proclaimed in Jesus name, is an example of Isaiah's prophetic words coming to fulfillment. This gathering would also exemplify the scattering or dispersion of faith as each returned to his/her perspective home with the message of the Messiah. It is important to notice that those present were not Gentiles from the nations, but as previously stated, God-fearing Jews from the nations.

> Then how is it that each of us hears them in his own native language? Parthians, Medes and Elamites; residents of Mesopotamia, Judea and Cappadocia, Pontus and Asia, Phrygia and Pamphylia, Egypt and the parts of Libya near Cyrene; visitors from Rome (both Jews and converts to Judaism); Cretans and Arabs—we hear them declaring the wonders of God in our own tongues! Amazed and perplexed, they asked one another, "What does this mean" (Ac. 2:8-12)?

It is not realistic to state that Pamphylia, Egypt and Libya were now reached with the gospel because speakers of those languages returned home as believers. Pentecost did not instantly precipitate an ingathering of much of the Middle East and Turkey. Mission to the whole world is elusive because the conscience can be as slippery as a watermelon seed in your fingers. Some jump to conclusions that a foreign student - now a believer in Jesus - will now go back and convert his or her nation. It is a nice thought, but overstated, or possibly premature in its conclusions. It is necessary for three things to be remembered in order to keep mission on track:

- Each of the Jews present that day in Jerusalem needed to internalize their new faith and allow it to flow in their own language. They needed to grasp the necessity to carry the good news back to their whole region. This is still true today.

- The enormous transfer of the Good News from Jewish speakers of Arabic, languages of Media, or languages of Pontus, etc. to Gentiles living in those regions must still take place. It must cross ethnic lines in their language community with the message, expressing the incarnational reality of the gospel. The incarnation in this case means that believers must become bicultural, while using nearly the same language. Bicultural expression in one city or region is difficult work.

- The message does not stop with the languages present. In time, believers will carry the message further into new language and ethnic groupings.

These stages will require revelation and obedience in order to cross social and ethnic lines with the gospel. The initial outpouring of the Holy Spirit set the direction for the nations. The Holy Spirit was far ahead of the early believers, pointing the way for them to follow. He is still far ahead of us today.

The idea that *only* nationals should reach their own people threatens world mission. This thought has, in its most extreme form, disqualified non-native speakers, or "clumsy foreigners," from entering a region with the gospel. God is saying that no nationality is excluded. Perfect speakers of a language may not be the best ones to convey the message. The other threat to world mission comes with the completion of the thought that "only nationals" are valid missionaries in their own countries. Those nationals will be stripped of the burden to go to regions beyond their home nation. If Indians, for example, believe that only Indians should be missionaries in India, they will mentally disqualify themselves from God's call to Turkey. The gospel is not from the earth but from above. The incarnational value of the message is that it comes from another realm. The message brought into any cultural setting must, by its nature, have a certain "foreignness" because it did not start with a human idea. Each person conveying the message must bring it with its "strangeness" of forgiveness and its "foreignness" of harmony with God. Both native speakers present in Acts 2 and strangers to regions whom we will encounter shortly need to find ways to convey this transforming message. The day for all nations to participate in world mission is still very much upon us.

Missiological Insight

The conclusion we reach is that on the day of Pentecost, the Spirit spoke into the languages of fifteen major peoples in the greater region. God is not locked into the Hebrew of Abraham's day or of Moses' day. The Spirit is freely moving into the languages and cultures of all nations. The Spirit speaking into each language will mean that the worldview of each people will be transformed, and life will be redefined through the Word of God in each language. We as co-laborers with God pick up on this significant missionary mantel, actively seeking to know the languages and cultural expressions of those still in darkness, those without the light of Christ.

We also understand that the Spirit of God seeks to utilize all language backgrounds in order to advance the Kingdom. Regardless of background, all people will need to welcome Jesus, learn to speak of Him, and live for Him. All will be challenged to move on with the message to others, possibly even into new regions.

The Spirit and All People

The Spirit of God is leading, not following, His people. Cultural constraints of nations and individuals, therefore, do not lead the Spirit. Peter quoted from the prophet Joel: "In the last days, God says, I will pour out my Spirit on all people" (Ac. 2:17). The significance of "all people" being the recipients of the Spirit of God was not yet understood by the disciples or by the newly developing party of the circumcision. Even though Peter grasped the word from Joel in context, which we will expand on later, the full meaning of this prophetic word was yet to be understood. It must be noted that the Spirit would move into the lives of believers of other backgrounds and would not be constrained by the cultural misunderstanding of Jewish believers. "I the Lord do not change" (Mal. 3:6) was fitting on Pentecost. Believing that the Lord desires to move into the lives of yet unreached people will encourage us to make the gospel message understandable to the masses.

The Spirit Continues to Fill His People

The Book of Acts records the words of Jesus that we are filled with the Spirit to "be my witnesses" (Ac. 1:8). Only one filling of the Spirit on the day of Pentecost would have limited the number of witnesses to 120 people and limited the power of God to one specific time period. Luke records the healing of a beggar at the Beautiful Gate during Peter and John's routine trip to the Temple at three in the afternoon (3:1-10). When questioned by the Sanhedrin as to how the beggar was now able to walk, Luke writes: "Then Peter, filled with the Holy Spirit, said to them . . ." (4:8). The significance is that God's people are repeatedly filled with the Spirit for many tasks. Normal life in the Book of Acts was for disciples to repeatedly move in the power of the Holy Spirit. This is the message Jesus spoke through the parable of the Ten Virgins (Mt. 25:1-13). The necessity to be refilled with the Spirit keeps us in God's work. Attitudes that result from unforgiveness, speaking slanderous remarks, and sin bring us into the flesh, departing from a walk in the Spirit. The enemy of our souls knows this tactic well. God wants us refreshed and refilled with His Spirit. It is necessary that we take time to be refilled with the Spirit (Eph. 5:18).

Fullness of the Holy Spirit was a requirement for those chosen to wait on tables of foreign (Grecian) Jewish widows (Ac. 6:3). They needed the wisdom of the Spirit to distribute food. Stephen was "full of God's grace and power" (6:8) in doing miraculous signs, and we must infer that it was the Spirit who led him into confrontation with the Jewish authorities. Some of us will find that God's amazing grace to see people healed in His name will bring a sharp conflict with religious authorities. The two are related. Inaugurating the Kingdom in new areas will initiate a clash between light and darkness. The darkness will be seen in both human institutions and in confrontations with demonic powers. Stephen's fullness of the Spirit is described as both his face being like the face of an angel (6:15), and as his ability to see "the Son of Man standing at the right hand of God" (7:54-56). Being full of the Spirit ushered in both his physical death and his life in the presence of Jesus. Do not be afraid if this is how the Spirit leads you or your loved ones.

Samaritans Receive the Spirit

Luke's gospel introduces us to Samaritans who knew that Jesus was en route to Jerusalem and, therefore, rejected Him (Lk. 9:51-53). We read a parable about a "Good Samaritan" (Ch. 10) and of a thankful Samaritan healed of leprosy (17:16). Luke not only tells us that Jesus promised His disciples that they would be witnesses in Samaria, but he records how the gospel entered this region. Philip was one of the seven chosen to minister to foreign Jewish widows (Ac. 6:5), and he was known to be full of the Holy Spirit. The scattering of believers after Stephen's martyrdom brought Philip to Samaria. Philip's ministry was accompanied by miraculous signs including healings, the driving out of evil spirits, faith in Jesus, and baptisms (8:4-13).

Why did it take Peter and John, traveling from Jerusalem, to pray for the Samaritans to be filled with the Holy Spirit? Three reasons are possible, none of which suggests that the "apostles" needed to arrive in order to carry out the ministry of the fullness of the Spirit. Believing that super anointed people must be present to validate a work has carried mission activity into oddities that bend toward cult worship of leadership. One possible reason could be that "all except the apostles were scattered throughout Judea and Samaria" (8:1). The words of Jesus, "Do not leave Jerusalem" (1:4), may have been mistaken either for waiting for the Spirit to be poured out or simply remaining in the city. The joy and curiosity of salvation in Samaria may have thrust them out to a new area. A second possible reason for these two original disciples arriving in Samaria could stem back to their being with Jesus when Samaritans believed and invited them to stay in their village (Jn. 4:39-41). Advancing the work Jesus had begun would certainly have been of interest to all of the apostles. A third reason Philip was not the one who prayed for the fullness of the Holy Spirit could be that he was young and too timid to move forward in this ministry, especially with non-Jewish recipients. All of us need to be encouraged to move in the gifts of the Spirit, not timidly holding back. God will bless boldness and faith.

The Spirit and God's People

There were immediate, measurable changes to the way God's people interacted after the coming of the Holy Spirit. The Spirit brought a great transformation of how people interacted with each other, regardless of background. Disciples who previously had compared their relative greatness, now had a hunger to be together: "They devoted themselves to the apostles' teaching and to fellowship, to the breaking of bread and to prayer" (Ac 2:42). The presence of the Spirit of God made them hungry to be with other believers and gave birth to the Church.

Note that the believers met both in the Temple courts and in their homes. Two traditions were still in place for the believers in Jerusalem: the significance of Jewish customs including the Temple and the new found joy of being with those of like faith in the risen Jesus. Meeting in the Temple courts would not be an option for new believers who came to walk with Jesus in Gentile lands, but meeting house to house would remain a viable option.

God loves to inhabit the praises of His people (Ps. 22:3), yet there are times that we struggle to know who is hungry for the living God. This was the case with Saul and his dramatic conversion on the road to Damascus (Ac. 9). Ananias was changed from a man who was afraid of Saul, even telling God of Saul's true intent, to one who believed God and acted. Ananias prayed in faith for Saul's sight to return, called Saul "brother" in an act of total acceptance, and prayed for Saul to be filled with the Holy Spirit (9:17-19). This was moving very fast on a human level, but obviously not too fast for the Spirit of God. The speed at which God moves is a challenge for us and a constant reminder not to set our own timetable for God to work. Saul's anointing and future ministry were revealed to Ananias in that same encounter.

> But the Lord said to Ananias, "Go! This man is my chosen instrument to proclaim my name to the Gentiles and their kings and to the people of Israel. I will show him how much he must suffer for my name" (Ac. 9:15-16).

Can we look beyond a person's background and allow the Spirit of God to speak prophetic vision of their future? Such faith will require placing our trust in God who calls, and not in our ability to train people to remain loyal to our personal ministry. Paul's ministry was marked by a boldness in the Holy Spirit, an acceptance of new leaders, by healings, and by power in preaching. Luke tells us that Paul was also filled with the Holy Spirit to rebuke Elymas the sorcerer (13:9). A fullness of the Spirit is needed when confronting dark powers or people operating in spiritual darkness. It is important that we ask God for His fullness daily because we do not know what a day might bring to our lives.

Peter also encountered the speed at which the Spirit of God operates. His simple message to Cornelius and his household related his personal eye witness account of Jesus: His life, His death, and His resurrection. The Scripture says, "While Peter was still speaking these words, the Holy Spirit came on all who heard the message" (10:44). The intentional prayer for the gift of the Holy Spirit in Samaria was absent in Cornelius' house. We must grasp how eager God is to fill the lives of people He calls out of darkness. This move of God would bring Peter's actions into question with the party of the circumcision, and eventually define the work of God among Gentiles. Learning to hear God's direction for new questions among people receiving the gospel drives us to our next topic: Theology in Context.

29. Theology in Context

How do we interpret the work of God in our midst? What is God saying that affects our ministries today? Scripture is alive and relevant for each people group on the planet, yet what God is saying will vary according to the priorities and needs of a people. Mission requires us to understand the times in which we live and interpret Scripture in light of these times.

Peter and Theology in Context

Luke tells us of Peter's leadership to restore the number of apostles to twelve. There are several lessons we glean from this passage. Some quickly conclude that the choosing of Matthias over Joseph was wasted energy because neither were heard of again after this point. Judgement of Peter's leadership should not be made on the point of silence in regard to these two names. The early Church eagerly acted on Scripture as it illuminated the paths of believers. Believers did their theology in context, according to their understanding of Scripture. Peter quoted, "May his days be few; may another take his place of leadership" (Ps. 109:8). It seemed best to them to choose one to take Judas' place of leadership, based upon Scripture and their sense of God's leading. The believers saw themselves living out a prophetic command inspired by the Holy Spirit. The early apostles should be commended for both their obedience and their initiative in their faith to make decisions based on Scripture.

Reflection

Those who judge the actions of the early believers as frivolous will fall under that same judgment and be weakened in their ability to make decisions.

The side lesson learned comes through the reality Joseph faced--he was not chosen to be counted with the other eleven apostles. Each of us will face opportunities for encouragement and advancement, as well as the humbling experience of the advancement of others, not ourselves. How each of us responds to similar circumstances reveals our heart for God and toward others around us. Remember though, Joseph was most likely anointed on the day of Pentecost to fulfill God's purpose through his life. Nothing held Matthias, Joseph, or Peter back from doing great exploits for Jesus as the Kingdom expanded. **Nothing holds us back from moving in great anointing and faith, regardless of a title or lack of title.**

What do we tell the crowd?

The Church was in a very significant stage as it began. The forty days the disciples spent together were, no doubt, spent pouring over the Scriptures, trying to understand the events that had taken place from the context of the Word of God. The message Peter gave drew deeply from the writings of the Prophet Joel and King David. Peter addressed the crowd, assuring them that the disciples were not drunk, and went on to give an explanation of what God was doing in their midst.

Peter related their current experience as confirmation that this was the outworking of the Holy Spirit predicted by the prophet Joel. Peter quoted to the crowd the prophetic words that the Spirit would be poured out upon all people.

> In the last days, God says,
> I will pour out my Spirit on all people.
> Your sons and daughters will prophesy,
> your young men will see visions,
> your old men will dream dreams.
> Even on my servants, both men and women,
> I will pour out my Spirit in those days,
> and they will prophesy.
> I will show wonders in the heaven above
> and signs on the earth below,
> blood and fire and billows of smoke.
> The sun will be turned to darkness
> and the moon to blood
> before the coming of the great and glorious day of the Lord.
> And everyone who calls
> on the name of the Lord will be saved (Ac. 2:17-21).

This was a scene we need to grasp. The God-fearing Jews heard from Scripture that all people would be filled with the Spirit even as the disciples were filled. Peter reminded them that prophesy would be part of the lives of both males and females. In the increasingly male dominated world of the first century, which is similar to many parts of the world yet today, it was essential that the Kingdom of God be taught as a spiritual heritage for both men and women. Hearing and speaking God's words was for both genders and all ages. Visions and dreams would be given regardless of age group. Older people in the faith must listen to what God is speaking through younger people, and vice versa. A vision of God on the heart of a young person must be nurtured and not dominated to fit into the dream of an older person.

Peter, quoting from Joel, placed the framework of their times into the last days before the coming of the great and glorious day of the Lord. This was not a scare tactic. We still live in those "last days," and no one knows how long they will last. Peter goes on to tell the crowd that ". . . everyone who calls on the name of the Lord will be saved" (2:21). By this, Peter signified that salvation is for all who call on the Lord. All are welcomed, regardless of ethnic background. How was it possible to understand this word in a highly Jewish context? God had just reiterated His heart for the world, which was outside the common worldview of many Jewish people. He was addressing the issues of God's open door for salvation and gift of the Holy Spirit to Jew and Gentile alike.

Many would probably have wrongly concluded that "all" referred to any Jew who called out to the Lord. It is often very difficult to hear Scripture outside of our cultural framework. Most people assume that they hear and interpret the Word of God correctly, while stuck in the complexities of their own cultural norms. This is why the issue of slavery took centuries to address in the West. In a similar way, the East struggles against pluralism and absolutes. Muslim background believers will be challenged to receive believers from other ethnicities as "clean" in God's eyes. These challenges require Scripture in context to address pressing needs.

Reflection

Believers who make judgments based on good common sense, rather than on the Word of God in context, will err in blindness and from a false sense of cultural superiority.

Peter recapped the story of Jesus before the crowd, including the necessity of both the death and resurrection of the Messiah, and he contrasted this with David's tomb. He quoted from a Psalm and brought new understanding to the context of his hearers in Jerusalem.

> Therefore my heart is glad and my tongue rejoices;
> my body also will rest secure,
> because you will not abandon me to the grave,
> nor will you let your Holy One see decay.
> You have made known to me the path of life;
> you will fill me with joy in your presence,
> with eternal pleasures at your right hand (Ps. 16:9-11).

Mission will require theology in context for the message of the day. The questions people have when they are exposed to the gospel will require an understanding of Scripture in a new light. Theology will not have strength if presented as a line of dogma. It must answer the questions of the people of a particular time. God's servants need the anointing and the freedom to expound on passages that meet the present needs of people.

Peter placed three items together to bring a convincing argument to the people.

- David died and is still buried.

- The resurrection of the Messiah fulfills this prophesy.

- We are eye witnesses to these events.

Peter, speaking by the Holy Spirit, went on to tell them to repent and be baptized. He told them that they would receive the gift of the Holy Spirit which "... is for you and your children . . ." He went on to say something that would only later be understood: *". . . and for all who are far off—for all whom the Lord our God will call"* (Ac. 2:39 Emphasis mine).

Theology in context did not simply address the immediate needs of the people present, but also stretched their hearts to hear the call of God to the nations.

The scene was set for the repentance, baptism, and fullness of the Holy Spirit for all people. The rest of Acts will highlight the struggles faced in living out this prophetic word from the whole of Scripture. It will also give us insight into how we must, in a similar way, find answers to questions we will face as the gospel continues to the ends of the earth.

Theology in context was evident when Peter rethought Scripture based upon his revelation from God in accepting all people.

> Then Peter began to speak: "I now realize how true it is that
> God does not show favoritism but accepts from every nation
> the one who fears him and does what is right" (Ac. 10:34-35).

Not allowing our theology to change will keep us locked into a ministry that reflects our religious understanding and our culturally approved lifestyle. Both Peter and James addressed the council in Jerusalem facing the question of the Gentiles being incorporated into the Kingdom, and both applied their theology in context. Peter recalled the work of the Holy Spirit in Cornelius' household, giving approval to the ministry among Gentiles. "God, who knows the heart, showed that he accepted them by giving the Holy Spirit to them, just as he did to us" (Ac. 15:8).

James and Theology in Context

The council in Jerusalem needed a theology for the Gentiles who had turned to the Lord. James quoted Amos 9:11-12, applying the passage to the Gentiles as a people for God. The clarity of thought allowed Gentiles to follow the Lord.

> After this I will return and rebuild David's fallen tent.
> Its ruins I will rebuild, and I will restore it,
> that the rest of mankind may seek the Lord, even all the Gentiles
> who bear my name, says the Lord, who does these things—
> things known from long ago (Ac. 15:16-18).

We need both the ability to recognize the work of God, as Peter did, and the ability to search the Scriptures, like James, to give an explanation to what God is currently doing in our midst. Both Peter and James came to the same conclusion but by different means. It is safe to conclude that the work of God and the Scriptures that bring to light His present work complement each other; both are necessary.

The party of the circumcision required Jewish law to be applied first. If the Law of Moses had been applied first, the Gentiles would not have been Gentiles, but rather Proselytes to Judaism. James picked up on "even the Gentiles who bear my name" and refused to make them Jewish converts first. God wants Gentiles to bear His name. This must take our thoughts to the thousands of cultures that God wants to bear His name. A short list of avoiding the immoral was appropriate, rather than a long list which would have required the Torah and the commands handed down by the elders of Israel. It also avoids a long list of what our own national heritage deems necessary. The denominational heritage we have is also an improper set of rules to hand to a newly emerging Church.

The rebuilding of David's fallen tent must be applied to all people. This Scripture speaks of the sanctuary God desires to make in all locations. David's tent and worship of Jesus must be established among all people, and not left in our minds as only a large physical tent where prayer occurs only for several nations.

Paul and Theology in Context

Paul's sharp mind and background in Scripture was a tool in God's hand to bring formation to the early church. Paul reasoned from Scripture, along with the Jews, that Jesus was the Christ (i.e. in Cyprus, Ac 13:5; Pisidian Antioch, 13:16-41; Thessalonica, 17:1-4), displaying great resourcefulness in bringing the risen Messiah into the context of Jewish Scripture. We, too, will find the need to focus on Scripture in ways that highlight both *truth* to people hearing the gospel for the first time, and *conviction of sin* in their context. Paul's freshness in interpreting Scripture shows he is not relying on old Jewish teachings or on the preeminence of Moses. His life changed and his understanding of Scripture lined up with his Damascus road experience. His clear description of Jesus as the Messiah throughout Scripture is needed today, clarifying the nature and role of the Anointed One for many people groups.

Reflection

Jews deny that Jesus is the Messiah. Muslims believe Jesus is the Messiah (i.e. Surat Al-Imran 3:45; Surat Women 4:157), but they do not understand the nature of Messiah. Sharp minds are needed today to reason from Scripture, describing the incarnational nature of the Messiah.

Circumcision and Context

The party of the circumcision arrived at a Gentile fellowship in Antioch and told the people, "Unless you are circumcised, according to the custom taught by Moses, you cannot be saved" (Ac.15:1). Fortunately, Paul and Barnabas were there to declare this teaching heretical. The question was of faith in the Messiah or faith in circumcision. The Messiah would shape Paul's ministry. His understanding of Scripture in this context would grow and his writings, to this day, help believers throughout the globe learn about freedom from works.

One of the first church plants in Paul's ministry was in Philippi. His letter to this fellowship warns them to:

> Watch out for those dogs, those evildoers, those mutilators of the flesh. For it is we who are the circumcision, we who serve God by his Spirit, who boast in Christ Jesus, and who put no confidence in the flesh (Php. 3:2-3).

His love for freedom in Christ necessitated warning the Philippians against true and false circumcision. His definition of the true circumcision spoke to the issue in terms of the intent of the heart. He agreed with James that they should remain Gentiles, but pressed the issue of transformation of the heart. Paul crafted his letter like a lawyer, making sure they got the point. He detailed his life in Judaism and the perfection with which he kept the law--to the point of persecuting the Church (3:6). He referred to all of his achievements in Judaism as rubbish, that he might gain Christ (3:8). Paul's complete transformation in Christ formed a theology that strengthened others against the heresy of "freedom through the law."

Through his letters, Paul warned all the churches to avoid false righteousness based on the law. His grief was evident when the Galatian church included the Jewish law in their belief system. The grief Paul felt when he said, "You foolish Galatians! Who has bewitched you?" (Gal 3:1), was really God's grief. Doing our theology in context is allowing the Holy Spirit to form a people who cling to Jesus. Paul told the Galatians, "Neither circumcision nor uncircumcision means anything; what counts is the new creation" (6:15).

Paul wanted transformation based upon faith in Jesus the Messiah. The goal of theology for each of us is to bless a people with freedom to know Jesus without the shackles of their past, or of our past laid upon them.

Questions

With your people group in mind, what past expressions become chains in their walk with Christ?

From what chains from the outside should they be protected and with what chains from the outside should they be strengthened?

Reflections

Theology in context requires carefully crafting answers to the current questions that believers face. Expect that questions will arise that demand attention. Always search for answers:
- through the flow of God's Word
- through the knowledge of His character
- in the presence of many counselors

Do answers that fit a culture ignore the commands of Christ? Answers cannot be imposed from the outside because they will lack ownership by the local believers. Individuals should not make decisions which will lead to manipulative hierarchy and control of the fellowship.

30. Leadership, Obedience, and the Kingdom of God

Leadership and Transitions

Transition times are always a challenge for leaders. The leadership on which we have relied, possibly for many years, can change in an instant. Critical times call for action on the part of young leaders to move into their God-given anointings. Joshua faced this stark transition when Moses, to whom he had looked for leadership for forty years, was no longer present. The command God gave to Joshua contained both direction and encouragement; it was indeed his time and place to lead.

> Moses my servant is dead. Now then, you and all these people, get ready to cross the Jordan River into the land I am about to give to them . . . Be strong and very courageous. Be careful to obey all the law my servant Moses gave you; do not turn from it to the right or to the left, that you may be successful wherever you go (Jos. 1:2, 7).

In the days shortly after Jesus' ascension, Peter spoke with the authority of a confident leader that one needed be chosen to take the place of Judas.

> In those days Peter stood up among the believers (a group numbering about a hundred and twenty) and said, "Brothers and sisters, the Scripture had to be fulfilled in which the Holy Spirit spoke long ago through David concerning Judas . . ." (Ac. 1:15-16).

Peter was the one who stood to speak and give direction in choosing a successor. His confidence to move forward was inspiring to all believers, and it should not be taken wrongly as grounds for others to sit back and wait for leadership to act. Peter could neither be in multiple locations, nor could he carry out multiple ministries. The Body of Christ needs leadership in many capacities and is crippled, at times, by waiting for others to make decisions.

A transition in leadership took place between Barnabas and Saul on their first missionary trip. The two left Antioch with Barnabas leading the team (13:2). By the time they transversed Cyprus, Paul was team leader (v. 13). Do not presume that a change in leadership indicates sin or weakness.

> But in fact God has placed the parts in the body, every one of them, just as he wanted them to be. If they were all one part, where would the body be? As it is, there are many parts, but one body (1 Co. 12:18-20).

God is free to place people for a season, and He transitions leaders in and out for His purposes. A leadership role is not permanent, but rather is only for a season. (For more discussion on this transition, refer to Chapter 31 of Acts and to Missionaries to the Nations, Let Leaders Grow.)

Peter at Pentecost

The day of Pentecost brought a sudden change in how the Spirit of God moved among His people. The crowd heard the disciples speak in at least fifteen languages. Some wondered, "What does this mean?" and some speculated that drunkenness was the reason for what they perceived to be babbling (Ac. 2:12-13). Leadership is needed during times of transition when uncertainty abounds. Peter brought current meaning and fulfillment to the prophetic writing of Joel (Joel 2:28-32).

Peter took leadership by standing up with a prophetic word and clarifying the overall vision of the Kingdom of God. Key elements of leadership include the immediate direction as well as the overall vision. Peter described the coming of the Spirit as Jesus had promised. He explained that the Spirit had been given freely to all, regardless of age or gender, unlike popular Jewish custom. Three points of Joel's prophecy were added that went beyond the present question of languages and clarified the overall vision of God. One was that the judgment of God was coming to the whole earth. The second was that the resurrected Jesus would return as had been prophesied. The third was an invitation for all to call upon the name of the Lord and be saved.

Just ten days before, the Apostles had asked Jesus, "Lord, are you at this time going to restore the kingdom to Israel" (Ac. 1:6)? Salvation could no longer be defined as restoration of a Davidic kingdom, but as the proper understanding of the transformation of all who turn to God in repentance through the Messiah. Peter now proclaimed Pentecost, Judgment, the Second Coming of the Messiah, and the open door for worldwide transformation. This is Spirit-led leadership. We must also marvel at the Spirit-led recording of Luke to capture this message in its fullness. The world looks for someone to "take leadership." But the Kingdom of God is advanced when leaders step forward and describe God's plan in clear terms, inviting all to participate.

A misunderstanding of the way God works can be heard when people pray for a move of the Holy Spirit and then divorce their prayer from taking any action. It is neither reasonable nor Scriptural to pray and be silent, taking no action and not proclaming that which the Lord has requested. It is important that we both pray and then act in accordance with the direction God gives.

Peter moved in a powerful evangelistic anointing of the Holy Spirit on the day of Pentecost, and at precisely the right moment needed. In this case, God's heart brought Peter to look at the audience made up of Jews from many ethnic backgrounds. He drew them to face their depravity without God. Most of the Jews would have been in Jerusalem for Passover, and certainly they had heard of the crucifixion of the Nazarene. Peter made it clear that Jesus had been raised from the dead according to prophecy (2:30-32).

Peter was generous in his leadership. The crowd in Jerusalem were ". . . cut to the heart . . . " and asked, "Brothers, what shall we do" (Ac. 2:37)? A leader must display God's heart for all people, even for those who have previously opposed the coming Kingdom. Peter invited the crowd to repentance, baptism, and to also share in the fullness of the Holy Spirit. He offered freedom from the curse that people had called down upon their lives and upon the lives of their children (Mt. 27:25) by offering God's blessing to all. Leadership in the Kingdom has God's heart to remove the curse and to bless. It is not His heart to reinforce old lines of conflict or seek revenge.

It is important that we understand Peter's words that drew people into both conviction and direction of what to do next. Our message is not simply to bring information, but conviction and decision, utilizing the internal work of the Holy Spirit.

Leadership at the Beautiful Gate

Peter moved rapidly from one situation to another, seizing opportunities for the Lord. We must receive the challenge that a creator God wants more out of our ministries than we can often envision. God expects great things from His people.

Peter spoke healing to a beggar who ". . . was over forty years old" (Ac. 4:22). We might tend to rejoice at such a healing, thinking it was the main point of our day! Peter utilized the opportunity, however, to preach salvation to the quickly gathering crowd. He spoke words that brought deep conviction and pointed toward the solution. His anointed message, which drew another two thousand people into the Kingdom of God, is worth our grasping (4:4). Spirit-inspired leadership displays God's heart for all to repent and be transformed into the likeness and image of Jesus. God leading us will either help us rejoice at His wisdom and power at work in ways we never imagined, or we will feel out of control, swamped by more happening than we can administrate.

The healing at the Beautiful Gate subsequently brought Peter and John before the Jewish authorities, opening another door to speak as leaders in a movement.

> When they saw the courage of Peter and John and realized that they were unschooled, ordinary men, they were astonished and they took note that these men had been with Jesus (Ac. 4:13).

Confrontation between the religious authorities and the people of God cannot be avoided. Mission people brought before authorities for questioning has happened throughout the ages. The "courage of Peter and John" came from the same source from which each of us draws, the Spirit of God. Do not question why you prayed for a person or shared the message of Jesus when interrogation or persecution come as a result. The Enemy wants us to doubt our actions that brought persecution. God wants our unwavering trust in trials.

Discipline and Church Expansion

Ananias and Sapphira

Discernment of heart motives by the apostles is sobering. Peter discerned the lie Ananias had portrayed. The conspiracy was to profit from the sale of their property, while appearing to give all to help the believers' movement.

Peter clearly left room for private ownership, for the sale of private property, and for using the proceeds as people choose. Judgment falls as a result of lying to the Holy Spirit which, in this case, was also lying to the Body of Christ. The Lord defends His name and His Church from believers who know better, those who are making a mockery of truth. The lesson to us today is clear: Never masquerade as someone whom you are not. Do not use worldly wealth to buy recognition in the Body of Christ. New movements cannot afford scandals that unravel the fabric of the fellowship.

Simon the Sorcerer

Simon the Sorcerer believed the message and was baptized (8:13). His new faith and lack of discipleship had not yet changed his inner urge to "amaze all the people of Samaria." Peter sharply rebuked Simon's desire to purchase the ability to grant the Holy Spirit. Simon was not struck dead, but he repented of his words.

The two stories show a contrast of discipline. Ananias and Sapphira knew they had lied and plotted against God's people, and thus against the Spirit. Simon received a crisp rebuke that brought growth to him and to his community. Be careful not to be too harsh with a new group of believers or judge them, as you might, as people who have been in the faith for a considerable period of time.

Leadership, Obedience, and the Seven

Stephen and Leadership

Luke focuses on the lives of another generation of leaders who move us closer to Light to the Nations. Hebraic Jewish widows received more attention than the Grecian Jewish widows (6:1). Ministries unfold and grow rather than come in a mature package. Growth meant the opportunity for new ministries rather than a negative view that leaders lacked the foresight to understand and deal with multi-cultural needs. Whether the Grecian widows were of Jewish background who had returned from the Diaspora--the dispersion of the Jews after the Babylonian exile-- only speaking Greek, or whether they were proselytes, is unclear. The seven men chosen to oversee the distribution of food to this group of widows all had Greek names. Stephen exercised his anointing for more than table waiting, doing "great wonders and miraculous signs" (6:8). It is an important lesson to utilize your talents and anointing for the work of God's Kingdom, not holding back because your job title seems mediocre. Stephen exercised great leadership qualities when conflict arose with "the Synagogue of the Freedmen" (6:9). The Freedmen were those who had previously been slaves under the Roman system and who had received their freedom to become citizens. They were not those who had been born citizens (The New International Dictionary of New Testament Theology, Vol 1, pgs. 715-716). Those freed proselytes were not only vigorously following their Jewish faith, but in deep conflict with Grecian Jews who followed Jesus as Messiah. Stephen faced their charges with a short history of the Jewish people from Abraham to Solomon's temple (7:2-50). He also landed a stinging rebuke of their hardened hearts (vv. 51-53), which led to his stoning and claimed his life as the first martyr of the Church. His leadership was evident through his stepping out to perform miracles and proclaiming the message of God to a hostile group. Leadership of the early Church must highlight the multiplication of leaders and their key roles in proclaiming the Kingdom of God. This is just as true today. We need to multiply fresh waves of leaders. Complacency will lead to stagnation and a poor ability to believe for "regions beyond."

The martyrdom of Stephen precipitated the watershed of mission in the New Testament. His death opened the door for believers to carry the eternal truth of God to new areas.

> On that day a great persecution broke out against the church in Jerusalem, and all except the apostles were scattered throughout Judea and Samaria (8:1).

Stephen's leadership brought the scattering of believers who were used of God to enter new lands with the message of the gospel. God is concerned that Light to the Nations is a reality. This scattering of the believers from Jerusalem mirrors the former scattering that brought light and truth to Babylon and Persia.

> Then the word of the LORD came to me: "This is what the LORD, the God of Israel, says: 'Like these good figs, I regard as good the exiles from Judah, whom I sent away from this place to the land of the Babylonians (Jer. 24:1-5).

Philip and Obedience

Philip found a ministry in Samaria. Entering this area was out of necessity as a result of persecution. It was not a deep sense of calling and personal choice to go to Samaria. Many miss opportunities to serve God as they wait for a particular calling or for deep feelings that will draw them to a particular people or region. As God's people, we must be available to Him in any location or circumstance. Rather than looking for shelter and mourning his losses, Philip moved in his anointing. His ability to overcome the foreignness of Samaria could have been, in part, the result of his Grecian, or non-traditional Jewish roots. His leadership led to miracles, to the casting out of evil spirits, and to "great joy in that city" (Ac. 8:6-8).

Philip obeyed the voice of the Lord and moved on from Samaria. It is evident from the text that he was unaware of where God was leading him. We, too, like our examples Philip and Abraham, learn to follow the One we trust, not knowing where we are going.

> Now an angel of the Lord said to Philip, "Go south to the road—the desert road—that goes down from Jerusalem to Gaza" (8:26).

The Ethiopian Eunuch was a seeker after God. He traveled one thousand six hundred miles to worship in Jerusalem. Philip's obedience in following the leading of the Lord, and approaching a stranger, is an example to anyone who wants to obey God. Overly cautious people would not encourage responding to something you hear because it could make you look like a fool. Vibrant faith in Jesus certainly calls us to step outside accepted cultural norms. Greeting someone you have never met before (clarifying Isaiah 53:7-8) and then baptizing that person needs to be repeated throughout our lives and not relegated to stories of old. After the baptism, Philip found himself about thirty miles away in Azotus. We are reminded of Elijah who was carried by the Spirit of the Lord to different regions (1 Ki. 18:12).

Leadership as a Shepherd

God's mission includes feeding and shepherding His people. After the resurrection, Jesus called Peter to feed His sheep (Jn. 21:17). Feeding the sheep meant tender care for their lives, feeding them with sound teaching, and presenting the call to service for the next generation of believers. The mission of God is not only to seek and to save the lost, but to care for them as family members, bringing instruction and dealing with sin and error. The tender care for new fellowships of believers is understood through Paul returning to the cities of "...Lystra, Iconium and Antioch, strengthening the disciples and encouraging them to remain true to the faith.... Paul and Barnabas appointed elders for them in each church" (Ac. 14:21-23).

The call we carry is to strengthen the believers in every stage of their lives in Christ. Random gatherings of believers, without leadership, will not have direction. Leaders are needed, but note that leaders were appointed on Paul's return trip, allowing time for qualifications necessary for oversight to become evident.

The Epistles, or letters to the Churches, are prime examples of God's tender leadership exemplified through early Church leaders. Paul's words of "Grace and peace to you from God our Father and the Lord Jesus Christ" (1 Co. 1:3) were spoken to the Churches in Rome, Corinth, Galatia, Philippi, Colosse, and Thessalonica, with similar greetings to the Church in Ephesus. The letters are filled with instruction on the divine nature of Jesus and His life given for us. The resurrection of Jesus from the dead and the authority we have as believers to walk in freedom are also highlighted throughout the Epistles.

Care of other believers is a gift of God and, like all gifts, needs to be used frequently to foster growth. Paul told Timothy that aspiring to leadership was a good thing (1 Ti. 3:1). Wanting to lead, teach, and nurture others in the faith is healthy. Older leaders must open the door for younger leaders to exercise their gifts in the Church. The future growth of the Church, both locally and to the ends of the earth, necessitates people with proven character, thriving in their giftings and callings.

31. Acts and Missionaries to the Nations

The heart of God is to bring all nations, all languages, and all tribes into relationship with Himself and with each other. Scripture conveys God's intense desire to make Himself known to the entire earth. We also understand that the task of bringing the good news of Jesus rests upon all of us as His people. How are missionaries developed? How do some learn to relate to new groups of people and convey a message that becomes their own? What helps some thrive despite opposition, overcoming tremendous odds? These are questions that anyone living as a missionary wants answered. These missionaries also desire to pass these answers on to the next generation.

Acts is the turning point in "ends of the earth" theology. Several of the leaders we meet in Acts witnessed the conviction of God transform both Jew and Gentile into the image of Jesus. We need to incorporate the insight we gain from missionaries in Acts and, like them, be filled afresh with the Holy Spirit for today's challenges.

Peter and Change

Christians often consider themselves adaptable to convey the message of Christ to people of different backgrounds. Change does, in fact, take conscious effort and some time to implement. All workers face the challenge of interpreting the new environment, initially through the grid of their own backgrounds. Peter faced a deep personal challenge when he needed to move among people he formerly considered to be unclean.

Peter traveled very little in his ministry compared to Paul, Barnabas, and Timothy. His face-to-face meeting with the risen Jesus gave him the determination to shepherd, feed, and take care of the flock of God (Jn. 21:15-19). His visiting the saints brought him about twenty miles northwest of Jerusalem to Lydda (Ac. 9:32). The miracle of Aeneas' healing brought an expanse of the Kingdom, and this news spread to the surrounding areas. Believers in Joppa heard that Peter was present in Lydda, just an additional twenty miles northwest, and they sent for him after Tabitha's death. Her resurrection from the dead was a powerful expression of the work of God in the lives of the believers. Following the path down which God led Peter, we begin to understand how He brought Peter into contact with Gentile "God-seekers" in Caesarea. It seems that the miracles among Jewish believers brought Peter geographically closer to the place of need with Gentiles in Caesarea.

> Peter stayed in Joppa for some time with a tanner named Simon
> (9:43).

Peter's time at the tanner's house is similar to the time Elijah spent being fed with unclean animals (1 Ki. 17:4). The ravens were unclean birds, but they were in Israel's east bank of the Jordan. Peter was staying within the confines of Judaism with Simon, but at the same time in a realm of impurity near dead carcasses. Elijah's next stop would be a Gentile widow's house in Zarephath (17:9), and Peter's next move was to Caesarea, to a Gentile home. It is our challenge in mission to move with God across ethnic lines we may have previously considered to be taboo. The work of God cannot be completed by ministering among one type of people. Ethnic and linguistic lines must be crossed repeatedly to embrace "ends of the earth" theology.

There are four involved in the meeting of Peter and Cornelius' household (Ac. 10:4-23). **God** is at work answering the cries of hungry hearts by giving visions, directing people, and sending an angel with the message to ". . . bring back a man named Simon . . ." (v. 5). **Cornelius** and "his household" represent the spiritually hungry or the unreached. He obeyed the angelic directive and sent for Peter, not knowing what would be the outcome of the meeting. **Peter** actively responded in obedience and traveled with the messengers over thirty miles north to Caesarea. There were also **six Jewish background believers** currently aligned with the "party of the circumcision" (11:12). There are times we take people with us on visits to the unreached and only later understand their cultural or religious bias. The worldview of those Jews joining Peter from Joppa is about to be challenged beyond their abilities to adapt.

God gave a vision to Cornelius, a "God-seeker," that was specific. It required obedience in order to move beyond his present understanding of God! God will also challenge people with whom you work to obey a specific word or revelation in order to grow into a deeper understanding of the Lord. Expect unreached people to have been given a word or a vision that challenges old thinking about God's revelation.

> The angel answered, "Your prayers and gifts to the poor have
> come up as a memorial offering before God. Now send men to
> Joppa to bring back a man named Simon who is called Peter.
> He is staying with Simon the tanner, whose house is by the sea"
> (Ac. 10:4-6).

God did not consider Cornelius to be fine if left in his present state. Cornelius feared God, gave to the poor, prayed, and was involved with the Jewish community. But this was not salvation for him or his household. God is not a humanist. Be clear in your goals in mission. What do you long for your people to become?

Being a good neighbor, praying, giving, and loving does not constitute salvation. Cornelius needed Christ and His forgiveness. This message will divide workers into two camps: those who understand the preeminence of the Messiah and those who are uncertain of His preeminence. The camp of your convictions will make all the difference in your ministry.

God did not preach the gospel message to Cornelius apart from human involvement. Neither does He send angels to preach the message of salvation. God's miracles are waiting to burst forth upon the unreached, but He waits for our involvement as believers to carry this message. Misguided thinking abounds when people pray for dreams and visions to be given to people half a world away, without understanding the necessity of a human life interacting with the unreached. Jesus instructed us:

> The harvest is plentiful, but the workers are few. Ask the Lord of
> the harvest, therefore, to send out workers into his harvest field"
> (Lk. 10:2).

Workers are needed in God's harvest. It is good to pray for the miracles of God that both bless people and draw their attention to the truth, but not without workers. Mission without workers is a mystical belief that is not founded in Scripture.

The vision given to Peter confirms this point. God wanted Peter to respond and to carry the message of salvation to Cornelius' household.

> About noon the following day as they were on their journey
> and approaching the city, Peter went up on the roof to pray. He
> became hungry and wanted something to eat, and while the
> meal was being prepared, he fell into a trance. He saw heaven
> opened and something like a large sheet being let down to earth
> by its four corners. It contained all kinds of four-footed animals,
> as well as reptiles of the earth and birds of the air. Then a voice
> told him, "Get up, Peter. Kill and eat" (Ac. 10:9-13).

Reflections

God gave Peter the vision of the sheet descending with animals while at the tanner's house. How was this different from receiving the vision while in Jerusalem?

Do you have examples in your life of God bringing you closer to your people, step by step?

432   God's Heart and Mandate for Mission

The vision came from heaven, yet heaven was not defiled. Peter's concern was for his personal purity rather than for heaven being defiled by the sheet returning to its origin.

We need to ask, "What do the animals in the sheet represent?" This is not a discussion of animals given for food, but rather a metaphor representing the people of the nations. The closest correlation for Peter between clean and unclean people was clean and unclean food. People, considered to be the animals and unworthy of attention, were held in the sheet from heaven. God already has room in heaven for all those types we think are very strange, dangerous, or politically opposed to our background.

Peter traveling to Cornelius' house required more than the words of Jesus that the gospel must be preached to all nations. He also needed more than the Old Testament prophecies of all people coming to the Son of Man. Peter needed to experience personal revelation that God's Kingdom was accessible to the Gentiles who believed in Jesus the Messiah. Peter did not comprehend Jesus' word that the Holy Spirit would develop witnesses "to the ends of the earth" (Ac. 1:9) before he had his encounter with the household of Cornelius. Nor did Peter understand on the day of Pentecost the real meaning of "I will pour out my Spirit on all people" (2:17) or the significance of "everyone who calls on the name of the Lord will be saved" (v. 21).

Peter found himself in uncharted areas when he entered Cornelius' home. Even though the disciples had been with Samaritans and Gentiles on different occasions, it was in the company of Jesus and the twelve. In those previous encounters, Peter and the others possibly felt they were a clean group and simply followed Jesus. This time Peter is entering into a Gentile's realm with six men who think they are clean.

> He said to them: "You are well aware that it is against our law for a Jew to associate with or visit a Gentile. But God has shown me that I should not call anyone impure or unclean. So when I was sent for, I came without raising any objection. May I ask why you sent for me" (Ac. 10:28-29)?

This certainly seems clumsy to enter a person's home and describe your past aversion to being with them. Asking Cornelius to explain the reason he sent for Peter also appears odd in light of the messengers previously telling Peter the complete vision (10:22). The beauty of Acts is that it tells us how first time encounters actually developed. It helps us as new missionaries, entering the homes of unreached people, to know that being nervous is nothing new. Even Peter felt this way.

Peter understood the tension between Jewish law that forbade association with Gentiles and the revelation of God declaring no people to be impure. Jewish law, which previously had described a clean community, now showed itself as an improper barrier that neither cleansed its members nor welcomed outsiders. Jewish law was now out of place when the Messiah was in place.

The question was: "What are the requirements for *everyone* far off to be brought into the kingdom of God?" Peter settled this question in Cornelius' home. He was fully convinced of the Lord's complete work with the household of Cornelius, which is evidenced by his later testimony: "Who was I to think that I could oppose God" (11:17)?

The movement called "The Way" could not afford to remain primarily a Jewish sect, with a few marginal Samaritan and Roman families attempting to fit into Jewish customs. Peter needed to promote this work among Gentiles, confessing with them that Jesus, the risen Messiah, was the central core of their faith. Christian leaders in a similar way today also need to remain committed to a theology of proclaiming Jesus to the ends of the earth. If it becomes lip service, or a lopsided focus upon their own ethnicity, the mission of God will wane. Likewise, denominational distinctives need to fade in light of Christ becoming the central core of new people groups with their own significant issues that need transformation.

Human Vision without Adaptability

The six Jewish believers who accompanied Peter from Joppa were certainly in for a challenge. They would have heard Peter's vision, told in great detail, and known of the Spirit telling Peter to go with the men from Caesarea. They also heard of Cornelius' angelic visit. Why did they accompany Peter to Caesarea?

> The circumcised believers who had come with Peter were astonished that the gift of the Holy Spirit had been poured out even on the Gentiles (Ac. 10:45).

The circumcised believers did not envision faith without the Law. We must ask who Peter was in the eyes of the circumcised (Jewish) believers? Was he a leader of a Jewish sect? Was Peter a Messianic believer? They certainly did not yet understand that Peter was a leader in the expansion of the Kingdom of God to all nations. Their astonishment would have held them back from entering a Gentile's home, presenting the gospel, praying for the Holy Spirit to come, and baptizing the new believers in water. They could only pass on a report (Ac. 11) that Peter ate and drank with Gentiles. Did these six plan ahead and bring food with them for the journey? It is evident from the text that they refused the hospitality of the newly believing community in order to remain "clean."

Peter was in an uncomfortable place of leadership. Was his primary vision to reach the Gentiles or to bring Jewish believers into a vision for the Gentiles? Most missionaries have a similar task of bringing the hearts of people in the Church with them to a new people. Each of us has to sort out our primary God-given direction. Peter's direction was two-fold: Do not call unclean what God calls clean, and go to Cornelius with the men he sent.

The contrast between Peter and his six companions from Joppa helps us in our calling to the nations. Peter adapted and blessed the expanding movement. The six onlookers were confined in their cultural backgrounds, expecting others to become like them. The Kingdom of God comes through faith in Jesus the risen Messiah, and not through Jesus with a cultural prerequisite.

Missiological Implications

Mission is carried out in uncertainty! Neither we nor Peter know what everything means. God used human messengers to convey the good news of the Kingdom, traveling into uncharted regions. We need a new wave of leaders who will follow the leading of the Spirit to bless unreached people with the gospel in our days. Risk is part of the missionary enterprise.

Mission must be carried out in the pilgrimage of downward mobility. This is often true for our financial pilgrimage, our social pilgrimage, and frequently true for a humanly perceived ethnic pilgrimage. Jesus' death makes all worthy to hear the message of salvation. No one's ethnicity suffices as a qualifying or disqualifying factor.

Paul, the New Missionary

Pre-faith Background

Saul, like Moses, defended his people from what he understood to be oppression and threat. Saul's approval of Stephen's death was similar to Moses killing the Egyptian who had oppressed a Hebrew. Both were wrong. The exclusive mentality of the Jewish system was embodied by the Pharisees, whose very name means a "separated one." Saul openly identifies his background with the party of the Pharisees (Ac. 26:5).

> If someone else thinks they have reasons to put confidence in the
> flesh, I have more: circumcised on the eighth day, of the people
> of Israel, of the tribe of Benjamin, a Hebrew of Hebrews; in re-
> gard to the law, a Pharisee; as for zeal, persecuting the church;
> as for righteousness based on the law, faultless (Php. 3:4-6).

Saul knew why he persecuted the followers of Jesus. He thought they defiled the
purity of Hebrew life and law. He understood clearly that people of his background
turned to Jesus as their Messiah, even confessing Jesus as the prophesied "Son of
Man" mentioned in Daniel 7:56. The Way taught Jesus as sufficient, not requiring
righteousness based upon the law--a belief Saul denounced. The two systems
clashed in Saul's mind, and he believed that the new sect needed to be eradicated.

We know Saul was able to navigate in Greek and in Aramaic (Ac. 21:37, 40). He was
also, no doubt, familiar with formal Hebrew as well from his training in Scripture
under Gamaliel (22:3). It is unclear if his background also exposed him to Latin,
the language of Rome. He clearly embraced his Roman citizenship when advanta-
geous (i.e. Ac. 16:37; 22:26-27). Born in Tarsus (22:3) as a Roman citizen (v. 28),
his background is vastly different from the other disciples of Jesus.

He lived a three hundred seventy-five mile journey from Jerusalem, best navigated
by ship porting at Caeserea. Saul was familiar with travel, understood some of the
expanse of the Roman Empire, navigated well in multiple languages, and had an
exceptional background in the Scriptures. This former enemy to the faith would
draw on so much of his background once his ministry began. God has given all of
us a rich background that encourages the ministry He releases through our lives.

Question

Can you list areas of your background, positive or negative, that uniquely prepare
you for ministry?

Explain why your background is a help in your walk with the Lord.

The Vision of Jesus

Saul received enough revelation to stop his attacks against the Church completely
and reverse his worldview. The Damascus Road vision should not be interpreted
as God intervening with unreached people. Saul has previous knowledge of Jesus

and His followers, albeit distorted. Saul's encounter with the light and voice told him to receive his direction for life from another person.

> "Who are you, Lord?" Saul asked. "I am Jesus, whom you are persecuting," he replied. "Now get up and go into the city, and you will be told what you must do" (9:5-6).

The formerly strong and confident Saul now needed to listen to the Lord's direction from a person. Visions come to prepare people for what they are about to hear, or to confirm a message previously heard. Saul received a message that dismantled his previous understanding of Jewish Law and prepared him to wait intently for the message that was to come. During his three days spent in blindness and fasting, he no doubt remembered the violent attacks against Jesus and His followers. His mind churned over his encouragement by Jewish leadership to destroy "The Way" (9:1-2), which countered his revelation of the Kingdom of God. He was hungry to hear the Lord speak direction to his life.

Ananias and Light to the Gentiles

The vision given to Ananias challenged him in two areas. The first area was the obvious fear of praying for a man known to be a destructive agent against The Way. Ananias was hesitant to approach someone known to harm followers of Jesus. The news reports against Saul conflicted with God's word spoken to Ananias. This is a clear warning for us who live with news media saturation. From the first century's word of mouth to today's internet, TV, radio, and newspapers, the necessity is to hear God and not filter his Word through media reports. The news poisons many in the Church against Muslim immigrants and creates hardness toward their native countries. Do we not miss God's call to bless the world as light and salt when fear quenches the Spirit? Saul's transformation from an attacker to a fellow member of God's grace is not isolated. People like Kamal Saleem, also once dedicated to killing Christians, was transformed by both a vision of Jesus and the love shown to him by believers in Jesus.[1]

The second challenge for Ananias was to accurately pass on the prophetic direction of Saul's ministry. Ananias heard God say:

> Go! This man is my chosen instrument to proclaim my name to the Gentiles and their kings and to the people of Israel. I will show him how much he must suffer for my name (9:15-16).

---

1   Unexpected Encounter, God's Love Conquers a Muslim Radical! http://www.cbn.com/tv/1403094459001

Luke records this word to Ananias before Cornelius and his household are transformed. This is before Antioch blossomed as a Gentile fellowship, and before the gathering of leaders in Jerusalem to decide what was required for a Gentile to enter the Kingdom. Ananias spoke what he had heard without tainting the message with cultural bias. His openness to non-Jews was likely aided by his living in Damascus, a Gentile "free city" of the Decapolis.

Ananias laid hands on Saul and called him brother, an act that needs to be understood in depth. Our acceptance of new believers whom we deemed far off from God is certainly a factor in how they feel God accepts them. Probation is not a biblical model for discipleship when great change and growth are evident. Saul was totally accepted without the stinging rebuke of his past evil. Ananias prayed for Saul's healing from blindness, most likely prophesied over him his future ministry with the laying on of hands (1 Ti. 1:18; 4:14), prayed for Saul to be filled with the Holy Spirit, and baptized him (Ac. 9:17-18). That was a full day in the life of an apostle-to-be. Our timetable for baptism in water, fullness of the Holy Spirit, and prophetic direction for ministry is casually slow in comparison. Do we desire the release of apostles or the addition of church members?

The prophetic ministry of Saul was to be in four specific areas: to the Gentiles, to the rulers of the Gentiles, to the people of Israel, and in an acquaintance with suffering. Saul did not immediately launch into a ministry with Gentiles, a formidable stretch for this Pharisee. Two of these areas came about almost immediately. One was a direct ministry with the Jews in Damascus. The Word of God and the fire in Saul's soul came together, "proving that Jesus was the Christ" (Ac. 9:22). The other area prophesied, "suffering for my name," also began with a plot to kill him.

Jesus promised persecution because of our walk with Him.

> But before all this, they will seize you and persecute you. They will hand you over to synagogues and put you in prison, and you will be brought before kings and governors, and all on account of my name (Lk. 21:12).

Saul was not moving prematurely into ministry. He was filled with the Spirit and boldly proclaimed Christ. Some of the best evangelists are those who just come to Jesus and who are deeply in love with Him. Help young believers, who may possibly be very mature in some areas of life, to move boldly into ministry. We need an Ananias in our lives who speaks the Word of the Lord, releasing us into great things for God.

Barnabas and Light to the Gentiles

Barnabas stepped into Saul's life, vouching for his vision of Jesus and resulting conversion. He also related that Saul preached "fearlessly," which spoke of the instant opposition faced by a Pharisee turned disciple (Ac. 9:27). We must assume Barnabas knew Saul and his story, including his healing, fullness of the Spirit, and the word spoken by Jesus: "you will be told what you must do." Like Barnabas, we must take time to listen to a person's background, to the call of God on his or her life, and to how that call was received. The focus must be on the expansion of God's Kingdom and not our personal preferences in ministry. We need a Barnabas in our lives who encourages us personally and speaks well of us to people who do not know our full story. But then we, as mature members of the Body of Christ, need to look out for younger members, sensing God's direction and encouraging their calling. The world needs believers released into broad, Kingdom ministries to the ends of the earth, those not placated by a limited, hometown vision.

Saul moved toward his calling to the Gentiles in Jerusalem by talking and debating with Grecian Jews (9:29). This same group, with whom Saul formerly plotted to kill Stephen, now sought to kill him also. The safe move that the believers in Jerusalem took was to send Saul home to Tarsus. Barnabas would have been aware of all these details, remembering the call of God on Saul's life. How can a young zealous believer stay in his calling and gifting?

Antioch, A New Gentile Church

The word of God spread to Greeks in Antioch and we know that ". . . a great number of people believed and turned to the Lord" (Ac. 11:21). This window into the spread of the gospel is a pivotal point in the Book of Acts. We read that persecuted and scattered believers shared the message initially with Jews (v. 19), and that some men from Cyprus and Cyrene (or Libya) shared the good news of the Lord Jesus with Gentiles (v. 20). We do not know the names of those distant travelers who broke through stereotypes of communication lines. We are later introduced to Lucis of Cyrene, one of the prophets and teachers in Antioch (13:1). It is unclear if he was part of the early venture into this Gentile region. Luke tucks in this gospel break-through after Peter's explanation of his action in Cornelius' house. Cornelius was well-known for his good deeds (10:1-2). Mission to Antioch takes the gospel a step further by presenting truth to some who seemed to be unknown individuals. Mission to Antioch was simply presenting the gospel to unreached people. Mission to Antioch confirmed God's heart for all people to have the good news of Jesus the Messiah. The joy they experienced encourages us to keep moving to new regions with the gospel.

The Church in Jerusalem was intrigued by the faith spreading to the Gentiles, and it sent Barnabas, also a Cypriot, to investigate (13:22). Our understanding of mission theology must be formed by the sharp mind and heart of Barnabas. Three items catch our attention with his facilitation (rather than control) in Antioch.

1. Barnabas was able to recognize the grace of God without the preconditions of Jewish worship forms or observance of the Law. The door remained open ". . . and a great number of people were brought to the Lord" (v. 24). The rapid ability of Barnabas to function in another context may be partly due to his being a Cypriot (i.e. from a non-Jerusalem background).

2. He did not move into the place of leading the Antioch movement, imposing his position or oversight from Jerusalem. Barnabas worked with the leadership, encouraging them to grow. We understand that each movement is precious in God's sight and should not be controlled from another people or region.

3. "Then Barnabas went to Tarsus to look for Saul" (v. 25). Barnabas left what appeared to be a fruitful ministry and traveled about one hundred miles to search for a man he knew to be anointed for this ministry to the Gentiles. He wanted to connect Saul with his need to grow the ministry with the Gentile fellowship in Antioch.

Ministries do not develop in a vacuum. Skills in preaching to a particular people group and use of local language must be cultivated. Barnabas looked to multiply the mission efforts to the Gentile world and not simply grow his personal ministry in Antioch. Do we grasp the significance of this passage, "Then Barnabas went to Tarsus to look for Saul," in light of world mission? Can we not take a less prominent role in order to train and release more missionaries for Kingdom service?

Barnabas was willing to help a young believer move forward with the specific call of God to the Gentiles. This call would not be realized without some practical experience. A prophetic prayer over a life cannot be taken passively; it must have a practical outlet that allows the person to grow into the call of God. We are not clear on the number of years that lapsed between Saul's initial prophetic call and Barnabas searching for him in Tarsus. Barnabas moved into the role as team leader to Gentile peoples. It is extremely important that team members are chosen for their callings, ministry gifts, and particular skills. Imagine the confusion in Antioch if Barnabas had chosen a believer from the party of the circumcision. The outcome would have been quite different.

Antioch was shaken by the teaching of circumcision and the law of Moses by "unauthorized individuals." The youthfulness of the church in Antioch, and we assume the same throughout the entire region, tells us about the need for sound instruction. Instant maturity is not realistic. Paul and Barnabas were "appointed, along with some other believers, to go up to Jerusalem to see the apostles and elders about this question of how they should live before God" (15:2). It is unrealistic to read "authority and sending structure in mission" into a group seeking direction on what they believe and how they should live. They had fear that they, and several Gentile churches, would need to come under a Jewish cultural system.

Reflection

Wrongly recruiting members of the party of the circumcision to move into a new ministry among Gentiles was a recipe for intense frustration and heresy. What criteria do you use to select team members?

Missionary Principles

Barnabas and Saul invested a year together in Antioch which opened the doors for future ministry. The following seven lessons are gleaned from the way God sent them and their teams, and the types of ministries in which they engaged.

1. Leading by God

The Holy Spirit spoke to the church and led in mission. We should expect the same today. Five major prophets and teachers were mentioned (Ac. 13:1) and 40% of them were set aside for mission. The biblical text makes a point saying, "So after they had fasted and prayed, they placed their hands on them and sent them off" (13:3). The point is that Barnabas and Saul were not given directions by a governing body. There was no mandate, no road map, no given agenda, and no time frame. The prophets and teachers heard the Holy Spirit say, "Specialize for me" or "Release to me"[2] the men I have already called (13:2).

Opinions vary regarding the role of the church in Antioch in overseeing mission; mission did not simply happen. From this passage we understand that the church in Antioch gave Barnabas and Saul to the Holy Spirit in order to complete the work to which they had been called. There was no sense of exercised authority structure from the three remaining prophets/teachers in Antioch over Barnabas and Saul. Back reading "authority over" into this context removes the awe and wonder of two men setting out on an apostolic venture to the Gentiles! Peers agreed on God's direction and a mission team, or apostolic band, was sent out. The emphasis

---

2   Ἀφορισατε δη μοι literally means "separate then to me," or "release to me," or "let me have."

was on God's leading, not on structures and authority over people. Churches and missions are not in error to have more direction in sending missionaries, but we must not miss the point of listening to the Holy Spirit and freeing others to do the same. The significance of this act of sending was that the Gentiles in Antioch had a heart for the gospel to continue to spread among non-Jews.

This was neither a surprise nor change in direction for either Barnabas or Saul. The other leaders in Antioch agreed with God's calling by laying hands on Barnabas and Saul and releasing them to do God's bidding. Field-led ministry is very important to understand. It is not an independence from any influence from church or mission, but it is the ability to hear God and to make decisions based in real time and on current perceptions. It grows leadership in field workers and releases leadership to the national believers. Mission becomes sluggish and unable to meet current needs when the central home base in another nation dictates responses and direction. When perceived leadership and decision-making power remain in foreign hands, a sterile church is often the result; it can have life but it will lack second generation mission vision. This authority structure leads to "larger than life" leadership personalities and eventually to papal concepts; it does not lead to a brotherhood of fellow believers.

Baptism in a similar way needs to be carried out by the living body who greets the newly resurrected members. Baptism should be conducted by the missionary initially presenting the message, like Paul did in baptizing Lydia and her household (Ac. 16:15) and the household of the Philippian jailer (v. 33). This new body of believers had full authority to baptize and to spread the gospel of the Kingdom. Waiting for Paul to return for future baptisms, or worse yet, asking an elder from Antioch to baptize believers in Philippi, would have distorted the authority they had from the Lord and slowed the process of growth.

There was a sense of wonder in Barnabas and Saul moving into this mission phase. The phrase, "the two of them sent on their way by the Holy Spirit..." (13:4), brings to mind the call of God upon Abraham.

> By faith Abraham, when called to go to a place he would later
> receive as his inheritance, obeyed and went, even though he
> did not know where he was going (Heb. 11:8).

There is a beauty and a wonder in people listening to God and obeying in faith, without promises or specific plans before launching out. This could make some very uncomfortable today, fearful of immaturity and heresy spread globally. Remember, Barnabas and Saul served in a variety of capacities and had recognized ministries. They did not represent floaters who were known for their independence or inability to work with others. Neither Antioch in that day, nor mission agencies today, should feel compelled to send zealous but irresponsible people to do the work of God.

Missiological Insight

This discussion brings us back to the nature of the mission venture that originated with the Holy Spirit. Leaders in Antioch recognized God's call upon mature, gifted, dedicated disciples. They had to concede that the work of the Kingdom of God was far broader than Antioch. Pioneering ventures in mission require a team effort whenever possible. One person, or one married couple, will be harder pressed to discern the will of God. The blessing of a committed team is highly prized in mission. A team who does not always agree is also a prize and a safeguard for direction.

Mission was a team effort from its beginning stages. Jesus set a pattern of sending disciples out two by two with the twelve (Mk. 6:7) and with the seventy-two (Lk. 10:2). If you do not have a team, wait until you raise up at least one more team member. A team of any size will confirm your call and broaden the vision you carry. The value of team strength multiplies the efforts of a few (Lev. 26:8). Paul always had a team member with him in either a peer capacity, like Barnabas, or in a mentoring capacity, like Timothy. Whether venturing into new areas, praying for the sick, or sharing the gospel, find others with whom to share your vision and be mentored by your experience.

Paul, Silas, Timothy, and Luke were stopped by the Spirit from entering Asia, and the Spirit of Jesus forbade them from entering Bithynia (Ac.16:7). The lesson we learn is that God directed the apostolic band and also directs us today. Paul found Lydia, a "person of peace," in Philippi, and he also found the jailer through a difficult introduction. The province of Asia and Bithynia were not avoided because Paul was fearful of those regions, but because the Lord did not give him peace to enter.

There were times when the disciples avoided areas known to be resistant to the gospel, or so they thought. A church planter in Africa shared his plan to avoid a fanatical Muslim village.

> In my strategy, I had taken a map and made a note for my team to avoid one community because it was too harshly Islamic and a very dangerous place for Christians (Desta quoted in Trousdale 2012:136).

Desta described the breakdown of his motorcycle at the very village he wanted to avoid. What followed were the subsequent miracles of a resurrection, prayer for the sick, and seventy-six new believers in Jesus in just two days. In this case, God's direction was demonstrated in the form of a breakdown in equipment rather than a vision coming to a person in the night. It is God who directs. Faith is believing that He is working all things for our good and for the expansion of His Kingdom.

Missiological Implications:

Mission is carried out without a complete roadmap. Paul, Silas, and Timothy traveled without an advanced itinerary. The message we must hear is that God wants to lead us daily. Their sensitivity to God kept them from entering what we now call southwestern Turkey or the northern Turkish Black Sea areas. We do not go and preach wherever and whenever we feel the urge. Our message and location must be led by the Spirit of God.

Paul, Timothy, Luke, and Silas saw fruit with Lydia and her household listening, believing, and being baptized. They took the time to connect with people whose hearts were open. They worked with their families and saw the family unit through to baptism. This is part of Paul's church planting vision: family units. His strategy of the day leads us to believe for the same results with whole families coming to know Jesus.

2. Facing Demonic Opposition

In Cyprus, this newly appointed missionary team encountered Elymas the Sorcerer (Ac. 13:9). Saul, now known as Paul, felt the opposition from darkness and moved with an anointing of God to oppose it. Encountering satanic opposition on a first mission trip is not abnormal. Workers who are unfamiliar with spiritual darkness are bewildered when they encounter phenomenon unfamiliar to their background. The reality of animism and satanic influence should never be called "local superstitions." To do so indicates a lack of understanding of the parameters of the battle. There is no mention of Barnabas and Paul discussing the case and wondering who would take the lead. Young or insecure leaders would have reacted to Paul exercising leadership on their team. A heavy chain of command will make some feel culturally at rest, quenching the leading of God's Spirit and growth in the life of a young apostle.

Questions

You are a team leader with a younger member that exercises leadership and authority.

What do you do?
What do you avoid?

On the second missionary venture, Paul and Silas encountered a slave girl with a spirit of divination (Ac. 16:16). Opposition often comes when freedom in Christ challenges either local status, or in this case, financial gain. Fortune-telling is fairly common throughout the world and needs to be met with the strength of Deuteronomy 18.

> When you enter the land the Lord your God is giving you, do not learn to imitate the detestable ways of the nations there. Let no one be found among you who sacrifices their son or daughter in the fire, who practices divination or sorcery, interprets omens, engages in witchcraft, or casts spells, or who is a medium or spiritist or who consults the dead. Anyone who does these things is detestable to the Lord; because of these same detestable practices the Lord your God will drive out those nations before you. You must be blameless before the Lord your God (Dt. 18: 9-13).

Unreached people and refugees from their nations entertain animistic systems that include divining the future, interpreting omens, casting spells, and interest in communication with the dead. One of our Iraqi friends turned over her coffee cup to prepare to "read her future." When directly confronted with the truth of God's word, she abandoned her cup and saucer with the conviction that she had hosted Satan's desires.

I have met people in other faiths who honor a demon possessed person as "gifted," believing there is a prophetic gift at work or a link with the world of the spirits. Others have their methods to drive out the spirits, like branding with a hot iron. The unsuccessful story of Sceva's seven sons teaches us how powerless they were in facing demonic spirits (Ac. 19:13-16).

The power of God does not coexist with the power of Satan. The beauty of walking with God in the Messiah is that He grants the power to remove sorcery, witchcraft, adultery, drunkenness, and the like. The fear of the Lord touched the residents of Ephesus, urging them to denounce all magic arts (vv. 17-20). Believers in Christ "now came and openly confessed their evil deeds" (v. 18). The events with the sons of Sceva brought revelation to the new believers--they could not live for the Lord and still entertain old sin; their repentance had to be deep and complete. Old leaven is to be cleaned out, never left to cohabit with new life in Jesus. Paul knew this and warned the Corinthians: "Don't you know that a little yeast leavens the whole batch of dough (1 Co. 5:6)? He also informed the Galatians: "A little yeast works through the whole batch of dough" (Gal. 5:9), pointing out the necessity of total, radical discipleship. This act of repentance in Ephesus led to a riot because the veneration of Artemis of the Ephesians, the main faith of the region, was threatened.

Dealt with Territorial Powers

Artemis of the Ephesians referred to the great temple built around ". . . her image which fell from heaven" (Ac. 19:35), which is understood to be a meteorite (New Bible Dictionary, pg. 88). Demetrius stated, ". . . the goddess herself . . . is worshiped throughout the province of Asia and the world" (v. 27). His claim was overstated, but it is safe for us to recognize that the veneration of Artemis was the main faith of the region. Artemis of the Ephesians was a ruling territorial spirit.

Territorial spirits with associated cult observances coexist with animistic practices. The two are integrated by an overall cosmic story of their people and human need for daily spiritual power. High religious practices and animism are found cohabiting throughout the world, except where Jesus is Lord. The first commandment, "No other gods" (Ex. 20:3), comes with the power to turn from religious darkness and animism in all forms, including magic, sorcery, and communication with the dead. Paul's effective preaching precipitated a reaction from territorial powers. The same is true today. Our communication of the gospel must be clear without syncretizing old and new faiths which reshape the overall human story. The gospel must also speak against dark allegiances with animism, allowing Jesus to fill our daily needs.

Reactions will come to the gospel of our Lord Jesus. Like Paul, we will find ourselves in confrontations we did not anticipate. The unreached world contains high religious systems that do not meet daily needs. People attempt to fill the void with animistic practices which bring further bondage. Our mission is to see people set free from both, finding their joy and strength in the Lord.

Civilization in Paul's day honored Greek and Roman democracy. A warning from the city clerk against an unlawful assembly was enough to quiet and dismiss the crowd (Ac. 19:35-41). The high value of democracy is absent in regions that prize the value of crowds and honor those who take personal responsibility to quiet the opposition. Our calling in the Lord includes denouncing words that proclaim others to be infidels and subhuman.

3. Allowing Leaders To Grow

Luke added a curious transition of order at the end of ministry in Cyprus. He said, "Paul and his companions sailed to Perga in Pamphylia where John left them to return to Jerusalem" (Ac. 13:13). There was an obvious transition from "Set aside Barnabas and Saul" to "Paul and his companions." Paul was now team leader. Barnabas must be admired for exercising humility before the Lord and encouraging Paul to lead. This does not seem to be an abdication of leadership on the part of Barnabas, but rather exercising his gift of encouraging leadership. Abdication means leaving the purpose and no longer being interested in meeting the goals. John (Mark) left the team for unknown reasons. Barnabas was vigorously exercising his gift of building new leaders, to the point that mission to "regions beyond" took second place.

> They had such a sharp disagreement that they parted company.
> Barnabas took Mark and sailed for Cyprus (15:39).

Paul's ministry to unreached people required dedicated team members. Barnabas knew God's work was not finished with John Mark and poured time into this young leader. A ministry strength of evangelism and of raising up leaders will indicate a person's area of gifting. People will thrive when exercising their gifts and anointing. Placing the wrong person on a team, or a support person in a pioneering role, will bring great frustration. Good leadership needs to recognize gifts, strengths, and weaknesses, and then helps people to grow in their anointing.

4. Clarifying their Direction

Paul gave an eloquent presentation in Pisidian Antioch of Jewish history and Scripture, proving that Jesus was the risen Messiah. His message was to Jews living in the region as a result of the Diaspora and to Gentile converts to Judaism (13:16). Paul quoted from Isaiah 49:6, highlighting the ministry of Jesus, now given to him personally, of "light for the Gentiles" and "salvation to the ends of the earth." The jealousy and rejection by the Jews in Pisidian Antioch did not make Paul give up, but confirmed his calling to the Gentiles. You will also have junctures in your ministry that need clarification, freeing you to be specific in your vision.

The situation was now very complex. Gentile converts to Judaism rejoiced in the freedom Paul's message brought. Two groups were solidified: the followers of an Old Covenant based on the law, and the believers in the New Covenant based on faith in the Messiah. Both groups would not be welcomed in the synagogue and would make secondary decisions on how they would live their lives. The deposit in Pisidian Antioch was a group of Gentile disciples "filled with joy and the Holy Spirit" (Ac. 13:52). The church in that region had begun. Paul and his companions had a breakthrough within the Gentile community; it was not a conversion of the synagogue to a messianic fellowship. Paul continued with a similar pattern in many areas, beginning with the synagogue. The results varied regarding Jew and Gentile believers and the opposition that came from one or both groups. We learn from his team ministry that they did not give up, but spent time clarifying that Jesus was the Messiah from Scripture.

5. Learning Cultural Lessons

Missionaries learn how to present ideas in the language and cultural background of the receiver. Knowing a second culture well does not automatically set the communicator in a place of understanding a third culture. I personally experienced this gap of perception in North Africa after spending two decades in the Middle East. My words brought a different reaction than expected. A local elder in Algeria confided to me that his wife was not yet a believer. My word to him, "I would love to come and visit at your house," was met with caution and his promising to get back to me if a visit would be possible. A normal Middle Eastern response would have been: "Of course, you are welcome!" Two similar languages and cultures can bring very different responses.

Paul understood Jewish culture and its effects on Gentiles. He spoke several languages and communicated with many people of various backgrounds. He entered Lystra unaware that his message and actions were misunderstood. Paul spoke in Lystra and a crippled man listened to his message and was healed (14:8-10). However, the miracle was perceived through the lens of their former Greek belief system. Their misplaced joy, shouted in the Lycaonian language, was not understood by any of the team members. The missionary's message, and the cultural perceptions of those receiving it, take time to understand and unpack. Paul and his team now dealt with those worshiping Zeus and not with those having a background in Hebrew history.

Fit into Culture

Paul circumcised Timothy because of the Jews who lived in the region (Ac. 16:3). This was a clear departure from the Paul we knew in Jerusalem, advocating for a Gentile church. Culture is overwhelmingly strong at times. Timothy, like Paul, was required to live in two worlds. They both ministered to Jews and to Gentiles.

Their ministries may have been mainly to Gentiles, but the necessity to relate to Jews, even occasionally, required cultural adaptations. Paul was not a weak-willed chameleon; he was willing to become culturally relevant to many people with the hope of bringing them to Christ.

> Though I am free and belong to no man, I make myself a slave to everyone, to win as many as possible. To the Jews I became like a Jew, to win the Jews. To those under the law I became like one under the law (though I myself am not under the law), so as to win those under the law. To those not having the law I became like one not having the law (though I am not free from God's law but am under Christ's law), so as to win those not having the law. To the weak I became weak, to win the weak. I have become all things to all men so that by all possible means I might save some. I do all this for the sake of the gospel, that I may share in its blessings (1 Co. 9:19-23).

Many of us find our ministries in more than one camp, requiring our presentation and demeanor to be acceptable in each one. A returning missionary can, for example, teach in a church while sitting cross-legged in a robe. It is a novelty for a week, but very odd after six months. Culture plays definite roles in order to convey a message. Theology will change emphasis to clarify the heart of God to each people group and culture.

A Specific Message for a Specific Culture

Paul entered different arenas in Athens. Luke tells us that Paul was "...greatly distressed to see that the city was full of idols. So he reasoned in the synagogue with both Jews and God-fearing Greeks, as well as in the marketplace daily with those who happened to be there" (Ac. 17:16-17).

Athens was stretching for Paul, observing widespread polytheism with its accompanying symbols, and then tucking into a monotheistic synagogue. Even though he was called to both, Luke only highlights the marketplace and subsequent messages to intellectuals. The Epicurean and Stoic philosophers whom Paul encountered were of a vastly different worldview than those in the synagogue. The Epicurians believed the universe was a "result of random motion and combination of atomic particles" (New Bible Dictionary, pg. 340). Similar to evolutionists, they believed in the indiscriminate nature of life and, therefore, in the lack of eternal judgment and love of all pleasure. On the other hand, Stoics sought to understand the working of nature and how to peacefully fit into its grand scheme (op. cit. pg. 1145). Their ancient philosophy had similarities with environmentalists who sought the harmony of the planet and willingly denied conveniences as unnecessary. The

Stoics found greater pleasure in affirming the world and their place within it, than in seeking their own personal pleasure on which the Epicurians thrived. In this setting, Paul could not afford to give a message that worked in Berea; the present audience was radically different. We, too, need to understand the audience we address and present truth in an understandable, relevant fashion.

Their remarks to Paul's message indicate that Paul was an outsider to their area, even though he spoke Greek. A "babbler" is one who is hard to follow and who advocates for foreign gods (17:18). The use of this word tells us that they perceived Paul to be talking about multiple gods. Luke explained the confusion, noting that Paul spoke of "the good news about Jesus and the resurrection" (17:18). Jesus was portrayed as God and, in their minds, so was Anastasin (αναστασιν) (adapted from Flemming 2005:73). Paul was attempting to be understood in a radically different worldview. We also will find ourselves misunderstood, and we'll seek to rephrase our message or use other illustrations. An evangelist needs to move in humility, knowing that the message is meaningless if misunderstood. My message to un-reached people initially speaks of the nature and character of God from Scripture, which develops a hunger for God rather than arguments about religious history. Defining sin brings conviction and the need for help. On the other hand, beginning with the story of God's help to free us from sin can be misunderstood if they do not know His character or the destructive nature of sin to which we have all suc-cumbed. Understanding what sin is precludes understanding the need for a Savior.

Paul's message at the meeting of the Areopagus was conceived by the misun-derstanding in the market. The Areopagus was the governing body in Athens, responsible to decide religious questions (Flemming 2005:73). The presentation of Paul's message has been written about extensively. For our purposes, we note the following points from Paul's message.

1. Paul began by honoring the "men of Athens" (Ac. 17:22) rather than starting from his Jewish background. Intellectuals would reject those unfamiliar with their philosophical discussions as uneducated and below their dignity. His message affirmed their being "very religious" (v. 22).

2. Can we with Bible backgrounds (like Paul) greet unreached people, affirming their religious fervor? The tendency for some is to speak against their audience's whole basis for philosophy, which anthropologists refer to as reductionism. Reducing another's background to ashes and then attempting to rebuild that person with your faith is demeaning. The Lord takes us where we are and transforms us.

3. He quickly moved to something they did not know, referring to the "Unknown God" (v. 23). The unknown was not from Paul's background but from

the Athenian background. Looking for gaping needs in the philosophy or psychology of a people can often reveal a waiting platform for truth.

4. Paul turned to Biblical truth in general terms, describing God's creative abilities and His nature. He then moved to the specific revelation of one man (Adam) being the mutual ancestor of all human life (v. 26). Our world today needs this specific revelation revisited in order to remove disgust toward nationalities or ethnicities.

5. The use of a Greek poet was brilliant, tying into the flow of God's creation and humanity's relation. Quoting "We are his offspring" (v. 28) did not validate a particular poet or elevate his work to that of Scripture. It simply stated that the Greeks were also hungry to belong to their Creator. Paul was persuading the audience that they, too, needed their Creator. Discussions on this point raise a lot of questions in mission. How much freedom do we take in quoting from the Qur'an, for instance, to validate truth from the Bible? The real challenge is to use a person's background to bring him or her to a knowledge of the truth, rather than drive the person deeper into philosophies that bring death. Paul was not aiming to help Stoics become better Stoics with Jesus added into their philosophy. He wanted transformed believers with a core value of belonging to the Lord.

6. Silver and gold and their use in idolatry were equated with ignorance. This was a sharp word against idolaters who thought of themselves as intellectuals. Paul brought a contrasting understanding of a truly intellectual act in repentance.

7. Jesus was introduced as the coming judge of the whole world (v. 31), which was a complete affront to Greek hedonism and stoicism. Paul's message did not introduce Jesus as a baby in Bethlehem or as the Messiah long prophesied to come. Paul's proof of Jesus coming as judge was His resurrection from the dead.

Paul left the Areopagus with believers committed to Jesus. Luke records their names as proof of fruit in the most pagan and wicked city of its day. What city or people are you believing God to touch through the foolishness of your preaching?

6. Encouraging and Defending the New Fellowships

The band of two ". . . returned to Lystra, Iconium and Antioch, strengthening the disciples and encouraging them to remain true to the faith" (14:21-22). Paul and Barnabas told the stories about the grace of God among others of Gentile backgrounds. Their stories encouraged all of the churches to press on, using their missionary anointing to describe the grace of God on a broad basis. Paul and Barnabas had a love for the new churches, which demonstrated a shepherd's heart. They wanted the believers to be free from heresy that would destroy pure devotion to the Lord Jesus. Shepherds today, in a similar way, defend their people from outside teachings that prove unfruitful and damaging.

We appreciate Paul's heart for the churches through his subsequent visits and his letters of solid teaching. Preaching in multiple locations without continued contact or letters shows a detached ministry, not one with the heart of an older brother caring for a needy family.

Paul had a rare occasion to work with a group that another had planted (19:1-7). Apollos had planted a fellowship that was committed to Jesus, but only familiar with John's baptism in water (18:24-25). Paul's heart for the fellowship was evident by clarifying the work of the Holy Spirit, which strengthened their faith and ability to minister. It requires maturity in the Lord to clarify the work of the Lord, inspiring a fellowship to press on, believing for more in the Kingdom of God. Churches with robust worship yet elementary concepts of mission to the nations need to be taught from Scripture rather than written off as uninterested. A shepherd's heart will look to regions beyond and strengthen churches in areas needing growth.

Early Church Practices

Early church planters initiated rituals in new fellowships. Baptism was part of every conversion and fellowship. Peter told the crowd to "repent and be baptized" (Ac. 2:38). Philip baptized the Samaritans and the Ethiopian eunuch (8:36-38). Paul baptized Lydia and the members of her household (16:15) and the Philippian jailer and his household (v. 33). Baptism is questioned by some today, citing the firestorm it creates as reason to avoid the practice. Practices of the early church leaders should not be abandoned because of current struggles. Creative means can be explored, but we are not to change the examples that are recorded for our guidelines.

The baptism of the Holy Spirit was a necessity for all believers. Jesus told His disciples to wait for the baptism of the Holy Spirit (Ac. 1:15). Peter instructed the crowd on the day of Pentecost to receive the Holy Spirit so that times of refreshing could come (2:38). Peter and John prayed for the Samaritans to be filled with the Holy Spirit (8:17). This is true for Cornelius and his household (10:44), disciples in Pisidian Antioch (13:52), and those in Ephesus (19:6). Today, discussions become heated on how the Spirit comes, or if the move of the Holy Spirit was limited to the days of the early apostles. Patterns from Scripture tell us to ask the Lord for His Holy Spirit, regardless of denominational background. Not only do we actively seek the fullness of the Spirit, but we pray for new believers to also receive this fullness.

Breaking of bread among early believers carried both the habit of enjoying meals together as well as receiving the elements in the Lord's Supper. The early fellowship in Jerusalem ". . . devoted themselves to the apostles' teaching and to fellowship, to the breaking of bread and to prayer" (2:42). The breaking of bread, in this case, was listed with the apostles' teaching and prayer, which indicateed the spiritual nature of the Lord's Supper. We also know that "They broke bread in their homes and ate together with glad and sincere hearts" (v. 46). This tells us that the Lord's Supper and meals were important in the house fellowships. "On the first day of the week we came together to break bread" (20:7) illustrates that Paul celebrated communion in Troas. He was not simply having a meal, but coming together on the first day of the week, or Sunday. Rituals do not have to be celebrated on a particular day, but the meeting day and celebration together need to be consistent.

7. Provision Being Made for The Missionary

Lydia strongly urged the apostolic team to stay in her home. "If you consider me a believer in the Lord," she said, "come and stay at my house" (Ac. 16:15). Some of the provision is inferred by being a guest in a city or in a home. This is true with the Philippian jailer as well (v. 34), providing a midnight snack. Mission provision happens along the way through the faith and hospitality of those receiving the ministers of the gospel.

John, in his third letter, commended Gaius the elder for providing for missionaries who passed through his area (3 Jn. 5-8). John wrote, "It was for the sake of the Name that they went out" (v. 8), verifying that the reason these believers passed through was for the sake of the gospel. John's understanding of mission support linked the giver with the ministry they supported, ". . . so that we may work together for the truth" (v. 8). The curious part of this letter is that it was sent to the elder Gaius, rather than to Diotrephes who took leadership of the church. The Apostle John, who was well advanced in age, was not welcome in this fellowship (v. 10). Neither were other missionaries. If you face a lack of church support, remember that the Apostle John faced the same rebuff.

Paul also made tents to supply his daily needs (Ac. 18:3). He did not use this profession to get past a political boundary, but to live among a people. When finances are low, it is not wrong to take a job to supplement income. Early missionaries in this sense were no different than we are today. In Paul's farewell address to the Church in Ephesus, he emphasized supplying his own needs and the needs of his companions.

> I have not coveted anyone's silver or gold or clothing. You your-
> selves know that these hands of mine have supplied my own
> needs and the needs of my companions. In everything I did, I
> showed you that by this kind of hard work we must help the
> weak, remembering the words the Lord Jesus himself said: "It
> is more blessed to give than to receive" (Ac. 20:32-35).

Paul, missionary to the Gentiles, worked hard to bring health and prosperity to the community, while preaching the eternal message of the Kingdom. He knew that "those who preach the gospel should receive their living from the gospel" (1 Co. 9:14), but went on in this context with the Corinthians to verify that he used none of his rights (v. 15). Mission and its provision is a process learned by community involvement. Its principles take time and maturity to fully grasp. In this context, Paul was not asking the Corinthians to support him in mission ventures to other groups of people. His point was that the group receiving the gospel should contribute to the needs of those preaching. This concept is normally reversed in western mission ventures where the missionary goes with provision and asks almost nothing of those receiving the blessing of the gospel. Affluent sending bases need to rethink models of provision that grow healthy churches.

Two principles must be grappled with. The first is that those who preach the gospel should receive their living from the gospel. Both the community who sends and the community who eventually receives need to take responsibility for providing, which means it must be taught. It is not the missionary's place to demand recompense, because no person or group owes the missionary. We ask people to join in the work of God, but the choice is theirs. They need to be taught about the blessing that is theirs when contributing to the furtherance of the gospel. When believers do give financially to help the ministry, be thankful. They have sacrificed, as you have, for the sake of the gospel.

The other principle is that it is more blessed to give than to receive. Second generation mission happens when the newly planted fellowship learns to give, support, and send their people to regions beyond. Those who give are blessed. If the new fellowship only receives, it misses the blessing associated with their giving. When giving is not taught, a fellowship is robbed of blessing. There are times the missionary works hard for the gospel with little support, struggling to remain in ministry. By faith, we must understand that the missionary is blessed through his or her giving; the final reward is not in this life.

Paul had a single church standing with his mission venture to the Thessalonians. Are we not deeply convicted today, knowing that the great apostle Paul had only one supporting group?

> Moreover, as you Philippians know, in the early days of your acquaintance with the gospel, when I set out from Macedonia, not one church shared with me in the matter of giving and receiving, except you only; for even when I was in Thessalonica, you sent me aid more than once when I was in need (Php. 4:15-16).

Some are better at raising finances for other ministries than for the ministry they personally represent. Imagine Paul advocating for Timothy's needs. All involved in the Kingdom of God will need to contribute to both local needs and to mission efforts. Tithing locally with no involvement in mission may indicate someone without God's heart for the nations, or it may indicate one who expects that it is only the church's responsibility to fulfill the great commission. However, we are God's Church.

32. Decisions through Conflict

Jerusalem Council I

Conflict is necessary when opinions vary, and this is not necessarily bad. Resulting discussions lead people to decisions that can be remembered. How news travels and what portion of it is conveyed are always mysteries. Complaints come via editors to make their version of the news persuasive. The "circumcised believers" had a complaint against Peter after his ministry at Cornelius' household. "Peter left his Jewish convictions!" This astonishing news was very different from the day of Pentecost when Jews of various geographic and linguistic backgrounds heard the newly anointed believers speaking in many languages. Until the time of Cornelius and his household, most of the believers were of Jewish descent. The Syrian-Phoenician, Ammonite, and Samaritan believers were not abundant at this point. In Jerusalem, the believers would be almost exclusively from a Jewish background, and all were circumcised. Why does Luke call them "the circumcised believers?" His point is not about ethnic traditions, but rather a point of theology.

Many peoples of the East were circumcised. Isaac was bearer of the promise and also the covenant of circumcision. Ishmael was bearer of the covenant of circumcision, along with all male members of Abraham's household. The Ishmaelites who transported Joseph to Egypt were most likely circumcised. Many of the Ishmaelite communities scattered eastward were circumcised. Luke takes us into this theological topic of the day.

How do western Roman "pagans" enter into faith?

Luke pointed out that the term "circumcised believers" had to do with requirements for faith. Peter and the other apostles who were of Jewish background and circumcised were not part of "the circumcised believers." Theological lines were forming quickly.

The point of open controversy was not that Peter preached the gospel to the Gentiles. That would have been far too direct and raised suspicions. The circumcised believers were operating within a cultural and theological heresy that, if not countered, would have shaped the entire Church. Their belief required any seeker of truth to be introduced to Moses and to Jewish customs before being introduced to Jesus. If this heresy had been allowed to lead the new "Church,"

Moses would have remained primary, backing the validity of Jewish customs. Jesus would, therefore, have remained lower in importance and lower in the essentials of faith. Faith in Jesus would have become a Jewish sect rather than the gospel of the Kingdom to the entire world. This point was so fundamental because it challenged the cultural norms of all peoples to fall in line behind the preeminence of Jewish customs. Paul clearly understood the argument to declare:

> There is neither Jew nor Greek, slave nor free, male nor female,
> for you are all one in Christ Jesus (Gal. 3:28).

Another line of attack against believers from a Gentile background was more subtle--one of a political allegiance. For example, how could a Roman officer and leader of an occupying power be welcomed in the Kingdom of God while serving a government that was opposed by the party of the circumcision? The question was especially important when the occupying authority lived in Palestine.

I have had similar discussions with believers in the United States who have asked if I taught Palestinians and Jordanians to lay down their weapons and no longer fight against Israel. Transformation only takes place in Jesus and leads us to agree with Paul that "we are all one in Christ Jesus." Political lines are not the door required for the gospel to first enter. The Kingdom of God is broader than the questions of democracy versus communism, of Shi'ite versus Sunni, or Muslim versus Jew. Peace requires the Prince of Peace. Reversing the order will drive a wedge of favoritism, alienating people from the gospel we claim to preach.

Peter explained in detail the events that led him to Cornelius' house. He traveled with six brothers of "the circumcision" (Ac. 11:12). Peter related that the gift of the Holy Spirit was given to those who believed in the Lord Jesus Christ.

> So if God gave them the same gift as he gave us, who believed
> in the Lord Jesus Christ, who was I to think that I could oppose
> God (Ac. 11:17)?

Peter's statement directs the believers' movement. Faith in the Lord Jesus is primary. The gift of the Father comes through the doorway of the forgiveness of Jesus, not through the cultural norms of the Jews or through the Law of Moses. The Holy Spirit was given to them at the moment Peter declared, "everyone who believes in him receives forgiveness of sins through his name" (10:43). Personal works through the Law do not bring the gift of the Father. People of all cultures can have the gift of the Holy Spirit and forgiveness of sins when Jesus is Lord.

Reflections

Do any people you know understand God immediately and obey flawlessly?

God is not out to build a "super people," with other believers and followers of Jesus becoming less important.

The struggles the believers faced in the book of Acts surrounding customs and culture should not be quickly dismissed by us today as juvenile questions. We also struggle with the same or similar questions. I dealt with a believer from a Muslim background who was weeks old in the Lord. Christian background believers dismissed him as not truly transformed because he still used Islamic phrases when he spoke. "Christianizing" one's speech is not a goal, but it is often used as a test of a believer/outsider to this day. Dress codes in some churches, for example, are more strict than those of the world around them; others are less strict than the surrounding society.

With what was Peter charged?

The charges against Peter were (1) entering a Gentile's home and (2) eating with the uncircumcised. Missing from the report was any mention of the outpouring of the Holy Spirit to a large gathering of Cornelius' family and close friends (10:24) and their subsequent baptisms (v. 48). The charges demonstrated the enormous stumbling block that the party of the circumcision had placed upon Kingdom expansion to regions beyond. Those believing that forgiveness of sins was for all people were buffeted daily by believers steeped in Judaism. Various scales, such as those on the following page, measured the distance needed for a people to understand the gospel. These same scales can be modified for believers who struggle with reaching people of a radically different background.

Peter's complete explanation brought peace to the assembly, at least for a period of time. Old habits were not removed quickly. It appeared God's moving upon Cornelius' household silenced the mouths of the opposition but did not remove the stigma of religio-cultural purity which bred superiority.

Preconceptions of distance to understanding the gospel

Violently Antagonistic - - - Antagonistic - - - Neutral - - - listening - - - somewhat formable - - - receptive - - - in the faith

| -10 | -4 | 0 | +2 | +4 | +5 | +10 |

Similar scales need to express the distance that must be _traveled by believers_ who are buried in their own culture and unable to minister to the nations.

Gentiles are unworthy of the gospel - believe it is sin to mix w/ Gentiles - aversion to share - reluctant to share - indifferent - willing, but uneasy - believe it is our duty with some - believe it is our duty with some -

| -10 | -9 | -7 | -4 | -2 | -1 | 0 |

(Continued) - involved with some people - - all nations equally welcome!

| +2 | +10 |

Questions Resurface - Jerusalem Council II

Circumstances were quite different the second time questions of "salvation to the Gentiles" came to the attention of leaders in Jerusalem. The first time was when a known leader, Peter, was accused. The second occurrence lacked a leader of the movement, and unknown "men from Cyprus and Cyrene" were questioned (Ac. 11:20). We must confess that the Spirit was leading in Antioch, which meant a central command was not controlling the spread of the Kingdom. The party of the circumcision would also say that events were out of control, in a negative way, because the principles they deemed primary were being overlooked. Delegates from the party of circumcision traveled to Antioch from Jerusalem to straighten out the theology of the Gentiles. They represented a second agenda from Jerusalem and took it upon themselves to set a "pure course" that they believed needed to be proclaimed. They felt that Barnabas, Paul, and the leaders in Jerusalem had missed the essential points of the Law and needed to be set straight. This dark wing of control was not willing to follow the early apostles, believing themselves to be the expression of the bulwark of truth.

People who come to "set a fellowship straight" are not always in error, yet they need to handle the discussion with utmost integrity, not seeking to draw the loyalties of the community to themselves, but rather to Christ. There have been many examples of outside "apostles, prophets, and teachers" who have attempted to draw people into their followings, rather than into a pure affection toward Jesus. Paul dealt with the intrusive arrogance of the party of the circumcision in Antioch and, no doubt, reflected on this when warning the believers in Ephesus.

> I know that after I leave, savage wolves will come in among you
> and will not spare the flock. Even from your own number men
> will arise and distort the truth in order to draw away disciples
> after them. So be on your guard! Remember that for three years
> I never stopped warning each of you night and day with tears
> (Ac. 20:29-31).

Paul warned of those who would "not spare the flock." They were not interested in the community of believers thriving, but rather in drawing people to follow them and their teachings. Popularity cults must cease when Jesus is Lord.

Serious questions face new fellowships today when people come to sway their thinking. These questions must be asked:

1.   Is the teaching presented helpful to the community and to its growth?

2. Does the teaching build the community or draw its affections to particular leaders?

3. Do the outside teachers care for the "flock," or are they primarily interested in their own teachings and being recognized?

Paul fought the heresy of *"Faith through circumcision, and then belief in Christ"* in most of his letters. Old heresies do not die quickly and amazingly can come back after many years in new and different forms.

Peter was a major player in the discussion in Jerusalem. His experience with Cornelius and previous confrontation with the party of the circumcision prepared him to address this council. When addressing the believers in Jerusalem, Peter spoke of his calling to minister to the Gentiles (15:7). Peter's word was clearly based on faith in Jesus, not on faith plus the law, thus rejecting the demands of the party of the circumcision.

Paul was far more involved in the ministry to Gentiles of many backgrounds than was Peter. Paul learned to know many people scattered in Galatia and some regions of Cappadocia. But it was Peter's voice that held weight in the Jerusalem Council. Paul was very useful in the ministry to Gentiles, but Peter's leadership in the Jerusalem Council was necessary to move their theology.

Ministry gifts in context hold enormous value. Ministry gifts outside of context may be undervalued or go unnoticed. One person cannot easily enter another's sphere of influence. Peter's words actually opened the hearts of those in the meeting to hear what Barnabas and Paul had described (15:12). The ministry of God to the Gentiles and the description of miracles were now able to be heard.

James issued his judgment with a very assertive word from Amos 9:11-12. He clarified that the Gentiles were to bear the name of the Lord (Ac. 15:17). This meant that the Lord's name and His banner were placed on those who were still Gentiles. He went on to say, "... we should not make it difficult for the Gentiles who are turning to God" (15:19). This takes conflict to point out that the party of the circumcision were making entrance into the Kingdom for Gentiles difficult.

The "difficulty" to which James referred was actually heresy. The heresy in this case would require Antioch, and the entire Gentile world still unknown to the band in Jerusalem, to become cultural Jews before they had the Messiah.

The "not make it difficult" cannot be taken out of context. He was not advocating an easy Gospel without difficulties. Saul was a chosen instrument to whom the Lord had promised: "I will show him how much he must suffer for my Name"

(Ac. 9:16). Suffering for Christ cannot be confused with a Gospel "we should not make difficult."

Question

James gave leadership in crafting a letter to the Church in Antioch. The requirements laid out included abstaining from the following things:

1 – Food sacrificed to idols
2 – Blood
3 – Meat of a strangled animal
4 – Sexual immorality

Discuss the items given in this check list. If you were on the committee in Jerusalem, how would you write the letter? Did the strong Jewish element in Jerusalem influence the letter? Is the checklist communicator or receptor oriented?

Adding religious requirements to faith in Jesus resembles old-fashioned scaffolding on a finished new building. It has no purpose. Some years ago, I visited a team in northern Iraq who saw fruit. They encouraged the new believers to fast Ramadhan. The believers replied, "We did not used to fast Ramadhan, why should we start now?" This is the type of question which the Jerusalem Council addressed.

The foreign workers wanted to be "contextual" and allow Jesus to grow within this cultural background. The workers quickly realized that their assumptions were in error and dropped the request. Remaining within culture is not the same question as restarting a previously dumped system of works. Imposition of Ramadhan would have been a heavy yoke "that neither we nor our fathers have been able to bear." The point we must learn is that cultural props, several years later, will be questioned and then abandoned. We as foreign workers do not want to teach insignificant points that, in time, will prove either empty or even against freedom in Christ. If Ramadhan is taught, why not the whole legal system of Islam? Why not? Because it works against the forgiveness of sins through the cross of Christ. It proposes a system that "might work," as opposed to our assurance through God's work in Christ. Islam tells its followers to do good to overcome the evil debt accumulated. God tells us that our works without Christ are as filthy rags. The two systems are not compatible.

33. Fruit and Suffering in The Kingdom

Jesus calls His disciples to righteousness, to let our light shine before others (Mt. 5:16). It was prophesied in Daniel that the ". . . wise will shine like the brightness of the heavens, and those who lead many to righteousness, like the stars for ever and ever" (Da. 12:3). Shining for the Lord and drawing others to righteousness is a fruitful life. Jesus also promised that His disciples would be hated by the world and, therefore, suffer for relating to Him (Jn. 15:19). The animosity of the world and its religious systems against Jesus and His people are increasing in our days.

Persecution and trials come in many forms. Trials range from sickness to accidents, some which cannot be explained outside of darkness attempting to push the people of God away from fruitfulness. Missionaries and national believers endure much to remain in service to the Lord. Persecution for national believers can be the loss of a job, the loss of family, prison, torture, and martyrdom. Mehdi Dibaj[1] was imprisoned for nine years in Iran because of his faith in Jesus. The guards came with the news that his wife had divorced him and had married a faithful Muslim. Mehdi would not relinquish his faith in Jesus, God's most precious gift. He told the Islamic court, "I would rather have the whole world against me, but know the Almighty God is with me; be called an apostate, but know I have the approval of the God of glory." Mehdi was martyred six months after his release from prison.

Missionaries expelled from a nation lose their possessions, ministry, and the fellowship enjoyed with nationals. Expulsion of missionaries is definitely on the increase in some areas. There are more missionaries laying down their lives for the testimony of Jesus than ever before. Some have personal friends who have been martyred. The reality of martyrs crying out to the Lord from beneath the altar tells us that they are close to God's heart and at the center of His attention.

> When he opened the fifth seal, I saw under the altar the souls of those who had been slain because of the word of God and the testimony they had maintained. They called out in a loud voice, "How long, Sovereign Lord, holy and true, until you judge the inhabitants of the earth and avenge our blood?" Then each of them was given a white robe, and they were told to wait a little longer, until the full number of their fellow servants, their brothers and sisters, were killed just as they had been (Rev. 6:9-11).

The Lord is listening to their cries, and the world will be judged. The expansion of

---

1   http://www.elam.com/articles/Final-Testament-of-Mehdi-Dibaj/

the Kingdom of God will necessitate persecution and martyrdom. It is not possible to have life, liberty, and the pursuit of personal happiness while abandoning our lives for the sake of the cross. Jesus said, "Whoever does not take up their cross and follow me is not worthy of me" (Mt. 10:38). The expansion of the early church was marked with joy, fruitful lives, and suffering. This world truly is passing away. Jesus wants our eyes fixed on Him and on His eternal Kingdom.

Peter, the Apostles, and Suffering

Peter boldly proclaimed righteousness and truth. The day of Pentecost was marked by a clear declaration of God's work, the sin of the people, and a call to repentance (Ac. 2:14-39). The addition of three thousand believers now marked Peter as a threat to the Jewish system. The subsequent healing of the beggar and the preaching of Jesus landed Peter and John in prison (4:30). This first arrest brought the following warning: ". . . not to speak or teach at all in the name of Jesus" (4:18). Their bold reply was: "Judge for yourselves whether it is right in God's sight to obey you rather than God" (v. 19). Their bold declaration was neither looking to appease the religious leaders of the day, nor coming to a quiet settlement that would allow them to keep their ministry. The Kingdom of God is not seeking a quiet coexistence with ruling spirits, religious systems, or political authorities. Peter and John were aware of all they had gained through Jesus and were not focused on what they could lose. This is a key in our testimony of Jesus.

The second arrest of the apostles was short lived when an ". . . angel of the Lord opened the doors of the jail and brought them out (Ac. 5:19). God sent an angel who defied the authority of the Jewish officials. God was more concerned for the masses to understand "the full message of this new life" (v. 20), than abiding by the laws of a court that opposed the Kingdom. Missionaries need priorities that free them to do the will of God. Preaching the gospel of Jesus is against the laws of many nations. Workers who succumb to national laws forbidding the gospel work against God's command. Traffic tickets and taxes need to be paid; people of the Kingdom are not a defiant group. But the gospel of the Kingdom cannot be suppressed, resulting in submission to the kingdom of darkness. Proclaiming the message will be misunderstood by those under darkness as defiance to authority, bringing swift persecution. The Pharisees and Sadducees would have killed the apostles for this perceived defiance had not Gamaliel stepped in with caution (5:33-40). The apostles received their first flogging because they refused to remain silent (v. 40).

Persecution of God's people should not result in depression, but rather joy in identifying with Jesus. "The apostles left the Sanhedrin, rejoicing because they had been counted worthy of suffering disgrace for the Name" (v. 41). The conflict we face is between the "good life" described in this world and "life in the Kingdom" described in the Word of God. The challenges faced by the disciples between the richness of these two lives was not settled through one encounter. Jesus told us that we cannot serve two masters (Mt. 6:24). His words take on new meaning when we become disciples who proclaim the Kingdom. The world will scoff at anyone committed to righteousness that results in suffering or loss of material goods. James, half-brother of Jesus told us:

> Consider it pure joy, my brothers and sisters, whenever you face trials of many kinds, because you know that the testing of your faith produces perseverance. Let perseverance finish its work so that you may be mature and complete, not lacking anything (Jas. 1:2-4).

James' words of encouragement to scattered believers marked the early Church. Believers gave everything to retain their testimonies of Jesus. Remember that we are passing through this life en route to our eternal home. Bonhoffer noted that "Earthly goods are to be used, not collected" (1963:194). We may make use of every means available in this life, but we must not be possessed by anything that challenges our loyalty to the Name of Jesus. Fleeing and leaving all possessions behind because of persecution must be taken as "pure joy." God knows we have suffered for His name and He will not forget.

Stephen was seized and brought before the Sanhedrin (Ac. 6:12), the same court that tried Jesus and the apostles. Accused before such a court was a great honor because of its defiance against the Messianic Kingdom. Stephen's death was marked by his seeing the Son of Man standing (6:56), a sign that he was being welcomed home. Today, believers who are killed for their testimony will receive the same welcome home. The martyrdom of Stephen brought about the scattering of the believers and the spread of the gospel to Gentile regions. The expanse of the Kingdom was worth the pain he faced in his service; it is, most certainly, worth the pain any of us will ever face.

James, brother of John, was the first martyr of the original twelve apostles. As one of the early disciples, James was with Jesus on the Mount of Transfiguration (Mk. 9:2) and close to Him in the Garden of Gethsemane (14:32-33). The early leadership marked by Peter, James, and John in the Church did not go unnoticed by the religious authorities. Peter's subsequent arrest came with the intent of pleasing the Jewish leaders (Ac. 12:3), and we can assume Herod planned the same demise he gave James. Leaders who carry the gospel into new areas normally face the enemy's fury. Church and mission leaders in unreached areas will face threats and, at times, pay the price with their lives. The death of James and the release of Peter were both in God's hands, one story is not greater or lesser. Some missionaries are welcomed home at a ripe old age; others lay down their lives in their youth. Use the life He has given you for His purpose today.

Paul, His Mission Team, and Suffering

Paul's ministry began with the prophetic word that he would know suffering (Ac. 9:16). How many do you know today who began a ministry with suffering prophesied? Suffering for this early apostle was marked by rejection from his Jewish people (9:23) and suspicion from the believers in Jesus (v. 26). Human opposition can, at times, have the marks of demonic spirits, stirring people to fear the good news. Some types of rejection have more impact than others. Rejection of trusted friends stings more than opposition from the other camp.

Suffering from Jealousy and Slander

Paul often suffered because of human jealousy (Ac. 13:45; 14:5; 14:9). At the end of his first missionary journey, he told the believers: "We must go through many hardships to enter the kingdom of God" (14:22). This was a word which clearly described his journey. Suffering can come from people whom we did not expect to oppose us or our message. David had opposition from enemies and from close friends. The former we expect; it is the latter that catches us off guard.

> When one of them comes to see me,
> he speaks falsely, while his heart gathers slander;
> then he goes out and spreads it around (Ps. 41:6).

Slander is marked by partial information meant to denounce or raise doubts toward a person or ministry. Slander is subtle because it comes with the appearance of truth, but it is mixed with doubt. David described a person who could dwell in the Lord's sanctuary and live in His holy hill. This blameless person is one whose tongue utters no slander, who does no wrong to a neighbor, and casts no slur on others (Ps. 15:3).

Great damage to the work of God and to the people of God results from slander, a form of persecution. Slander needs to be confessed without the need to tell your side of the story. Hardness of heart will keep brothers estranged; repentance will bring healing.

Suffering as a Result of Obedience

Paul's mission team encountered dark spiritual activity in Philippi. A spirit of divination identified them: "These men are servants of the Most High God who are telling you the way to be saved" (Ac. 16:17). The spirit announcing them was really claiming supremacy by announcing the work of God. The pure presence of God and His work should never be announced by unclean spirits. It is an evil confusion that attempts to place the old darkness and the new Kingdom on the same level. (Refer to Mark 5:6-8.) Authority must be taken over other spirits claiming territory or recognition. Paul cast a spirit out of a girl, bringing financial loss to her owners. In this case, dark spirits and finances worked together. Jesus cast multiple spirits out of a man in the region of the Gerasenes (Mk. 5:1-19). The town focused on the financial loss of their pigs rather than on the healing of a tormented man. Both Jesus and Paul experienced rejection after freeing a person from the bonds of demons.

Paul and Silas were stripped, beaten, flogged, thrown in prison, and had their feet locked into stocks (Ac. 16:22-24). A violent day with this level of suffering would lead some to question their guidance. Paul and Silas sang hymns and prayed.

The believers in Philippi knew that Paul and company had suffered and had faced prison because of the clash of the gospel with wicked forces and human desire for financial gain through evil means (Ac. 16:18-19). The letter from Paul and Timothy to this Gentile church came from another prison setting – Rome (Php. 1:7, 12-14). Paul's view of prison was an opportunity to advance the gospel.

> Now I want you to know, brothers, that what has happened to me has really served to advance the gospel. As a result, it has become clear throughout the whole palace guard and to everyone else that I am in chains for Christ. Because of my chains, most of the brothers in the Lord have been encouraged to speak the word of God more courageously and fearlessly (Php. 1:12-14).

This was true for Paul in Philippi and in Rome. Prison in Philippi led Paul to the jailer who, with his whole household, was led to faith in Christ and baptism that very night (Ac. 16:32, 33b). Paul's imprisonment in Rome brought the knowledge of Christ to the whole palace guard (Php. 1:13) and emboldened the believers to speak fearlessly (v. 14). Suffering in these cases extended the Kingdom of God.

Suffering can often confirm the direction of a disciple rather than challenge its legitimacy. Paul's overwhelming message to the Philippians was: "Rejoice!" Our entire worldview must be shifted from self to Christ. Only then, when Christ is the center of your world, can deep joy be the normal way of living. Paul was so ready to suffer that his departure from this life was placed on hold. He was willing to remain and help believers grow in their faith (Php. 1:25). He urged them to live a life worthy of the gospel. This means that the message is more than a story to believe. Worthy of the gospel means to work together, overlooking differences. Worthy of the gospel means, in this context, not to shrink back in the face of opposition. Worthy of the gospel means to receive Christ and the suffering this faith brings.

Reflection

People emulate the life and faith of their leaders. As a missionary, Paul raised up a group in Philippi who embraced pain for Christ's sake. This Church knew how to stand in adversity. In contrast, believers nurtured by wealthy, successful, and pain-free leaders have little hope of remaining steadfast in adversity. To them, the cross is a story, not a life-style. Our responsibility in mission is to live for Christ, embracing our present struggles (2 Co. 4:17) with an eye on our promise of eternal life.

Suffering is not always God's plan; it can be self-inflicted through disobedience. Paul warned the Philippian believers not to embrace circumcision (Php. 3:2-4). His only confidence was Christ. He considered as rubbish his list of religious accomplishments. The message to the Church was to not imitate Paul's worthless background, but to imitate his life in Christ. Paul wanted the resurrection and all that came with it by associating with Christ. God wants the same for each believer.

Paul was eager to travel to Jerusalem and to arrive by Pentecost (Ac. 20:16), and we conclude that God put that desire in his heart. He obeyed under threat of persecution. The prophetic act and word from Agabus regarding Paul facing arrest was true (21:11), but the conclusion reached by the believers in Caesarea was to avoid suffering (v. 12). Paul's obedience brought a beating by the Jews (21:31), arrest by the Romans (v. 33), interrogation by the Sanhedrin (22:30), forced transfer to Caesarea (23:31-33), trial before Felix the governor (24:1-22), trial before Festus the new governor (25:8), and witness of faith to King Agrippa, great grandson of Herod the Great[2] (25:23-27). He was also sent as a prisoner to Rome (27:1), endured a hurricane for two weeks (27:27), was shipwrecked in Malta (27:41), and was transferred to Rome (28:11-14). His years of testimony and his time in prison must be viewed in light of the prophetic word over his life.

---

2   Commentary on the Whole Bible, page 1130.

> This man is my chosen instrument to proclaim my name to the
> Gentiles and their kings and to the people of Israel. I will show
> him how much he must suffer for my name (Ac. 9:15-16).

Paul fulfilled the call of God on his life. He served one Master. Can you say the same?

Drop past sin and pride of achievements!

Paul gave advice to the Philippian Church and to us today. His word, "forgetting what is behind and straining toward what is ahead" (Php. 3:13), is based on his understanding of forgiveness of sin and placing personal achievements in the dumpster. The past is no longer our jailer, and achievements are not our foundation. Human development and its opposite, human scars, do not determine our life in Christ. Christ breaks the bonds of sin and fades the scars of the past. Faith looks to God and to His strength to grasp His calling on our lives. The Kingdom of God offers fruitful, anointed service that disqualifies the self-righteousness of every believer.

Opportunities to complain come our way daily. Paul, as a servant of Christ who suffered repeatedly, gave advice to missionaries and to the Church. Focus on the true, the pure, the praiseworthy. We cannot live with opposite attitudes simultaneously. We cannot focus on complaints and on praise items at the same time. Prayer items should not be masked complaints. Praise items cannot be disguised frustrations. We are built up when our eyes are on God and on His expanding Kingdom. We are, in a similar way, allowing our spirits to be eroded when our words and attitudes focus on the difficult or impossible nature of our task, which is a sign we do not see God at work.

Conclusion

Persecution was common to the early church, not something to avoid through alliances with political or religious powers. Paul's encouragement to his disciple Timothy stated, "In fact, everyone who wants to live a godly life in Christ Jesus will be persecuted" (2 Ti. 3:12). Persecution can come from unbelievers, institutions of government or religion, and from trusted friends who slander the work of God. Suffering must be placed in the hands of God and not used as a measuring device of our obedience or level of spirituality. Suffering is used by the Lord to advance the work of the Kingdom.

34. Revelation, Epic Battles and Ultimate Victory

Introduction

The Bible is to be read as one complete work rather than fragmented stories with unrelated subject matter. Revelation culminates the story of the Bible which began with Creation and the entrance of sin through Adam and Eve. The story of God's redemptive mission to the world He created forms the Bible. This book of Revelation allows us to look at future events that are meant to comfort us in the struggles of this life.

John recorded Jesus identifying Himself as the Alpha and the Omega (Rev. 1:8), a word picture that describes the One who is both the Source and the Consummation. The creation story tells us that God created the sun, moon, and stars in a single day (Ge. 1:16-19). This glimpse of His awesome power in creating the universe helps us understand the greatness of one who, "In his right hand he held seven stars, and coming out of his mouth was a sharp, double-edged sword. His face was like the sun shining in all its brilliance" (Rev. 1:16). Genesis helps us understand Revelation.

But Jesus is also the Shepherd of Psalm 23 who:

> makes me lie down in green pastures,
> he leads me beside quiet waters,
> he refreshes my soul.
> He guides me along the right paths
> for his name's sake (vv. 2-3).

John recorded Jesus saying, "I am the good shepherd; I know my sheep and my sheep know me (Jn. 10:14). Our faith must embrace both the greatness of one who caused John to fall ". . . at his feet as though dead" (Rev. 1:17a), and the one who calls us with the words: "Do not be afraid" (v. 17b). He walks on the water and calms His disciples saying, "It is I; don't be afraid" (Jn. 6:20). After the trauma of the crucifixion, Jesus walked into a room with a locked door and said, "Peace be with you" (20:19). We need to embrace His greatness and His tenderness.

Half of this complete picture of Jesus twists our theology and ruins our life and witness. Some in the Church who tolerate adultery and homosexual lifestyles as acceptable see only a tender shepherd with tolerant compassion. Tolerance of sin redefines holiness, ignores the price of the cross, and denies judgment. The "tolerant" falsely define others with moral standards as "intolerant" and lacking compassion. Another imbalanced representation of God is a distant creator, frozen in time as the One at Sinai who was unapproachable by the Children of Israel.

> Put limits for the people around the mountain and tell them, 'Be careful that you do not approach the mountain or touch the foot of it. Whoever touches the mountain is to be put to death' (Ex. 19:12).

God made provision to cleanse us and bring us near to Himself. The writer of Hebrews contrasts the fearful sight of Mount Sinai and the giving of the Old Covenant, when the people begged not to hear another word (Heb. 12:19), with Mount Zion which is filled with acceptance and people who are redeemed to God. The reasons for this acceptance are "Jesus the mediator of a New Covenant and the sprinkled blood" (12:24). The full picture of Jesus as Creator, Redeemer, Shepherd, and Judge brings us to respect His Word and obey His leading with joy. We agree with John that "His commands are not burdensome" (1 Jn. 5:3).

The Book of Revelation describes future events, the vision of God for His creation and coming judgment. It is important that we listen to the opening greetings of the Apostle John and the Lord Jesus to the seven churches of Asia before reading the scrutiny placed on each church.

> John,
> To the seven churches in the province of Asia: Grace and peace to you from him who is, and who was, and who is to come, and from the seven spirits before his throne, and from Jesus Christ, who is the faithful witness, the firstborn from the dead, and the ruler of the kings of the earth. To him who loves us and has freed us from our sins by his blood, and has made us to be a kingdom and priests to serve his God and Father—to him be glory and power for ever and ever! Amen.
> "Look, he is coming with the clouds,"
>   and "every eye will see him, even those who pierced him;"
>   and all peoples on earth "will mourn because of him."
> So shall it be! Amen.
>   "I am the Alpha and the Omega," says the Lord God, "who is, and who was, and who is to come, the Almighty" (Rev. 1:4-8).

God greeting the churches demonstrates that He wanted them to prosper. Reminding them of the death of Jesus to redeem them was God's heart to continue their transformation.

The Mission of God in Revelation

1. **The supremacy of Jesus** as ". . . firstborn from the dead" is highlighted by the gospel writers and by Paul in his letter to the Philippians (Php. 2:6-11). The cross, death, and resurrection open a new representation of the Incarnate Son of God. The baby we knew in the manger is "ruler of the kings of the earth." This theme honors Jesus as Lord over all things and as the Sovereign Ruler. Revelation confirms the vision of the Son of Man "coming with the clouds of heaven," prophesied by Daniel (Da. 7:13), taught to the disciples (Mt. 24:30), and proclaimed to the Sanhedrin (26:64). The theme of His second coming will describe events that keep us from deception by false christs.

2. Another theme in this book will be **a kingdom of priests**, reinforcing the mandate to be Light to the Nations. God's desire to form Israel into a kingdom of priests (Ex. 19:6) was partly realized in the gospel records by sending the twelve (Lk. 9:1) and the seventy-two (10:1), and more fully in Acts by bringing the message to the Romans (Ac. 10:34-43), to the Greeks (11:19-21), and to regions beyond (16:29-34). This theme is also our mandate as co-laborers with Christ.

3. **Salvation to the ends of the earth** is a clear theme in this book. God's vision is for all to know Him and be cleansed by His blood, forever. We have a part in its fulfillment. Revelation is a call to God's mission to have every tribe, language, people, and nation redeemed and gathered to Him.

4. **God is judge** of both the Church and the wicked who refuse Him. Revelation will give us insight into the strength, struggles, and depravity of those claiming to be His people. God's ultimate judgment will come upon the world, Satan, and death itself. Ultimate judgment is in God's hands. He will carry out His purposes at the right time. The purity of God's character is evident throughout this book.

5. Revelation defines **our obligation as the Bride of Christ**. We are called to holiness, which includes the price of suffering and even death for some. Faithfulness to God brings future hope.

6. The Lord will bring **healing to all who know Him**. Tears will be wiped away and wounds healed. Revelation describes His healing and eternal life with His people.

To the Churches: Repent, Be Strengthened

Seven short letters were spoken to John for him to record with the instructions: "... send it to the seven churches" (Rev. 1:11). All seven churches were to receive this entire work. This tells us that the words to the churches were public knowledge to strengthen all of them in the fear of the Lord and to call them to repentance. All churches in the world need to be called to continuous repentance and to be strengthened for the tasks before them. The mission of Jesus is to strengthen His Church, expose its shortcomings, and rebuke its evil deeds. We take comfort in the fact that ". . . the Lord disciplines the one he loves, and he chastens everyone he accepts as his son" (Heb. 12:6; Rev. 3:19). God's love for the Church is evident through the Letters of the Apostles, which have brought teaching and correction to the Church through the centuries.

Churches of Asia	Corresponding Turkish City Today [1]
Ephesus	Uninhabited Excavations
Smyrna	Izmir
Pergamum	Bergama
Thyatira	Akhisar
Sardis	Uninhabited Excavations
Philadelphia	Alasehir
Laodicia	Denizli

The strengths and weaknesses of the cities will be looked at in broad terms without labeling any of the churches, which are all non-existent today.

Positive Qualities of Churches

Hard work and perseverance

Hard work and perseverance are part of spiritual health and please Jesus. This requires battling evil on all fronts while invitationally drawing all to repentance in Christ. It includes responsibility to take the gospel to regions beyond. The Church is commended for confronting evil and not caving in to the relentless demands of society. "I know your deeds, your love and faith, your service and perseverance, and that you are now doing more than you did at first" (Rev. 2:19). A touch of the Holy Spirit is necessary to both persevere and to grow.

---

1   New Bible Dictionary

Cannot tolerate "believers" living in sin

A healthy Church cannot "tolerate wicked men" (Rev. 2:2) is a reference to those inside the Church. Sin is destructive and God wants us to be kept pure as a bride waiting to meet the bridegroom. Because of this, the Church should be a gathering of those committed to the cross, not to their own pleasures. However, refusal to mix with unbelievers because of disgust regarding their lifestyles destroys mission. No mission activity in an evil world changes a church into a "saved community" who believes their lives are synonymous with purity. God wants a "saving community" that is able to reach across moral and cultural lines for the sake of the Kingdom.

Hates the practices of the Nicolaitans

The Nicolaitans were libertarians, or people who rejected moral laws (The New International Dictionary of New Testament Theology, Vol 2, pg. 677). They believed that salvation came through a right belief system and did not affect lifestyle. The Nicolaitans would tolerate anyone who had correct theology, regardless of moral standards. This word from Revelation divides churches and members into two camps: (1) those who believe God is a compassionate moral being with standards by which we must live, and (2) those who believe "tolerance" more clearly defines God. How you live and what you teach others must present a true and balanced picture of God.

Faithfulness

Jesus commends His people who remain ". . . faithful even to the point of death" (Rev. 2:10). The context for faithfulness is in poverty, slander, and the onslaughts of Satan. Faithfulness means that we retain our testimony of Jesus in all circumstances, both in belief and in practice. Compromise to avoid persecution does not describe faithfulness. The Church in the West has enjoyed many peaceful years. The word peaceful will be redefined for many in the days to come, and faithfulness will be a description of those standing with Jesus.

Negative Qualities of Churches

"You have forsaken your first love"

This is spoken from a tender heart, wanting His bride to return (Rev 2:4). There is no hint of rejection on God's part as He woos the Church, wanting the members to remember how they first fell in love with the Lord. Revelation does not portray a judgmental God against the Church, and then against the world. Sometimes people forget what they used to do when they first came to Jesus--including prayer meetings, sacrificial offerings to the work of the Kingdom, an eagerness to share their faith with anyone, and deep repentance of past sins. "Repent and do the things you did at first" (v. 5) reminds us to return to the tender place we once had in our hearts for Christ.

Holding to the Teachings of Balaam

Balaam was a non-Hebrew prophet hired to curse Israel. He could not curse Israel nor say anything outside of what God would allow him to speak (Nu. 22:18). However, he knew God's hand of protection would lift if Israel entered into sin, bringing a curse, or in this case, judgment upon themselves. Synonymous with the teachings of the Nicolaitans and the immoral teachings of "Jezebel" (Rev. 3:20), the end result would be God's judgment on the immoral. Those who taught these evil doctrines would be judged severely for causing God's people to sin (Lk. 17:2). Jesus called these people to repentance. If they did not repent, they became His enemy (Rev. 2:16).

Reputation without Life

"I know your deeds; you have a reputation of being alive, but you are dead" (Rev 3:1). Reputation is important. It reminds of past deeds still associated with a particular person or group. Jesus tells us that our past deeds are not indicative of our current life in the Lord. This is true for churches, denominations, mission organizations, and individuals. Examine where you are in your life in Christ today. Do not allow "soiled clothes" in your life.

Acceptance of sin brings people into a lukewarm state where they are neither in the world (cold), nor alive in Jesus (hot). The words, "I am about to spit you out of my mouth" (3:16), meant judgment was at the door. Do lukewarm believers know when they are judged? Or like Samson, are they unaware that the Spirit of God departed (Jdg. 16:20)? Even at this point, the Lord called His people to repent, not yet casting them aside as hopeless.

Worthy is the Lamb of God

The greatness of the Son of God depicted in this book was not just about size and strength or an ability to crush His enemies. People worshiped Him because His life was given to ". . . purchase men for God" (Rev. 5:9). This passage is foundational to our faith. It ties together the biblical theme of God's redemption for all.

> You are worthy to take the scroll and to open its seals,
> because you were slain, and with your blood you purchased for
> God persons from every tribe and language and people and na-
> tion. You have made them to be a kingdom and priests to serve
> our God, and they will reign on the earth (Rev. 5:9-10; 7:9-10).

The vision God gave to Daniel highlighted both the authority given to the Son of Man, and that ". . . all nations and peoples of every language worshiped him. His dominion is an everlasting dominion that will not pass away, and his kingdom is one that will never be destroyed" (Da. 7:14). The vision of God is yet to be fulfilled. Clearly He cares that all nations come to know Him. It requires that we prioritize our mission efforts, sending mission workers to the least evangelized areas of the world in order to complete the task. Priorities will press us to rethink budgets of churches, companies, and individuals, making sure that we follow the Spirit's leading to care for the poor, the foreigner living in our midst, and those ignored to this day. This vision of all nations, given to Daniel, repeated in the gospels, begun in Acts, and highlighted in Revelation must be taken seriously. It must change the way we live.

Judgment of People and Satan

The judgments of God on the earth and its inhabitants are numerous. We need to allow God to be judge and sovereign King and, like Ezekiel, find comfort in agreeing that He will bring judgment for a reason (Eze. 14:23). Another warning is to keep our eyes on Jesus and the coming fullness of His Kingdom, not looking back as did Lot's wife, still longing for a depraved world that was being destroyed (Ge. 19:26).

The seals opened by the Lamb are specific events, most of which are in the hands of God. We are not asked to enter into God's judgments by taking " . . . peace from the earth and make men slay each other" (Rev. 6:4), or raise the price of wheat and barley (v. 6). The **fifth seal** reveals martyrs under the altar of God, praying for Him to bring judgment to the earth for their shed blood. God's anger will be poured out when the number of martyrs is complete. Martyrs and their prayers speak of events to come that move the heart of God. The **seventh seal** brings judgment to the earth which is partly fueled by the combined prayers of God's people, contained for many years for this time. These two seals tell us that our involvement in the Kingdom of God is significant, but that the timing of the events is in His hands. We agree with the angel and those under the altar.

> You are just in these judgments, O Holy One, you who are and
> who were; for they have shed the blood of your holy people
> and your prophets, and you have given them blood to drink as
> they deserve."
> And I heard the altar respond: "Yes, Lord God Almighty, true and
> just are your judgments" (Rev. 16:5-7).

Opposing God's judgment are ". . .the kings of the earth who committed adultery with her and shared her luxury" (18:9-19). Their world and its treasures will pass away. The world did not recognize the people of God or care for the redemption offered by the Lord through the centuries. The distinctions between the world and God's Kingdom, and between the lives that long for one or the other, are evident. A life on fire for Christ will long for His Kingdom to be established.

Satan's end is clear. His being bound for a thousand years and further deceiving the world tells us that God is aware of events to come. Nothing will catch God by surprise or bring the Lord to form an alternate plan. God's judgment on Satan will come with precision.

> In number they are like the sand on the seashore. They marched
> across the breadth of the earth and surrounded the camp of
> God's people, the city he loves. But fire came down from heaven
> and devoured them. And the devil, who deceived them, was
> thrown into the lake of burning sulfur, where the beast and the
> false prophet had been thrown. They will be tormented day and
> night for ever and ever (20:8-10).

The description of epic battles brings comfort to our hearts. This vast army marching against God and His people is gone in an instant. Life with the Lord is forever a life without Satan and people marching with him against the Lord. Revelation is a book of many battles and judgments. Our place is to walk in purity, fulfilling His call on our lives. The battles are the Lord's.

The Bridegroom and the Bride

A great theme in Revelation is the joining of the Messiah and His Bride, the Church. Isaiah used the language of "garments of splendor, O Jerusalem, the holy city" (Isa. 52:1), akin to the description of the Bride wearing "Fine linen, bright and clean" (Rev. 19:8). We put on clean clothes which are a gift of God's grace. Self righteousness is not a wedding gown worth wearing. Isaiah also spoke comfort to the widow in her reproach: "For your maker is your husband - the Almighty is

His name" (Isa. 54:4-5). We have the mystery of Jesus the Bridegroom who said, "I am the Living One; I was dead, and now look, I am alive for ever and ever (Rev. 1:18)! This love story tells us of a Bridegroom who gave His life to form a Bride worthy of His attention.

Matthew recorded the following words of Jesus the night of His suffering:

> While they were eating, Jesus took bread, and when he had given thanks, he broke it and gave it to his disciples, saying, "Take and eat; this is my body." Then he took a cup, and when he had given thanks, he gave it to them, saying, "Drink from it, all of you. This is my blood of the covenant, which is poured out for many for the forgiveness of sins (Mt. 26:26-28).

The words of Jesus are the words of a bridegroom to His bride in first century Palestine; my body for yours, my life blood for your life. When a Jewish man selected his bride, He offered her a cup of wine that his father had passed to him with the words, "This cup is the new covenant in my blood, which I offer to you."[2] Jesus is asking us as His disciples to become His bride. Passover, the blood of the lamb, and a marriage covenant in blood are brought together in these passages. This mystery is God transforming us into a clean spotless bride, forever.

The description of the Bride and the new Jerusalem are synonymous as one prepared for Jesus.

> I saw the Holy City, the new Jerusalem, coming down out of heaven from God, prepared as a bride beautifully dressed for her husband. And I heard a loud voice from the throne saying, "Look! God's dwelling place is now among the people, and he will dwell with them. They will be his people, and God himself will be with them and be their God. He will wipe every tear from their eyes. There will be no more death or mourning or crying or pain, for the old order of things has passed away" (Rev. 21:2-4).

God met with His people for centuries at the tent of meeting (Ex. 30:6). We understand that God wants to be with us, He wants to meet with us daily. No other nation had God meet with them in this way. Revelation tells us that His desire is to be with the tribes and peoples who acknowledge Him, forever. God sets in place a new order that is incomparable with our former lives on earth, even as believers. The dream we now carry in our hearts is to be with Jesus and to start all things over. But having no tears, "no more death or mourning or crying or

---

2   His Body, His Blood, by Ray Vander Laan, Focus on the Family, April 1999, page 7

pain," is only possible in an environment that is constantly purified from sin. The world where we presently live is so permeated by sin that we cannot imagine a life without war. Imagine life without theft, no need for locks or codes of any kind. Imagine a life with no lying or twisted stories, but only truth. What would life be like without any other gods but the Lord and those who love Him? There would be no reason to wait for death, having lost functions and abilities, because our bodies and minds would be whole. How wonderful to know that our Lord is eternal, pure, creative, and all powerful. He promised to bring this dream into an eternal reality for those who love Him.

> Nothing impure will ever enter it, nor will anyone who does what is shameful or deceitful, but only those whose names are written in the Lamb's book of life (Rev. 19:27).

It appears that some live in the new city and others are able to travel to it. All who have walked without the Lord, in their sin, have already been judged eternally (19:8). Revelation ends with a description of those in the city who have washed their robes and those outside the city.

> Outside are the dogs, those who practice magic arts, the sexually immoral, the murderers, the idolaters and everyone who loves and practices falsehood (22:15).

Conclusion

We must agree with Jesus--"You are the light of the world. A town built on a hill cannot be hidden" (Mt. 5:4). Currently we are that city that cannot be hidden. Be careful that your bright light in Him shines in the corruption around us. The day will come when there will be no night and we shall see Him face to face (Rev. 22:4). Remain faithful as you look forward to that day.

Selected Bibliography

Ahlstrom, Sydney E.
> 1972   *A Religious History of the American People.* Binghamton, NY: Vail-Ballou Press, Inc.

Bediako, Kwame
> 2000   *Jesus in Africa.* Waynesboro, GA: Paternoster Publishing.

Bonhoeffer, Dietrich
> 1963   *The Cost of Discipleship.* New York, N.Y.: Macmillan Publishing Company.

Bright, John
> 1985   *The Kingdom of God.* Nashville, TN: Abingdon Press.

De Ridder, Richard
> 1985   *Discipling the Nations.* Grand Rapids, MI: Baker Book House.

Elliston, Edgar J. ed.
> 1999   *Teaching Them Obedience In All Things.* Pasadena, CA: William Carey Library.

Flemming, Dean
> 2005   *Contextualization in the New Testament: Patterns for Theology and Mission.* Downers Grove, Ill: InterVarsity Press.

Glasser, Arthur
> 1986   *Kingdom and Mission.* Pasadena, CA: Course Sylabus, Fuller School of World Mission.

Hesselgrave, David J.
> 1994   *Scripture and Strategy: The Use Of The Bible In Postmidern Church And Mission.* Pasadena, CA: William Carey Library.

Kaiser, Walter C.
> 2000   *Mission in the Old Testament.* Grand Rapids, MI: Baker Book House.

> 1978   *Toward and Old Testament Theology.* Grand Rapids, MI: Zondervan.

Kraybill, Donald B.
    1990   *The Upside Down Kingdom.* Scottdale, PA: Herald Press.

Kostenberger, Andreas J., and Peter T. O'Brien
    2001   *Salvation To The Ends Of The Earth.* Downers Grove, IL: Inter
             Varsity Press.

Ladd, George Eldon
    1959   *The Gospel of the Kingdom.* The Paternoster Press.
             (Reprinted 1998, Grand Rapids. MI: Wm. B. Eerdmans.)

Mbiti, John
    1986   *The Bible And Theology in African Christianity.* Nairobi,
             Kenya: Oxford University Press.

Muzorewa, Gwinyai Henry
    1991   *An African Theology Of Mission.* Lampeter, Dyfed, Wales,
             UK: The Edwin Mellen Press, Ltd.

Peters, George W.
    1972   *A Biblical Theology Of Missions.* Chicago: Moody Press.

Piper, John
    1993   *Let the Nations be Glad.* Grand Rapids, MI: Baker Book
             House.

Taylor, William D.
    2000   *Global Missiology For The 21st Century.* Grand Rapids, MI:
             Baker Academic.

Trousdale, Jerry
    2012   *Miraculous Movements.* Nashville, TN: Thomas Nelson.

Winter, Ralph D.
    2007   *The Unfinished Epic, In Five Acts.* Unpublished, Yet.

Wright, Christopher J. H.
    2006   *The Mission of God: Unlocking the Bible's Grand Narrative.*
             Downers Grove, Ill: InterVarsity Press.

Reference Material

1961   *Matthew Henery's Commentary on the Whole Bible in one Volume*. Grand Rapids, MI: Regency Reference Library.

1979   *The Open Bible*. La Habra, CA: Thomas Nelson Publishers.

1979   *Commentary on the Whole Bible*. Grand Rapids, MI: Zondervan Publishing House.

1986   *New Bible Dictionary*. Leicester, England: Inter-Varsity Press.

1986   *The New International Dictonary of New Testament Theology*. Colin Brown, ed. Exeter, Devon, England: The Paternoster Press, Ltd.

1992   *The Full Life Study Bible*. Grand Rapids, MI: Zondervan Publishing House.

The Qur'an
        Muhammad Ali Beydoun, Beiruit, Lebanon: Dar Al-Kutub Al-Aalamiya.

Scripture Index

Old Testament

Book	Page

Genesis

1 – 11	29
1 – 2	31
1:12	33
1:16-19	471
1:21	31, 33
1:24	31
1:25	33
1:26	33
1:27	31, 32
1:28	32, 33
1:28-31	33
3:9	34, 41
3:15	34, 53
4:9	36
4:17	36
5:32	36
6:6-8	37
6:9	37
6:13	37
7:6	36
11	39
11:4	54
11:32	53
12	324
12:1	62
12:2	54
12:3	54
12:1-3	53, 87
12:7	343
12:13-20	58
15:1	56, 73
15:2	56
15:4	56
15:5	56
15:16	81

16:1	235
16:2	57
16:5-6	57
16:6-15	57
17:15	57-58
17:23-27	58
18	163
19	163
19:26	477
21:4	58
20:11	58
21:10	57
21:14	57
22:2	58
22:14	59
22:17-18	59
24:1-4	133
24:24	62
25:23	60
25:28	60
26:3-6	59
26:35	60
27:13-29	60
27:27-29	59
27:31	60
27:28-29	60
27:39-40	60
27:46	61
28:1-5	59
28:14-15	59
28:15	61
29:31	61, 235
30:32	62
30:37-43	62
31:19	62
31:53	62
37:4	63
37:7-8	63
38	234
39:8-10	63

39:20-23	64
40:4-8	64
41:16	147
41:26	147
45:4-7	64
46:31-34	67
50:16-17	303
50:18-19	67

Exodus

1:7	67
1:10-11	67
1:15	67
1:22	67
2:12-15	67
3:2	68
3:5-6	229
3:10	68
3:12	68
3:14	68
3:19-20	68
3:21-22	68
4:2-4	69
4:6-9	69
4:10-14	69
5:1	344
7:16	275, 344
8:1, 20	344
9:1, 13	344
9:13-16	70
9:20	71
12:2	79
12:12	71
12:38	71, 196
12:43-51	71
13:4	79
13:7	76, 106
13:21-22	73
14:15-20	73

15:18	347
17	126
17:3	21
18:10-11	74
19:5-6	74
19:6	473
19:12	472
20:1-6	160
20:3	229, 445
23:14-17	75
23:15	79, 333
28:3	345
30:6	479
30:6-10	346-347
30:10	308
33:19-23	393
34:15, 16	196
34:18	79

Leviticus

9:7	345
10:10	264
16	277
16:6	345
16:29	346
17:10-14	266
23:15-16	75
23:16	404
23:22	76, 77, 404
23:39-43	77
26:8	442

Numbers

11:24-27	405
14:8-9	81-82
14:29-33	253
16:39-40	90
18:1-7	90
22:18	476

Deuteronomy

5:7	229
16:1	79
16:16-17	75-76
18:9-13	444
29:4	327
31:6	73
31:10-11	78
32:35	317

Joshua

1:2, 7	421
1:9	81
2:1	82
2:12-14	82
5:1-8	253
5:2-5	82
5:13	118
5:13-15	82
5:14-15	82
6:22-23	82-83
6:25	83
9	88
21:2	241
24:2	53

Judges

2:19	62
13:3, 5, 7, 9-20	236
16:20	476

Ruth

1:4	84
1:16-17	84
1:22	85
2:3	234
2:23	85
3:16	85
4:17	84

1 Samuel

1:5	235
2:30-36	265
3:10-16	351
3:11-14	265
13:13-14	265
15:28	351
16	86
18:8	351
20:31	351
24:1-5	86

2 Samuel

2	86
3:28-34	86
7:1	90
7:3	90
7:5-7	90
7:5-17	86
14:14	88
15:6	88
16:5-8	351
18:33	88
21:2	88
23:13-17	89
23:20-23	89

1 Kings

4:20-28	89
6:1,37	79
6:38	79
8	304
8:2	79
8:31-53	91
8:41-43	363
8:43	125, 379
10:1	371
10:22	99
11	348
12:10-11	89
17	344
17:1-9	95
17:1-16	371

17:4	430	26:16-23	90	3:2, 5	204
17:7	296	28:1	104	4:1-2, 11	202
17:9	430	28:5-8	106	4:7	379
17:17-24	96	29:3-5; 17-19	105	6:1-14	203
18	96	30:5-9	106	6:15	79
18:12	427	30:13-14	106	8:1, 7-8, 13-18	207
18:20-39	356			9:38	207
19:14-18, 19-20	265			13:4-5	205
		Ezra		13:6-9	379
		1:2-4	175	13:6, 10-13, 15, 21,	
2 Kings		2:40-60	176	24	206
2:9-10	96	2:59-63	176	13:23	262
4:8-10	97	2:68	176	13:24	206
4:18-36	344	3:11-13	367		
4:42-44	345	4:1-2	177		
5	97	4:1-3	178, 380	**Esther**	
5:1-14	371	4:4-5	178	1:1	187
5:2-3	98	5:1	180	1:5	187
5:14	345	5:6-7	185	1:9	187
5:17	97	6:9-10	185	1:10-12	187
5:17-19	304	6:15	79	2:12	188
5:18-19	97	6:21	185, 197	2:16	79
5:27	96	7:12-15, 19, 21, 23,		2:19	191
10:29	102	25, 26	193	3:2	189
15:19, 29	194	8:21-23	195, 201	3:7	189
17:24	107	9	162	3:7, 13	79
17:26	185	9:1	195	4:14	190
17:26-27	107	9:2	197	8:9	79
17:29-34	107-108	9:11-12	196	8:12	79
17:33	177	10:10-11	355	9:1-21	79
18:9-12	107	10:18-24	196		
19:34	349			**Job**	
		Nehemiah		1:3	39
1 Chronicles		1:1	79	1:6	46
8:12-13	92	1:6	199	1:7	41, 49
12:4	89	1:6-9	200	1:8	41
22:8-10	90	2:1	79	1:9-11	41
24:19	308	2:1, 4, 6	201	1:11-12	42
29:11	229	2:10	202	1:14-15	40
		2:11-12	201	1:15	43
		2:16-18	202	1:16	40, 43
2 Chronicles		2:19	202	1:17	40, 45
3:1	58	3:1, 8, 9, 12, 17,		1:18-19	40, 45
26:16-20	243	26, 31	204	1:20-22	40, 41

2:7	40, 45	137	131	11:6	86
2:9	49	145:13	229	11:6-7	120
4:7	48			11:9	285
4:12-15	48			11:10	119, 242, 344
4:16	39	**Proverbs**		12:1	344
4:16-20	49	2:16-17	89	12:4	120, 344
4:17	49	14:12	127	22	304
4:18	49	14:26	342	22:3	112
4:19	49	16:33	189	27:1, 7-11,13	120
7:6	113	19:2	viii	29:3-8	112
19:25-27	50			40:1-5, 10	113
42:7-9	45	**Ecclesiastes**		40:3-5	370
42:8-10	50	3:19-20	45	40:28	123
42:16	39			41:5	123
				41:8-10	351
				42:1	352
		Isaiah		42:6-7	352
Psalms		1:1	111	42:10	123
2:8	87	1:9	112	45:22-25	123
5:5-6	37	1:16-17	112	49:5	245
15:1	121	2:2-3	242	49:5-6	116
15	229	2:3	120, 121, 403	49:6	377, 386, 446
15:3	466	2:4-5	120	52:1	119, 478
16:9-11	415	2:16-17	112	51:4	299, 377
19:9	100	3:5-7	112	52:7	117
22:3	410	3:14-22	112	52:10	123
22:12-14	281	4:2, 5	119	52:13-14	352
22:17	72	5:1-7	165	53:4-5	352
23	48	5:5, 7, 9, 13, 23	112	53:4-6	245
23:2-3	471	5:20-23	113	53:6	152
37:21-22, 26	211	6:6	125	53:6,11, 12	119
41:6	466	6:8	114	53:7-8	428
67	87, 230	6:11, 13	113	54:2-3	117, 128
69:9	379	7:14	118, 239	54:4-5	119, 478
80:1	354	9:1	114, 359	55:5	117
84:5	91, 132	9:1-2	377	55:8	26
89:3-4	349	9:1-3	114	55:8-9	241
89:20-29	349-350	9:2	122, 359	56:3-7	122
90:10	39	9:4	115	56:6-7	366-367, 379
96:3	131	9:6	118	56:8	123
96:3-4	99	9:6-7	115, 229, 392	61:1-2	351
97:10	229	9:7	265, 347	61:1, 5	86
109:8	22, 413	10:2	112	61:2	256, 350
110:1	237	10:6-7	113	61:3	113
118:6-7	73	10:20, 27	344	61:5	123
126:1-3	87	11:3-5, 12	118		

Jeremiah

1:4-5	125
1:6	134
1:8	134
1:9-10	125
1:17	126
2:13	126, 159
2:21	127
3:8, 11	127
3:12	25
3:22	128
3:26	127
4:1-2	304
4:2-4	128
4:19	127
5:30-31	127
7:23	86
9:1	128
10:20	128, 132
10:21	101
11:18-24	134
12:1, 5, 8	134
13:12	25
14:11, 21-22	129
15:1	129
15:15-18	134
15:19	135
15:15-21	265
23:5	347
24:1-5	129, 426
24:4-8	130
24:5-7	230
24:6-7	131
24:7	344
25:11-12	175
29:4-7	133

Ezekiel

1:26	157
2:3	157
3:4-6	157
3:18-21	157
9:9	159
10:4	158
10:18-19	158
13:2, 15, 18	159
13:18-19	160
13:22	160
14:3	161
14:14-23	161
14:23	477
16:1-6	162
16:46, 49-50	163
16:60	162
18:24	164
20:31	164-165
21	165
22:7-12	165
22:30-31	166
33:1-6	166
33:23-29	167
34:17-24	168
36:25-27	224
37:15-17	169
37: 22	170
37:26-28	170
47:21-23	167-168

Daniel

1:4	144
1:8	145, 147
1:17	147
1:21	175
2:12	147
2:16	147
2:27-28	147
2:34-35	275
2:44	229
2:46	147
2:47	147, 185
3:17-18	148
3:28	149
4:1-18	149
4:34-37	149-150
5:4	150
5:11	194
5:21	131
5:22	150
5:31	194
6:25-27	185
6:26-27	151
7:9-10	151
7:13	151, 473
7:14	151-152, 477
7:56	435
8:10-12	152-153
9:2	125
9:2-5	153
9:11-14	153
9:16, 18	154
10:12-13	154
12:1-3	154-155
12:3	463
12:10	155

Hosea

1:2	109
1:10-11	109
6:2	109
6:6	110, 319
13:14	110
14:2-3	110

Joel

2:28-29	378
2:28-32	422

Amos

1:2	101
3:4-6	102
5:2	102
5:10-12	102
5:27	102
7:1, 4	102
7:10	102
8:11	104
9:11-12	104, 417, 460

Jonah

1:2	98
1:3	99
1:9-10	99
1:16	99
2:7	99
3:4-9	100
4:11	98
4:1-3	100
4:4	101

Habakkuk

2:14	285, 346

Haggai

1:1	181
1:1-3, 8, 9	180
2:3-4	180
2:10-19	181
2:18-19	181

Zechariah

1:1	181
1:7	79
1:8-2:13	182
1:21	182
2:10-11	182
3:5	183
3:8-9	184
3:9	224, 347
4:2, 6	184
7:1	79
8:20-23	184-185
9:9	386

Malachi

1:5-8	262
1:6, 7-9	209
1:10-11	210
1:14	210

2:1-9	262
2:10-16	211, 262
3:1	213, 223
3:2-3	239
3:6	408
3:8-12	211, 262
3:12	212
3:13-18	212
4:5	214
4:6	262

New Testament

Matthew

1:5	83-84
1:6	235
1:16	235
1:18	238
1:20	48, 237
1:23	233, 239
2:2, 4, 11	242
2:2-3	220
2:3	243
2:3, 16	392
2:3, 16-18	286
3:2	224, 251, 392
3:3	233
3:3-23, 44	355-356
3:7-10	224, 250
3:9	252, 277
3:10	251
3:7-11	224-225
3:12, 17	392
3:17	254
4:1	254
4:1-3	276
4:1-11	393
4:3, 4	277
4:5-6, 7	277-278
4:8-9	151, 359
4:13-16, 17	309
4:15	359

4:18	289
4:18-20, 21	290
4:19	301
4:23	215, 393
4:24	360, 393
4:25	355, 360
5:3-12	323-324
5:4	480
5:8	393
5:13-14	293, 361
5:14-16	324
5:16	463
5:17	361
5:17-19	335
5:17-48	324
5:19-20	206
5:22, 24	261
5:23-24	309
5:38	311
5:43-44	311
5:45	361
6:1-34	325
6:3-4, 24	292
6:6, 9	356
6:8, 32	261
6:10	350
6:12	312
6:24	465
6:31-33	361
7:1-2, 3-5	312-313
7:1-6, 7-12, 13-20	325-326
7:21, 24, 26	361-362
7:24	321
7:24-27	333
7:26	330
7:26-27	363
8	323
8:2	97
8:4	345
8:10-12	362
8:14	356
8:16	258, 353
8:20	101, 260
8:30	364

9:1	314	16:6	333	27:27-31, 32-44	351
9:10	356	17:18	282	27:51	308, 347
9:12-13	315	18:11	200	28	23
9:32-33	282	18:12-14	335	28:5	48
9:34	264	18:15	317	28:9-10	269
9:36	355	18:15-17	183	28:16	299
10:1	293, 354	18:21-35	316	28:16-20	359, 369
10:1, 24-25	293-294	19:16-23	293	28:19-20	54, 299
10:4	219	20:19	268	28:18	369
10:5-6, 18	365	20:26	353	28:20	206
10:8	97	20:28	268, 352		
10:11-13, 42	322	21:12-13	379	**Mark**	
10:29	49	21:12-16	366	1:1	233
10:38	464	21:18-22	367	1:4-6	225, 308
11:2-6	354	21:23	264	1:9-11	290
11:4-5	391	21:28-32	336	1:12	290
11:7-15	223	21:33-46	265	1:15	230, 309
11:21, 28	355	21:38-39	118	1:17	293, 301
11:21-24	365	21:45-46	327	1:21	215
12:1-8, 9-14	284	22:2-14	362	1:23-26	282
12:6	346	22:10	337	1:32-34	257
12:7, 14	319-320	22:15-16	220	1:40	97
12:10	263	23:4	344	2:1	314
12:15	258, 353	23:11	353	2:1-2	356
12:18-21	352	23:13	283	2:1-12	285
12:22	282	23:15	295	2:6-7	263
12:22-32	320	23:17	25	2:23-28	284
12:41	345	23:27	159	3:1-6	284
12:42	348, 350	23:37	351	3:2-4	284
13:1-9, 36	331	24:1-3	389	3:11-12	282
13:11-13	327	24:14	368, 390	3:13-15	293
13:24-30	340	24:24	44	3:15	115
13:33	333	24:30	473	3:20-30	320
13:44-45	334	24:30-31	151	3:22	264
13:47-50	340	25:1-13	408	4:1-9, 13	331
13:52	334	25:14-30	338	4:21	332
13:54	215	25:31-46	341	5:1-19	467
14:3-5	224	26:1	389	5:1-20	364
14:13-21	257	26:26-28	479	5:6-8	467
14:23	356	26:27-28	307	6:7	442
15:1-10	366	26:57-68	346	6:17-18	250
15:2	264	26:63	286	6:30-44	257
15:20-31	257	26:64	151, 473	7:1-4	264
15:21-28	344	26:67-68	351	7:4-7, 9-13	295
15:26-27	366	27:25	423	7:9, 24, 31	296

7:28	366	2:22, 29-32	243-244	8:4-8	331
7:31-37	257	3:2	225	9	322
7:32-37	361	3:3, 6	306	9:1	354, 473
8:15	294	3:3-6, 7	250-251	9:1-2	45, 321
8:31	267	3:4-6	370-371	9:10-17	257
8:32-33	279	3:10-14	250	9:22	268
8:34-38	291	3:11, 13, 14	252-253	9:23	293
9:2	465	3:23	235, 245, 250	9:30-31, 54-56	372
9:25	282	4:6-8	151	9:42	282
10:45	268	4:14-15	371	9:53	372
11:7	122	4:16	215, 290	9:51-53	409
11:15-18	366	4:16-21	255-256, 350	9:58	260, 343
11:20, 25-26	310	4:16-30	285	10	409
11:25	310	4:18-19	344, 371	10:1	473
12:12	332	4:18-21	351	10:2	431, 442
13:10	368	4:21, 24, 25-27	371	10:3	116
13:32-33	368	4:24-25	366, 371	10:8-9	230
14:32-33	465	4:24-27	398	10:8-15	372
16	23	4:24-30	115	10:19	47, 115
16:7	272	4:27	371	10:25	341
16:6-7, 9-10, 15-18	270	4:28-29	96	10:25-37	373
16:15	369	4:28-30	371	11:8	264
16:15-16	299	4:38-39	290	11:9-13	401
		5:1-9	290	11:14	282
		5:4-11	272	11:14-23	320
Luke		5:5, 7, 8	289-290	11:15	264
1:3	370	5:8	301	11:29-32	371
1:5	218	5:11	290	11:31	348
1:8-10	308	5:12	97	12:1	258
1:13	48, 235-236	5:17	314	12:30	261
1:15	236, 318	5:21, 24	22, 263	13:6-9	365, 372
1:17	236, 305	5:22, 30, 33, 36-39	297	13:10-17	284
1:26-27	236	5:27-32	292	13:16	344
1:30	48	6:1-5, 6-11	284	13:29-30	362
1:30-33	347	6:1-5	295	13:32-33	267
1:36-37	236	6:7	263	13:33	333
1:39	237	6:12-13	356	14:1	337
1:41	213	6:12-49	323	14:3	263
1:41, 44, 49	319	6:47-49	333	14:1-6	285
1:54-55	305	7:9-10	362	14:16-24	338
1:67-79	304-306	7:11-17	97, 345	14:26	295
2:5	240	7:16	345	15	335
2:7	233, 240	7:36-50	315	15:2	313
2:8, 9, 13	241	7:39	263	15:4	335
2:10	48	7:48-50	285	15:7-10	88

16:13, 31-46	266	1:6	213
16:15	342	1:7	325
16:16-17	342	1:11, 12	260, 377
17:2	476	1:14	376
17:3-4	317	1:21-26	225
17:12	97, 345	1:28	253
17:14	345	1:29	251, 254, 289, 378
17:15-19	374	1:29, 36	318
17:16	409	1:29-31	224
17:18	97	1:31-40	289
18:11	200	1:33	250, 254, 378
18:32-33	374	1:35-36, 37-40, 41,	
19:1-10, 11-27	339	45	290
19:7	261	2:1-11	353
19:47-48	262	2:11	255
20:1-8	264	2:15	378
20:9-19	265	2:17	379
20:16	332	3:6	401
20:19	265, 327	3:16	57
20:27	218	3:16-17	380
21:5-6	389	3:28, 29-31	225
21:9	367	4	323
21:12	437	4:2	321
22:15-16, 18	391	4:4, 6	381
22:20	268	4:10	355
22:3, 53	280	4:7, 9, 10, 15, 18	382
22:29-30	391	4:9, 12, 19	382
23:2	286	4:14	126
23:23, 25	375	4:21-24	383, 401
23:35-39	280	4:35, 39, 40, 42	384
24:1-10, 13-35, 38-42,		4:39-41	409
45, 47	270-272	5:1-17	285
24:6-8	375	5:14	314, 345
24:13-24	299	5:24-29	378, 385
24:21	375	5:28	393
24:25-26, 33, 39,		5:28-29	155
41-42	319	5:39	27
24:45	299	6:1-3, 14	355
24:25-27, 36, 46-49	376	6:1-13	257, 345
24:47	319	6:15	258
24:50	369	6:20	471
		6:26	289
		6:26-27	258-259
John		6:35	265
1:4-5	377	6:38	366

6:44-45	385
6:54	266
6:60	327
6:68	355
7:14	356
7:16	366
7:38	126
7:49	262
8:11	253, 298, 377
8:12	377
8:26, 28, 38, 40	326
8:48	384
8:51	343
8:56, 58	343
9:1-34	285
9:16	263
9:22	286
10:3-5	49
10:6	119
10:7, 9, 11, 14	385
10:10	260
10:10-11	268
10:14	471
10:16	169, 253, 385
10:33	286
12:3	152
12:7, 22	386
12:20-23	386
12:31, 32	387
12:34	86
13:4-17	353
14:12	354
15:12	283
15:19	463
16:8	314
17:1-5	346
17:15, 20-23	386
18:19-24	346
19:30	345
20:1-5, 15-17, 19, 21,	
22, 24-29	272
20:19	471
20:19-23	299-300
20:21	116
20:21-23	404

20:24-31   300
20:31   234
21   301
21:1-3, 11   272
21:15-19   429
21:17   427

Acts
1:1   370
1:3   269
1:4   401, 409
1:5   401
1:6   402, 422
1:7-9   402
1:8   76, 408
1:9   432
1:13   399
1:15   451
1:15-16   421
2   407
2:5, 8-12   406
2:12-13   422
2:14-39   464
2:17   408, 432
2:17-21   414
2:21   415, 432
2:21-22   115
2:30-32, 37   423
2:38   451
2:39   416
2:42   410, 452
2:46   452
3:1-10   408
4:4   424
4:8   408
4:13   424
4:18-19   464
4:22   423
4:30   464
4:32   397
5:19, 20, 33-40,
    41   464-465
6   397
6:1   425

6:3   409
6:5   409
6:8   409, 425
6:9   425
6:12, 56   465
6:15   409
7:2-53   425
7:54-56   409
8:1   409, 426
8:1, 4   143
8:4-13   409
8:6-8, 26   426
8:10   319
8:11   315-316
8:13   424
8:15   319
8:17   451
8:36-38   451
9:1-2   436
9:2   215
9:5-6   436
9:15-16 436, 468-469
9:15-19   410
9:16   460, 466
9:17-18, 22   437
9:23, 26   466
9:27   438
9:29   438
9:32   429
9:43   430
10:1-2   438
10:4-23   430
10:9-13   431
10:22   432
10:24   457
10:28-29   432
10:34-43   473
10:34-35   416
10:43   456
10:44   411, 451
10:45   433
10:48   457
11   119, 433
11:12   430, 456
11:17   433, 456

11:18   132
11:19-21   438, 473
11:20   459
11:29-30   397
12:3   465
12:15   44
12:21-23   397
13:1   438
13:1-3   440
13:2   421
13:4   441
13:5   418
13:9   411, 443
13:13   421, 446
13:14   215
13:16   446
13:16-41   418
13:22, 24, 25   439
13:45   466
13:52   447, 451
14:1   215
14:5   466
14:8-10   447
14:9   466
14:21-22   450
14:21-23   427
14:22   466
15   119
15:1   418
15:2   440
15:7   460
15:8   417
15:12   460
15:16-18   417
15:17, 19   460
15:39   446
16:3   447
16:7   442
16:15   441, 451, 452
16:16   444
16:17, 18-19   467
16:19-34   473
16:22-24   467
16:32   467
16:33   441, 451, 467

16:34	452	**Romans**		**Ephesians**	
16:37	435	1:21, 24	164	1:4-5	238
17:1	215	5:12	33	2:2	45
17:1-4	418	6:10	370	2:11-22	170
17:16	215	8:3-4	35	2:12	113
17:16-17	448	8:16	370	5:18	408
17:18, 22, 23	449-450	8:23-25	238	6:16	56
17:26, 28	450	9:3-5	238		
17:30	35	10:4	212		
17:31	450	10:9	341	**Philippians**	
18:3	452	10:14	212		
18:4	215			1:7, 12-14	467
18:24-25	451			1:13, 14, 25	467-468
18:26	215	**1 Corinthians**		2:5-11	269
19:1-7	451	1:3	427	2:6-11	473
19:6	451	1:27-29	189	2:7	292
19:8	215	3:6	331	2:9	292
19:13-16, 17-20	444-445	3:9	132	3:2-3, 6, 8	418-419
19:27	445	3:16	171	3:2-4	468
19:35	445	4:20	231	3:4-6	434-435
19:35-41	445	5:6	445	3:10	109
20:7	452	6:19	121, 171	3:13	469
20:16	468	9:14, 15	453	4:8	212-213
20:29-31	459	9:19-23	448	4:15	397
20:32-35	453	11:1	209	4:15-16	454
21	119	12:18-20	422		
21:11, 12, 31, 33	468	15:31	184		
21:37, 40	435			**Colossians**	
22:3	435			1:27	399
22:26-27, 28	435	**2 Corinthians**		4:14	398
22:30	468	4:17	468		
23:8	218	6:10	334		
23:31-33	468	6:14	196	**2 Thessalonians**	
24:1-22	468			1:3	309
25:8	468			2:9-11	44
25:23-27	468	**Galatians**			
26:5	434	1:15	126		
27:1	468	3:1	419	**1 Timothy**	
27:24	48	3:28	456	1:18	437
27:27	468	3:28-29	170	3:1	427
27:41	468	5:9	445	4:14	437
28:11-14	468	6:15	419		

2 Timothy
3:12   469

Hebrews
2:14   255
11:7   37
11:8   441
11:13   343
11:14-16   131-132
11:19   59
11:31   83
12:6   474
12:19, 24   472
13:5   73

James
1:2-4   465
1:13   43, 276
1:26   212
1:27   259
2:5   83
2:15-16   259
2:25   83

2 Peter
3:12   37

1 John
1:5   392
1:7   72
2:6   342
2:15-17   260, 342
3:8   34, 276
5:3   472

3 John
5-8, 10   452

Revelation
1:4-8   472
1:7   151
1:8   471
1:11   474
1:16   471
1:17   471
1:18   478
2:2   474
2:4, 5   475-476
2:10   475

2:16   476
2:19   474
3:1, 16   476
3:4   292
3:19   474
3:20   476
5:8-10   210
5:9   224
5:9-10   476-477
6:4, 6   477
6:9-11   463
7:9-10   477
12:9   47
12:10   183
12:11   47
13:13-14   45
16:5-7   477-478
18:9-19   478
19:8   478, 480
19:27   480
20:4-6   148
20:8-10   478
21:2-4   479
21:3-5   91
22:1   119
22:4   480
22:15   480